Secure Architectures
with OpenBSD

Secure Architectures
with OpenBSD

Brandon Palmer

Jose Nazario

✦✦Addison-Wesley

Boston · San Francisco · New York · Toronto · Montreal
London · Munich · Paris · Madrid
Capetown · Sydney · Tokyo · Singapore · Mexico City

Many of the designations used by manufacturers and sellers to distinguish their products are claimed as trademarks. Where those designations appear in this book, and Addison-Wesley was aware of a trademark claim, the designations have been printed with initial capital letters or in all capitals.

The authors and publisher have taken care in the preparation of this book, but make no expressed or implied warranty of any kind and assume no responsibility for errors or omissions. No liability is assumed for incidental or consequential damages in connection with or arising out of the use of the information or programs contained herein.

The publisher offers discounts on this book when ordered in quantity for special bulk purchases and sales. For more information, please contact:

U.S. Corporate and Government Sales
(800) 382-3419
corpsales@pearsontechgroup.com

For sales outside of the U.S., please contact:

International Sales
(317) 581-3793
international@pearsontechgroup.com

Visit Addison-Wesley on the Web: www.awprofessional.com

Library of Congress Cataloging-in-Publication Data

Palmer, Brandon.
    Secure architectures with OpenBSD/Brandon Palmer, Jose Nazario.
        p. cm.
    Includes bibliographical references and index.
    ISBN 0-321-19366-0 (pbk. : alk. paper)
    1. OpenBSD (Electronic resource) 2. Operating Systems (Computers)
3. Computer security. 4. Computer architecture. I. Palmer, Brandon. II. Title.
QA76.76.O63N388 2004
005.4'32—dc22   2004001163

For information on obtaining permission for use of material from this work, please submit a written request to:

Pearson Education, Inc.
Rights and Contracts Department
75 Arlington Street, Suite 300
Boston, MA 02116
Fax: (617) 848-7047

ISBN 0-321-19366-0

Text printed on recycled paper.
1 2 3 4 5 6 7 8 9 10—CRS—0807060504
First printing, April 2004

Contents

Chapter 1

Introduction

The OpenBSD operating system (OS) is a secure, stable, and powerful operating system that is attracting many new and old UNIX users to it. The OS is well designed for both workstation and server use. OpenBSD supports many mainstream applications and also offers great hardware support. Because OpenBSD doesn't face many of the business pressures to increase sales and employ trendy gimmicks that Linux and other BSD systems have to deal with, it is able to be designed on technical merit. This means that while the system works very well, it isn't targeted at the user who wants to be able to "point and click" and not read the documentation. This book is written to help new users understand the features of the OpenBSD system and to give more seasoned users the education to fully exploit all that OpenBSD has to offer.

OpenBSD came into existence on October 18, 1995, at 08:37 when Theo de Raadt committed the first branch into the CVS server from the NetBSD tree. The first release, OpenBSD 2.0, became available in autumn 1996. Release dates have been every six months since then, with the most recent version, 3.4, being released on November 1, 2003.

There are no firm numbers on a user base for OpenBSD. Even though CD sales could give an estimate, CDs are used to install only some systems. A huge number of installations are done over the Internet. The user base is, however, "pretty incredible," says Theo.

1.1 What Will This Book Cover?

This book will cover the hardware that most users will be faced with, and some notes about other hardware they may not encounter. The i386 architecture is used for most of the examples as that is where most users first encounter it. Note, however, that OpenBSD works almost the same on all architectures.

The book is broken down into the following sections:

- **Introduction**   This chapter.
- **Overview of OpenBSD**   A quick overview of what OpenBSD is and some of its main features.
- **Installation**   A walkthrough of an installation detailing what various options mean, why one should make certain decisions, and what's really happening in the background. This up-to-date discussion applies specifically to the OpenBSD 3.4 installation, but also to most other versions.
- **Basic Use**   Basic system usage and some of the major usage differences between OpenBSD and other UNIX systems.
- **Basic Default Services**   Usage and management of services that run by default on a freshly installed system.
- **Online Help Resources**   Descriptions of the "man," GNU Info, and "perldoc" facilities for online help.
- **X Window System**   Information regarding the X Window system on an OpenBSD host.
- **User Administration**   Addition and deletion of users and management of the space that these users will work in.
- **Networking**   Setting up basic networking, advanced networking topics, and bridging.
- *inetd*   Function and configuration of services that are run from *inetd*.
- **Other Installed Services**   Additional information about services that are installed on a default system, but not enabled on start-up.
- **Precompiled Third-Party Software: Packages**   Use of the precompiled packages that are available for OpenBSD.
- **The Ports Tree: Third-Party Software from Source**   Use of the ports tree and compiling applications from source.
- **Disks and Filesystems**   The creation and care of filesystems and disk devices.
- **Backup Utilities**   Tools and techniques for system backup.
- **Housekeeping**   Regular system housekeeping chores.
- **Mail Server Operations**   SMTP services in OpenBSD.
- **The Domain Name Services**   The domain name system setup and use.
- **Web Servers with Apache**   Web services with the Apache and mod_ssl servers.

- **OpenSSH**   The OpenBSD secure shell daemon and client.
- **The OpenBSD Development Environment**   Languages and software development tools.
- **Packet Filtering and NAT**   Using OpenBSD as a firewall and setting up systems to do NAT (Network Address Translation).
- **NFS: The Network Filesystem**   Setting up and using an OpenBSD NFS server and client.
- **NIS and YP Services**   Configuration of an NIS server and clients.
- **Kerberos**   Configuration and operation of OpenBSD as a Kerberos V client and server.
- **Authentication Methods**   The numerous login methods for OpenBSD, including S/Key.
- **IPsec: Security at the IP Layer**   Configuring an OpenBSD client and gateway for secure IP networking.
- **IP Version 6 (IPv6)**   Overview of how OpenBSD is able to use IPv6 and basic usage in normal activities.
- **Systrace**   A system call policy mechanism, which can safely limit the actions of any application on an OpenBSD system.
- **Network Intrusion Detection**   While not a standard part of OpenBSD, use of tools in the ports tree to allow OpenBSD to be used as a network security monitor.
- **Upgrading**   Upgrading an OpenBSD system.
- **Kernel Compilation**   The GENERIC kernel, the few reasons to compile a new kernel, and tweaks to the kernel without compilation.
- **Bug Reports with OpenBSD**   Checking for and reporting system bugs.
- **CVS Basics**   Use of CVS on OpenBSD to access the kernel source and for system deployment.
- **Applying Source Code Patches**   Ways to apply system and application patches.
- **Tuning the Kernel with *sysctl***   Tunable kernel parameters.
- **A *dmesg* Walkthrough**   Information available from *dmesg* and how it applies to system use.
- **Core File Evaluation**   Evaluation of core files from system and application crashes.

- **Other OpenBSD Tools and Resources**   Documentation reference for OpenBSD and other sources of information.
- **IPsec *m4***   *m4* processing scripts for the IPv6 chapter.

During the preparation of this book, a friend who was reviewing the table of contents asked me, "Where is the chapter on security?" Just as in OpenBSD, security is everywhere. We sprinkle it in almost every chapter, because this is how security is best done. A chapter or two at the end of a book simply cannot demonstrate how OpenBSD has integrated security into almost every facet of the system.

1.2 Whom Is This Book For?

This book targets both the user who is new to OpenBSD and the user who has been using the system for a while. It is not intended to be a beginner's guide; it presumes that the user knows UNIX and is moving to OpenBSD or looking to expand his or her knowledge base. In addition, given that networking is a core function of any OpenBSD system, having a basic understanding of networking is important. This book will not cover the specifics of editors like *vi* or *emacs*; the user is expected to be able to edit his or her own files. Finally, this book concentrates on the use of server-end tools; it will not cover the clients being used to access these services, except in terms of how that might change decisions during server configuration.

The first section of the book can probably be skimmed by experienced and savvy UNIX administrators, but many will want to read these chapters in depth. These chapters include the basics of the layout of the OpenBSD system and its installation.

1.3 Book Syntax

In this text the following typographic standards are used to indicate the nature of the environment:

/home	Directory names in text
ls	Commands in text
`uname -a`	Output from scripts or commands
`# adduser`	Command examples to be run from the command line as root
`$ repquota -a`	Command examples to be run from the command line as a user

The book assumes default paths whenever possible. Thus the ports tree is installed in **/usr/ports**, the source tree is installed in **/usr/src**, the X11 source tree is installed in **/usr/XF4**, and ports and packages are installed in the **/usr/local** filesystem. All of these can be modified, of course.

All code and examples are available at **http://www.crimelabs.net/openbsdbook.**

1.4 About the Authors
1.4.1 Brandon Palmer

Brandon has been working with UNIX for many years. He has industry experience with Linux, Windows, Solaris, and OpenBSD systems, from small home environments up to enterprise trading systems and networks. Professionally, he is the IT Director for a trading company. He spends a lot of his free time working with the PostgreSQL database system. Brandon is a member of the Crimelabs Security Research Group.

1.4.2 Jose Nazario

Jose recently finished a Ph.D. in biochemistry at Case Western Reserve University, where he met Brandon. After playing with Linux for a number of years, he got frustrated by the inconsistent code quality, the dramatic number of changes, the confusion of distributions, and general frustrations ... and came to OpenBSD at version 2.4. He's been at home ever since.

Jose has been an OpenBSD team member since mid-2003. When he's not doing ports or minor bug notes to the OpenBSD core team, he hacks code, and tries to have fun. He works for a small network security company in the Midwest.

1.4.3 Contributing Authors

Because OpenBSD is a large, complex system, it is impossible for any one or two people to know it all. We had some help from other authors and wish to acknowledge their contributions.

Todd Fries, who works in the OpenBSD project, contributed lots of fixes and corrections to the book. His work in the X11, IPsec, IPv6, and backup chapters is especially notable.

Florian Kohl, who runs the Hairy Eyeball systrace policy repository, was kind enough to chip in many pages of material.

Jolan Luff helped us with his great notes on running dynamic content inside an Apache chroot environment. Thanks, Jolan.

Peter Valchev served as an excellent technical filter and pointed out many places for corrections.

1.5 Acknowledgments

The authors are grateful to the OpenBSD community for their forthright information and assistance. Several key people have been especially helpful in the writing of this book: Niels Provos, for his enlightening discussions on PF, IPsec, sshd, and systrace; Mike Frantzen, for his insightful discussions on PF and the related areas; Todd Miller, for his help in the mail subsystem and S/Key cleanups; and Dug Song, for inspiring work with systrace on monkey.org. Itojun and Brian Hatch were also crucial to the review process and their contribution is noted.

A special thanks to everyone at Addison-Wesley for publishing this book. This includes our editor Jessica Goldstein, our friend in production Patrick Cash-Peterson, and their respective staffs. Without them, this book wouldn't have been the light of day nor been as well put together as it is.

Part I

Getting Started

## Chapter 2

Overview of OpenBSD

OpenBSD is one of the most secure and well-designed operating systems available today. It has its roots in countless hours of research and development based on some of the best UNIX flavors of the past, and it boasts all the features of modern operating systems. The OS is widely considered one of the most secure general-purpose operating systems available today and it supports many key parts of the global Internet infrastructure.

2.1 A Brief History of OpenBSD

Although the roots of OpenBSD go all the way back to the 1970s and the early days of UNIX development, OpenBSD has since evolved into a leading UNIX system that has a strong following and is deployed in many places around the world. UNIX first forked off into BSD in the late 1970s and then again into FreeBSD and NetBSD in the early 1990s. Theo de Raadt, still the current project leader, split NetBSD into OpenBSD in October 1995 and released the 2.0 version of OpenBSD in mid-1997. This new flavor was designed to be ultra-secure and elegant in design.

OpenBSD shares a great deal with FreeBSD and NetBSD, and the development team has added many well-known packages for use on systems such as OpenSSH and *pf*. OpenBSD is a different system from Linux, but most UNIX applications that work under Linux are or will be available for OpenBSD systems.

2.2 OpenBSD Security

OpenBSD's top priority is to be secure, and it was designed with security in mind throughout every stage of development. OpenBSD has remained immune to most of the exploits and attacks that have surfaced during its lifespan. The code for the core OS and the packages required for its installation have been carefully audited, and are generally considered to be secure. An additional constraint placed on the OpenBSD secure development model is that the base system must attempt to be cohesive with the original BSD model, preventing applications from breaking when possible.

This can all change, of course, when the next insecurity paradigm arises—for example, with the discovery of format string attacks in the summer of 2000. The OpenBSD group tries to stay ahead of the curve and implement preventive security measures; so far, it has proved successful. The code undergoes continual scrutiny and audits, and apparently innocuous bugs are fixed on the chance that they may be deemed exploitable at some later date. The OpenBSD team can typically provide a vendor response along the lines of "This was fixed at some earlier date." By remaining an open development model (everyone can view the CVS change logs), OpenBSD is constantly sharing its experiences with the larger community. Additionally, some developers within the project work on other software projects and incorporate OpenBSD security fixes into their own software; OpenBSD also benefits from these other projects by incorporating some of their code or ideas.

The OpenBSD team was one of the first large-scale development teams to adopt the now basic software engineering standard: Fix bugs, and classes of bugs, rather than just vulnerabilities. This means that system security can be enhanced by ensuring code correctness. Handling error conditions wisely is another part of correct development. Lastly, OpenBSD attempts to operate with as little privilege when possible, by having programs drop privileges as soon as feasible or by increasingly using the privilege separation mechanism. By applying these principles throughout the system, OpenBSD enhances overall system security.

2.2.1 The OpenBSD Security Model

One of the major goals of OpenBSD is to be a secure BSD-based UNIX system, and remaining BSD-centric is important to the project. For example, the developers have decided against incorporating features such as POSIX.1e capabilities, commonly referred to as "Orange Book" features. The system is to remain as generic a UNIX version as possible, but as hardened as possible within that constraint. Enough room exists within the traditional UNIX model to allow for a very secure and reliable system.

To accomplish this goal, facets of security have been incorporated into the system in a variety of places. Within the kernel, for example, subtle changes have been in place for years, such as randomized process IDs. This may seem unimportant, but it is a useful measure. Several applications use process IDs as security markers, and their predictability can be exploited to abuse the system. The kernel also has a strong random number generator, which it employs to hand out "entropy" to processes. Likewise, TCP initial sequence numbers are extremely random—far more unpredictable than on any other operating system available.[1]

Cryptography has been extensively developed and fully incorporated into the system as well, including the Blowfish and Advanced Encryption Standard (AES) algorithms (the latter is based on Rijndael). This feature is available to applications through the regular APIs. The advantages of this approach are numerous. An example is the ability to encrypt pages of swapped memory. If an attacker is able to obtain access to pages of swap that contain sensitive information, he or she would have to decrypt the data first before using it for nefarious purposes.

2.2.2 The Audit

Most people know about the full code audit of OpenBSD that began in the summer of 1996 and found thousands of bugs, including new types of software bugs leading other OSs to perform further security audits. This effort has produced a system well known for its reliability and correctness, plus an overall reputation of security throughout.

What few people realize is that the audit is continual. Almost every line of code is thoroughly audited, bugs are fixed, and many security vulnerabilities are eliminated.

One of the key facets of the OpenBSD approach to code auditing is the idea that "Bugs are what lead to security vulnerabilities, so bugs should be fixed." This is in contrast to many development efforts, which focus on vulnerabilities ahead of bugs. In taking its approach, the OpenBSD team has found that classes of programming errors produce a common bug pattern. This immediately leads to the notion that it is important to scour the source code for similar bugs, which the team periodically does when new classes of bugs are found.

This isn't to say that every bug that could be fixed is. In several cases OpenBSD has fallen victim to security problems, and in a few cases this OS has been the only one with a security bug. The development team is a group of humans and makes mistakes. Bugs get fixed and everyone moves on.

2.2.3 Cryptography

Along with strong security comes the use of cryptography wherever possible. A very secure operating system is useless unless you can do work securely with it. This is where cryptographic tools come into play. OpenSSH is used to allow secure connections and

---

[1] As was shown in a summer 2001 report by Michal Zalewski of the Bindview Group.

file transfers over the Internet. A strong random number generator is used throughout the system for everything from process numbers to salts for password generation. String hash transformations are used for the generation of MD5 hashes, S/Key passwords, and other items. The default cryptographic scheme of DES has been replaced with Blowfish to create much stronger user and system passwords. OpenBSD even supports a wide range of encryption hardware.

2.2.4 Proactive Security

OpenBSD is unique among operating systems because of its pervasive security goal; it has proactive security. OpenBSD developers are constantly working to find new security problems before they appear in the wild, and to apply these findings to current and future sources in the form of audits. In addition to making extensive use of tools and techniques such as chroot and privilege separation, everything is designed in such a way that problems are prevented and circumvented even before they came into being.

2.3 Which Applications Are and Are Not *Secure*?

Although the base installation is considered to be *secure*[2] the applications in the ports tree aren't generally considered to meet this standard. No thorough code audits of the applications in the ports tree are usually done by the OpenBSD team. Ports are, however, installed in such a way to help avoid most potential problems, and security problems sometimes do get detected and fixed in the porting process. Due to the large number of total ports, this cannot be said for the whole ports tree.

2.4 Licensing

Another goal of OpenBSD is to keep all of the source code free. To achieve this goal, as much software as possible that is included with OpenBSD is covered by the Berkeley Copyright.[3] This also means that almost all software that is included with OpenBSD must be at least as free as the Berkeley copyright. Recently, the entire OpenBSD source code and

---

[2] Saying that something is or isn't secure is hard to do. Even if an application has been audited, new techniques may arise that were never taken into consideration when the audit was done. Thus, while it is easy to say that a system is insecure, it is difficult to say with authority that an application is secure. The OpenBSD team works diligently to find most of the potential problems and to be as safe at they can be. OpenBSD does not attempt to employ any provable security mechanisms, however.
[3] **http://www.openbsd.org/policy.html.**

ports tree went through a massive license audit. This led to the change of many licenses by the respective code's authors and, in some drastic cases, the removal of code from OpenBSD source and ports.[4] In most situations it suffices for the authors of the software to be contacted to clarify their licenses. It is uncommon for software to be removed or replaced due to licensing issues.

As a consequence, OpenBSD can be used in commercial settings safely and with little fear of licensing issues. No fees—only the respect of the copyright and its statement—is required to use OpenBSD in a commercial product. In fact, there are numerous commercial products based on OpenBSD underpinnings.

2.5 The *Feel* of OpenBSD

OpenBSD feels different than many other UNIX systems. Its filesystem layout is more controlled and is designed primarily for security and functionalty, rather than to satisfy the needs of the marketing department.

Furthermore, OpenBSD attempts to adhere to its BSD 4.4 roots and do things "the BSD way" when possible. Many commercial and even some other free operating systems have adopted many System V features and characteristics.

2.5.1 Filesystem Layout

One of the first things that most new users will notice about OpenBSD is how the layout feels different than that of most other UNIX systems. One of the goals of OpenBSD is to make the system elegant. The result is that files are where you expect them to be. All system binaries are stored in **/sbin** folders, while the userland binaries are in **/bin**. As the software was developed mostly from the ground up, OpenBSD doesn't have any extra backward compatibility, like the support for **/opt** or **/usr/ccs/bin** seen on some other UNIX systems. This is possible because the number of people who are able to make changes to the system is kept to a minimum.

There is similar control for the ports tree—the main way new applications are installed. There is good control to prevent ports from installing files outside of **/usr/local**. All of these constraints help the operating system have a clean feel throughout, which many users see as a great selling point for the system.

---

[4]As an example, the license for the old firewall code used under OpenBSD kernels, *ipf*, had to be removed because the license was not compatible with the spirit of the Berkeley copyright.

2.5.2 Security

OpenBSD is different from most other systems in another way: It is built to be secure by default. On a new OpenBSD installation, there are very few daemons running and few network services started. Many other systems don't behave in this manner. Most systems turn on almost every service possible to save the user from having to do the setup. In contrast, on an OpenBSD system, the user needs to go through the configuration steps to enable a service. This "secure by default" stance has prevented security problems on many occasions. Although a threat may occur on many other systems, since it wasn't configured or enabled on OpenBSD systems, the security of the system remains intact.

This stance also applies to all services that are enabled by default; the least necessary access is given and the most secure setup is configured. This sometimes does have the side effect of closing off some expected functionality. As an example, by default the *OpenSSH* daemon is configured with X forwarding disabled. Most users would prefer to have this service turned on, but it's an unnecessary feature and it might turn out to be a security threat.

This isn't to say that OpenBSD is a minimalist system. The basic installation contains an SSL-enabled Apache Web server, an FTP server, an NIS client and server, an SSH server (enabled by default), a routing server, and much, much more. Most of these services are controlled via central configuration files (discussed in later chapters). The system also supports a number of third-party packages, such as the Network Time Protocol (NTP), by enabling it in the start-up of the system when it is installed.

2.5.3 User Friendliness

As can be seen from the discussion of its security in Section 2.4.2, OpenBSD seems to be designed differently than a lot of other UNIX systems. Most systems are designed to be easy to use and friendly to the user, to the point of sacrificing security. The development of OpenBSD is driven solely by the ideals of its team of developers. Although many people are upset by some of the opinions of the leading group, this strategy has the side effect of keeping the system clean.

Another place where this attitude can be seen is in the support (and lack of support) for some hardware. NetBSD aims to support as many hardware architectures as possible and has support for almost any piece of hardware that can be bought. Solaris is designed to run well on the SPARC and i386 processor lines. The hardware that is supported by OpenBSD is directly related to the task most OpenBSD systems perform: networking services. As a result, a good number of strong and stable network cards are supported, but other, more error-prone cards (e.g., old NE2000 cards) are not as well supported. Any hardware that OpenBSD does support, however, typically works well.

2.6 Packages and Ports

OpenBSD supports the concept of packages and ports. As with other operating systems, packages are programs that can be installed without the need to compile them (in binary form). A vast number of packages are shipped with the OpenBSD CDs, and more are available on the OpenBSD FTP mirrors, to fill the needs for most users. Along with the collection of packages, OpenBSD comes with a ports tree (discussed in later chapters), which contains the recipes used for building the packages. The ports tree is designed to identify dependencies needed to build and install packages automatically as necessary. The resulting packages can be installed and distributed across systems. Packages and ports are discussed more in Chapters 12 and 13, respectively.

2.7 Where Is OpenBSD Used?

Most people do not use OpenBSD as a desktop OS, though there are some people who swear by it. Some mainstream applications are not supported by OpenBSD, causing many newer-generation UNIX users to shy away from it. Many people do decide to use OpenBSD as a desktop due to its numerous advantages, and they either make sacrifices by not being able to use the missing software or actually make it work. However, OpenBSD is untouchable as a secure network services platform. Most OpenBSD systems are deployed as firewalls or other edge servers where high security is vital. The systems also shine as Web, e-mail, DNS, and intrusion detection servers. Almost anywhere that security is a high concern, OpenBSD is well designed to fit the role.

For users who wish to have modern office, multimedia, and productivity applications, OpenBSD may not be the best choice. The support for third-party applications that meet these requirements is growing, but relatively thin. Java support in OpenBSD, for example, is poor.

OpenBSD also forms the base of several commercial applications—specifically, networking and security applications. Several of the project members are employed as software architects at different companies. The license of the project allows for the reuse of the software in commercial, closed-source applications. Nevertheless, many of the benefits and bug fixes of commercial development eventually return to the project as reliability patches and enhancements.

Chapter 3
Installation

New OpenBSD users often complain that the installation process is hard and, consequently, give up before they have even gotten a system up and running. For most of these people, simply reading the documentation for the installation process would have solved most of their problems. Unlike many other systems, OpenBSD isn't designed to be configured with the click of a button—there is no graphical installation process.[1] This chapter will walk through some of the more important parts of the installation process and give information about some of the options. It will not try to guide the user through a normal installation, as that process is well documented on the OpenBSD Web site[2] and included with the official CDs.

3.1 Supported Hardware

OpenBSD supports a great deal of hardware, but it's more centered on being a server operating system, so support for fancy desktop hardware sometimes lags behind. People seeking support for the newest hardware should look more closely at FreeBSD or Linux as a way to satisfy their needs. Because the list of supported hardware is a moving target, it has not been included in this text. Consult the list at the OpenBSD Web site, which is kept current.[3] Careful consideration must be taken before installing OpenBSD on a system. While Linux will support almost any given piece of hardware, the same cannot be said of an OpenBSD system. Review the Web site listing to make sure the system will be supported before proceeding with an installation.

---

[1]Although a graphical installation process is being developed by some folks outside of the OpenBSD project, it is not a part of the main installation process. More information about this project is available at **http://www.gobie.net**.
[2]The installation guide is available at **http://www.openbsd.org/faq/faq4.html**.
[3]Check **http://www.openbsd.org/plat.html** for more information.

3.2 System Preparation

One of the most important steps in the installation process is getting to know the hardware. Make sure the documentation for the main parts of the system is at hand, or at least readily accessible from the Internet. Having this information will make the installation go much more smoothly if any problems occur.

Before an installation is started, it is good practice to review the hardware used in the system and to make notes to be used during the installation. The main components include the following:

- CPU and system architecture
- Network interface card or cards
- Disk devices and controllers
- Video hardware
- Sound hardware

The hardware in the system can be referenced against the supported hardware list for each system type and the drivers that OpenBSD will use for each device. Note that limited models of some platforms, like the Digital Alpha platform, are supported due to the diverse hardware used in their product lines. The Intel i386 platform is very well supported, however.

If the machine already has an operating system loaded, it is important to perform a full backup before installing OpenBSD. When installing the new OS, you have two options: replacing the entire hard drive with OpenBSD or partitioning the hard drive such that both operating systems can coexist. When you have multiple operating systems on the same computer, you can choose which will run when the machine is started, a practice commonly called "dual booting." You may find it easiest to back up your data, repartition the hard drive to have dedicated space for both operating systems, reinstall the original OS, reinstall your data from backups, and only then install OpenBSD. For pointers see **ftp://ftp.openbsd.org/pub/OpenBSD/3.4/i386/INSTALL.linux**. Some free boot loaders for dual booting an OpenBSD i386 system are provided in the **ftp://ftp.openbsd.org/pub/OpenBSD/3.4/tools** directory; several commercial boot managers also work with a dual-boot scenario for your OpenBSD system.

Another thing to be considered before the installation begins is what the machine will be used for. Not only can this affect which programs are installed, but it can also change how the disk should be partitioned. If the machine is to be used as a workstation, more space should be allocated for applications; if it will be used as a mail or Web server, space for the respective data files and logs should be reserved.

As when working with any new system, be prepared to reinstall a few times to get the hang of the installation and to find the best possible disk layout. Because Linux, Solaris, and OpenBSD all spread themselves across the hard disk in different ways, a disk partitioning scheme that may have worked for one OS may not work for another.

3.3 Getting the Files for Installation

The main ways to install OpenBSD are either by using the installation CD or by doing an FTP installation through the Internet or from a local mirror, if one exists. Many people who are new to OpenBSD search in vain for a downloadable copy of the OpenBSD ISO image to create a CD for themselves. Unlike with most other free operating systems, OpenBSD ISO images are not available online because the official CD image itself is trademarked. Although this practice may seem restrictive, sales represent one of the main ways to fund the project. Many people even buy the CD every six months[4] even if it won't be used, just to support the project.

Until recently, the fact that OpenBSD used strong cryptography meant that serious export restrictions applied to it. Now that the United States has modified these restrictions, many of these concerns for U.S. citizens do not exist.

3.4 Selecting Boot Media

Some architectures, such as i386, give several floppy disk choices. These accommodate various configurations and device options. Because of the small capacity of a floppy disk, only a smaller kernel with a limited amount of drivers is available for installation purposes.

The most commonly used installation image is **floppy34.fs**. It supports most IDE i386 systems and most generic laptop systems. The image **floppyB34.fs** contains several SCSI and RAID drivers enabled, and the image **floppyC34.fs** supports additional PCMCIA and cardbus devices.

For the Alpha platform, the floppy images **floppy34.fs** and **floppyB34.fs** differ in their supported hardware. Because of the diversity of Alpha hardware, these images are mutually exclusive and specific to various hardware lines. Check the documentation to determine which one to use.

As always, boot the CD if possible. It is a much easier approach to installation, with most drivers and configurations being rolled into one system. Some architectures don't

---

[4]OpenBSD releases a new version about every six months; OpenBSD 3.3 was released May 1, 2003, and 3.4 was released November 1, 2003.

have such installation choices, such as HP300 and Mac68k. Here an alternate operating system or netbooting is used for the installation purposes. Mac68k, for example, installs from an existing MacOS installation.

3.5 Booting

For most systems, booting and installing are as easy as putting the OpenBSD CD[5] in the system and away you go. On some architectures, however, this is not the case. In addition, many systems don't have a CD drive, or even a floppy disk drive for that matter. If these systems have newer network cards, network boots can be done. If they lack all of these options, more creative methods need to be used.

3.5.1 The Boot Configuration

Configuration of the boot process is done in the file **/etc/boot.conf**. Various options can be set here, including the ability to have the device boot via the command *set device root_device* (e.g., *set dev hd1a*). Notice that IDE devices are hd* devices, not wd* devices as they are listed in the booted kernel.

The *boot* keyword tells the system to boot immediately. A timeout can be set using the *set timeout* command—for example, *set timeout 30* to wait for 30 seconds. The kernel file can be specified here as well. Use *boot/bsd.new* to boot a new kernel named **/bsd.new**, or even *boot hd1a:/bsd* to boot the kernel **/bsd** from the device **hd1a**.

Serial console options can also be set here using the *stty* command. To set the serial port 0 to 19,200 baud, use the command *stty com0 19200*. Login prompts will still be displayed on screens 1–7 as normal.

To boot into single user mode—for example, to edit a lost root password or a broken root shell—use *boot -s*. Note that you will have to remount the disks with read-write privileges to access and edit files. No root password is needed to perform this option. The command *boot -a* can be used to specify an alternate root device (the system defaults to **wd0a**).

If you have a kernel problem to debug, you can issue the command *boot -c* to boot while configuring the kernel. This option is very time intensive, but it does allow you to enable or disable devices and options as needed, one by one. Lastly, use the command *boot -d* to drop to the ddb prompt immediately, which is useful for kernel testing.

---

[5]This section presumes that a CD installation will use a bootable OpenBSD CD that was purchased from the OpenBSD Web site.

3.5.2 Creating a Serial Console

For systems that run "headless," or without a monitor and keyboard, the next best thing to use is a serial console. Connecting two computers via a NULL serial cable, a serial console gives almost all of the same benefits available with a monitor and keyboard attached to the system but without extra equipment. Some form of non-networked console is needed for operations such as installation, firmware or BIOS-level operations, and kernel debugging. Serial console setup differs between the major hardware platforms.

On a typical i386-class PC, a serial console can be used to control the system almost entirely. Most desktop PCs and servers will begin using the serial device once the OpenBSD boot loader software begins, configured through the file **/etc/boot.conf** and described in the previous section. While most PC systems forbid BIOS access via the serial console, some more expensive server hardware does allow for this possibility.

Sun SPARC and UltraSPARC systems are designed to operate using serial consoles in the absence of a monitor or keyboard being attached. Simply attach a serial cable with a NULL modem adapter, and it should work without issue (as long as a keyboard isn't plugged in, the PROM automatically switches to serial mode). To create a serial console in the presence of a monitor, you need to edit two firmware values and save them:

```
ok  setenv input-device ttya
ok  setenv output-device ttya
ok  reset
```

By configuring **/dev/ttyc0** in the file **/etc/ttys**, the keyboard and monitor can still be used for normal login operations, just not console access.

MacPPC hardware, which uses OpenFirmware, is quite similar in the setup of a serial console to the SPARC family. Once at the firmware (arrived at by booting the system with the key sequence of command-option-O-F), edit the values for the input and output devices:

```
ok  setenv output-device scca
ok  setenv input-device scca
ok  reset-all
```

This will activate the serial console at 57,600 bps with 8N1 settings. Note that some older MacPPC machines default to using the serial console for OpenFirmware access. Newer models, required for using OpenBSD on the MacPPC platform, typically do not do so.

For Mac68k machines, the MacOS-based boot program can be used to select the serial console. The modem port is **tty00** and the printer serial port is **tty01**.

For all of the above systems, you will have to activate the login processes on the serial terminal as well. This is controlled through the file **/etc/ttys**. By default, the serial consoles (known as devices **tty00** and **tty01**) are off, but they can be enabled. Simply set the terminal type (in this example, *vt100*) and enable it (using the *on* keyword) and allow for root logins (with the keyword *secure*):

```
tty00   "/usr/libexec/getty std.9600"   vt100   on secure
```

For MacPPC machines, the setting *std.57600* should be used rather than the 9600 baud setting.

From an OpenBSD machine, you can access this serial console on another system by using a serial terminal program such as *minicom*, available in ports, or the built-in command *cu*:

```
# cu -l cua00 -s 9600
```

This would launch a serial console to the device **cua00** (the first serial port) at 9600 baud. Serial consoles are also used to access embedded devices and networking equipment.

3.5.3   Platform-Specific Information

i386 Hardware

Most i386 systems are easy to work with using either a CD player or floppy drive and a network card to perform the installation. The BIOS simply needs to be told to use the CD as the boot source. On some very old systems, the CD drive isn't bootable and the floppy installation path must be used. If the system has an adequate network card, the install-ation can be done using just the network card by doing a network installation with the help of a network boot server. If none of the options will work, a last-ditch method is to simply remove the system disk, install it in a different computer, and put the disk back in. As long as the architecture is the same, OpenBSD is very forgiving. The same software is installed no matter what hardware is on the system.

SPARC and SPARC64

For the most part, installation of OpenBSD on non-Intel i386 platforms is very much the same as installation on Intel platforms. The major differences come in booting and setting the machine to boot the OpenBSD kernel. In some cases the booting firmware needs only a few options set to boot correctly.

On Sun SPARC hardware, booting from a floppy disk is the most straightforward method to install the OpenBSD system. You can boot from the floppy disk by getting to the PROM, typically by pressing Stop-A on the keyboard. Once there, you can type the following to boot from the floppy disk:

```
ok  boot floppy
```

(The "ok" is the PROM prompt.) The installation procedure at this point closely resembles the i386 installation procedure. Once that completes, you will need to modify your PROM settings to boot from the hard disk and to load the file **bsd**, rather than the **vmunix** file that is expected by the Sun hardware. To do this, at the PROM type the following:

```
ok  setenv boot-file bsd
ok  setenv boot-from sd@0,0        for SCSI ID 0
 or
ok  setenv boot-from disk          for the default disk
                                     at SCSI ID 3
 then
ok  nvramrc                        to make these changes
                                     permanent
```

If additional information is needed about the devices on the SCSI chain, the PROM can be used to query the devices and show their names:

```
ok  probe-scsi-all
ok  probe-scsi                     an optional command
```

Systems that lack a CD or floppy drive can also easily be booted off a network server for their installation:

```
ok  boot net
```

This requires knowledge of the boot server's Ethernet address as well as a properly configured boot server that can serve the appropriate files.

For additional information, read the file **INSTALL.sparc** in the distribution directory.

3.5.4 Boot Example

```
boot>
booting fd0a:/bsd: 4162256+710560=0x4a5bf8
entry point at 0x100120


Copyright (c) 1982, 1986, 1989, 1991, 1993
The Regents of the University of California.  All rights reserved.
Copyright (c) 1995-2003 OpenBSD. All rights reserved.
http://www.OpenBSD.org

OpenBSD 3.4 (RAMDISK_CD) #127: Wed Sep 17 03:49:42 MDT 2003
deraadt@i386.openbsd.org:/usr/src/sys/arch/i386/compile/RAMDISK_CD
cpu0: Intel Pentium III ("GenuineIntel" 686-class, 512KB L2 cache)
    499 MHz
cpu0: FPU,V86,DE,PSE,TSC,MSR,PAE,MCE,CX8,SEP,MTRR,PGE,MCA,CMOV,PAT,
    PSE36,MMX,FXSR,SIMD
real mem  = 268009472 (261728K)
...
...


....
rootdev=0x1100 rrootdev=0x2f00 rawdev=0x2f02
de0: enabling Full Duplex 100baseTX port
erase ^?, werase ^W, kill ^U, intr ^C, status ^T
(I)nstall, (U)pgrade or (S)hell?  i

Welcome to the OpenBSD/i386 3.4 install program.

This program will help you install OpenBSD in a simple and rational
way. At any prompt except password prompts you can run a shell
command by typing '!foo', or escape to a shell by typing '!'.
Default answers are shown in []'s and are selected by pressing
RETURN. At any time you can exit this program by pressing Control-C
and then RETURN, but quitting during an install can leave your
system in an inconsistent state.

Terminal type? [vt220]  enter
```

```
Do you wish to select a keyboard encoding table? [n]  enter

IS YOUR DATA BACKED UP? As with anything that modifies disk
contents, this program can cause SIGNIFICANT data loss.

It is often helpful to have the installation notes handy. For
complex disk configurations, relevant disk hardware manuals and a
calculator are useful.

Proceed with install? [n]  y
Cool!  Let's get to it...
```

3.6 Filesystem Partitioning

The layout of a disk is highly dependent on the nature of the system being created. Four major system types are described below: a personal system (e.g., a laptop), a shell server, various server types, and a firewall. These constitute the major points on the spectrum of security and convenience. The *disklabel* program, which is used to set up the partitions in the installation program, is described in Chapter 14.

Filesystem sizes are relatively easy to figure out, but some thought must be given to them. The base system, with a separate **/usr** filesystem, takes up approximately 150MB to 250MB of space plus some room in which to move around. The **/usr** filesystem takes up 1GB to 1.5GB of space with all of the base system and a small set of common ports and packages installed. If the system source is installed, such as in **/usr/src**, and the ports tree is installed in **/usr/ports**, additional space is required. Letting the **/usr** filesystem be the remainder of a filesystem is probably the most convenient way to ensure that adequate space is allocated.

Many users also choose to separate their **/usr/local** and **/home** directories. This allows filesystems to be segmented for security and maintenance purposes.

3.6.1 A Private System

A personal system, such as a laptop, has dramatically different needs than a multiuser system. Because typically only one user is using the system, and it is often used as a primary machine, additional third-party packages are usually installed. For developers with source code installed, the size requirements can increase dramatically.

The largest changes will occur in the **/home** and **/usr** filesystems. At least 3GB of space for the **/usr** filesystem to hold the OpenBSD source tree, the ports tree, and dozens of distribution files for the packages is sufficient. A large **/home** filesystem is also important. Typically 2GB to 5GB of space is sufficient. Developers will also want to keep their **/home** directories executable for source code testing. Another solution is to place home directories on the **/usr** filesystem in a location like **/usr/home**. This will permit the remaining disk space on the drive to be allocated to the **/usr** filesystem without worrying about space needs.

3.6.2 A Multiuser System with Untrusted Users

World writable filesystems are the greatest concern for a system with many users, most of whom are untrusted. The need for world writable filesystems arises because of temporary files, such as editor recovery files or mail spools. They simply cannot be escaped, but their risk can be mitigated. World writable directories include temporary storage locations such as **/tmp** and **/var/tmp**, a user's own directory in **/home**, and the mail queue directory **/var/spool/mqueue**.

The simplest option for preventing an attack is to partition the disk according to this set of concerns and to specify mount options for those filesystems requiring greater security. With this in mind, a general-purpose server system with shell users would be partitioned as follows:

- **/usr** to hold executables
- **/tmp** to hold temporary files
- **/home** for the users' home directories
- **/var** for system volatile files
- **/** for everything else

The concerns here are space and security. Space concerns come from logfiles or temporary storage space filling the root filesystem and causing a crash.

For security issues, there are four mount options to consider:

- **nodev**   No device files are allowed on the filesystem.
- **noexec**   No application can be executed on this filesystem. This can be circumvented through a variety of techniques, however.
- **nosuid**   No application can run with a privilege level different than the user's level.
- **rdonly**   Mounts a device as a read-only device.

The option **rdonly** forces a filesystem to be mounted as read-only, preventing any write attempts to it. It can be used with base system filesystems (such as **/** and **/usr**) to prevent alteration of the system's executables. Note that the filesystem will have to be remounted with read-write privileges enabled to update the system. The root and **/usr** filesystems should not be mounted with the **noexec** or **nosuid** options as they *must* be able to execute applications and *setuid* binaries.

An additional consideration is the backup of the system. If the system is being backed up to tape, the relationship between the size of the tape and the filesystem needs to be considered. If, for example, a DDS2 tape is being used to back up the **/home** filesystem, the partition should not be larger than about 6g[6] so it can all fit onto one tape.

3.6.3 Server Partitioning

The size of the partitions on a server system greatly depends on the use of the system. If the server will be used for only one task, such as being a Web server, then space considerations are easy to resolve. If, however, the system will be a database server, a mail server, and a Web server, then obviously more must be considered.

For each service that the machine will be running, space will be needed. For a mail server, that means a large **/var/spool** filesystem. For an FTP server, space must be set aside for **/home/ftp**. The only server that doesn't really have disk requirements would be a DNS server, as it takes almost no space and doesn't log excessively. An important issue is the **/var** filesystem for a nameserver. Because the *named* process runs in a jail located in **/var/named**, it has to create a logging device to replace **/dev/log**. For a nameserver running on such a system, a separate partition for **/var/named** should be created and allowed to have a device for the system logger. In addition to the space for each application, the space that the log files will take up needs to be evaluated. In a Web server, for example, Apache will keep its logs in **/var/www/logs** by default. How much traffic will the Web server get that will be logged? Will Web log processing software be running on the system that will generate more information as well? In general, a lot of space should be allocated for the **/var** filesystem to allow for logging, even with log rotation in operation.

Because these systems will be servers, they will change a lot less than other types of systems. As a consequence, they won't need XF86 installed and may not even need the system source code or ports. Thus the **/usr** filesystem can be smaller and the **/home** filesystem can even be ignored given that there should be no users on the machine.

---

[6]The 6g estimate assumes 33 percent compression.

3.6.4 Firewall

Although setting up and running a firewall can be tricky, the partitioning for it is quite easy. The only space consideration arises for **/var** if *pflogd* is being used to log data. A firewall system also shouldn't need much of anything installed from the ports tree. In addition, filesystems should be mounted with *noexec, nosetuid*, and *nodev*. The **/usr** filesystem could even be mounted as read-only if there will be few changes.

3.6.5 Swap Space Allocation

Swap size calculation is something that is sometimes debated, but relies on a set of simple principles. While it is important to have enough memory to run all of your applications, in the event of a large-scale system fault, you'll want to have enough memory to handle a full dump of the physical RAM pages and any affected applications. This amount is typically twice the amount of physical RAM in the system. Thus, for a system with 128MB of physical RAM, a 256MB swap space should suffice for both running the system and allowing all of the system pages to be dumped to disk should the need arise.

3.6.6 Partitioning Example

The following is an example of partitioning for a firewall system.

```
You will now create an OpenBSD disklabel inside the OpenBSD MBR
partition. The disklabel defines how OpenBSD splits up the MBR
partition into OpenBSD partitions in which filesystems and swap
space are created.

The offsets used in the disklabel are ABSOLUTE, i.e. relative to
the start of the disk, NOT the start of the OpenBSD MBR partition.

# using MBR partition 3: type A6 off 63 (0x3f) size 26699967
    (0x19768bf)

Treating sectors 63-26700030 as the OpenBSD portion of the disk.
You can use the 'b' command to change this.

Initial label editor (enter '?' for help at any prompt)
>  p
device: /dev/rwd0c
```

```
type: ESDI
disk: ESDI/IDE disk
label: WDC AC313600D
bytes/sector: 512
sectors/track: 63
tracks/cylinder: 16
sectors/cylinder: 1008
cylinders: 16383
total sectors: 26712000
free sectors: 0
rpm: 3600

16 partitions:
#        size    offset    fstype   [fsize bsize  cpg]
  a:    262017        63    4.2BSD    2048 16384   260
  b:    262080    262080      swap
  c:  26712000         0    unused       0     0
  d:    262080    524160    4.2BSD    2048 16384   260
  e:   2097648    786240    4.2BSD    2048 16384   328
  f:  23816142   2883888    4.2BSD    2048 16384   328
```

As can be seen above, OpenBSD was set up on this system before. We are going to delete all of the old partitions and create new ones.

```
> d a
> d b
> d d
> d e
> d f
> p
device: /dev/rwd0c
type: ESDI
disk: ESDI/IDE disk
label: WDC AC313600D
bytes/sector: 512
sectors/track: 63
tracks/cylinder: 16
sectors/cylinder: 1008
```

```
cylinders: 16383
total sectors: 26712000
free sectors: 26699967
rpm: 3600


16 partitions:
#        size    offset    fstype    [fsize bsize   cpg]
  c: 26712000         0    unused        0      0
>  a a
stray interrupt
offset: [63]  enter
size: [26699967] 128M
Rounding to nearest cylinder: 262017
FS type: [4.2BSD]  enter
mount point: [none]  /
>  a b
offset: [262080]  enter
size: [26437950] 128M
Rounding to nearest cylinder: 262080
FS type: [swap]  enter
>  a d
offset: [524160]  enter
size: [26175870] 128M
Rounding to nearest cylinder: 262080
FS type: [4.2BSD]  enter
mount point: [none]  /tmp
>  a e
offset: [786240]  enter
size: [25913790] 1024M
Rounding to nearest cylinder: 2097648
FS type: [4.2BSD]  enter
mount point: [none]  /var
>  a f
offset: [2883888]  enter
size: [23816142]  enter
FS type: [4.2BSD]  enter
mount point: [none]  /usr
>  p
```

```
device: /dev/rwd0c
type: ESDI
disk: ESDI/IDE disk
label: WDC AC313600D
bytes/sector: 512
sectors/track: 63
tracks/cylinder: 16
sectors/cylinder: 1008
cylinders: 16383
total sectors: 26712000
free sectors: 0
rpm: 3600

16 partitions:
#        size    offset    fstype    [fsize bsize   cpg]
  a:    262017        63    4.2BSD    2048 16384    16  # /
  b:    262080    262080      swap
  c:  26712000         0    unused       0     0
  d:    262080    524160    4.2BSD    2048 16384    16  # /tmp
  e:   2097648    786240    4.2BSD    2048 16384    16  # /var
  f:  23816142   2883888    4.2BSD    2048 16384    16  # /usr
>  w
>  p
device: /dev/rwd0c
type: ESDI
disk: ESDI/IDE disk
label: WDC AC313600D
bytes/sector: 512
sectors/track: 63
tracks/cylinder: 16
sectors/cylinder: 1008
cylinders: 16383
total sectors: 26712000
free sectors: 0
rpm: 3600

16 partitions:
#        size    offset    fstype    [fsize bsize   cpg]
```

```
  a:    262017        63      4.2BSD      2048 16384     16  # /
  b:    262080    262080       swap
  c: 26712000         0      unused         0     0
  d:    262080    524160      4.2BSD      2048 16384     16  # /tmp
  e:   2097648    786240      4.2BSD      2048 16384     16  # /var
  f: 23816142   2883888      4.2BSD      2048 16384     16  # /usr
> q
No label changes.
The root filesystem will be mounted on wd0a.
wd0b will be used for swap space.
Mount point for wd0d (size=131040k)? (or 'none' or 'done') [/tmp]
Mount point for wd0e (size=1048824k)? (or 'none' or 'done') [/var]
Mount point for wd0f (size=11908071k)? (or 'none' or 'done') [/usr]
Mount point for wd0d (size=131040k)? (or 'none' or 'done') [/tmp]
Mount point for wd0e (size=1048824k)? (or 'none' or 'done')
    [/var] done
No more disks to initialize.



You have configured the following partitions and mount points:

wd0a /
wd0d /tmp
wd0e /var
wd0f /usr


The next step creates a filesystem on each partition, ERASING
existing data.
Are you really sure that you're ready to proceed? [n] y
Warning: cylinder groups must have a multiple of 2 cylinders
Warning: 64 sector(s) in last cylinder unallocated
/dev/rwd0a: 262016 sectors in 260 cylinders of 16 tracks, 63 sectors
        127.9MB in 1 cyl groups (260 c/g, 127.97MB/g, 16384 i/g)
/dev/rwd0d: 262080 sectors in 260 cylinders of 16 tracks, 63 sectors
        128.0MB in 1 cyl groups (260 c/g, 127.97MB/g, 16384 i/g)
Warning: cylinder groups must have a multiple of 2 cylinders
/dev/rwd0e: 2097648 sectors in 2081 cylinders of 16 tracks,
    63 sectors
```

```
      1024.2MB in 7 cyl groups (328 c/g, 161.44MB/g, 20608 i/g)
Warning: cylinder groups must have a multiple of 2 cylinders
Warning: 884 sector(s) in last cylinder unallocated
/dev/rwd0f: 23816140 sectors in 23628 cylinders of 16 tracks,
   63 sectors
      11629.0MB in 73 cyl groups (328 c/g, 161.44MB/g, 20608 i/g)

/dev/wd0a on /mnt type ffs (rw, asynchronous, local,
   ctime=Sat Nov 15 14:16:10 2003)
/dev/wd0d on /mnt/tmp type ffs (rw, asynchronous, local, nodev,
   nosuid, ctime=Sat Nov 15 14:16:10 2003)
/dev/wd0f on /mnt/usr type ffs (rw, asynchronous, local, nodev,
   ctime=Sat Nov 15 14:16:11 2003)
/dev/wd0e on /mnt/var type ffs (rw, asynchronous, local, nodev,
   nosuid, ctime=Sat Nov 15 14:16:11 2003)
```

3.7 Network Configuration

During the installation process, there isn't much configuration to be done in terms of networking. The installation will set the hostname for the system and the domain name. Static or dynamic IP addresses are set for any interfaces that are seen with the base kernel. Some drivers may not be supported by the installation kernel and can be configured only after the system's normal kernel has booted.

3.7.1 Network Setup Example

The next step in the installation process is to configure the networking on the machine.

```
System hostname? (short form, e.g. 'foo') server
Configure the network? [y] enter
Available interfaces are: de0.
Which one do you wish to initialize? (or 'done') [de0] enter
Symbolic (host) name for de0? [server] enter
The default media for de0 is
       media: Ethernet autoselect (100baseTX full-duplex)
Do you want to change the default media? [n] enter
```

The first option is to set the IP address for the interface using DHCP.

```
IP address for de0? (or 'dhcp')  dhcp
Issuing hostname-associated DHCP request for de0.
Internet Software Consortium DHCP Client 2.0p15-OpenBSD
Listening on BPF/de0/00:40:05:a3:36:56
Sending on   BPF/de0/00:40:05:a3:36:56
Sending on   Socket/fallback/fallback-net
DHCPDISCOVER on de0 to 255.255.255.255 port 67 interval 1
DHCPOFFER from 10.0.10.10
DHCPREQUEST on de0 to 255.255.255.255 port 67
DHCPACK from 10.0.10.10
New Network Number: 10.0.0.0
New Broadcast Address: 10.0.255.255
bound to 10.0.0.201 -- renewal in 21600 seconds.
No more interfaces to initialize.
DNS domain name? (e.g. 'bar.com') [crimelabs.net]  enter
DNS nameserver? (IP address or 'none') [10.0.0.2]  enter
Use the nameserver now? [y]  enter
Default route? (IP address, 'dhcp' or 'none') [dhcp]  enter
```

The second option, using static addresses, is not much different.

```
IP address for de0? (or 'dhcp')  10.0.10.50
Netmask? [255.255.255.0]  255.255.0.0
No more interfaces to initialize.
DNS domain name? (e.g. 'bar.com') [my.domain]  crimelabs.net
DNS nameserver? (IP address or 'none') [none]  10.0.0.2
Use the nameserver now? [y]  enter
Default route? (IP address, 'dhcp' or 'none')  10.0.0.1
add net default: gateway 10.0.0.1
```

At this point you can invoke a shell and modify networking as needed. This can include setting the media options on the device or manually adjusting any DHCP leases you received.

```
Edit hosts with ed? [n]  enter
Do you want to do any manual network configuration? [n]  enter
Password for root account? (will not echo)  password
Password for root account? (again)  password
```

3.8 Base Software Set Installation

The OpenBSD sets are distributed as a collection of compressed tar files, usually ending with the extension **.tgz**. They should not be confused with the ports and packages system, which also uses this filename extension. These files are not added with the *pkg_add* commands (see Chapter 12), but instead are unpacked directly with *tar* and *gunzip*.

The installation program will prompt you for which sets to install and provide you with a way to select all or groups of sets. These include the base system, compilers, manual pages, and the X11 windowing system. They also include the kernel file, **bsd**, which is not compressed.

3.8.1 Types of Installations

The sets to install depend on the installation itself. For example, a NIDS sensor or a firewall may be better suited to installation without the X11 system, the games packages, and the compiler package. However, a workstation or a laptop would be fairly useless for most people without a windowing system.

Additional sets may be selected and installed after the initial round of sets is added. Thus, if you change your mind later, you can modify the installed sets by adding a set.

Sets may be added after the installation program is long gone and the system is running normally because they are simply compressed tar files. However, the right flags must be used to preserve file ownership and modes. The files should be unpacked in the root directory (/). The following example shows how to add the compiler package, located in **/tmp/comp34.tgz**, to a running system:

```
#  tar -C / -zxvpf /tmp/comp34.tgz
```

The files will be unpacked relative to the root of the filesystem and prepared for immediate use. This is not the official way to unpack installation sets, but it has been used by the authors on several occasions.

Filesets may be deleted as well, albeit with a bit more difficulty. This is because the files are not registered with any packaging system. However, as described in Chapter 15, the *tar* command can list the contents of the archive. The following commands will remove the contents of any of the sets:

```
#  cd /
#  rm -f ' tar -ztvf /tmp/comp34.tgz | awk '{print $9}'
```

This code will show only the filenames from the output of the contents argument to *tar* and remove the files. We do not want to remove directories, as they may be used by other packages. Although example shows the package installed above, the same technique should work for any of the base packages. Note that this is also a very unofficial and unsupported method of removing software, but it has been used by one of the authors on several occasions to alter installations.

3.8.2 Descriptions of the Installation Sets

The binary sets from an installation (or upgrade) are named to indicate what they hold and what they provide. The asterisk indicates the version independence of the name (typically the name includes the system version, such as 34 for OpenBSD 3.4). The sets are listed below.

- **base*.tgz**   The base OpenBSD system is installed from this set, which includes core system functionality in userland. **You must install this set**.
- **etc*.tgz**   This set contains the **/etc** files for configuration of the system. **You are required to install this set**.
- **comp*.tgz**   The compilers (C, C++, F77) are installed from this set. This set is not required, but it is recommended for a typical server or system use.
- **man*.tgz**   The manual pages are installed in this set, documenting the system. This set is not required, but is recommended.
- **misc*.tgz**   This set contains miscellaneous information, such as the BSD 4.4 manuals (SMM, USD, PSD).
- **game*.tgz**   This set contains the system games, typically console games.
- **xbase*.tgz**   The base of the X11 system is installed from this set.
- **xfont*.tgz**   This set contains fonts for the X11 system; it is required for the X11 system.
- **xserv*.tgz**   The X11 server is required for the X11 system.
- **xshare*.tgz**   The manual pages and locale settings in this set include files for the X11 system.
- **bsd**   The BSD kernel is **required for a working system**.
- **bsd.rd**   This ramdisk version of the kernel is suitable for booting from a CD-Rom device. Download it if you plan to build your own bootable CD filesystems for installation. This set is not suitable for a running kernel.

3.8.3 Installation Example

The example installation will be done from a local FTP mirror server. We will install all
packages except the games package.

```
You will now specify the location and names of the install sets you
want to load. You will be able to repeat this step until all of you
sets have been successfully loaded. If you are not sure what sets
to install, refer to the installation notes for details on the
contents of each.


Sets can be located on a (m)ounted filesystem; a (c)drom, (d)isk
or (t)ape device; or a (f)tp, (n)fs or (h)ttp server.
Where are the install sets? (or 'done')  f
HTTP/FTP proxy URL? (e.g. 'http://proxy:8080', or 'none')
    [none]  enter
Display the list of known ftp servers? [y]   enter
Getting the list from 129.128.5.191 (ftp.openbsd.org)...done.
  1  ftp.openbsd.org/pub/OpenBSD            Alberta, Canada
  2  mirror.aarnet.edu.au/pub/OpenBSD       Canberra, Australia
  3  ftp.it.net.au/mirrors/OpenBSD          Perth, Australia
....
....


....
 74  mirror.cs.wisc.edu/pub/mirrors/OpenBSD    Madison, WI, USA
Server? (IP address, hostname, list#, 'done' or '?')  10.0.0.2
Does the server support passive mode ftp? [y]  enter
Server directory? [pub/OpenBSD/3.4/i386]  enter
Login? [anonymous]  enter


The following sets are available. Enter a filename, 'all' to select
all the sets, or 'done'. You may de-select a set by prepending a
'-' to its name.

        [X] bsd
        [ ] bsd.rd
        [X] base34.tgz
```

```
        [X] etc34.tgz
        [X] misc34.tgz
        [X] comp34.tgz
        [X] man34.tgz
        [X] game34.tgz
        [ ] xbase34.tgz
        [ ] xshare34.tgz
        [ ] xfont34.tgz
        [ ] xserv34.tgz

File name? (or 'done') [xbase34.tgz]   +x*

The following sets are available. Enter a filename, 'all' to select
all the sets, or 'done'. You may de-select a set by prepending a
'-' to its name.

        [X] bsd
        [ ] bsd.rd
        [X] base34.tgz
        [X] etc34.tgz
        [X] misc34.tgz
        [X] comp34.tgz
        [X] man34.tgz
        [X] game34.tgz
        [X] xbase34.tgz
        [X] xshare34.tgz
        [X] xfont34.tgz
        [X] xserv34.tgz

File name? (or 'done') [done]   -ga*

The following sets are available. Enter a filename, 'all' to select
all the sets, or 'done'. You may de-select a set by prepending a
'-' to its name.

        [X] bsd
        [ ] bsd.rd
        [X] base34.tgz
```

```
         [X] etc34.tgz
         [X] misc34.tgz
         [X] comp34.tgz
         [X] man34.tgz
         [ ] game34.tgz
         [X] xbase34.tgz
         [X] xshare34.tgz
         [X] xfont34.tgz
         [X] xserv34.tgz


File name? (or 'done') [game34.tgz]  done
Ready to install sets? [y]  enter
Getting bsd ...
0% |*                                   |    16 KB     00:00
...
...


...
Getting xserv34.tgz ...
100% |*********************************| 14797 KB     00:08


Sets can be located on a (m)ounted filesystem; a (c)drom, (d)isk or
(t)ape device; or a (f)tp, (n)fs or (h)ttp server.
Where are the install sets? (or 'done')  done
Do you expect to run the X Window System? [y]  enter
Saving configuration files...done.
Generating initial host.random file...done.
```

3.9 Post-Installation
3.9.1 Time Zone Information and Example

The last stage of the installation sets the time zone.

```
What timezone are you in? ('?' for list) [US/Pacific]  US/Eastern
You have selected timezone 'US/Eastern'.
```

If you need to change this selection in the future, you can change the link in the file **/etc/localtime**, which points to an entry in the directory **/usr/share/zoneinfo**.

3.9.2 After Reboot

Once the system has finished installing, a reboot is needed. Note that the system will generate its OpenSSH keys on this first boot. This rather CPU-intensive process may take considerable time depending on the hardware type.[7]

3.10 Customizing the Installation Process

For some users, a customized installation may be desirable. This can be useful for large-scale rollouts, reinstallations from backups, installation support for hardware needed to complete the process, or local setups (e.g., a university campus). There are three major ways to customize the process, characterized by differing capabilities and levels of difficulty.

3.10.1 Creating Site-Specific Files

The easiest way to customize the installation process is to create a local archive to install along with the base system. This is handled gracefully by the normal installation floppy. Along with the installation sets (such as **base34.tgz**), a corresponding file named **site*.tgz** is listed. The version of this file matches the version of the installation sets being loaded (i.e., **site34.tgz** for an OpenBSD 3.4 installation). This file is installed last, after any other sets are installed (even if additional sets are chosen).

This file is unpacked in the root directory of the root filesystem, and therefore provides a way of customizing the installation for the particular site. For example, **/etc** files can be created for a local configuration (such as Kerberos files), additional or different binaries can be installed, and even some basic packages can be installed this way.

Because this file overwrites any file that previously existed, it cannot be used to remove files. However, it can be used to modify permissions on files and executables or to zero files out, thereby effectively removing them.

Creating this file is easy. After a system is installed and configured, simply use *tar* and *gzip* to build the **site*.tgz** file. In this example, a system is configured for a local Kerberos V realm and has a default user added to the **/etc/passwd** file. These will be installed on all other machines in this laboratory setup:

---

[7]SSH key generation took about 20 minutes on a 60 MHz SPARC system, but only a few seconds on a modern Pentium IV processor.

```
modify the system for the local settings
# tar -zcvf /tmp/site33.tgz /etc/krb5.conf /etc/kerberosV
/etc/passwd /etc/master.passwd /home/guest
now copy the file to the FTP server next to the install sets
```

Now the other machines will receive the Kerberos configurations and the information for the guest user account, along with the home directory for the guest user account. Permissions and file modes are preserved by the installation program.

3.10.2 Jumpstarting Installations

The next method to customize an installation is to replicate the process using a custom installation process.[8] This method is similar to the RedHat "Kickstart" installations and the Sun Solaris "Jumpstart" method. The basic premise is that you build a system image that meets your needs and then automate the installation process. This option requires that the source code to the system be checked out and available for alteration.

One of the most challenging aspects of this installation method is the need to automate the disk partitioning. The easiest way to do this is to use the *disklabel(8)* command and to write the predefined label to the system. Once the prototype system is installed, the *disklabel* command can be used to automatically build a disk label for the disk you will be using:

```
# disklabel -t wd0 >> /etc/disklabel   (or sd0)
```

This method assumes that all of the systems will have identical hardware and disks. If this is not the case, but a small number of disk types will be seen instead, build the disklabel for each one and write them to the **/etc/disklabel** file.

Having set up the disks and fileystems, the next step is to edit the file **/usr/src/distrib/miniroot/dot.profile**. Change the lower part to read as follows:

```
        # Installing or upgrading?
        /install
fi
```

This will force an installation, rather than querying for the next step.

---

[8]This section is based on a message to the misc@openbsd.org mailing list by Chuck Yerkes on December 23, 2002, with the subject "Re: Jumpstart install." Chuck was also very helpful in private e-mails in clarifying some information.

Next, edit the files **/usr/src/distrib/miniroot/install.sh** and **/usr/src/distrib/miniroot/install.sub** to remove the "ask" functions. Instead, set a default answer to autopartition the disk and create filesystems (using *newfs*), and then mount these created filesystems. Setting the installation server and choosing the sets are relatively easy tasks at this point. This technique requires a tremendous amount of editing of the installation script, which is not detailed here. However, advanced users will find that it is a reasonably well-documented script and, by removing the "ask" functions and replacing them with variable settings, the process can be automated rather smoothly. Note that the hard disk's root filesystem is mounted on the boot system's **/mnt** filesystem, so all paths are relative to it.

The remaining challenge is to set the hostname and IP address of the system. A DHCP server can be used to assign both, which can then be parsed and inserted automatically into the booting system. This will requiring reordering of the settings, as the installation process asks for the hostname before the IP address (or the use of DHCP).

Having edited the installation scripts (in **install.sh** and **install.sub**) to automatically select the operations and choices, now rebuild all of the boot floppies (or choose one of the floppies):

```
#  cd /usr/src/distrib/i386
#  make
```

This will create the kernel and populate the ramdisks, leaving you with a floppy-sized image to copy to a floppy disk using *dd*, just as you would for a normal installation with the provided floppies:

```
#  dd if=floppy34.fs of=/dev/fd0c
```

This command copies the entire floppy image to the floppy disk itself, suitable for booting.

Now, when you boot this crafted disk, the ramdisk will use its new **/etc/dot.profile** and launch into the script **install.sh**, which performs the installation process. This set will complete the installation process and leave the system ready for disk ejection and a final reboot.

This method is the most labor-intensive process, by far, and is recommended only for experienced developers. The level of detail required to make it work is beyond the scope of this book.

3.10.3 Customized Installation Floppies

The next method available to customize the installation process is to alter the kernel configurations of the boot floppies. This approach is needed for hardware that lacks, support on the installation floppies provided—for example, a new Ethernet device or a disk driver.

By modifying the kernel configurations in **/usr/src/sys/arch/i386/conf**, which are used by the **Makefile** files in **/usr/src/distrib**, new kernels can be built. The kernel configurations **RAMDISKA, RAMDISKB**, and **RAMDISKC** are used by the installation floppies. **RAMDISK_CD** is used by the CD installation process. For other architectures, different kernel configuration files are listed.

The main step is to modify the kernel configuration to support your hardware as needed. For example, one may enable the Ethernet device *bge*, which is only supported on the CD configuration[9] for the installation sets. Once that step is complete, simply run *make* in **/usr/src/distrib/i386** or whatever architecture you are using (e.g., *sparc64, alpha*).

Note, however, that size is a crucial factor for the installation floppies. If a device is added, another one (or two) must be taken away. The easiest set of devices to remove comprises unneeded Ethernet drivers, which merely consume space. It may take several attempts to get the size changes correct.

It is much easier to just boot the larger CD image. More options and devices are available using that method.

3.11 Upgrading an Installation

For those who wish to upgrade an existing OpenBSD installation, a variety of approaches are feasible. The easiest is to use the binary upgrade path. Alternatively, upgrading from a source is available. These steps are discussed in Chapter 31.

---

[9]The *bge* device is a gigabit Ethernet device.

Chapter 4

Basic Use

Once you have a good grasp of any particular UNIX system, almost all others feel about the same. Indeed, only a few small quirks need to be dealt with to move to any other system. These quirks can include anything from flags for the *ps* command, to filesystem layout differences, to RC scripts, to the installation of applications. This chapter will walk through some of these points on the OpenBSD system and explain why these differences exist.

4.1 General Filesystem Layout

Most UNIX systems have a fairly similar filesystem layout. The difference between OpenBSD and most other systems is that OpenBSD keeps programs and files in set places. Because there is much better control over the applications (a tightly knit group of developers builds the trusted set), all programs are put in the *correct* places. Other systems such as RedHat 9.0 and Solaris 9 don't follow this strategy. They have many applications installed by different authors or significant backward compatibility requirements that lead to a messy filesystem layout. On OpenBSD, everything is where you would expect it to be on a BSD 4.4 system.

The filesystem hierarchy is described in the manual pages. The reasons for this layout are both technical and administrative.

4.1.1 /bin and /sbin

When the system boots, it needs a base set of files. These files, and nothing more, should live in **/bin** and **/sbin**. When the system is brought up in single-user mode, it should not need any files in **/usr**. Some systems NFS-mount **/usr** or mount **/usr** off a different partition. All the files that are needed to use NFS or to mount an additional filesystem would then need to reside in the **/bin** or **/sbin** directories. These should always be on the **/** partition of your hard drive. Keep in mind that to also have **/etc** on the partition you put **/** on to spare you a lot of grief when something goes awry and you don't remember which partition contains your **/etc** directories.

4.1.2 /usr/bin and /usr/sbin

Once the system starts up and has all disks mounted, programs in **/usr/bin** and **/usr/sbin** can be used. These folders contain the system installed binaries (those that came with the base installation). The **/usr/bin** directory contains the programs for users on the system. For the most part, files in **/usr/sbin** are used by the system itself or an administrator. Users will normally not need to run binaries in **/usr/sbin**. The system daemons also live in **/usr/sbin** (e.g., *httpd, sendmail, inetd*).

Also on the **/usr** partition, though not in **/usr/bin** or **/usr/sbin**, are several other folders. Two notable directories are **/usr/src** and **/usr/ports**. The **/usr/src** folder, which was originally empty after the installation, is the usual place for the source code of the base system (which you get via *cvs*, as described in Appendix A). The **/usr/ports** folder, which doesn't exist after the installation, will be created when you untar the ports tarball. The ports tree lives in **/usr/ports**. More information on the **/usr/ports** and **/usr/src** folders is provided in Chapters 12, 13, and 32.

One additional filesystem that needs some explanation is **/usr/libexec**. It contains system binaries, as does **/usr/sbin**, but most of these are used by the system rather than being called from the command line. For example, **/usr/libexec/locate.updatedb** is called weekly to rebuild the *locate(1)* database.

4.1.3 /var

Like most UNIX systems, OpenBSD makes heavy use of the **/var** partition. It differs from most other partitions in that it contains variable data (hence the name). Things like logfiles, mail spools, and print files are all found here. Unlike many other OSs, OpenBSD stores all logs in the **/var/log** folder as separate files based on the *syslog* facility. Many other operating systems store logs in both **/var/adm** and **/var/log**, or shove all messages into one huge file instead of breaking them down based on *syslog* facilities.

Make sure the partition where **/var** is located doesn't get full. If it does, your system can come to a quick halt. Ideally, you should put this directory on its own partition if you can afford the space.

4.1.4 /tmp

The **/tmp** directory is the place where anyone can write. This is a great benefit, but can also cause security problems because some programs create files in **/tmp** with predictable filenames. For example, if it's known that a program creates a file called **/tmp/.abc123** that is run as root, we could create the file ahead of time and symlink it to, for example, **/etc/passwd**. The program would then happily overwrite the password file. This outcome can be prevented only by good coding, as has been done by the OpenBSD audit team.

Another thing to note about **/tmp** is that all files contained in it are erased upon rebooting. This can be prevented by editing the **/etc/rc** file. As this space can be used for scratch space sometimes, it may be wise to not have it erased upon a reboot.

If **/tmp** is located on the **/** partition, any user can crash the system. Because the system needs the ability to write to **/**, if the user fills up the partition by putting files in **/tmp**, the system can lock up.

Some filesystem options can be used to speed up the use of the **/tmp** directory. They will be covered in Chapter 14.

4.1.5 /usr/local

Any applications or files that are installed that are not part of the base installation should be installed in their respective **/usr/local** counterpart folders, such as **/usr/local/bin, /usr/local/sbin, /usr/local/lib,** and **/usr/local/include**. OpenBSD discourages ports and packages from creating their own top-level folders in **/usr/local**. This strategy keeps the filesystem cleaner. On some systems, **/usr/local/** will be NFS-mounted from a remote server. This allows for better administration in an environment with many machines.

4.1.6 /home

As with most operating systems, users' home directories are located on the **/home** partition with OpenBSD. This partition can and should be mounted with the *noexec* and *nosuid* mount options to restrict the potentially malicious actions available to users. See Chapter 14 for information on how to achieve this.

4.1.7 /dev

As Table 4.1 shows, a major difference between OpenBSD and other UNIX systems relates to the naming of the devices in **/dev**.

Table 4.1. Names of Devices in **/dev**

	RedHat Linux	**Solaris 8 (i86)**	**OpenBSD**
IDE disk 0	hda	dsk/c0t0d0s0	wd0
SCSI disk 2	sdc	dsk/c0t0d2s0	sd2
Parallel	lpt0	lp0	lpt0
Serial port	cua0	cu/a	cua00

Obviously, when more than one device is present, the last number is increased. For example, the second serial device is **/dev/cua01** in the OpenBSD kernel. Ethernet and other networking devices will be covered in Chapter 9.

4.1.8 /sys

The symlink **/sys** points to the source directory that lives in **/usr/src/sys**. This is where the source files for the kernel reside.

4.1.9 /stand

The directory tree that starts in **/stand** holds programs and applications that are needed in a stand-alone environment. It is typically empty and is maintained for backward computability with older BSD systems.

4.2 Start-up and Shutdown

In Linux and Solaris systems, the file **/etc/inittab** is read by the kernel when it attempts to bring the whole system up. The kernel parses through that file and runs various scripts depending on the desired run level. On an OpenBSD system, the *init* process reads a different file, the **/etc/rc** file. This script starts filesystems, networking, daemons, and other components.

The following is a walkthrough of the boot process with excerpts from the script. When possible, the entire action is shown; otherwise, it is abbreviated.

1. Configure the CCD (Concatenated Disk Driver) and RAIDframe Disk Driver. These will be described in Chapter 14.

```
# Configure ccd devices.
if [ -f /etc/ccd.conf ]; then
        ccdconfig -C
fi

# Configure raid devices.
for dev in 0 1 2 3; do
        if [ -f /etc/raid$dev.conf ]; then
                raidctl -c /etc/raid$dev.conf raid$dev
        fi
done

# Check parity on raid devices.
raidctl -P all
```

2. Enable the system's virtual memory swap space using *swapctl*.

```
swapctl -A -t blk
```

3. The system runs FSCK (Filesystem Consistency ChecK) on all disks in the
   /etc/fstab file.

```
if [ -e /fastboot ]; then
      echo "Fast boot: skipping disk checks."
elif [ $1x = autobootx ]; then
      echo "Automatic boot in progress: starting file system checks."
      fsck -p
...
fi

trap "echo 'Boot interrupted.'; exit 1" 3
```

4. Mount all system disks except those that are NFS mounts.

```
umount -a >/dev/null 2>&1
mount -a -t nonfs
mount -uw /          # root on nfs requires this, others aren't hurt
rm -f /fastboot      # XXX (root now writable)
```

5. Read in the settings from the **/etc/rc.conf** file.

```
. /etc/rc.conf
```

6. If PF is enabled, set up a default block policy allowing only *sshd* in while the rest of the system is loaded.

```
if [ "X${pf}" != X"NO" ]; then
    RULES="block all"
    RULES="$RULES pass in proto tcp from any to any port 22 keep state"
...
    echo $RULES | pfctl -f - -e
fi
```

7. Parse the **/etc/sysctl.conf** file and set the kernel state from the information in the file.

```
if [ -f /etc/sysctl.conf ]; then
(
        # delete comments and blank lines
        set -- `stripcom /etc/sysctl.conf`
        while [ $# -ge 1 ] ; do
                sysctl -w $1
                shift
        done
)
fi
```

8. Start networking by launching the **/etc/netstart** script.

```
echo 'starting network'
. /etc/netstart
```

This script does the following things:

(a) Re-parse the **/etc/rc.conf** file for settings and options.

(b) Set the system hostname, which lives in **/etc/myname**.

(c) Set the system domain name, held in **/etc/domainname**.

(d) Enable the loopback (lo) interface and set up routing for it.

(e) If IPv6 is enabled, load the IPv6 routes for the loopback interface.

(f) For each interface in **/etc/hostname.*** files, parse the file and configure the interface using *ifconfig*.

(g) Set the default gateway, configured in **/etc/mygate**.

(h) Set up multicast routing using static routes, if enabled.

(i) Set up GIF/GRE/bridge interfaces if any are configured.

9. If you're using PF, load the ruleset from the default **/etc/pf.conf** file as specified in the **/etc/rc.conf** file.

```
if [ "X${pf}" != X"NO" ]; then
        if [ -f ${pf_rules} ]; then
                pfctl -f ${pf_rules}
        fi
fi
```

10. Make sure the **/var/db/host.random** file exists. Create it if it does not.

```
# if there's no /var/db/host.random, make one through /dev/urandom
if [ ! -f /var/db/host.random ]; then
        dd if=/dev/urandom of=/var/db/host.random bs=1024 count=64  >
    /dev/null 2>&1
        chmod 600 /var/db/host.random >/dev/null 2>&1
else
        dd if=/var/db/host.random of=/dev/urandom bs=1024 count=64 >
            /dev/null 2>&1
        dd if=/var/db/host.random of=/dev/arandom bs=1024 count=64 >
            /dev/null 2>&1
fi

# reset seed file, so that if a shutdown-less reboot occurs,
# the next seed is not a repeat
dd if=/dev/urandom of=/var/db/host.random bs=1024 count=64 >
    /dev/null 2>&1
```

11. Clean up lingering lock files and boot files.

```
rm -f /etc/nologin
rm -f /var/spool/lock/LCK.*
rm -f /var/spool/uucp/STST/*

...
```

12. Make a backup copy of the *dmesg* output, storing it in **/var/run/dmesg.boot**.

```
dmesg >/var/run/dmesg.boot
```

13. Start *syslog*, and, if required for the *named* chroot environment, set up *syslog* for that environment by creating the needed socket **/dev/log**. Begin listening on that device.

```
echo 'starting system logger'
rm -f /dev/log
...
syslogd ${syslogd_flags}
```

14. If PF and *pflogd* are being used, enable them via *ifconfig*.

```
if [ X"${pf}" != X"NO" -a X"${pflogd_flags}" != X"NO" ]; then
        ifconfig pflog0 up
        pflogd ${pflogd_flags}
fi
```

15. If enabled, start *named* in a chroot jail in **/var/named**.

```
if [ "X${named_flags}" != X"NO" ]; then
...
        echo 'starting named';          named ${named_flags}
fi
```

16. If enabled, start *isakmpd* for IPsec.

```
if ["X${isakmpd_flags}" != X"NO" -a -e /etc/isakmpd/isakmpd.policy];
then
        echo 'starting isakmpd';        isakmpd ${isakmpd_flags}
fi
```

17. Start the following enabled RPC daemons:
    (a) *portmap*, which handles port redirection for services
    (b) *yp* services, which handle the NIS subsystem

18. Enable NIS binding if necessary.

```
if [ -d /var/yp/binding -a X`domainname` != X ]; then
        if [ -d /var/yp/`domainname` ]; then
```

```
                 # yp server capabilities needed...
                 echo -n ' ypserv';        ypserv ${ypserv_flags}
                 #echo -n ' ypxfrd';        ypxfrd
        fi

        echo -n ' ypbind';                 ypbind
...
```

19. If enabled, start the NFS daemon.

```
if [ X${nfs_server} = X"YES" -a -s /etc/exports -a \
    `sed -e '/^#/d' < /etc/exports | wc -l` -ne 0 ]; then
        rm -f /var/db/mountdtab
        echo -n > /var/db/mountdtab
        echo -n ' mountd';            mountd
        echo -n ' nfsd';              nfsd ${nfsd_flags}
        if [ X${lockd} = X"YES" ]; then
                echo -n ' rpc.lockd';  rpc.lockd
        fi
fi
```

20. If enabled, start *amd*, the automount daemon.

```
if [ X${amd} = X"YES" -a -e ${amd_master} ]; then
        echo -n ' amd'
        (cd /etc/amd; amd -l syslog -x error,noinfo,nostats -p \
            -a ${amd_dir} `cat ${amd_master}` > /var/run/amd.pid )
fi
```

21. If enabled, start *rdate* and *timed*.

```
if [ X"${rdate_flags}" != X"NO" ]; then
        echo -n ' rdate';     rdate -s ${rdate_flags}
fi
if [ "X${timed_flags}" != X"NO" ]; then
        echo -n ' timed'; timed $timed_flags
fi
```

22. Mount any NFS partitions specified in **/etc/fstab**.

```
mount -a -t nfs
```

23. If enabled, start *afs*, the Andrew filesystem.

24. If enabled, start quota management and run *quotacheck* on applicable filesystems.

```
if [ "X${check_quotas}" = X"YES" ]; then
        echo -n 'checking quotas:'
        quotacheck -a
        echo ' done.'
        quotaon -a
fi
```

25. Create kernel and **/dev** databases.

```
echo -n 'building ps databases:'
echo -n " kvm"
kvm_mkdb
echo -n " dev"
dev_mkdb
...
```

26. Run ACL and owner sanity checks on **/dev** and **/etc/passwd**.

```
chmod 666 /dev/tty[pqrstuvwxyzPQRST]*
chown root:wheel /dev/tty[pqrstuvwxyzPQRST]*
```

27. Clear **/tmp** by removing any files in it.

```
(cd /tmp && rm -rf [a-km-pr-zA-Z]* && ...
```

28. Create necessary UNIX sockets for X.

```
if [ -d /usr/X11R6/lib ]; then
        for d in /tmp/.X11-unix /tmp/.ICE-unix ; do
...
```

29. Set the system security level, defaulting to 1 (secure mode) as specified in the **/etc/rc.securitylevel** file. This choice cannot be reversed. It increases the system security by preventing kernel memory from being written to from userland programs, enforcing extra filesystem safety for immutable and append-only files, and prevents the loading of kernel modules. Any initialization tools that need to modify these parameters must appear in the script **/etc/rc.securelevel**. This value is controlled by the *sysctl* variable "kern.securelevel" in the file **/etc/sysctl.conf**.

```
if [ -f /etc/rc.securelevel ] && . /etc/rc.securelevel
if [ X${securelevel} != X"" ]; then
        echo -n 'setting kernel security level: '
        sysctl -w kern.securelevel=${securelevel}
fi
```

30. Rewrite the **/etc/motd** file to the system default.

```
if [ ! -f /etc/motd ]; then
        install -c -o root -g wheel -m 664 /dev/null /etc/motd
fi
...
```

31. Recover any lost *vi* files.

```
if [ -x /usr/libexec/vi.recover ]; then
        echo 'preserving editor files'; /usr/libexec/vi.recover
fi
```

32. Turn on process accounting via *accton*, storing information in the file **/var/account/acct**.

```
if [ -f /var/account/acct ]; then
        echo 'turning on accounting';   accton /var/account/acct
fi
```

33. Create a runtime link editor directory cache, which configures the location of shared libraries.

```
if [ -f /sbin/ldconfig ]; then
        echo 'creating runtime link editor directory cache.'
        if [ -d /usr/local/lib ]; then
```

```
                        shlib_dirs="/usr/local/lib $shlib_dirs"
            fi
   ...
```

34. Generate new SSH, RSA, and DSA host keys if none are present. This usually is done during your first boot up after the installation is complete.

```
if [ ! -f /etc/ssh/ssh_host_dsa_key ]; then
        echo -n "ssh-keygen: generating new DSA host key... "
        if /usr/bin/ssh-keygen -q -t dsa -f /etc/ssh/ssh_host_dsa_key
        -N '';
        then
   ...
```

35. Start enabled network daemons:

    (a) *gated* (available in ports and packages) or *routed* (supplied with the system). These support dynamic routing protocols.

    (b) *mrouted*, which supports dynamic multicast routing protocols.

    (c) *dhcpd*, which processes requests for DHCP clients.

    (d) IPv6 routing services, such as router solicitation messages via *rtsold*, or becoming an IPv6 router using dynamic routing protocols via *route6d* and advertising the local subnet information via *rtadvd*.

    (e) *rwhod*, which allows others to query the list of who is logged into the local machine from remote machines.

    (f) *lpd*, which handles printing services.

    (g) *sendmail*, which handles electronic mail delivery. The system defaults to a localhost-only service, so that messages can be handled for scheduled jobs and the like.

    (h) *httpd*, the Apache Web server.

    (i) *ftpd*, the FTP service.

    (j) *identd*, a network socket identification program, which is queried by some remote services such as *sendmail* or IRC.

    (k) *smtpfwdd*, the SMTP forwarding daemon.

    (l) *inetd*, which acts as a super-server for many network daemons.

    (m) *rarpd*, which handles reverse ARP requests.

(n) *bootparamd*, which handles boot parameters for diskless clients.

(o) *rbootd*, which serves diskless clients information needed to boot.

(p) *mopd*, which handles MOP requests from diskless clients.

(q) *sshd*, which handles incoming secure shell (SSH) connections.

(r) *wsconsctl*, which sets the console state.

(s) *kbd*, which sets the keyboard translation.

(t) *kerberos* KDC server, the Kerberos Domain Controller service. More information will be given in Chapter 25.

(u) *kerberos* slave server, which allows a slave KDC to exist.

The start-up of these processes is typically controlled by two factors. First, the option must be enabled in the file **/etc/rc.conf**, which is typically done by setting the parameter to something other than "NO" or by providing arguments. Second, the executable required must exist. Very few of these processes are started by default in the base OpenBSD system.

36. Run programs added by the user in **/etc/rc.local**. This looks similar to the start-up script **/etc/rc** but contains commands added after the base system has been loaded.

```
[ -f /etc/rc.local ] && . /etc/rc.local
```

37. If enabled, load *apmd*, the automatic power daemon.

```
if [ "X${apmd_flags}" != X"NO" -a -x /usr/sbin/apmd ]; then
        echo -n ' apmd';          /usr/sbin/apmd ${apmd_flags}
fi
```

38. Enable *screenblank*, which preserves the screen by blanking it after a period of inactivity.

39. Start *crond*, the scheduler service.

```
echo -n ' cron';              cron
```

40. If enabled, start *wsmoused*, which allows a mouse to be used in console-only mode.

```
if [ "X${wsmoused_flags}" != X"NO" -a -x /usr/sbin/wsmoused ]; then
    echo 'starting wsmoused...';  /usr/sbin/wsmoused ${wsmoused_flags}
fi
```

41. If enabled, start *xdm*, the graphical login manager.

```
if [ "X${xdm_flags}" != X"NO" ]; then
    echo 'starting xdm...';        /usr/X11R6/bin/xdm ${xdm_flags}
fi
```

Although this script is long, it has a rather simple structure. When a full installation is done, very few services are enabled by default. This minimalism is by design. Because the inexperienced user has to learn how to *enable* different services instead of how to *disable* services, the system is more secure and less prone to user configuration mistakes.

Creating a new service that can be controlled in the same way is very simple. Just perform a two-part test for any service: (1) Is enabled in a configuration file? and (2) Can the needed executable be run? This can be done in the file **/etc/rc.local**, for example, via the use of a **rc.local.conf** file. At the top of **/etc/rc.local**, add a line to source this configuration file:

```
. /etc/rc.conf.local
```

This will load the file and any of its settings. Next, begin using them to control services. First, we will test for a setting for a service—in this case *firewalld*, for "YES." Next, we will ensure that the needed executable is available:

```
if [ "X${firewalld} != X"NO" -a -x /usr/local/sbin/firewalld ]; then
    echo -n ' firewalld';  /usr/local/sbin/firewalld ${firewalld_flags}
fi
```

We set the variable *firewalld=YES* and the needed flags for the command in the variable *firewalld_flags* in the file **/etc/rc.local.conf**. We can turn off this service by simply setting the flag to "NO."

4.3 Logging In

Most Linux users will be familiar with the procedure for adding and removing terminals via the **/etc/inittab** file. On the OpenBSD system, this is done in the **/etc/ttys** file.

```
ttyC0    "/usr/libexec/getty Pc"        vt220   on   secure
ttyC1    "/usr/libexec/getty Pc"        vt220   on   secure
ttyC2    "/usr/libexec/getty Pc"        vt220   on   secure
```

```
ttyC3    "/usr/libexec/getty Pc"        vt220   on  secure
ttyC4    "/usr/libexec/getty Pc"        vt220   off secure
ttyC5    "/usr/libexec/getty Pc"        vt220   on  secure
ttyC6    "/usr/libexec/getty Pc"        vt220   off secure
ttyC7    "/usr/libexec/getty Pc"        vt220   off secure
```

As can be seen here, five virtual terminals are started. These are accessible by pressing Ctrl+Alt+F[12346], respectively. Note that *ttyC5* is off and is used for the X Window system. These terminals can be enabled, though, and X will happily use *ttyC7*. The program *getty* is the process that prompts for the username and password on the console.

Using one of the serial ports on the system for a console (for remote management, VT100 terminals, or other purposes) is simple. In the **/etc/ttys** file, change the following line:

```
#tty00   "/usr/libexec/getty std.9600"    unknown off
tty00    "/usr/libexec/getty std.9600"    vt100 on secure
```

For our system, we've turned on *getty* on the first serial port (known as com1 to DOS folks). We've set the term type to be *vt100* and set it to *secure* so root can log in from that terminal. A system reboot or *kill -HUP 1*[1] is required to activate it. To also see the boot prompt, enabling you to choose which kernel to boot and other boot-time options, run this command:

```
#  echo ''set tty com0 >  /etc/boot.conf''
```

You will then see the boot messages flying by on the attached serial console.

4.4 RC Scripts

In other UNIX systems, start-up scripts are typically stored in **/etc/init.d**, **/etc/rc.d**, or a similar location. In the OpenBSD boot process, everything works from the **/etc/rc** script. To start a daemon from a running system, you simply call it (rather than using a start-up script). To stop a process, you simply kill it (rather than using the stop script).

Although you can add your own start-up commands to the **/etc/rc** file, it is better to add them to the **/etc/rc.local** script. This allows for better management, whose benefits

---

[1]Sending a HUP signal to the *init* process, which is always process ID 1, will cause *init* to reread the **/etc/ttys** file.

become apparent at upgrade time. By locating all changes to a single file that is accessed after normal system boot time, fundamental system behavior is unlikely to be disrupted.

4.5 Default Processes

OpenBSD doesn't start much by default. Here is a quick *ps -ax* listing and a description of what each program really does:

```
PID     TT  STAT  TIME      COMMAND
1       ??  Is    0:00.01  /sbin/init
20406   ??  Is    0:00.04  syslogd
16749   ??  Is    0:00.00  inetd
9367    ??  Is    0:00.65  /usr/sbin/sshd
29875   ??  Is    0:00.24  sendmail: accepting connections (sendmail)
26405   ??  Is    0:00.03  cron
4307    C0  Is+   0:00.00  /usr/libexec/getty Pc ttyC0
24017   C1  Is+   0:00.00  /usr/libexec/getty Pc ttyC1
23993   C2  Is+   0:00.00  /usr/libexec/getty Pc ttyC2
17088   C3  Is+   0:00.01  /usr/libexec/getty Pc ttyC3
27814   C5  Is+   0:00.00  /usr/libexec/getty Pc ttyC5
```

- */sbin/init*   *init* is the master parent process. Most daemon processes have *init* as their parent.

- *syslog*   *syslog* is the system logging service. Applications log to the *syslog* port, and *syslog* logs to files as specified in the **/etc/syslog.conf** file. *syslog* is documented in Chapter 5.

- *inetd*   *inetd* is the master process that spawns most of the Internet services, such as *ftp* and *telnet*. *inetd* is documented in Chapter 10.

- */usr/sbin/sshd*   *sshd* is the secure login process and is discussed in Chapter 20.

- *sendmail: accepting connections (sendmail)*   *sendmail* is the default mail server for OpenBSD and is documented in Chapter 17. By default, it listens for mail on the localhost address, which is not accessible via the outside network. This allows for normal intra-system mail delivery, as well as the delivery of messages off the system.

- *cron*   *cron* is used by OpenBSD for scheduling tasks. It is documented in Chapter 16.

- */usr/libexec/getty Pc ttyC[01235]*   There are five login consoles listening on this machine, controlled by the **/etc/ttys** file.

4.5.1 Random PID Values

As an added security feature, OpenBSD picks random process numbers for each process that is spawned. This helps to prevent attacks against predictable process ID values. It also adds some security to files that use the process ID to create random filenames. The only process to which this rule doesn't apply is the *init* process; its number is always 1.

4.6 Ports and Packages

Most add-on programs should be installed from the packages collection or ports tree. This seems like a strange paradigm relative to what most Linux users are used to. Once the ports tree file has been extracted, all that needs to be done is to *cd* into the right folder and to do a *make install* as root. The *make* script will go through a list of FTP servers, download the source for the package, check for dependencies, get and install files as necessary, and install the original package. This process will be covered more in Chapters 12 and 13.

4.7 Networking in Brief

Networking is one of main strengths of OpenBSD and most systems take advantage of its strength to fill network-related roles. Networking is discussed in depth in Chapter 9, but a quick overview is given here as well. At boot time, the networking systems are begun via the script **/etc/netstart**, which is called from **/etc/rc** and executed before the script **/etc/rc** is completed.

The main tool used to check the status of the current network configuration is *ifconfig*. Using *ifconfig -a* to show all network devices we get something like this

```
root@server:/root# ifconfig -a
lo0: flags=8049<UP,LOOPBACK,RUNNING,MULTICAST> mtu 33224
        inet 127.0.0.1 netmask 0xff000000
        inet6 ::1 prefixlen 128
        inet6 fe80::1%lo0 prefixlen 64 scopeid 0x4
lo1: flags=8008<LOOPBACK,MULTICAST> mtu 33224
xl0: flags=8802<BROADCAST,SIMPLEX,MULTICAST> mtu 1500
        address: 00:06:5b:d8:8a:37
        media: Ethernet autoselect (none)
        status: no carrier
pflog0: flags=0<> mtu 33224
```

```
sl0: flags=c010<POINTOPOINT,LINK2,MULTICAST> mtu 296
sl1: flags=c010<POINTOPOINT,LINK2,MULTICAST> mtu 296
ppp0: flags=8010<POINTOPOINT,MULTICAST> mtu 1500
ppp1: flags=8010<POINTOPOINT,MULTICAST> mtu 1500
tun0: flags=10<POINTOPOINT> mtu 3000
tun1: flags=10<POINTOPOINT> mtu 3000
enc0: flags=0<> mtu 1536
bridge0: flags=0<> mtu 1500
bridge1: flags=0<> mtu 1500
vlan0: flags=0<> mtu 1500
        address: 00:00:00:00:00:00
        vlan1: flags=0<> mtu 1500
        address: 00:00:00:00:00:00
gre0: flags=9010<POINTOPOINT,LINK0,MULTICAST> mtu 1450
gif0: flags=8010<POINTOPOINT,MULTICAST> mtu 1280
gif1: flags=8010<POINTOPOINT,MULTICAST> mtu 1280
gif2: flags=8010<POINTOPOINT,MULTICAST> mtu 1280
gif3: flags=8010<POINTOPOINT,MULTICAST> mtu 1280
```

This output shows only one physical interface, *xl0*. This interface has no cable plugged in and no IP address assigned. We also see the *lo0* interface, the lookback interface. Interface configuration takes place through files in **/etc**, such as **/etc/hostname.xl0**. The *netstat -rn* command shows the current routing table, just as it does on most other UNIX systems.

4.8 APM: Automatic Power Management

OpenBSD supports the ability to suspend the computer's using APM. The daemon *apmd* responds to user requests made by the *apm* tool. The *apmd* service is enabled in the control file **rc.conf**.

Sometimes a few actions must be performed before a laptop is suspended, resumed, or powered up. These activities can be controlled by scripts in the directory /etc/apm/. The scripts are named for the actions to which they are tied, such as suspend, standby, resume, powerup, and powerdown. For example, if the disks on the system should be synchronized before suspending a laptop, the script /etc/apm/syspend would contain the command */bin/sync*. These scripts must be executable to be run. Also, this directory does not exist by default and must be created.

The /etc/apm/powerup and /etc/apm/powerdown scripts are run by *apmd* when the system's power state changes. For a laptop, this occurs when AC power is plugged in or disconnected.

The *apm* userland tool is employed to query and manage *apmd*. It has several flags that can be used to ask about the state of the battery and power usage. When called without any flags, the program displays the current state:

```
user@laptop:/home/user$  apm
Battery state: high
Battery remaining: 89 percent
Battery life estimate: 239 minutes
A/C adapter state: not connected
Power management enabled
```

The two main flags that will be used by most people are **-z** and **-S**. They will suspend (heavy sleep) or stand-by (light sleep) the system, respectively. A quick way to run *apm -z* is to use the *zzz* command. Although **-z** is supported by most systems, **-S** may not be.

By default, only the root user and users in the wheel group are allowed to change the system state. Control is exerted via the access settings in the **/var/run/apmdev** file. If the user is allowed to read from or write to the file, he or she can use *apm* to change the system state.

You can configure the flags to the APM system in the kernel configuration file. These flags are needed on some laptop models or for some versions of the APM protocol. The configuration line looks like the following:

```
apm0 at bios0 flags 0x0000 #flags 0x0101 to force protocol version 1.1
```

Ways to change the value and recompile the kernel, and ways to edit a running kernel, will be covered in Chapter 32.

4.9 Mouse Control with *wsmoused*

Although most people will use OpenBSD either with X running or in the pure console mode as a server, the system has support for using a mouse in the console mode. This is done via the *wsmoused* daemon. For most people, simply enabling the service in the **/etc/rc.conf** file will give console mouse support. Some flags can be set to tell *wsmoused* how to behave and are well documented in the *wsmoused(8)* manual page. The only flag that may be needed is the *-p* flag. It is used to specify the device where the mouse is connected. As an example, if a serial mouse was attached on the first serial port, the following would be used:

```
#  wsmoused -p /dev/cua00
```

Likewise, the same flag could be specified in the **/etc/rc.conf** file to be set on start-up:

```
wsmoused_flags=''-p /dev/cua00''
```

Even though the system can now have mouse support in console mode, no conflicts should arise when using the mouse in X.

Chapter 5
Basic Default Services

OpenBSD comes with the ability to run many services, but for the sake of security and simplicity, most of them are disabled by default. The *inetd* server is used to start servers that don't need to run all the time like *telnetd* or *ftpd*. The *cron* service is used to schedule tasks on the system. The *syslog* server handles the collection of logging information for the system. The *sendmail* server acts as the mail server for OpenBSD (by default it is set up to listen on the loopback interface only, enabling it to send but not receive mail). The *sshd* secure login server replaces the functionality of *rsh, rcp*, and *telnet* securely and with encryption.

5.1 *inetd*: The Super-Server

Having programs running on a system that aren't in active use takes up unnecessary memory and CPU time. Most servers are now able to be launched from one program, *inetd*. Not only is this a less resource-intensive approach, but it also allows for better access control, which otherwise would have to be individually implemented in each server and managed independently. The program *tcpd*, used in conjunction with *inetd*, can control inbound connections based on the remote host. Again, although many services can be run from *inetd*, most are disabled for the sake of security.

The following services are enabled by default in *inetd*:

- **ident 4/6**   Identity server for IPv4 and IPv6 via the *identd* program. It provides a way for remote systems to ask who is using what connection (identified as a source port–destination port pair). This service is mainly used by SMTP servers and some client services, such as IRC. Disabling *identd* can slow down mail delivery and in some rare cases make it impossible to submit mail to some systems. Running it usually does not represent a security hazard. The *identd* service binds to TCP port 113.

- **comsat 4/6**   Biff server for IPv4 and IPv6. It is used for the notification of *biff*-aware applications of incoming mail to eliminate the need to constantly poll for e-mail and instead inform the application when mail for the user has arrived. It uses UDP port 512.
- **daytime 4/6, time 4/6**   Internal time servers for IPv4 and IPv6. It has been largely superseded by NTP servers. It uses TCP port 13.
- **rstatd**   Kernel statistics server for IPv4. It has been largely superseded by SNMP queries. This RPC service uses the *portmap* daemon.
- **rusersd**   Information about users who are logged in to the system. It uses IPv4 UDP RPC ports, and also requires *portmap* to be running.

The last two services, *rstatd* and *ruserd*, are considered by some to constitute information leaks about the system. In addition, better services are available to gather such information for those users with authorized access. These services are often disabled early in the configuration stages by many users and administrators. The *identd* service is generally used only by SMTP server operators.

The configuration file for *inetd* is **/etc/inetd.conf**. Each line in the file has seven whitespace-delimited fields:

- **Service name**   Mapped to a port number via the file **/etc/services**. Numbers may also be used.
- **Socket type**   The type of socket the application uses—either a stream (TCP services) or a dgram (UDP).
- **Protocol**   Communication protocol (usually TCP or UDP), or *tcp6* for TCP over IPv6 and *udp6* for UDP over IPv6.
- **Wait/nowait[.max]**   Tells *inetd* whether it should wait until a connection is finished before allowing subsequent connections. The *nowait* directive allows for multiplexing of services. Some services can have a maximum number of clients configured using the *max* directive.
- **User[.group] or user[:group]**   Specifies which user to run the program as. Some programs do not need to run as root or with elevated access and thus can be executed as a different user by using this parameter.
- **Server Program**   The full path to the binary.
- **Server program arguments**   The name of the executable and the parameters to pass to the application.

Taking a look at the *ftpd* service, we see the following:

```
ftp stream tcp  nowait root /usr/libexec/ftpd ftpd -US
ftp stream tcp6 nowait root /usr/libexec/ftpd ftpd -US
```

These configuration directives tell *inetd* to listen on the FTP port and launch **/usr/libexec/ftpd** when a request arrives. The components of this line are broken down as follows:

- **ftp**   ftp is port 21 from **/etc/services**.
- **stream**   The *ftpd* program uses a stream-oriented protocol (TCP).
- **tcp/tcp6**   This is the TCP protocol for IPv4, and the TCP6 protocol for IPv6.
- **nowait**   Don't wait for the program to return before allowing another connection.
- **root**   Run **/usr/libexec/ftpd** as the root user.
- **/usr/libexec/ftpd**   Use **/usr/libexec/ftpd** as the binary, which sets up the execution environment of the application.
- **ftpd -US**   Run *ftpd* with "-US" for parameters. This specifies the program name again so that the right executable will run with any arguments it needs.

5.1.1 The Use of TCP Wrappers

If you were to replace (in the previous example) */usr/libexec/ftpd* with */usr/libexec/tcpd* and replace *ftpd-US* with */usr/libexec/ftpd-US*, the server would then be controlled by *tcpd*. This allows for numerous advantages:

- All connections are logged with *syslog*.
- Connections can be restricted based on location using the **/etc/hosts.allow** and **/etc/hosts.deny** files.
- The *tcpd* service can protect the program by using hostname verification, *ident* restrictions, and address spoofing protection.

One of the most important parts of *tcpd* is the restriction of hosts based on location. Hosts connecting to the system are checked through analysis of two files. First, if a connection's parameters match the file **/etc/hosts.allow**, it will be allowed. Second, exceptions to the rules are listed in the file **/etc/hosts.deny**. If the connection doesn't match anything in either file, it will be allowed; the first match wins, allowing for a default deny policy with the entry "ALL:ALL" in **/etc/hosts.deny**.

For example, if we wanted to allow anyone from our 192.168.1.0 network and from the localhost to connect using *telnet*, but no one else, we would use the following file: **/etc/hosts.allow**.

```
telnetd:    192.168.1.0/255.255.255.0 LOCAL
```

In the file specifying networks to deny access to, **/etc/hosts.deny**, we can specify options as follows:

```
telnetd:    ALL
```

This command denies all connections to the *telnet* daemon unless otherwise listed in the allowed connections file. It serves as a "catch all" rule. The "LOCAL" keyword will match any hostname that is not fully qualified, such as local network hostnames.

The *tcpd* service is far more flexible and allows for many more options. The *tcpd* and **hosts.access** manual pages have more information covering a variety of scenarios. For **libwrap** linked applications that run on a stand-alone basis (such as popa3d), these files can be used to provide access control.

5.2 *syslog*: The Logging Service

Before *syslog*, all applications logged into their own files, and watching logs was a nightmare. Now programs can log to one place and can be taken care of that way. It's also very easy to implement logging to *syslog* in your own applications using the libraries provided by *syslog*.

The most important parameters for *syslogd* are described here:

- **-f** *file*   Specify the configuration file.
- **-m #**   Put a mark in the log file every **#** minutes. This parameter can be used to give a "heartbeat" indicating that logging is still active even though nothing else is being logged, such as on a slow server.
- **-u**   Use insecure ("Unsecure") mode, allowing connections to the server from the network. This parameter allows anyone to log to a remote *syslog* server. It is very useful, but also very dangerous, as anyone can create an attack by intentionally flooding a logging host and filling its filesystem.

Configuration for *syslogd* is done in the **/etc/syslog.conf** file. It consists of the following entries:

```
authpriv.debug              /var/log/secure
```

The first part specifies what type of event to filter for and the second part controls what level of importance of information is logged. In this example, if the log message has a facility of *authpriv* and a level of *debug*, then it will be logged to **/var/log/secure**. Although the configuration file can be as granular as the example, it can also contain information like the following:

```
*.err:authpriv.none            /dev/console
```

This command tells *syslogd* to log any *err*-level events but not to log any *authpriv* events to the console.

To log to a remote host, the @ symbol can be used. For example:

```
*.*                    @logserver.example.net
```

This setting would log everything to the host **logserver.example.net**. Presumably that host would filter the events and log them as necessary. Lines can be in any order in the file and events can be repeated (the same events being logged to more than one file or to multiple hosts, for example).

5.3 Electronic Mail with *sendmail*

The mail server *sendmail* is started by default with a configuration that allows only local or outbound e-mail. No machines can connect to *sendmail* from the network. Due to the complexity of *sendmail* configuration, it is covered in detail in Chapter 17.

5.4 The Secure Shell Server *sshd*

Once upon a time, computers used clear text logins for everything. Anyone who was in the right location on the network could then read everything that was typed, obtain other users' passwords, and cause disruption. A secure connection tool was needed. The *ssh* program, developed by Tatu Ylonen in Helsinki, Finland, was such a tool. It allows secure logins and encrypted tunneled traffic. Its sister program, *scp*, allows secure file transfer as well. Although the tools were designed as replacements for *rsh, rlogin*, and *rcp*, they have replaced *telnet* and *ftp* in many cases as well.

When the group that developed *ssh* released version 1.2.13, they radically changed the license. As a result, many people were no longer willing or able to use the software. At this point, people from the OpenBSD group stepped in and wrote a replacement, OpenSSH, based on SSH 1.2.12, the last fully free version. The majority of the UNIX world has since moved to OpenSSH and it is quickly becoming the standard SSH client.

The *ssh* program is a simple tool to use:

```
bpalmer@client:$  ssh root@server
The authenticity of host 'server (192.168.1.30)' can't be established.
RSA key fingerprint is e6:85:92:ff:5d:9d:0f:45:67:9e:82:47:c0:3e:a2.
Are you sure you want to continue connecting (yes/no)?  yes
Warning: Permanently added 'server' (RSA) to the list of known hosts.
root@server's password:
. . .
. . .
. . .
root@server#
```

As we can see here, this connection was from being logged in as *bpalmer* on the host **client** and connecting to the host **server** as the user root. Had we left off the username, the username would be presumed to be that of the current user, *bpalmer*. If we have not connected to this host before, the *ssh* program will inform us of this fact and ask us to verify the RSA key fingerprint. For the truly paranoid, this key can be obtained beforehand to check against possible security breaches. We accept the key and connect as root[1] to the host.

The *scp* command also works in roughly the same way as it does for the older, insecure command *rcp*. The command takes the general form of an *scp* source destination, which can be local or remote. Usernames for remote hosts can be specified in the format of an e-mail address. The path to the file (relative or absolute) is specified after a colon separator from the hostname for the remote host.

```
$  scp username@host:~/file file
```

We can use *scp* to copy files from anywhere to anywhere. Most of the time, this involves the localhost and a remote host. Consider this example:

```
bpalmer@client$  scp OpenBSD.tex bpalmer@server:
bpalmer@server's password:  enter password here
OpenBSD.tex       100% |********************************| 11900 00:03
```

---

[1]*ssh* is allowed to connect as root, unlike in most other protocols. Because *ssh* is secure, it is allowed here.

This command copies the **OpenBSD.tex** file from **client** to *bpalmer*'s home directory on **server**. We could have also specified a remote location and filename:

```
user@client$  scp OpenBSD.tex jose@server:/home/jose/openbsd-main.tex
```

The remote file would then be in a folder called **doc** in Jose's home directory and be named **openbsd-main.tex**.

Configuration for *ssh* is done in the **/etc/sshd_config** and **/etc/ssh_config** files for the server and the client, respectively.

Although most of the settings in the files can be left as the defaults, some are worth looking at. These parameters are configured in the file **/etc/sshd_config**:

- *ListenAddress*   This explicitly configures the IP address on which *sshd* listens. By default, it listens on all assigned IP addresses.
- *Port 22*   *sshd* runs on port 22 by default. If you want it to run on a different port for some reason, this choice can be set here.
- *LoginGraceTime 600*   This sets the timeout for login. Ten minutes is quite a long time and you may want to trim this value.
- *PermitRootLogin yes*   By default, SSH does not allow root to connect via *ssh*. On some systems, this is not a desired setting.
- *X11Forwarding no*   Setting this to "yes" will allow X applications to be tunneled over SSH from the server. This option is disabled due to some security concerns in the networked X11 protocol.
- *SyslogFacility AUTH and LogLevel INFO*   SSH allows the administrator to specify which facility and log level are used for logging messages to *syslogd*.
- *ChallengeResponseAuthentication no*   This setting will allow for alternate authentication methods to be used, such as S/Key. It would allow a user to log in with his or her private "identity" without having to send passwords over the wire. To use this facility, a setting must be placed in the **/etc/ssh_config** file as well. For a detailed description, see Chapter 26.
- *Banner /etc/issue.net*   Though not supported by all SSH clients, this will allow a banner message to be displayed before the user logs in. For most systems, it will comprise a notice about usage policy.

Client settings are controlled in the file **/etc/ssh_config**. Some of the major options are described here:

- **Host *** The file has settings for individual hosts and for default hosts. The **Host *** is for default hosts and is what most people want to change. Settings for a host are maintained until the next **Host** command is found.

- *ForwardX11 yes* This also needs to be set to "yes" to allow X applications to be forwarded over the SSH connection. Both the client and the server ends need this option enabled for X tunneling to work. Set it to "yes" for systems on which you trust the root account, as it allows a rogue root user to eavesdrop on communications.

- *ChallengeResponseAuthentication yes* If S/Key is enabled on the server end, this will cause the client to use S/Key in an attempt to connect. It should be set on a per-host basis, as most servers will not be set up with this feature enabled.

- *Port 22* If the server runs on a port other than 22, this can be set so that the port doesn't need to be specified on the command line every time you connect.

- *EscapeChar ~* In *telnet*, to break out of the connection without closing it, you would use *Ctrl-]*. With SSH, the default escape character is the ~ character. To break from a SSH connection, you would use *escape-~*. If you were to nest connections, it would be useful to specify alternate characters.

Per-user settings can be controlled in the file **.ssh/config** in the user's home directory. While some options cannot be overridden, most major options can be set to accommodate a user's preferences.

Additional details of the OpenSSH system are covered in Chapter 20. Even greater detail is available in the book *SSH, the Secure Shell, the Definitive Guide* by Barret and Silverman (O'Reilly).

Chapter 6
Online Help Resources

While the chapters in this text are intended to help you navigate parts of the OpenBSD system, the information given in this book can never be fully complete. Fortunately, OpenBSD includes a wealth of additional information sources to help you get around your OpenBSD system. These include the typically excellent manual pages, the GNU info pages, the Perldoc information sets, and other means of documentation. These internal resources are enhanced by other, external sources of information.

6.1 Manual Pages

OpenBSD includes, in the **man*.tgz** set, the manual pages for the system. These include descriptions of commands, the layout of the system, development information, and the like. The development team has worked hard to ensure that the information in the manual pages is complete, accurate, and worthwhile to study. The manual pages often include examples and discussions of bugs or other unexpected behavior as well.

To access a manual page, use the *man* command. This will call up the manual page and format it for the screen. An example manual page, for the *intro* section, is shown below:

```
INTRO(1)                 OpenBSD Reference Manual              INTRO(1)

NAME
    intro - introduction to general commands (tools and utilities)

DESCRIPTION
    The manual pages in section one contain most of the commands
    which comprise the BSD user environment. Some of the
```

73

```
commands included in section one are text editors, command
shell interpreters, searching and sorting tools, file
manipulation commands, system status commands, remote file
copy commands, mail commands, compilers and compiler tools,
formatted output tools,and line printer commands.

All commands set a status value upon exit which may be
tested to see if the command completed normally. The exit
values and their meanings are explained in the individual
manuals. Traditionally, the value 0 signifies successful
completion of the command.

SEE ALSO
    man(1), intro(2), intro(3), intro(4), intro(5), intro(6),
    intro(7), intro(8), intro(9)

    Tutorials in the UNIX User's Manual Supplementary Documents.

HISTORY
    An intro manual appeared in Version 6 AT&T UNIX.

OpenBSD 3.4                    December 30, 1993
```

Each manual page is divided into a number of clearly demarcated sections, several of which are visible in the preceding example. The **NAME** section, not surprisingly, contains a name and one-line summary of the command or topic of the manual page. In this case, it identifies the *intro* manual page. A **SYNOPSIS** section is sometimes included to provide a concise summary of the command and its options. The **DESCRIPTION** is a lengthy commentary on the topic of the manual page. For example, a command's manual page would define its actions, inputs, and outputs, and describe the possible-command line arguments. Many manual pages include an **EXAMPLES** section, which is especially helpful for illustrating features of the command or programming feature. Several manual pages for programming options also include caveats and recommended use of the library call. The final major section is a list of further readings, called **SEE ALSO**. This will point to additional manual pages, perhaps some example files, or other resources, such as Internet RFCs or additional documentation in the system.

Often, a manual page will presume that you know the gist of the command. This is an unfortunate limitation imposed by the size of the manual page. Some are better than others, certainly, but learning to use the online manual is, in general, a valuable skill to gain. The convention, often used in this book, is to list the manual page title along with the section in parentheses. For example, "man(1)" will point you to the manual page for "man" in section 1 of the online manual.

In the X Window system, an additional UNIX manual page viewer is available, called *xman*. It allows for a prettier display of the UNIX manual. However, some sections are not available for browsing due to their nonstandard locations. A prettier, colored graphical interface to the UNIX manual is the *tkman* tool, available in the ports tree as **misc/tkman**.

6.1.1 Which Manual Page?

Sometimes you may know the topic that you wish to learn about, but not the exact manual page. Two utilities can be useful here. The first is an option to the *man* command, *man -k* (which is synonymous with the *apropos* command). For example, to find out which manual pages are worth reading to understand the SMTP protocol, a list would be obtained using a command such as the following:

```
$  man -k smtp
smtpd (8) - Obtuse Systems SMTPD message storing daemon
smtpfwdd (8) - Obtuse Systems SMTPFWDD message forwarding daemon
starttls (8) - ESMTP over TLS
```

Three manual pages are returned that you may want to investigate. Using the *man* command on any of them would return the manual page and associated information. The **SEE ALSO** sections of these manual pages may prove useful if they do not answer your question.

Often, *man -k* will return several manual pages that do not pertain to the topic you are investigating. Consider the command *man -k ls* to find out which manual pages deal with the *ls* command. Currently approximately 126 manual pages are returned for that one query due to the way in which *man -k* works. Namely, it uses substring matching in both the title *and* the one-line synopsis of the manual page. As you might expect, a common fragment like "ls" will return many unrelated manual pages using this method.

A second, improved method relies on the *whatis* command. Using *whatis* you can find the exact match using only the title of the manual page and string (not substring) matching. An example is shown below for the *kill* command, which using *man -k* returns nine entries:

```
$  whatis kill
kill (1) - terminate or signal a process
kill (2) - send signal to a process
```

Two exact matches are returned for the *kill* command, one of which is probably the one you want.

This example illustrates an additional feature of the online manual. In the early days of UNIX, the manual consisted of one large section. Today, with so many commands, library calls, and informational pages, the manual is split into several sections. In the preceding example for *kill*, two instances of "kill" were returned. How would you select one over the other to read about? It's simple: Use the section number as an argument to the *man* command, such as *man 2 kill* to read the "kill(2)" manual page. To read all of the possible entries in succession, use the command *man -a*.

6.1.2 The Layout of the Manual

The original layout of the online UNIX manual was established in the early days of AT&T UNIX. Since then, the BSD tradition has made a few modifications. OpenBSD has made a few additional choices to include extra manual pages for informational sections, for example.

The basic layout of the online manual, found under **/usr/share/man**, is as follows:

- **Section 1**   General user commands.
- **Section 2**   Common system library calls used in programming.
- **Section 3**   Additional C programming library calls. Some systems include sections **3p** and **3M** to refer to the Perl programming language and the Motif library calls, respectively. OpenBSD uses the subdirectory **/usr/X11R6/man** for X11-related manual pages, while the general layout remains the same.
- **Section 4**   Core system drivers. Note that section 4 manual pages are also available for specific architectures supported by OpenBSD.
- **Section 5**   System runtime commands and configuration files.
- **Section 6**   Manual pages for installed system games (from the **games*.tgz** installation set).
- **Section 7**   Various informational pages.
- **Section 8**   System administration commands and informational pages.
- **Section 9**   Kernel API and system calls.

Additional manual pages, installed from ports and packages, are found in **/usr/local/ man**. The same basic hierarchy is followed.

6.1.3 Notable Manual Pages

While all manual pages are worth reading, several are especially noteworthy for their content and assistance to new users or introduction to new topics:

- **afterboot(8)**   This manual page introduces the new OpenBSD user to the system. Several things to check after a new system is brought up, configuration files worth examining, and ways to build a new kernel from a source are covered.
- **ssl(8)**   This manual page introduces the reader to the SSL and TLS libraries, which are included in the base system.
- **ipsec(4)**   This section introduces the IPsec system to the reader. IPsec is a set of extensions to IPv4 (installed by default in IPv6) providing for encryption and authentication.
- **vpn(8)**   Virtual private networking facilities in OpenBSD are introduced in this section of the manual.
- **intro(*)**   Since the early days of UNIX, this manual page has provided a brief introduction to the UNIX system. The OpenBSD variant is an excellent introduction to the system for new users as well. Note that every section in the OpenBSD manual has an introductory manual page.

6.1.4 Added Sections

Some software packages, such as Tcl, install their own manual pages in a directory hierarchy not searched by the *man* tools. In this case, you can append the section name and the directory path to the *man* command configuration file **/etc/man.conf**. The resulting addition in the case of a default Tcl installation would be as follows:

```
n                    /usr/local/lib/tcl8.3/man
```

Tcl manual pages would now be accessible in the *n* section of the manual, and can be accessed via the command *man n* command.

6.1.5 Writing Your Own Manual Pages

If you are developing software for your own use and wish to use the UNIX manual pages for documentation, a handy introduction to the *nroff* macros used in manual pages, along with an explanation of how to process them, appears in the *mandoc(7)* manual page. Although many of the macros listed are specific to BSD and OpenBSD, the general concepts underlying writing manual pages can be learned through this manual page and *mdoc.samples(7)*.

6.2 GNU Info Pages

Citing several limitations of the traditional UNIX manual system, the Free Software Foundation (FSF) has created the GNU Info document markup language. It provides a rich, readily navigated method for gaining information on the commands documented. A related system, Texinfo, can be used to simultaneously create online and printed documentation. Info files are processed using the *makeinfo* command, which will not be covered here.

When initiated, *info* displays the top-level node (described below) in an *emacs* style editor on the console. You can move forward and backward, as well as quickly navigate using menus, via the cursor. The use of the spacebar will move you forward, as expected, and the Delete key will scroll back a page. To quickly move to the beginning or the end of a node, use the "b" and "e" keys, respectively. To navigate between nodes, use "n" to move to the next node and "p" to reach the previous node. To quit the viewer, press the "q" key. Additional navigation commands are available in the "info" Info page.

The command-line interface to *info* is rather simple. The main argument to the command is the name of the module you wish to view, such as "info" or "emacs." To specify a particular file not in the *info* search path, use *info -f file.info*.

Like manual pages or *perldoc* documents, GNU Info pages have a defined structure, which allows for the quick perusal of the documents. They typically start with a brief synopsis and then, for larger documents, a top-level menu to browse. Smaller documents don't have detailed menus. At the end of many Info documents, suggested further reading sources are provided.

Menus in Info pages are navigable and interactive, which is perhaps one of the biggest strengths of the Info system. Simply hover the cursor over the menu item and press Enter. This will take you to the specified section or subsection.

Central to the GNU Info system is the idea of "nodes," or subsections of data. These break the document into manageable sections. Furthermore, they can be moved directly to the command line. For example, to jump right to the "Repository" node of the *cvs* Info page, use the command *info cvs repository*. This method can help you more quickly navigate larger Info documents.

Like the *man* command, *info* allows you to search the database of documents it contains. The command is very similar to the *man -k* and *apropos* commands. The command *info --apropos=key* will search the database. For example, to find information on the "bash" shell contained in the Info database, use a command such as the following:

```
$ info --apropos=bash
"(cvs)Specifying a repository" -- .bashrc, setting CVSROOT in
"(kpathsea)configure shells" -- bash,recommended for running configure
"(bash)Bash Variables" -- BASH
"(bash)Bash Variables" -- BASH_ENV
"(bash)Bash Variables" -- BASH_VERSINFO
"(bash)Bash Variables" -- BASH_VERSION
"(bash)Basic Installation" -- Bash configuration
"(bash)Basic Installation" -- Bash installation
```

The first part, in parentheses, is the Info repository. The second part is the name of the node; sometimes it is a subsection in a node. The third section is a brief summary of the section. Using the Info browser you can navigate to the subsection you need to read.

To get full details on the *info* command, along with information on how to write your own Info pages, use *info info*.

6.2.1 Converting Info to Manual Pages

While *Info* pages certainly are powerful, they are not to everyone's liking. For example, their format isn't widely accepted as a UNIX standard. However, several GNU utilities rely on the Info pages as their online documentation. As a result, it may be desirable to convert GNU Info pages to other formats—namely, the *man* page format. A set of third-party scripts can be used to convert between the Info format and the Pod format (described in Section 6.3), and from there to almost any other popular format. A pair of scripts, *info2pod* and *info2man*, can be used to accomplish this conversion. They are available from Cameron Simpson on his Web site at **http://www.zip.com.au/~cs/scripts/**.

6.3 *perldoc* and Pod

The powerful programming language Perl includes its own method for viewing its documentation (found in the 3p subsection of the manual), named *perldoc*. Using the Pod format, *perldoc* can convert between several popular reading interfaces, including *man* and GNU Info pages. For a description of the Pod document markup system, see the manual page *perlpod(1)*. For example, when *perldoc* is run from the command line, the Perl documentation is run through the *pod2man* program, which formats the document using the *groff* macros for the UNIX manual. This then provides a familiar interface for the reader using the standard UNIX pager.

The *perldoc* command offers a few advantages over the regular UNIX manual interface. They include formatting options (useful if you want to interface with other document markup systems, such as PostScript), searching, and extraction. These are useful features given the plethora of documentation on the Perl programming language. The *perldoc* command is installed in most Perl installations, including most Win32 installations.

By default, the documentation in Pod format is located in **/usr/libdata/perl5/pod**. Several modules—particularly those central to the Perl language—include Pod documentation in their headers, which can be later put into the *perldoc* system using *perldoc -F*:

```
$ perldoc -F /usr/libdata/perl5/Pod/Text.pm
Pod::Text(3)   User Contributed Perl Documentation   Pod::Text(3)


NAME
     Pod::Text - Convert POD data to formatted ASCII text

SYNOPSIS
         use Pod::Text;
         my $parser = Pod::Text->new (sentence => 0, width => 78);
...
```

As its argument, the command *perldoc -F* uses a filename from which to extract Pod data.

An interface to the FAQ is even provided, using *perldoc -q*. The FAQ is searched and related entries are sorted, formatted, and then displayed. This feature is especially useful because the Perl FAQ is so large. The questions can be found on the *perlfaq(1)* manual page. For example, to find FAQ entries dealing with HTML, a typical session might look like this:

```
$ perldoc -q html
Found in /usr/libdata/perl5/pod/perlfaq9.pod
     How do I remove HTML from a string?

     The most correct way (albeit not the fastest) is to use
     HTML::Parser from CPAN.  Another mostly correct way is to
     use HTML::FormatText which not only removes HTML but also
     attempts to do a little simple formatting of the resulting
     plain text.
...
```

Lastly, to generate an unformatted entry shown in raw Pod format, use the command *perldoc -u*. For example, to view the POSIX information page, use a command such as the following:

```
$ perldof -u POSIX
=head1 NAME

POSIX - Perl interface to IEEE Std 1003.1

=head1 SYNOPSIS

    use POSIX;
    use POSIX qw(setsid);
    use POSIX qw(:errno_h :fcntl_h);
...
```

The output of this command can be piped to other formats—for example, by using the *pod2** commands. To format the above output using *pod2man* (which uses *groff* macros as an output mechanism), which can then be prepared as PostScript output, a command such as *perldoc -u POSIX | pod2man | groff -Tps* could be used. One interesting way to get only the header information in the **USAGE** section of a Pod document is to pipe the output through *pod2usage*.

This section merely touches on some of the more popular features of *perldoc* and the Pod format. Many of these features are worth studying in depth, as they combine the complexity and power of Perl with the portability of the Pod format.

6.4 Package-Specific Documentation

Software will often include files named **README** or something similar, discussing the software's use. These documents typically offer a more general overview of how the software works than the manual pages or other online documentation associated with a package. Thus they are often a better way to learn how to use the software than reading the manual pages.

By convention, ports and packages install these files in the directory **/usr/local/share/doc**, with a subdirectory existing for each package. Often you will find the **README** file here, as well as examples, bug lists, or other information you may find important.

This is merely a convention used by many port and package maintainers. As a consequence, not all ports and packages will have this information available. However, it is quite common practice, and the directory is a worthwhile location to hunt for additional information on software.

6.5 Other Sources

A large number of additional reasources are available in the form of Web sites, mailing lists, and Usenet newsgroups. For a list of some, see Appendix F. Of course, this book is designed to be a comprehensive information source as well.

## Chapter 7

X Window System

Like any good UNIX system, OpenBSD has full support for the X Window system, the graphical user interface (GUI) used by most versions of UNIX.[1] Using the default installation process, the X Window system, commonly referred to as just X, can be installed with a good range of default supporting applications. X (the implementation is formally known XFree86) is a very advanced system that boasts support for virtual screens, high resolution, multiple monitors (known as xinerama), and a wide range of window managers.

The bottom line is that X is a graphical windowing system that can be found on all major UNIX(R) and UNIX-like operating systems, including OpenBSD.

In X, there are two major aspects of displaying graphics. One special program, known as the server, talks to the graphics hardware directly. All other programs talk to the server to display anything. An X application, then, is a program that talks to an X server, which in turn talks to the graphics hardware.

Although X is a very advanced system, most video hardware is designed to work under Windows and each card comes with its own drivers. Because most of these cards are not designed to be supported under X,[2] the user needs to choose video hardware that is supported by this system. The X Web site[3] has a list of the currently supported cards.

While X is a great desktop solution, many OpenBSD systems are used as servers and hence there is no need for a GUI.[4] X can use up a good deal of CPU and memory depending on how it is used.

---

[1] Solaris still uses Openwin.
[2] Although most video card vendors do not support X, with the growth in the Linux user population, many are starting to offer X drivers. Both Linux and OpenBSD use the same X software. Thus any card that is supported with the Linux driver is also supported under OpenBSD as well.
[3] **http://www.xfree86.org.**
[4] Some people choose to run X applications on their servers via an SSH connection, which can securely redirect an X application to another machine.

On the i386 platform, the system uses 3.3.6 servers for older hardware, and 4.x series servers for newer hardware. This means that some graphics cards may need to be used with the newer server software. All i386 platforms (and other platforms) use the XFree86 4.x series userland and libraries outside of the core server. The HP300 platform uses MITX, a very old release, for the *Xhp* server. As a consequence, performance and support for some server-intensive applications will be lacking; this platform, however, is not very performance intensive. The SPARC64, SPARC, MacPPC and Alpha platforms use *wsfb* for unaccelerated X.

7.1 Installation

To install the X Window system during an OpenBSD installation, choose the following sets along with the other sets:

- **xbase34.tgz**   This is the core component set, outside of the X server itself, for running X. It includes shared libraries for X11 applications.
- **xfont34.tgz**   This set contains the fonts needed to display X applications, including the basic terminal.
- **xserv34.tgz**   This is the core server that interacts with the hardware and drives the display. This package contains the X server versions 3.3.6 (or later) and 4.x (currently 4.3).
- **xshare34.tgz**   This contains the components of X that are shared across all architectures. It includes application text configuration files, header files, and other such files common to all OpenBSD platforms.

Installation of these sets, which requires approximately 300MB of installation space in the **/usr/X11R6** hierarchy and a few megabytes in the **/etc/X11** hierarchy, proceeds normally as with other installation sets. Note that the version numbers will change depending on which version of OpenBSD is being installed.

During the installation process, the installer will ask, "Do you expect to run the X Window system?" If X is added at installation time, it will correctly set the *sysctl* variable *machdep.allowaperture* to 1. If X is added post-installation, you must set this to 1^5 in **/etc/sysctl.conf** for X to work properly. This kernel parameter allows the X server to change the display properties.

---

[5]On i386 systems, setting *machdep.allowaperture* to 2 is required for most video hardware in the 4.x servers.

7.2 Quick Setup

In the past, X was tricky to set up and get working properly. There were some tools to help you through the process, but the user had to know a vast amount of information about the hardware to get everything set up correctly. With the incorporation of version 4 of XFree86, more advanced drivers and better setup software have greatly facilitated this process.

The **README** files that come with the XFree86 server are valuable resources and can assist with nonstandard installations. Autoconfiguration, described below, works for most of the displays and video cards in use on typical systems. When installing OpenBSD and preparing to set up X, one should always consult the provided **/usr/X11R6/README**, which will contain notes specific to your particular platform as well as those applicable to OpenBSD in general.

To begin, you should make sure that the directory path **/usr/X11R6/bin** is in your shell's *PATH* variable. Without it, the binaries needed to run the X Window system will not be found. If your system has a well-supported video card and the monitor is detected, the setup for X can be this simple:[6]

```
root@client:/root#  X -configure


XFree86 Version 4.3.0 (for OpenBSD)
Release Date: 27 February 2003
X Protocol Version 11, Revision 0, Release 6.6
Build Operating System: OpenBSD 3.4 i386 [ELF]
Build Date: 18 June 2003
        Before reporting problems, check http://www.XFree86.Org/
        to make sure that you have the latest version.
Module Loader present
Markers: (--) probed, (**) from config file, (==) default setting,
        (++) from command line, (!!) notice, (II) informational,
        (WW) warning, (EE) error, (NI) not implemented, (??) unknown.
(==) Log file: "/var/log/XFree86.0.log",Time: Tue Nov 11 22:35:30 2003
List of video drivers:
        atimisc
```

---

[6]If you are using a platform other than i386, you may not need to do any configuration. If you are using the i386 platform, there are a number of other ways to configure X automatically. Consult your local **/usr/X11R6/README** for more details.

```
            r128
            radeon
            mga
            glint
            nv
            tga
            s3
            s3virge
            sis
            rendition
            neomagic
            i740
            tdfx
            savage
            cirrus
            vmware
            tseng
            trident
            chips
            apm
            fbdev
            i128
            nsc
            ati
            i810
            ark
            cyrix
            siliconmotion
            vesa
            vga
            dummy
(++) Using config file: "/root/XF86Config.new"

XFree86 detected your mouse at device /dev/wsmouse.
Please check your config if the mouse is still not
operational, as by default XFree86 tries to autodetect
the protocol.
```

```
Your XF86Config file is /root/XF86Config.new

To test the server, run 'XFree86 -xf86config /root/XF86Config.new'

root@client:/root#
```

Starting X with the *-configure* flag tells X to scan the hardware and set up a good configuration file. There is little output from this activity, but the details of what was found and set can be seen in **/var/log/XFree86.0.log**. As the output from the command explains, you can now start X with the new configuration file.

If everything works well, a gray screen should show up and your mouse should work. Use Ctrl-Alt-backspace to kill the X server and return to console mode. If the server started and video was acceptable, you can move the **/root/XF86Config.new** file to **/etc/X11/XF86Config** and then start the server:

```
someuser@client:/home/someuser$  startx
```

The default window manager of *fvwm* will be started and you can continue to work.

7.2.1 Troubleshooting Configuration

There are a few common problems that people experience when trying to set up X. One problem is having the wrong color bit depth set (number of colors). Another common mistake is using the wrong resolution. Both errors can be fixed by editing the **XF86Config** file. When X creates the configuration file for the first time, no special settings are used, which means that the settings you want may not have been specified. The first thing we want to change is to add a *DefaultDepth* directive in the Screen section:

```
Section "Screen"
        Identifier "Screen0"
        Device     "Card0"
        Monitor    "Monitor0"
        DefaultDepth    24
        SubSection "Display"
             Depth    1
...
...
```

Our one (and only) screen here has been set to a default depth of 24. X will try this depth first and then use lower depths if it fails.

The next setting is the desired resolution (also in the Screen section):

```
SubSection "Display"
        Depth     24
Modes    ''1600x1200'' ''1024x768''
EndSubSection
```

We added this Modes line under the Display subsection for the depth that we will be using (one Modes line would be added for each depth we wanted to use). When the server starts, it will first try the "1600 × 1200" resolution; next it will try the "1024×768" resolution. You can also switch between resolutions while the system is running using the *Ctrl-Alt*-plus and *Ctrl-Alt*-minus key combinations (you must use the plus and minus on the numberpad, not on the keys on the normal keyboard).

7.3 *xdm*

Although it is mostly used in a lab or shared workstation environment, X supports the use of XDM (X Display Manager). This allows a graphical login to X, bypassing the need to run *startx* manually from a text *tty*. Using *xdm* is as easy as enabling it in the **/etc/rc.conf** file:

```
xdm_flags='' ''
```

Upon start-up, the login window will appear and users can log in. Alternate window managers can be used by specifying them in the user's **.xsession** file. Configuration files for *xdm* are contained in **/etc/X11/xdm**. A few files may be of interest:

- **Xaccess**   If this feature is set up properly, users can log in to an *xdm* session remotely. Because passwords would flow in plain text over the network for such a login, it is disabled by default. This file has settings for allowing remote logins.
- **Xresources**   This file has all of the settings for the login window—everything from fonts to colors to image logos. If a customized login window was needed, changes would be made here.
- **Xsession**   If the user has no **.xsession** file, the defaults from this file are used.

- **Xsetup_0**   The login window contains a console in the corner by default. This can be disabled or more windows can be added by editing this file, such as with **Xsetup_1** for the display on :1.

Using *xdm*, you can enable machines or X terminals to present a login from a remote machine. This feature is, however, disabled by default in OpenBSD for security reasons. It can be enabled by editing two configuration files, one for the resources (**Xresources**), and one for the access file (**Xaccess**).

7.4 Window Managers

Once the X server has started, any number of window managers can run on top of it. These control how windows are placed, stacked, controlled, and decorated. The default system comes with *fvwm*, but some users may prefer a less spartan look. Two other window managers come with the basic OpenBSD installation: *twm* and *fvwm2*. The "original" X window manager, *twm* is a bit on the minimalistic side, but definitely usable. Intended as an extremely minimalistic window manager, both in memory consumption and flexibility, *fvwm2* is very clean and functional—just not very good looking.

Most of the common window managers are supported and available in the ports tree. This group includes the window managers for Gnome, KDE, and Enlightenment. They are found in the ports tree in the **/usr/ports/x11** subtree. If the user is not using *xdm*, he or she can simply add a line in the **.xinitrc** file.

```
/usr/local/bin/enlightenment
```

When X starts, if the user has this file, it is read and executed. As a result, more than the window manager could be used.

```
/usr/local/bin/netscape &
/usr/X11R6/bin/xterm -reverse -ls &
/usr/local/bin/xbatt &
/usr/local/bin/enlightenment
```

Note that the last line is the only one that is not put into the background. If the others were not run in the background, the start-up of X would wait to proceed until they had completed running and returned. Likewise, if the window manager was run in the background, the script would complete and the X server would exit. If *xdm* has been enabled on the system, the **.xsession** file is used instead of the **.xinitrc** file. Its use is exactly the same.

7.5 Basic X Applications

X is most often used to open more console windows (the default number enabled on the console is 5). The application used by default is *xterm*. This simple terminal window works the same way that the console does. Most window managers will have an *xterm* entry in their menus. Although we will not detail how to change the menus for the window managers, note that when the *xterm* is launched, some flags can be set to customize the window to your liking.

- **-ls** Process the login scripts as though we were logging in from a login shell/console *tty*, placing an entry in *utmp*, and appearing in the output of the *w* command.

- **-reverse** By default, *xterm* are black text on a white background. This setting makes them appear as white text on a black background.

- **-font fontname** A smaller or larger font may be desired. If, for example, you were to keep a window open to hold just logs, you might want to use the "5×7" font.[7]

Default settings for applications can also be controlled through the **Xdefaults** file. Global application attributes are controlled in the directory **/etc/X11/appdefaults/**, with one file per application. Default settings for each user are held in the **.Xdefaults** file in the user's home directory.

The two files differ in that the attributes for the global configuration already know which application is being altered. In the per-user configuration, the application must be explicitly stated. A systemwide *xterm* configuration would therefore look like the following:

```
! we like scroll bars, scrolls back 1024 lines
*scrollBar:    true
*saveLines:    1024


*SimpleMenu*BackingStore: NotUseful
```

The per-user configuration explicitly states the application name per attribute:

```
XTerm*font 6x10
XTerm*VT100*background:        blue4
XTerm*VT100*foreground:        white
```

---

[7]Some fonts are listed in the configuration for *xterm* in the **/etc/X11/appdefaults/XTerm** file.

Note two things: (1) The file can be commented using the *!* marker, not a pound sign (#) like other files; and (2) user-configured settings can override system settings by default.

If you need more information on the configuration of X applications, the XFree86 organzation maintains a list of useful resources at **http://www.xfree86.org/support.html**.

7.6 Remote Display

Another feature of X is the ability to display programs that run on other machines, even ones that are not running X servers. There are two ways to use this feature. The first, and preferred, strategy is through *ssh*. The second is by specifying the *DISPLAY* variable for the application you want to display.

As discussed in Chapter 5, *ssh* can be set up to forward X session information. To see if this feature is enabled, *ssh* to the server and check the *DISPLAY* variable:

```
bpalmer@desktop:/usr/home/bpalmer$  ssh -X remote
bpalmer@remote's password:
Last login: Sun Jun  2 18:29:31 2002 from client.crimelabs.net
bpalmer@remote:/usr/home/bpalmer$ echo $DISPLAY
localhost:10.0
bpalmer@remote:/usr/home/bpalmer$  xeyes
```

Note that the *DISPLAY* variable points to the localhost, which from the standpoint of the machine "remote" would be itself. SSH will intercept any graphical application that connects to localhost:10.0 and tunnel the packets back to your desktop to be displayed there, cleanly and securely.

While *ssh* is *far* more secure, sometimes it cannot be used. Some applications, like streaming video, would be too slow going through an *ssh* tunnel, but would work well with just direct X hosting. In other cases, and more often, *ssh* has not yet or cannot be installed on the remote system. Most importantly, one should not use *ssh* to forward X connections if one does not trust the administration of the remote machine. Any administrator on a remote machine with whom you set up an X session can gain access to your X display, and even log what you are typing.

To use X hosting without using *ssh*, only two steps are needed. On the remote machine,[8] you do the following:[9]

```
bpalmer@remote:/usr/home/bpalmer$  export DISPLAY=desktop:0
```

---

[8]Which you logged into on the console or via some insecure protocol like *telnet*.
[9]This example uses *ksh*. If you use a different shell, you may need to modify the syntax.

On the desktop:

```
bpalmer@desktop:/usr/home/bpalmer$  xhost +remote
```

The first line tells all X11 applications on the remote machine to send their displays to the desktop machine over the network. The *xhost* command run on the desktop says to allow X11 connections from the remote server. By default, *xhost* is set to allow only connections from the local machine. Be warned, however, that with *xhost* set, any user on *remote* can gain compete control over the session on the desktop. If you are using *ssh* with X forwarding enabled, manually setting the *DISPLAY* variable will eradicate the *ssh* port forwarding, destroying security.

7.7 X and Security

Because the X Window system is network aware, it introduces new network ports and therefore new security issues. Chief among these new elements is the server itself. The X server listens on TCP ports 6000–6010 (associated with displays 0–10) for network connections and events. As described earlier, this setup allows network X clients to contact the server. These ports should be firewalled at the border to prevent unauthorized use, because X itself has only weak security mechanisms turned on by default. Use *ssh* X forwarding when possible, and be careful when using *xhost* because it can open more holes than are needed.

Also, note that some X services use network ports themselves. The X font server *xfs* uses TCP port 7100 for its communications. This can be disabled by using the argument *no listen = tcp* in the configuration file along with the *droppriv* option to ensure that *xfs* doesn't open a listening socket (on TCP port 7100) and doesn't run as the root user. Most network-aware X applications can perform similar functions.

Part II

System Configuration and Administration

## Chapter 8

User Administration

On the basic level, user administration is the same on OpenBSD as it is for any UNIX system. Most information about a user is stored in the **/etc/passwd** file and the user's password is stored in **/etc/master.passwd**. The tools to manage users are a bit different and the restrictions set up by OpenBSD are as well. OpenBSD also has default support for quotas and process management, whereas most other systems require some changes to make these features work.

8.1 User Creation and Deletion

One way to create users on OpenBSD is via the *adduser* command. This interactive tool will walk you through the creation of a user and allow you to set many of the available options.

The first time *adduser* is run on a system, it will prompt the operator to set the default options:

```
# adduser
Couldn't find /etc/adduser.conf: creating a new adduser
    configuration file
Reading /etc/shells
Enter your default shell: csh ksh nologin sh [sh]:  ksh
Your default shell is: ksh -> /bin/ksh
Enter your default HOME partition: [/home]:  enter
Copy dotfiles from: /etc/skel no [/etc/skel]:  enter
Send message from file: /etc/adduser.message no [no]:  enter
Do not send message
Prompt for passwords by default (y/n) [y]:  enter
Default encryption method for passwords blowfish des md5 old
```

```
[blowfish]:  enter
Use option ''-silent'' if you don't want to see all warnings
    and questions.
```

Because the file **/etc/adduser.conf** didn't exist, it is created and the default parameters are set. For this system, the default shell was set to *ksh* and the user's home directories are in **/home**. The dotfiles are the default **.profile, .login**, and **.cshrc** files that are copied from the directory **/etc/skel**. The *adduser* program will ask for passwords by default and uses the Blowfish algorithm for the default encryption[1] of the password. The **/etc/adduser.conf** contains the default settings for user addition and can be edited as necessary. The list of shells that are available is generated from the **/etc/shells** file and is dynamically read each time the *adduser* command is run, checking for new or removed shells.

```
Reading /etc/shells
Check /etc/master.passwd
Check /etc/group

Ok, let's go.
Don't worry about mistakes. I will give you the chance later to
    correct any input.
Enter username [a-z0-9_-]:  bpalmer
Enter full name []:  Brandon Palmer
Enter shell csh ksh nologin sh [ksh]:  enter
Uid [1000]:  enter
Login group bpalmer [bpalmer]:  enter
Login group is ''bpalmer''. Invite bpalmer into other groups: guest no
[no]:  wheel
Enter password []:  enter
Enter password again []:  enter

Name:     bpalmer
Password: ****
```

---

[1]Most systems use DES to encrypt passwords. DES isn't considered a very strong algorithm and can be defeated in a fairly short time. The Blowfish algorithm is far stronger and is used for most of the encryption internal to the OpenBSD system. Another nice feature of Blowfish is that you're now welcome to e-mail an encrypted string to a friend as your password. With DES, almost any password could be cracked (using brute force). With Blowfish and with passwords that can be up to 128 characters long, this task is far more difficult and would take many powers of magnitude more resources and time to defeat.

```
Fullname: bpalmer
Uid:       1000
Gid:       1000 (bpalmer)
Groups:    bpalmer wheel
HOME:      /home/bpalmer
Shell:     /bin/ksh
OK? (y/n) [y]:  enter
Added user ''bpalmer''
Copy files from /etc/skel to /home/bpalmer
Add another user? (y/n) [y]:  n
Goodbye!
```

The user *bpalmer* was created with a *ksh* shell. This user was also added to the *wheel* group. Only people who are members of the *wheel* group are allowed to *su* to the root account. The user's password was set[2] and information about the account was given for confirmation. Most UNIX systems will allow the user to have a maximum name length of 8 characters; OpenBSD will allow a maximum of 31 characters. Note that the user's home directory has been created with access rights of 0755, which means that anyone on the system can look in that user's folder. Depending on the system's need for security, this value should be changed to 0750 or 0700 for those who want an even more closed system.

By default, added users are logged to the file **/var/log/adduser**. Here the time and date when the user was added are stored, in addition to some basic information about the account. This can be used for an audit trail in the system. For example:

```
2003/10/27 09:23:30 bpalmer:*:1000:1000(bpalmer):Brandon Palmer
2003/10/28 08:44:39 jose:*:1001:1001(jose):jose
```

Here we can see that two users have been added with the user ID and group ID values of 1000 and 1001, respectively, on two successive days.

To remove the user's account, there is a complementary tool, *rmuser*:

---

[2]Although when creating users this isn't the case, in general the *passwd* program is very restrictive on passwords being selected. It will enforce a minimum length and some degree of variance. The *passwd* settings are specified in the **/etc/passwd.conf** file. In that file, the minimum password length can be set along with hooks to programs to check the quality of the password. Passwords can be up to 128 characters long (unlike the 8 characters allowed on many other systems).

```
# rmuser
Enter login name for user to remove:  jose
Matching password entry:

jose:$2a$3...sJT66:1001:1001:Jose Nazario:0:0:jose:/home/jose:/bin/ksh

Is this the entry you wish to remove? y
Remove user's home directory (/home/jose)? y
Updating password file, updating databases, done.
Updating group file:Removing group jose -- personal group is empty
 done.
Removing user's home directory (/home/jose): done.
```

The program, when not given any command-line options, will ask which user to delete. It will make sure that you do not delete the wrong person by showing that user's information from the **/etc/master.passwd** file.

The program will also ask if you want the user's home directory to be deleted. This allows for the home directory to be backed up in case the account later needs to be re-created. User removals via the *rmuser* command are not logged to the *adduser* logfile.

The examples shown here have used the interactive mode for both of these tools, but they also support command-line options so the programs do not have to work interactively. This allows for scripts to be written for the addition or deletion of users. The *-batch* argument to the *adduser* command can be used, along with either a series of options or explicit arguments to command arguments:

```
# adduser -batch jose jose,guest,staff 'Jose Nazario' MyPassword
```

This batch command will add the user *jose* to the groups *jose, guest*, and *staff* and install the user with the password of *MyPassword*.[3] Alternatively, explicit arguments to the command can be used:

```
# adduser -group USER -batch jose
```

This command will add the user *jose* to the group *jose* (indicated by specifying the group *USER*) but not set a password for the user.

An alternative way to add many users in batch mode relies on the *useradd* command. Here users can be added in batches as well but with more flexible options. The passwords

---

[3] This is a huge security hole, as anyone running *ps* at the time will notice the arguments to the *adduser* command, which include the user's password in clear text.

on the command line *must be* encrypted already. These passwords are generated by the command *encrypt*. To add the same user as was done in the *adduser* batch command above, the following *useradd* command would be used:

```
#  encrypt MyPassword
$2a$06$jDyTmHcw/aPKOUBGs1SmF.QqNV39d7mdANYhQIVcQpS1F2FrKKAYi
#  useradd -g staff -d /home/jose -s /bin/ksh -p
  $2a$06$jDyTmHcw/aPKOUBGs1SmF.QqNV39d7mdANYhQIVcQpS1F2FrKKAYi jose
```

The *useradd* command can also be used to specify the login class for the new user, in the file **/etc/login.conf**. This information can be used to fine-tune the limits placed on the new user at the time of its creation. Unlike *adduser*, the *useradd* command does not create the home directory of the user by default.

8.1.1 Altering the Default New User Options

If the options selected at the time of the first run of *adduser* were incorrect or need to be changed, they can be edited in the configuration file **/etc/adduser.conf**. The options are designated as key-value pairs and are typically well described in the configuration file. For example, if the default home directory for new users should be set to **/export/home**, then the following value would be edited:

```
# default HOME directory ("/home")
home = "/export/home"
```

A common operation for users who are moving from Linux to OpenBSD is to change the default shell from *ksh* to *bash* after installing it from packages.

An interested reader may wish to review a 1999 Usenix paper by Niels Provos, which covers this file format and design. The paper can be found at **http://www.usenix.org/events/usenix99/provos.html**.

8.2 *vipw* and Group Management

The preferred way to edit user accounts on OpenBSD is to not edit the password file by hand, but rather to employ the *vipw* tool. This program is an editor that uses *vi* (this is the default editor, but the program respects the **EDITOR** environmental setting, allowing you to choose an editor with which you're more comfortable) to edit the **/etc/passwd** and **/etc/master.passwd** files. It locks the file for the edit and then performs an integrity check on the file when a write is attempted. If there are errors in the file, *vipw* won't allow the changes to be committed.

Some UNIX systems put users into one group, usually named *users* or something similar. As described earlier, by default OpenBSD creates a group for each user. This allows for more granular control and makes the user's home folder more secure for group access.

Another feature of OpenBSD that most operating systems omit by default is to restrict who can run the *su* command. Only people who are in the *wheel* group are allowed to run the command. Even if an attacker had root's password, he or she couldn't *su* to root.[4]

8.2.1 Self Account Administration for Users

Regular system users do not have access to the *vipw* command to edit their own information or the information of others. Instead, they can access their basic account information using the command *chsh*. Designed primarily to allow users to change the shell, it can also be used to edit the GECOS (originally named for the General Electric Comprehensive Operating System) information, such as a name or phone number. If invoked as *chsh*, an interactive editor window (which uses *vi* by default or the value of the *EDITOR* shell variable) is invoked:

```
# Changing user database information for jose.
Shell: /bin/ksh
Full Name: jose
Office Location: upstairs
Office Phone: 867 5309
Home Phone:
```

Non-interactive mode can also be invoked by using *chsh -s* to set the new shell value—for example, *chsh -s /bin/csh* to change to the *csh* shell.

In NIS (YP) environments, *chsh* will first attempt to access the local authentication database and then the remote NIS information. To force a change to only the local information, *chsh -l* is used; *chsh -y* is used to force a change to the NIS database.

The superuser (root) can use *chsh* to alter other users' records.

---

[4] An attacker could still log in or use *ssh* depending on the local environment and the setup of the machine, however.

8.3 User Limits with *ulimit*

Disk space usage is restricted with quotas as discussed in Chapter 14; other system resource limits are restricted by *ksh ulimit* commands. These resources include CPU time, the maximum amount of memory that can be allocated, and the maximum number of open files.

The file used to manage *ulimit* resources is **/etc/login.conf**. It consists of different login classes for groups and a default setting. The default is as follows:

```
default:\
        :path=/usr/bin /bin /usr/sbin /sbin /usr/X11R6/bin
        /usr/local/bin:\
        :umask=022:\
        :datasize-max=256M:\
        :datasize-cur=64M:\
        :maxproc-max=128:\
        :maxproc-cur=64:\
        :openfiles-cur=64:\
        :stacksize-cur=4M:
```

There are two settings to make note of here: the *-max* and *-cur* settings. When users log in, their limits are set to the soft level but they can request that the limits be raised to the hard limit with the *ulimit* command, which is part of the *ksh* shell. For example, the default user can run only 64 programs from the process group (login session). The current limit is 64 and the max limit is 128. Using *ulimit* with a *-a* parameter will show the current limits and *-aH* will show the hard limits.

```
$  ulimit -a
time(cpu-seconds)      unlimited
file(blocks)           unlimited
coredump(blocks)       unlimited
data(kbytes)           65536
stack(kbytes)          4096
lockedmem(kbytes)      38410
memory(kbytes)         115232
nofiles(descriptors)   64
processes              64

$  ulimit -aH
time(cpu-seconds)      unlimited
```

```
file(blocks)            unlimited
coredump(blocks)        unlimited
data(kbytes)            262144
stack(kbytes)           32768
lockedmem(kbytes)       115232
memory(kbytes)          115232
nofiles(descriptors)    1024
processes               128
```

To raise the limit to the hard limit of 128, use the following commands:

```
$  ulimit -p 128
```

```
$  ulimit -a
time(cpu-seconds)       unlimited
file(blocks)            unlimited
coredump(blocks)        unlimited
data(kbytes)            65536
stack(kbytes)           4096
lockedmem(kbytes)       38410
memory(kbytes)          115232
nofiles(descriptors)    64
processes               128
```

We can see that the hard limit for processes is now set to 128. Many more parameters can be set for the user. Check *login.conf(5)* for more information.

8.4 Process Accounting

OpenBSD offers full support for process accounting. Once enabled, process accounting lets you see who has been using CPU time on the machine and what programs they have been running. Process accounting data records the following data for each process that has been executed:

- The name of the command
- The amount of time (for the user, the system, and elapsed real time) for the process, together with the start time of the process
- Who ran the process, with what user and group IDs

- Memory statistics
- How the process ended

Process accounting records only the base name of the process (none of its arguments), and only when the process has completed. As a result, a subversive executable with an otherwise normal name (such as *ls*) will not by itself indicate a compromised system. Additionally, any arguments to the programs, such as destinations for a network client, are not recorded. Process accounting should not be used as a security monitor but rather as a rough measurement of resource consumption by users or as a profile of a host's activity by process.

To enable process accounting, you simply tell the kernel where to log the information:

```
#  touch /var/account/acct
#  accton /var/account/acct
```

Now the kernel will log information to the **/var/account/acct** file. Because this file doesn't exist by default, it must be created for accounting to work (using *touch*).

The file that is created is viewed by using the *lastcomm* program. We can see that the user *bpalmer* logged in at 21:53, checked his mail, made a folder, looked at processes, and used *grep* to look for something. The total login session was 1:45 minutes and used 0.04 second of CPU time.

```
ksh    -S  bpalmer     ttyp0  0.02 secs Tue May  8 21:53 (0:01:45.59)
grep   -   bpalmer     ttyp0  0.00 secs Tue May  8 21:53 (0:00:00.23)
ps     -   bpalmer     ttyp0  0.02 secs Tue May  8 21:53 (0:00:00.23)
mkdir  -   bpalmer     ttyp0  0.00 secs Tue May  8 21:53 (0:00:00.06)
mail   -   bpalmer     ttyp0  0.00 secs Tue May  8 21:53 (0:00:00.02)
```

The nightly scripts that run on the system know to look for the accounting log files and rotate them for three days' history by default. This can be configured by altering the configuration for the *newsyslog* command. Specific commands executed by a user or on a specific terminal can be viewed using the *lastcomm* command:

```
#  lastcomm ssh root
```

This command would show all of the recorded actions by the user root of the command *ssh*.

The system accounting logs can be processed for summarizing and aggregation via the *sa* tool, which can also be used to generate small reports. Without any arguments, *sa* will print the summary of accounted actions:

```
       32         0.80re         0.01cp       15avio        0k
        8         0.10re         0.00cp       27avio        0k    ***other
        2         0.03re         0.00cp       69avio        0k    tex
        5         0.00re         0.00cp        2avio        0k    ls
        2         0.05re         0.00cp       14avio        0k    make
```

In this case the ***other* entry is the collection of commands that were run once or that contain unprintable characters. This output can be expanded by using *sa -a*. A more useful metric of resource consumption on a multiuser system is *sa -m*:

```
#  sa -m
root              25         0.00cpu          170tio          0k*sec
smmsp              1         0.00cpu           26tio          0k*sec
jose              13         0.01cpu          343tio          0k*sec
nobody             1         0.00cpu            0tio          0k*sec
```

Finally, system accounting data can be truncated and summarized by merging the similar data sets into summary files using the command *sa -s*.

System accounting is turned off by issuing the *accton* command with no arguments.

8.5 Privileged Users with *sudo*

Often it is required to grant a user some extended privilege, but giving the user full access to the superuser account would be too dangerous. Some examples of this include the following:

- A server with shared administrative duties, clearly delineated by applications and requirements
- A shared resource, such as a CD burner, that requires elevated privileges to use
- Privileged access to a system file

Rather than using convoluted group membership and file permissions, as well as a possibly modified kernel, you can use the *sudo* command as a solution.

The *sudo* mechanism uses a file, **/etc/sudoers**, listing users and the privileges they can execute with superuser privileges. Users, groups of users, their authentication requirements, and limits on the actions they can take provide an elegant solution to the issue of divided administration. The advantages of this setup are simple:

- The specific commands executable by the user are well defined.
- The unprivileged user never needs to know the superuser password.

For these reasons, the use of *sudo* is recommended for setups with users who require just a few extra privileges.

The *sudo* facility is used extensively in the OpenBSD *Makefile* infrastructure. A regular user can do most of the building but installation mandates the user have the required privileges.

8.5.1 The sudoers File

The use of and allowed actions from *sudo* are controlled by the file **/etc/sudoers**. A simple listing has the following format:

```
user    host = authentication: command command ...
```

Aliases can be set up to make this file easier to manage, for both users and hosts as well as commands. Commands should always use their full path names.

This file is created and edited with the command *visudo*, as it maintains a database of structured binary data (similar to the *vipw* command to edit the password database). To specify, for example, that users in the *src* group can run the command *make* at an elevated privilege, an entry would look like this:

```
src    ALL = /usr/bin/make
```

Users in the *src* group from any host (*ALL*) are allowed to run the command */usr/bin/make* at an elevated role (such as *make install*). Users in this group would have to authenticate their permission to run this command:

```
$  id
uid=1276(jose) gid=1276(jose) groups=1276(jose), 900(src)
$  sudo make install
We trust you have received the usual lecture from the local System
Administrator. It usually boils down to these two things:
```

```
#1) Respect the privacy of others.
#2) Think before you type.
```

```
Password:  type my own password here
```

Once you authenticate as yourself, using your password, you can run the command as the superuser.

The use of aliases can make a complex **sudoers** file more readable. For example, the three groups listed below are easily understood thanks to the use of aliases (by convention, aliases are in all capital letters):

```
User_Alias    WEBBIES = jose, brandon, michelle
User_Alias    DATABASE = brandon, chelsea, markus, andy, beth,
                           greg
User_Alias    TAPERS = jose, chris
```

Similarly, command aliases allow for the easy grouping of commands for use in the **sudoers** file:

```
Cmnd_Alias    BACKUP = /bin/tar, /usr/bin/gzip, /sbin/dump, /sbin/restore
Cmnd_Alias    REBOOT = /usr/sbin/reboot, /usr/sbin/fastboot
```

Lastly, host aliases allow for the grouping of hosts:

```
Host_Alias    SGI = octopus, squid
Host_Alias    SUN = saturn, jupiter, pluto, venus
Host_Alias    HOMENET = 10.10.0.0/16, 192.168.1.0/24
```

As you can see, this logical grouping allows you to more quickly build an easy-to-understand **sudoers** file.

To put this all together, you can create a very complex **sudoers** file:

```
TAPERS     HOMENET = BACKUP, REBOOT
```

Additional options include the lack of authentication (via the *NOPASSWD* token), negation (via *!token*), and the ability to use a different privilege level than that of the superuser. See the manual pages for *sudo(8)* and *sudoers(5)* for more information on these combinations.

8.5.2 Logging with *sudo*

The use of *sudo* facilitates auditing of actions taken on a system. For example, you can see what happened in this log message and what actions were taken:

```
Apr 23 19:24:20 tank sudo: jose :TTY=ttyp1 ; PWD=/home/jose/rats-1.4 ;
USER=root ; COMMAND=/usr/bin/make install
```

This is far easier than backtracking through logins and actions on a host to determine what happened. The *syslog* facility is normally used for this purpose, allowing for log filtering or remote logging as well.

8.5.3 Security of *sudo*

While *sudo* was designed to enhance security, it can be used to undermine it if you are not careful. If a command has a shell interaction feature, it can be used to start a shell with privileges. Additionally, if a command can be broken via a security flaw to execute arbitrary commands, these commands will run as the privileged user. An example would be the following scenario: A user is given *sudo* access to the *make* command to install software. The user can build and install a modified command that, when run by the superuser, can install a backdoor for the user to gain unfettered access to the system.

Also, note that the simple **sudoers** file

```
username ALL = (ALL) ALL
```

can be a very dangerous file to have around. To obtain a root shell, a user would simply have to execute *sudo sh*.

For all these reasons, it is vital to understand the full scope of any commands to which you grant privileged access. A well-designed and properly limited **sudoers** specification will enhance security, not provide more leaks.

Lastly, note that *sudo* caches the credentials for a brief period of time, typically a few minutes. This time span can be configured via the *timestamp_timeout* option in the **/etc/sudoers** file. Once someone has authenticated, if that person steps away from his or her workstation, an attacker could utilize the cached credentials to abuse the privileged access granted to the user. Lock the terminal that is using *sudo* to prevent this simple attack.

8.6 Restricted Shells

An additional method to control the actions of users works via a restricted shell. This limited-action shell has long been a popular choice for open-access UNIX systems, such as ISP shell servers. The restricted shell is almost a fully working shell with only a few limitations relative to the normal shell:

- The current working directory cannot be changed (typically done with the *cd* command).
- The Shell parameters *SHELL, ENV*, and *PATH* cannot be altered after start-up.
- Commands cannot specify relative or absolute path names; they must respect the established *PATH*.
- File creation redirection cannot be used.

Other than these restrictions, the shell appears to be a normal shell.

From within a restricted shell, a session cannot escape the current working directory:

```
$   pwd
/home/jose
$   cd
rksh: cd: restricted shell - can't cd
```

Hence, if a user's login shell is a restricted shell, the user cannot leave and explore other parts of the system. This constraint can be useful to allow users to have basic mail program access but to prevent them from exploring the system fully.

A restricted shell can be started in two ways: by directly calling *rksh*, and by using *ksh -r*. Note that a restricted shell is merely one part of a secure environment, coupled to binary restrictions (via permissions) and filesystem options.

Restricted shells are not perfect security measures and have several holes. One obvious security hole in *rksh* is closed by ensuring that the *PATH* variable contains only system executables but no local or user-controlled directories. This prevents the execution of user-supplied binaries (e.g., in the user's home directory or **/tmp**). A second security hole on *rksh* is child shells of some processes. For example, in the *vi* editor a child shell can be spawned by the *!* operator (as *:! sh*). This produces an unrestricted shell. Care must be taken to leave the shells open only to users of the *rksh* (and other restricted shells) facility.

8.7 Restricting Users with *systrace*

An additional mechanism to restrict processes and users is to control execution with the *systrace* command. By controlling the actions of processes at the system call level, *systrace* can provide kernel-level security policy enforcement. The *systrace* facility is described in Chapter 29. Note that while a much more secure system can be created by using the *systrace* command, it requires substantial setup effort.

Chapter 9

Networking

Networking is one of the main focuses for the OpenBSD project. While systems like Microsoft Windows suggest that video, sound, and other capabilities are of great importance, networking is a core part of the OpenBSD system. OpenBSD supports Ethernet, wireless, gigabit, ATM, FDDI, and some WAN adapters. Also native to OpenBSD is support for IPv6, which is discussed in Chapter 28. This chapter focuses on Ethernet adapters and PPP links.

9.1 Device Support

OpenBSD names the networking devices with the driver name. This is in contrast to Linux systems, in which all Ethernet devices use the common prefix "eth." The device name in OpenBSD is a combination of the device type (and driver name) and the index number within the system. Examples include **fxp0** for the first Intel Etherexpress Pro 10/100 device (which uses the fxp* driver), **bge1** for a Broadcom BCM570x-based PCI gigabit Ethernet device, and **wi0** for a Prism2-based 802.11b interface. Most Ethernet device drivers have their own manual pages describing the options applicable to the device and supported hardware manufacturers. The loopback device is created with the lo* device name.

Driver support is enabled in the kernel configuration file, with the GENERIC kernel containing most (but not all) device drivers enabled. To enable an fxp* driver device, the following line would be used in the kernel configuration:

```
fxp*  at pci? dev ? function ?   # EtherExpress 10/100B ethernet
```

This attaches the fxp device to the PCI bus. Similar device drivers are available in the configuration file. Chapter 32 describes how to configure and build a kernel.

9.1.1 Virtual Interface Drivers

A number of virtual interface types are also supported by the OpenBSD kernel. These include tunnel devices, 802.1q virtual LAN devices, and encryption interfaces. A similar strategy for kernel support is employed for the virtual devices, but typically using the *pseudo-device* directive. Some devices support the installation of multiple virtual devices.

One commonly used virtual device is the gif* device, which provides a generic tunnel interface. It can be used to tunnel IPv4 within IPv4 traffic, IPv6 within IPv6 traffic, or a mixture of the two. The gif driver uses the *tunnel* keyword for the *ifconfig* command to enable the two endpoints of the tunnel:

```
#  ifconfig gif0 tunnel 10.10.32.1 1.1.1.1
#  ifconfig gif0
gif0: flags=8051<UP,POINTOPOINT,RUNNING,MULTICAST> mtu 1280
    physical address inet 10.10.32.1 --> 1.1.1.1
    inet6 fe80::205:5dff:fef2:cb11%gif0 -> prefixlen 64 scopeid 0x11
```

To clear the tunnel address, use the *ifconfig gif0 deletetunnel* command. The GENERIC kernel on i386 contains support for four gif interfaces by default.

Virtual LAN (VLAN) devices conforming to the IEEE 802.1q specification can also be used using the **vlan*** virtual device. These are enabled in the kernel configuration file:

```
pseudo-device vlan 2
```

Additional VLAN devices can be configured by using the *ifconfig* command and then associated with a VLAN tag and a physical device. To create the first VLAN device with a VLAN tag of 1 and associate it with the physical device **wi0**, use the following command:

```
#  ifconfig vlan0 vlan 1 vlandev wi0
#  ifconfig vlan0
vlan0: flags=8843<UP,BROADCAST,RUNNING,SIMPLEX,MULTICAST> mtu 1496
        address: 00:05:5d:f2:cb:11
        vlan: 1 parent interface: wi0
        inet6 fe80::205:5dff:fef2:cb11%vlan0 prefixlen 64 scopeid 0xe
```

VLAN device configurations are cleared using the *ifconfig vlan0 -vlandev* command. This removes the VLAN device from the physical interface, clears the VLAN tag, and shuts the interface down. The GENERIC kernel on i386 is configured to support two VLAN devices by default. Note that not all physical devices support VLAN tagging due to the additional frame overhead incurred. Those that do not offer such support will drop VLAN Ethernet frames as corrupted input. Additionally, with a large number of VLAN devices and physical devices, an OpenBSD host can be made into an expensive VLAN-aware switch.

To use the GRE virtual device in OpenBSD, you follow steps similar to those used in the configuration of a **gif** tunnel. The **gif** pseudo-device is enabled in the kernel configuration with a number of virtual devices to create:

```
pseudo-device   gre      1
```

GRE tunnels have two endpoints—one local and one remote—and an associated netmask and route. Configuration using *ifconfig* takes place in two steps. The first sets the interface and the netmask, and the second adds the tunnel:

```
#  ifconfig gre0 10.10.32.1 10.11.10.1 netmask 0xffff0000 link0 up
#  ifconfig gre0
gre0: flags=9011<UP,POINTOPOINT,LINK0,MULTICAST> mtu 1450
        inet 10.10.32.1 --> 10.11.10.1 netmask 0xffff0000
#  ifconfig gre0 tunnel 10.10.32.1 10.11.10.1
#  ifconfig gre0
gre0: flags=9011<UP,POINTOPOINT,LINK0,MULTICAST> mtu 1450
        physical address inet 10.10.32.1 --> 10.11.10.1
        inet 10.10.32.1 --> 10.11.10.1 netmask 0xffff0000
#  route add 10.11.10.2 10.11.10.1
```

The last step adds a route to be used over the GRE tunnel—in this case, a remove system on the 10.11/16 network (via 10.11.10.1). To begin passing GRE traffic, the system must be configured both to allow incoming GRE traffic and to forward IPv4 traffic:

```
#  sysctl -w net.inet.gre.allow=1
#  sysctl -w net.inet.ip.forwarding=1
```

Now traffic destined for 10.11.10.2 will use the GRE tunnel between 10.10.32.1 and 10.11.10.1. To clear the GRE device, you must issue two commands: *ifconfig gre0 delete* to delete the address and *ifconfig gre0 deletetunnel* to clear the tunnel between the two hosts. To fully bring the GRE interface down, use the command *ifconfig gre0 down*. The GENERIC kernel contains support for one GRE device. This GRE tunnel is not compatible with the Microsoft PPTP use of GRE, however, and must be disabled if the system will be used with a PPTP client or server package. To configure the GRE tunnel to use IP protocol 55, Mobile IP, as described in RFC 2004, use the *-link0* link protocol in the *ifconfig* command. GRE tunnels can also be used with Cisco routers and, on OpenBSD systems, require a slightly different configuration due to the router's GRE routing. The manual page for *gre(4)* contains instructions on how to create this configuration.

OpenBSD supports the **bridge** virtual device. Bridging is described in detail later in this chapter.

Encapsulating interfaces, using the **enc** driver, work with IPsec and are described in Chapter 27.

9.1.2 Kernel Messages

We can get information about the card from *dmesg* output, showing us how the kernel identified the device:

```
#  dmesg | grep ^fxp0
fxp0 at pci0 dev 6 function 0 "Intel 82557" rev 0x05: irq 9,
    address 00:90:27:07:a1:01

#  dmesg | grep ^dc0
dc0 at pci0 dev 15 function 0 "Lite-On PNIC" rev 0x21: irq 3,
    address 00:a0:cc:39:db:41

#  dmesg | grep ^ep0
ep0 at isa0 port 0x300/16 irq 10: address 00:60:97:1b:73:60,
    utp/bnc (default utp)
```

The first card is the internal Intel 10/100 card on the motherboard, the next is a PCI Netgear 10/100 card, and the last is an ISA 3Com-509 card. These names relate to those seen in the output of the *ifconfig* command.

9.2 Basic Setup

Networking for OpenBSD is configured by working with just a few main files. The first file of concern is **/etc/netstart**. This script is called by **/etc/rc** during start-up. The *netstart* script reads from several other files to get the information it needs.

The first task in working with networking is to learn the names of the network devices. As with Solaris, the name of the device is connected to the hardware or the vendor. An example system has the following identifying information:

```
#  ifconfig -a
lo0: flags=8009<UP,LOOPBACK,MULTICAST> mtu 32972
        inet6 fe80::1%lo0 prefixlen 64 scopeid 0x5
        inet6 ::1 prefixlen 128
        inet 127.0.0.1 netmask 0xff000000
lo1: flags=8008<LOOPBACK,MULTICAST> mtu 32972
fxp0: flags=8843<UP,BROADCAST,RUNNING,SIMPLEX,MULTICAST> mtu 1500
        media: Ethernet autoselect (100baseTX full-duplex)
        status: active
        inet 192.168.1.20 netmask 0xffffff00 broadcast 192.168.1.255
        inet6 fe80::290:27ff:fe07:a101%fxp0 prefixlen 64 scopeid 0x1
dc0: flags=8802<BROADCAST,SIMPLEX,MULTICAST> mtu 1500
        media: Ethernet autoselect (none)
ep0: flags=8822<BROADCAST,NOTRAILERS,SIMPLEX,MULTICAST> mtu 1500
        media: Ethernet 10baseT
...
...
```

We can see that there are three network cards in the machine: *fxp0, dc0*, and *ep0*. The "lo" interfaces are loopback devices, which allow the system to network with only itself.

Boot-time networking configuration occurs during system initialization and is run by the */etc/rc* script, which itself is run by the script */etc/netstart*. This script uses a series of files to control configuration information about the devices and networking setup. To make changes persistent across different system boots, edit these files.

IP addresses are assigned to the interface from the respective **/etc/hostname.if** file, where **if** is the name of the interface. For example, the **/etc/hostname.fxp0** file contains the following, information, which configures the interface **fxp0**:

```
inet 192.168.1.20 255.255.255.0 NONE
```

The first field sets the address type—in this case, an Internet type. The interface address family is typically either **inet** or **inet6** for IPv4 or IPv6, respectively. The next two fields set the IP address of the interface to 192.168.1.20 with a netmask of 255.255.255.0. The *NONE* option can specify a broadcast address or an interface setting for the card.

In addition, a line in the file starting with "!" specifies a command-line program to be run. For example, if we had a wireless network card, we might want to specify the SSID:

```
!ancontrol -n MYSSID
```

Arbitrary commands can be executed for the interface upon configuration. The macro **$if** can be used to expand the name of the current interface. The *ancontrol* program is explained more in Section 9.2.1.

The default gateway for the network is set in the **/etc/mygate** file. The only information in this file is the address of the gateway device:

```
#  cat /etc/mygate
192.168.1.1
```

No comments are allowed in this file.

If your system is multihomed (it has more than one network connection installed) and you want to use different routing gateways for different networks, you will need to modify the system start-up scripts for these changes to take effect at boot time. This is most efficiently done via changes to the **/etc/rc.local** script:

```
# handle local routing instances.
# fxp0 (192.168.1.20/24) -> 192.168.1.1, default (mygate)
# fxp1 (172.13.1.4/16) -> 10.0.0.0/8 via 172.13.1.1
route add 10.0.0.0/8 172.13.1.1
```

At this time no easy methods exist by which you can set up a static route map to be parsed by the system initialization scripts.

9.2.1 Interface Media Options

The extra options can be media options, such as a half-duplex connection. To get a list of supported options for a given interface, use the command *ifconfig -m interface*:

```
$  ifconfig -m de0
de0: flags=8863<UP,BROADCAST,NOTRAILERS,RUNNING,SIMPLEX,MULTICAST>
mtu 1500
        media: Ethernet autoselect (10baseT)
        status: active
        supported media:
                media 10baseT
                media 10baseT mediaopt full-duplex
                media 10base2
                media 10base5
                media autoselect
```

This is sometimes needed to force an interface to the proper settings when autonegotiation fails.

Wireless interfaces using the 802.11b standard are supported by two main drivers: the **wi** driver and the **an** driver. While the basic address information and fundamental media options can be configured using the *ifconfig* command, options specific to the 802.11b networking standard can be configured using the programs *ancontrol* and *wicontrol*. Both the *ancontrol* and *wicontrol* commands have similar options, though **wi**-based interfaces are also capable of performing *host AP* functions. The *wicontrol* commands are decribed below; see the manual page for *ancontrol* for the compatible commands.

Without any arguments selected, the *wicontrol* command displays the current settings for the interfaces:

```
$ wicontrol
NIC serial number:                        [ 001214004472 ]
Station name:                             [ WaveLAN/IEEE node ]
SSID for IBSS creation:                   [ IBSS ]
Current netname (SSID):                   [ linksys ]
Desired netname (SSID):                   [ ]
Current BSSID:                            [ 00:06:25:51:54:41 ]
Channel list:                             [ 2047 ]
IBSS channel:                             [ 6 ]
Current channel:                          [ 6 ]
Comms quality/signal/noise:               [ 48 95 0 ]
Promiscuous mode:                         [ Off ]
Process 802.11b Frame:                    [ Off ]
Port type (1=BSS, 3=ad-hoc, 6=Host AP):   [ 1 ]
MAC address:                              [ 00:05:5d:f2:cb:11 ]
TX rate (selection):                      [ 3 ]
TX rate (actual speed):                   [ 11 ]
Maximum data length:                      [ 2304 ]
RTS/CTS handshake threshold:              [ 2347 ]
Create IBSS:                              [ Off ]
Antenna diversity (0=auto,1=pri,2=aux):   [ ]
Microwave oven robustness:                [ On ]
Roaming mode(1=firm,3=disable):           [ 1 ]
Access point density:                     [ 1 ]
Power Management:                         [ Off ]
```

```
Max sleep time:                          [ 100 ]
Intersil Prism2-based card:              [ 1 ]
Card info:                               [ PRISM2 HWB3163 SST-flash,
                                           Firmware 0.8.2 ]
Encryption:                              [ Off ]
Encryption algorithm:                    [ Firmware WEP ]
Authentication type
(1=OpenSys, 2=Shared Key):               [ 1 ]
TX encryption key:                       [ 1 ]
Encryption keys:                         [   ][   ][   ][   ]
```

If multiple **wi** interfaces are present, the information for each will be shown.

The following options relate to the use of Wired Equivalent Privacy (WLP), a security standard for 802.11b networking. Note that the use of WEP is trivial to circumvent and IPsec is the preferred wireless security mechanism.

- **-e**   Enable or disable the use of WEP.
- **-k [1|2|3|4]**   Specify the four default WEP encryption keys to use.
- **-T 1|2|3|4**   Specify which WEP key will be used for the transmission.

There are four modes of operation for a wireless interface, specified with the *wicontrol -p number* command and indicated with a number for the type:

- 1 specifies BSS mode, where the interface associates with an access point.
- 3 specifies ad hoc mode, where two or more interfaces communicate directly without an AP.
- 4 indicates IBSS mode is to be used, where the station takes the role of an AP.
- 6 specifies that host AP mode is to be used.

The last option, host AP mode, is available only on certain types of **wi** interfaces. The manual page for *wicontrol* specify which types.

The name of the station to associate with the device can be specified with the *wicontrol -n* command. Note that the station name is case sensitive. An additional option, -P, can be used to enable or disable power conservation mode—a useful feature for laptop systems.

Other options that are used less frequently are listed on the manual page for *wicontrol*.

9.3 DNS Client Configuration

The OpenBSD machine needs to know with which DNS servers it should communicate for name resolution. This information is covered in Chapter 18.

9.4 DHCP

Using DHCP on OpenBSD is a trivial matter. To set your interface configurations to use DHCP at boot time, simply do the following:

```
# echo dhcp > /etc/hostname.fxp0
```

Make sure that the filename corresponds to the interface driver for your network card. That's it. During the initial network configuration at start-up, OpenBSD will then try to get an IP address, default gateway, DNS servers, and other data from the server and set up this connection for the host. This is done by the system by invoking *dhclient* with the interface name as its argument. The *dhclient* program is left running to handle lease renewal. It will overwrite the **/etc/resolv.conf** file with the information it got from the DHCP server. If the system is using DHCP, the *netstart* script will also ignore the **/etc/mygate** file. The **/etc/dhclient.conf** file contains information for the *dhclient* program regarding which options from the DHCP server are and are not used.

   If, for some reason, you need to renew your lease from the server, the *dhclient* program can be re-run. However, you must first *kill* the initial *dhclient* process to stop it from handling leases, potentially incorrectly, with the new instance of *dhclient.* Use the interface name as the command-line argument to *dhclient.* Continuing the earlier examples, to renegotiate the lease on the interface **fxp0**, you would use the command *dhclient fxp0* after first stopping the initial *dhclient* process with *kill.* Lease information is stored in the **/var/db/dhclient.leases** file. This file should not be edited by the user, but is used to maintain information even during a reboot.

   Autoconfiguration for IPv6, done via router solicitation, is specified via the *rtsol* keyword. It causes OpenBSD to query the local IPv6 routers for stateless autoconfiguration information. More information on IPv6 autoconfiguration is given in Chapter 28.

   Both IPv4 and IPv6 autoconfiguration can have additional interface options specified in the configuration line. These are typically media options, as described earlier.

9.5 Alias Addresses

Sometimes you need more than one IP address for an interface—perhaps for virtual Web servers or testing. OpenBSD readily supports this setup. To add a second IP address to the **fxp0** interface, we would place the following line in the **/etc/hostname.fxp0** file:

```
inet alias 192.168.1.21 255.255.255.255
```

When the system boots, it will now have the new address bound to the **fxp0** interface. This goal can also easily be achieved without restarting the system:

```
#  ifconfig fxp0 inet alias 192.168.1.21 netmask 255.255.255.255
#  ifconfig fxp0 inet -alias 192.168.1.21
```

We see the address being added to the **fxp0** interface and then removed in the next step.

9.6 ARP: Address Resolution Protocol

Ethernet interfaces use ARP to map layer 2 MAC addresses, which are part of the networking hardware, to layer 3 IP addresses. IP addresses are fluid and can be manipulated without great difficulty; in contrast, layer 2 addresses can be changed but require additional overhead. The mapping is similar to the mapping between IP addresses and hostname entries in DNS tables. ARP entries are added for hosts and gateways directly connected to the interface on the same broadcast segment. Hosts on another routed segment do not have ARP entries added for them. ARP maps between these two address layers by sending requests to the broadcast address and receiving replies:

```
16:42:34.320468 arp who-has 10.10.2.20 tell 10.10.10.1
16:42:34.320476 arp 10.10.2.20 is-at 00:80:ad:4a:23:f0
```

ARP addresses are 48-byte addresses typically represented in hexadecimal format. Leading zeroes may be omitted, such that 08:1a and 8:1a are equivalent. Trailing zeroes may not be omitted. Every field must have at least one character. Thus 00:00 collapses to 0:0.

To view the ARP table, the simple *arp* command is used with the *-a* flag:

```
$  arp -a
uriel.crimelabs.net (10.10.10.1) at 00:a0:cc:7b:af:92 on wi0
hoover.crimelabs.net (10.10.10.23) at 00:80:ad:41:22:10 on wi0
```

Normally, the displaying program will attempt to resolve the host name, but this behavior can be overridden using the *arp -n* command. Entries that lack a mapping are marked as *incomplete* by the ARP program output.

The ARP discovery and mapping process occurs automatically. The host that needs the mapping makes a request, which is answered only if the host is on and configured to respond. ARP entries can also be added manually. Normal users and the superuser can request a mapping for a host by issuing the command *arp hostname*, where *hostname* is the name or address of the host for which you want an entry added automatically. Entries may also be added manually by the superuser:

```
#  arp -s 10.10.2.20 00:80:ad:4a:23:f0
```

This command will add an ARP entry for the host 10.10.2.20 at the MAC address of 00:80:ad:4a:23:f0.

ARP entries are normally aged and removed unless explicitly renewed. This allows for new hosts to be moved into the same IP address without causing problems. Ethernet frames that are intended to deliver their payload to the given IP address will not be accepted by the new interface with a differing MAC address.

```
#  arp -s 10.10.2.20 00:80:ad:4a:23:f0 permanent
```

The *permanent* keyword indicates that this entry is not to be removed until the system is shut down. Permanent entries are often useful to ensure that layer 2 hijacking attacks cannot succeed. If important systems reside on the same segment and are not subject to change, some network administrators will add permanent entries for them. This group includes DNS servers and the gateway device.

One interesting use of the *arp* command is to perform proxy-*arp*. In this scenario, one host replies on behalf of another IP address. The *pub* keyword is used to publish the ARP entry sent in reply for other IP addresses:

```
#  arp -s 10.10.2.21 00:80:ad:4a:23:f0 pub
#  arp -s 10.10.2.22 00:80:ad:4a:23:f0 pub
```

Here two proxy-*arp* entries have been added for other hosts with the same MAC address as the host 10.10.2.20. This allows 10.10.2.20 to see the traffic destined for 10.10.2.21 or 10.10.2.22, which is useful in scenarios such as IDS monitoring. These mappings can be made permanent by using a file containing the arguments to the *arp -s* command:

```
10.10.2.21 00:80:ad:4a:23:f0 pub
10.10.2.22 00:80:ad:4a:23:f0 pub
```

If we add this information to the file **mappings** and run the command *arp -f mappings* at boot time, these entries will always be added. While no explicit support for this action

exists in the OpenBSD network boot scripts, it can be easily added to the final stage of
the boot process in **/etc/rc.local**:

```
if [ -e /etc/mappings ]; then
        echo "Adding proxy-arp entries ..."
        arp -f /etc/mappings
fi
```

This will cause the entries to be added to the kernel ARP table at every start-up and can
be manipulated via the file **/etc/mappings**.

ARP entries can also be deleted from the kernel mapping. They can be removed one
entry at a time:

```
#  arp -d 10.10.2.21
```

Alternatively, they can be flushed entirely:

```
#  arp -d -a
```

This ability can be useful if an entry has changed but needs to be updated immediately,
before the kernel timeout occurs.

9.6.1 Diagnostic Information

There are two main messages from the kernel with respect to ARP tables that can signal
a problem. The first is a warning from the kernel that a collision has occurred, where two
differing MAC addresses have been mapped to the same IP address:

```
Apr  7 16:18:12 uriel /bsd: arp: attempt to overwrite entry for
    10.10.32.1 on de0 by 00:05:5d:f2:cb:11 on sis1
```

In this scenario, confusion may occur on the machine and cause failures in reliable delivery
of the packets to the destination.

The second message is the warning that the kernel's ARP table is full:

```
Nov  9 17:04:54 uriel /bsd: arpresolve: can't allocate llinfo
```

This can occur when the kernel has too many mappings and is unable to allocated more
information for the mapping. This problem usually does not persist for more than a few
minutes on most networks.

9.7 Routing

By default, the kernel will route packets to any interfaces it has. It won't, however, forward any packets. Thus, even if the machine is set as a gateway device, it won't send any packets through. To enable this feature, you need to enable forwarding in the kernel. This is done via a command-line tool *sysctl*:

```
# sysctl -a | grep forward
net.inet.ip.forwarding = 0
net.inet6.ip6.forwarding = 0
# sysctl -w net.inet.ip.forwarding=1
net.inet.ip.forwarding: 0 -> 1
```

To maintain this setting during rebooting, it must be placed in the **/etc/sysctl.conf** file by setting *net.inet.ip.forwarding* variable to 1 and uncommenting that line.

Static routing tables are queried, created, and adjusted using the *route* command. The basic concept underlying routing is that the path chosen by the kernel is the most specific route listed for a destination. Routes can be for a specific host, a network, or a default entry or a gateway of last resort; routes are used in that order.

Routing tables can be displayed using the *route show* command. Use the command *route -n* to suppress name lookups for the addresses:

```
# route -n show
Routing tables

Internet:
Destination        Gateway              Flags
default            10.10.10.1           UG
10.10.0.0          link#21              U
10.10.10.1         0:a0:cc:7b:af:92     UH
10.10.10.23        0:80:ad:41:22:10     UH
127.0.0.0          127.0.0.1            UG
127.0.0.1          127.0.0.1            UH
224.0.0.0          127.0.0.1            U
```

This table contains all three types of routing entries. The first line is for the gateway of last resort, which on this network is the address 10.10.10.1. The next line is for a network address, in this case 10.10.0.0/16, using the interface with an index of 21. The next two entries are for hosts directly connected to the machine's local subnet; hence they have layer 2 addresses displayed as their gateway addresses.

To add an IPv4 (or IPv6) route to the kernel routing table, use the *route add* command:

```
#  route add 1.1.1.0/24 10.10.32.2
add net 1.1.1.0: gateway 10.10.32.2
```

This will add the network 1.1.1.0/24 to the system with the gateway address of 10.10.32.2. The addition could have also used the syntax *route add -net*, although it was implied in the destination syntax. To add a host, the same syntax is used:

```
#  route add -host 10.10.2.20 10.10.10.1
add host 10.10.2.20: gateway 10.10.10.1
```

To suppress name lookups, use the *route -n* command for these operations.

Deleting specific routes is easy and uses the same syntax structure for the *route delete* command. To undo the two additions from the previous examples, the following two commands would be used:

```
#  route delete -host 10.10.2.20 10.10.10.1
delete host 10.10.2.20: gateway 10.10.10.1
#  route delete 1.1.1.0/24 10.10.32.2
delete net 1.1.1.0: gateway 10.10.32.2
```

To delete the default gateway, specify the "default" destination. Note that the local network—the broadcast for any given interface on the machine—cannot be deleted and is added automatically. To remove all configured routing entries except for those directly connected, use the *route flush* command.

Routing entries can also be changed without the need for removal and readdition of an entry. The *route change* command can change a routing entry in place:

```
#  route change 224.0.0.0/4 10.10.10.1
change net 224.0.0.0: gateway 10.10.10.1
```

Again, hosts or networks can specified for the update.

Route lookups can be performed against the current routing table as well. This can be useful in examining the path a connection would use in a complex routing table or for debugging purposes. The command uses the *route get destination* syntax:

```
$  route get 10.10.10.1
   route to: 10.10.10.1
destination: 10.10.10.1
  interface: wi0
      flags: <UP,HOST,DONE,LLINFO>
 recvpipe sendpipe ssthresh rtt,msec rttvar hopcount    mtu   expire
        0        0        0        0      0        0      0       57
```

A brief summary of statistics is also given.

One use of routing in security for a network attack is to NULL route a destination. This is done by establishing a route for a network or for a host with a gateway using the localhost address (127.0.0.1). This effectively prevents the packets to that destination from being passed.

All of the examples in this section have used IPv4, but they can also be performed using IPv6. Simply substitute IPv6 addresses for their IPv4 counterparts.

9.8 Bridging

Bridging, where two network segments are joined together by a device creating a shared segment (not a routed segment), is configured using the *brconfig* command. Many of its main options are similar to those of the *ifconfig* command. By default, the GENERIC kernel ships with support for two bridging devices:

```
# brconfig -a
bridge0: flags=0<>
        Configuration:
                priority 32768 hellotime 2 fwddelay 15 maxage 20
        Interfaces:
        Addresses (max cache: 100, timeout: 240):
bridge1: flags=0<>
        Configuration:
                priority 32768 hellotime 2 fwddelay 15 maxage 20
        Interfaces:
        Addresses (max cache: 100, timeout: 240):
```

To configure a bridge, interfaces are added to it and the bridge then is brought up:

```
# brconfig bridge0 add dc1 add gif0
# brconfig bridge0 up
```

```
#  brconfig bridge0
bridge0: flags=41<UP,RUNNING>
        Configuration:
                priority 32768 hellotime 2 fwddelay 15 maxage 20
        Interfaces:
                gif0 flags=3<LEARNING,DISCOVER>
                        port 19 ifpriority 128 ifcost 55
                dc1 flags=3<LEARNING,DISCOVER>
                        port 2 ifpriority 128 ifcost 55
        Addresses (max cache: 100, timeout: 240):
```

Interfaces can be removed from the bridge configuration via *brconfig del interface.* Not all interfaces can be added, but almost all physical Ethernet interfaces can be, as well as several virtual devices, such as the ***gif*** devices (used in IPsec and IPv6 tunnels). Interfaces do not need to have addresses, which will give your bridge a transparent face to the outside world:

```
#  ifconfig dc1 up
#  ifconfig fxp0 up
#  brconfig add dc1 add fxp0 up
```

This code will create a two-member transparent bridge suitable for filtering. A third interface (such as **dc0**) would be used as a management interface.

Using a bridge device as a subnet filter allows for even greater flexibility in filtering. Because a bridge operates at the link layer, link-layer addresses (MAC addresses) can be filtered. Using the *brconfig rule* command, pass and block rules can be specified for individual MAC addresses:

```
#  brconfig bridge0 rule pass in on dc1 src 0:1:2:3:4:5 dst
   5:4:3:2:1:0
#  brconfig bridge0 rule pass out on dc1 src 5:4:3:2:1:0 dst
   0:1:2:3:4:5
#  brconfig bridge0 rule block in on gif0
#  brconfig bridge0 rule block out on gif0
#  brconfig bridge0
bridge0: flags=41<UP,RUNNING>
  Configuration:
    priority 32768 hellotime 2 fwddelay 15 maxage 20
```

```
Interfaces:
  gif0 flags=3<LEARNING,DISCOVER>
     port 19 ifpriority 128 ifcost 55
   block in on gif0
   block out on gif0
  dc1 flags=3<LEARNING,DISCOVER>
     port 2 ifpriority 128 ifcost 55
   pass in on dc1 src 00:01:02:03:04:05 dst 05:04:03:02:01:00
   pass out on dc1 src 05:04:03:02:01:00 dst 00:01:02:03:04:05
Addresses (max cache: 100, timeout: 240):
```

This code will selectively filter all traffic so that Ethernet frames between 00:01:02:03:04:05 and 05:04:03:02:01:00 can send traffic in and out of **dc1**, but not through **gif0**. This technique can be used, for example, on three or more member bridges to selectively isolate and segment traffic. A simple bridge filter can also be applied to block non-IP traffic (i.e., traffic that is not IPv4, IPv6, ARP, or RARP traffic) on bridges. This is useful for segmenting broadcast-based protocols, such as AppleTalk and DECNet, from the remainder of the network:

```
# brconfig bridge0
bridge0: flags=41<UP,RUNNING>
      Configuration:
            priority 32768 hellotime 2 fwddelay 15 maxage 20
      Interfaces:
            gif0 flags=3<LEARNING,DISCOVER>
                  port 19 ifpriority 128 ifcost 55
            dc1 flags=7<LEARNING,DISCOVER,BLOCKNONIP>
                  port 2 ifpriority 128 ifcost 55
      Addresses (max cache: 100, timeout: 240):
```

The PF packet filter can be used with a transparent bridge as well. To do so, create a bridge with IP-less interfaces as shown above, and then apply the rules for inbound and outbound traffic to the interfaces (not the bridge). This will create a transparent firewall, suitable for filtering at the network or IP address layer.

Bridges have extensive ARP tables to map link-layer addresses to their interfaces. As with a normal Ethernet switch, frames for which no MAC address to port mapping has been made will be forwarded on all interfaces. This discovery can be turned off for selected interfaces:

```
#  brconfig  bridge0 -discover dc1
#  brconfig bridge0
bridge0: flags=41<UP,RUNNING>
        Configuration:
                priority 32768 hellotime 2 fwddelay 15 maxage 20
        Interfaces:
                gif0 flags=3<LEARNING,DISCOVER>
                        port 19 ifpriority 128 ifcost 55
                dc1 flags=5<LEARNING,BLOCKNONIP>
                        port 2 ifpriority 128 ifcost 55
        Addresses (max cache: 100, timeout: 240):
```

The default action is to perform this discovery. Learning is disabled on a per-interface basis with the option *brconfig bridgename -learn interface*. Static mappings of a MAC address to an interface can be generated as well:

```
#  brconfig bridge0 -learn gif0 static gif0 0e:ff:80:ca:fe:dd
#  brconfig bridge0
...
        Addresses (max cache: 100, timeout: 240):
                0e:ff:80:ca:fe:dd gif0 1 flags=1<STATIC>
```

Similarily, these mappings are made visible, along with MAC addresses that have been learned, by using the *brconfig bridgename addr* command.

All of the preceeding examples use the *brconfig* command interactively. This provides a temporary configuration, which will be lost upon a reboot. To make these settings permanent, use the file **/etc/bridgename.bridge0** (and **bridge1** and so forth). In this file place the arguments to the *brconfig bridge0* command:

```
add dc1
add gif0
-learn gif0
static gif0 0e:ff:80:ca:fe:dd
up
```

This file can contain comments (prepended with a pound sign) as well as shell commands, which are indicated by the use of an a "!" character. This file is read by the *netstart* script at system start-up, and the bridge is configured accordingly.

A variety of other options for bridging, including 802.1D parameters, can be tuned. The manual pages for the *brconfig* command, and the *bridge* subsystem are worth reading. Some developers have tested bridge sizes of up to 16 member bridges or even 16 bridges per system. The stability of bridges for most users should suffice.

9.9 PPP

Dial-up is quickly becoming a dying technology in most parts of the world as more and more people move to broadband. Even though this access method is on the way out, there is still a great need for OpenBSD to support it. Most people use a PPP connection to get Internet access over dial-up, which is what OpenBSD supports. The PPP support for OpenBSD is very mature and simple to use.

9.9.1 User Dial-up with PPP

Configuring PPP for a dial-up user with OpenBSD is very easy. The file **/etc/ppp/ppp.conf** contains all the information needed for the dial-up session.

```
default:
 set log Phase Chat LCP IPCP CCP tun command
 set device /dev/cua00
 set speed 38400
 set dial "ABORT BUSY ABORT NO\\sCARRIER TIMEOUT 5 \"\" AT OK-AT-OK
          ATE1Q0 OK \\dATDT\\T TIMEOUT 40 CONNECT"

myispname:
 set phone 12125551234
 set login "ABORT NO\\sCARRIER TIMEOUT 15
          ogin:--ogin: USERNAME word: PASSWORD"
 set timeout 120
 set ifaddr 10.0.0.1/0 10.0.0.2/0 255.255.255.0 0.0.0.0
 add default HISADDR
 enable dns
```

Note that the *set dial* and *set login* lines should be joined together into one line separated by a space.

This file is separated into two sections. It could be just one section, but using two will enable us to create other connections more easily. In the *default* section, we assign values to settings that will be used for any connection. The device relates to the COM ports on the system. In our case, our modem is attached to COM1 (as viewed from DOS) and so is set to **/dev/cua00** (UNIX traditionally starts numbering devices from 0, not 1). We have also set the speed of the modem to be 38,400 baud.

We then create a second section for the ISP we will be using. Our internal name for this connection is *myispname*. The phone number to dial for the connection is 1-212-555-1234. The *login* section is the chat script [read the *chat(8)* manual page for more information]. It waits for "ogin:", will then send "USERNAME" in response, waits for "word:", and will then send "PASSWORD" in response. These settings should be changed to reflect the username and password for your ISP. The *ifaddr* setting helps to assign the IP address for the connection. We will attempt to get a local IP address of 10.0.0.1 for our end of the connection, but the /0 means that we will allow anything. The next section means that we are requesting 10.0.0.2 for the remote end, but the /0 again means that we will accept anything. The last two sections are the respective netmasks. The *add default* setting means to set our end of the PPP connection to be the default gateway if the session is successful. There are many other settings for PPP, which are all well documented in the *ppp* manual page.

9.10 Listening Ports and Processes

To get a listing of processes actively listening for incoming connections or even processes that are active with a peer, you can use the *netstat* command to obtain the network status. It can show you active and listening sockets for TCP and UDP servers, as well as IPsec routing and UNIX domain sockets. (IPsec is covered in detail in Chapter 27.)

To find out which process is listening on a port, we can go from the *netstat* output to other programs and tie this information together. A portion of the *netstat* output is shown below:

```
$ netstat -na
Active Internet connections (including servers)
Proto Recv-Q Send-Q  Local Address       Foreign Address     (state)
...
udp        0        0  10.10.3.45.123      *.*
udp        0        0  127.0.0.1.123       *.*
udp        0        0  *.123               *.*
udp        0        0  *.514               *.*
...
```

Here we see two active listening sockets on UDP ports 123 and 514. We can identify the listening process by using the *fstat* command and looking for the class "internet." The use of UDP port 123 will be obvious:

```
$  fstat -n
...
root      ntpd       22223    3* unix dgram 0xd0b72400 <-> 0xd0b72d40
root      ntpd       22223    4* internet dgram udp *:123
root      ntpd       22223    5* internet6 dgram udp *:123
root      ntpd       22223    6* internet dgram udp 127.0.0.1:123
root      ntpd       22223    7* internet6 dgram udp [::1]:123
root      ntpd       22223    8* internet6 dgram udp [fe80::1%lo0]:123
root      ntpd       22223    9* internet dgram udp 10.10.3.45:123
...
```

We can see that the user *root* is running the process *ntpd* with the process ID *22223*. We can confirm this by examining the output of the *ps* command:

```
$  ps -ax | grep ntp
22223 ??  Is    0:02.63 /usr/local/sbin/ntpd -p /var/run/ntpd.pid
```

We have now been able to tie a listening socket to a process through the use of the *fstat* command.

9.11 Troubleshooting

1. I am unable to contact other hosts via my wireless interface.

   After basic configuration checks, such as checking for a proper address and the endpoint being available and within range, the next three most common problems are the network name being incorrect, the mode of the interface (such as ad hoc or BSS mode) being incorrect for the networking setup, and the use of WEP being misconfigured (or misapplied, if none should be used).

Chapter 10
inetd

OpenBSD starts many services from the *inetd* server. Although the programs don't have any known vulnerabilities, the way some of them are used brings an inherent risk. For this reason, most of the services are disabled by default. It's wise to leave the services disabled unless their use and the security ramifications are well understood.

This chapter describes some of the more common services that are configured for *inetd*. The layout of this configuration file, **/etc/inetd.conf**, was discussed in depth in Chapter 5.

10.1 *ftpd*

OpenBSD's FTP server is considered to be one of the most secure, but its use can still be dangerous. The FTP protocol doesn't support encryption or secure logins. It also allows users to log in anonymously—a risky feature. FTP's use needs to be thoroughly assessed with regard to the environment in which it will operate.

The FTP server is configured from several sources. The first is the command line with which the server is started. The relevant flags are set in the **/etc/inetd.conf** file. Some of the most useful and common flags are the following:

- **-A**   Allow anonymous connections to the server. Without this flag, only users with accounts on the system would be allowed to log in and anonymous users would be shut out.

- **-l**   Log all file retrievals using *syslog*. If this option is used twice, any action that the user performs will also be logged.

- **-S**   All downloads are logged to the **/var/log/ftpd** logfile.

- **-U**   All logins are logged in **utmp**.

For anonymous connections, the base of the FTP directory is determined by using the home directory of the *ftp* user account. The session is chroot-ed and the user can't *cd* below the base directory.

The *ftpd* server can prevent users, such as root, from logging into the system by putting their names in the **/etc/ftpusers** file. No user in that file is allowed to log in.

As an additional layer of security, if a username is specified in the **/etc/ftpchroot** file, the user is chroot locked into his or her home directory on the system. This way, users are allowed to get only their own files, but not any other system or user files on the system.

The *ftpd* tool also has support for S/Key. When a user logs in, if S/Key is set up for the account and the user appends ":skey" to the username, the challenge is presented. Note that S/Key won't work with most non–command-line programs. Netscape, for example, doesn't care about S/Key and won't give you the challenge.

```
bpalmer@client:/usr/bpalmer$  ftp server
Trying 192.168.1.20
Connected to server.crimelabs.net.
220 server.crimelabs.net FTP server (Version 6.5/OpenBSD) ready.
Name (server:bpalmer):  bpalmer:skey
331- otp-md5 98 vict33672
331 S/Key Password:
Password:
230 User bpalmer logged in.
Remote system type is UNIX.
Using binary mode to transfer files.
ftp>
```

10.1.1 *sftp*

FTP can be a real security risk for non-anonymous environments, but the ability to browse for files is a much-needed feature. For this reason, the folks who developed SSH also have developed *sftp*. It's documented in Chapter 20, which covers OpenSSH.

10.2 *telnetd*

The *telnetd* service is well known and supported by OpenBSD systems. It does have some settings that can be specified from the command line, but most users won't have any need for it. The main difference between *telnetd* on OpenBSD and on other systems is that the OpenBSD version supports S/Key logins. The use of S/Key requires that the user has it enabled as documented in Chapter 26:

```
bpalmer@client:/usr/bpalmer$  telnet server
Trying 192.168.1.20...
Connected to server.
Escape character is '^]'.

OpenBSD/i386 (server) (ttyp3)

login:  bpalmer:skey
otp-md5 97 vict33672
S/Key Password:
Last login: Sun Apr 21 19:37:45 on :0
OpenBSD 3.1 (GENERIC) #59: Sat Apr 13 15:28:52 MDT 2002

bpalmer@server:/usr/bpalmer$
```

When prompted for the login name, enter the username followed by ":skey".[1]

10.3 *shell*

The "r" tools, as they are known, allow remote login, execution, and file transfer from hosts without the use of passwords. The *rlogin* program allows the user to log in remotely, *rsh* allows for the remote execution of a command, and *rcp* allows files to be transferred. The ability to connect without a password is controlled by the **.rhosts** file in the user's home directry. This file specifies which hosts are trusted. Nevertheless, several major security risks are associated with the "r" tools:

- If a rogue user could edit the **.rhosts** file, he or she could log in as the user. If the access rights on the user's folder are incorrect, the file could be viewed or, worse, edited.
- When the "username" is sent to the remote host, it's not checked for validity (with the right tool, anyone could log in claiming to be root).
- Because host authentication is done by hostname, if DNS were tricked or changed, login would be authorized from the wrong host.
- The "r" tools also support a **hosts.equiv** file. All hosts in this file are considered to be equals, and any remote user can log in to the host from any of them.

---

[1]You can log in using several different authentication methods. For more information on other authentication methods, look at the *login.conf(5)* manual page.

Although these tools can be dangerous, they do have practical applications. In an environment where all hosts are trusted, they work well. An example of this would be a Beowulf[2] system. All nodes in these systems trust the master node and allow remote execution and login. SSH would work, but the overhead imposed by encryption could be a problem.

SSH was designed to replace these tools. The tools that make up SSH also have the ability to be used without passwords. An example can be seen with the OpenSSH documentation in Chapter 20.

10.4 *fingerd*

The *finger* tool was used far more extensively in the past than it is now. It allows the user to see who is logged into a machine and gives some general information about the user. The *fingerd* process can run on a server so that remote users can see who is logged in. This process is not enabled by default. With it enabled, the user would see the following on a remote server:

```
bpalmer@client:/usr/home/bpalmer$  finger @server
[server/192.168.88.208]
Login     Name            Tty   Idle   Login Time Office    Office Phone
bpalmer   bpalmer         *C1     -       Thu 19:53
bpalmer   bpalmer         p0      -       Thu 20:05
root      Charlie Root    *C0     -       Thu 19:48
```

In this example, we can see that three users are logged into the system. The first is *bpalmer* on console 1 (*C1*). The next is *bpalmer* again, this time through a network connection pty0 (*p0* for short). The last is the *root* user logged into console 0 (*C0*).

The *finger* tool can also be used to get a user's information on a remote machine:

```
bpalmer@client:/usr/home/bpalmer$  finger bpalmer@server
[server/192.168.88.208]
Login: bpalmer                        Name: bpalmer
Directory: /usr/home/bpalmer          Shell: /bin/ksh
On since Thu May 29 19:53 (EDT) on ttyC1 (messages off)
On since Thu May 29 20:05 (EDT) on ttyp0, idle 0:04, from client
New mail received Thu May 29 20:09 2003 (EDT)
     Unread since Thu May 29 20:09 2003 (EDT)
```

---

[2]http://www.beowulf.org.

```
Plan:
This is my .plan file.
```

This information can be gathered for any user on the system, which makes it a rather serious security concern. The *fingerd* process is disabled by default for this reason.

10.5 *identd*

The *identd* program is used by remote applications to confirm that the username we are claiming is the same as the one we are logged in with. It is most commonly employed with SMTP and IRC servers. For example, most IRC servers require clients to run *identd* so they can match the username you claim with the username you are logged in with.

10.6 *comsat*

The *comsat* service is used to tell users about new mail. If *comsat* is enabled and the user logs in with *biff* enabled, the user will receive messages on the console about new mail that arrives. Enabling *biff* is as easy as putting the following line in the user's login script:

```
biff y
```

When the user gets new mail, interesting parts of the message will now scroll on the console screen:

```
New mail for bpalmer@crimelabs.net has arrived:
----
From: jose@crimelabs.net
Subject: CVS: seraph.crimelabs.net: OpenBSD-book

CVSROOT:        /mnt/cvs
Module name:    OpenBSD-book
Changes by:     jose@crimelabs.net      2003/05/29 20:23:08

Modified files:
        .                   : networking.tex

Log message:
Cleanup some errors in text
```

Most people no longer use *comsat* because they check their mail using POP clients.

10.7 *ntalkd*

The *ntalkd* service is required to use the *talk* program between two remote systems. The *talkd* server will inform the local user that a remote user would like to "talk" with the user (using the *talk* program). The *talk* program has largely fallen out of favor due to the rise of instant messaging software.

10.8 *popa3d*

The *popa3d* service can be enabled to allow a user's e-mail to be popped to a remote system. There are no configuration options. One problem with POP servers is that passwords are sent in plain text. To avoid security breaches, users who have POP accounts should not have shells. If there is no shell, an attacker can't log into the server even with the user's password. If a user needs both a shell account and POP, a different POP server should be used that supports either SSL or APOP. The ports tree contains several other more advanced POP servers.

10.9 Internal Services

Internal services are servers that don't have any external binaries, but rather are part of *inetd*. They include both IPv4 and IPv6 services, and are typically turned off by default. They are represented in the **inetd.conf** file as follows:

```
# Internal services
#echo         stream  tcp    nowait  root    internal
#echo         stream  tcp6   nowait  root    internal
#discard      stream  tcp    nowait  root    internal
#discard      stream  tcp6   nowait  root    internal
#chargen      stream  tcp    nowait  root    internal
#chargen      stream  tcp6   nowait  root    internal
#daytime      stream  tcp    nowait  root    internal
#daytime      stream  tcp6   nowait  root    internal
#time         stream  tcp    nowait  root    internal
#time         stream  tcp6   nowait  root    internal
#echo         dgram   udp    wait    root    internal
#echo         dgram   udp6   wait    root    internal
#discard      dgram   udp    wait    root    internal
```

```
#discard          dgram     udp6     wait     root     internal
#chargen          dgram     udp      wait     root     internal
#chargen          dgram     udp6     wait     root     internal
#daytime          dgram     udp      wait     root     internal
#daytime          dgram     udp6     wait     root     internal
#time             dgram     udp      wait     root     internal
#time             dgram     udp6     wait     root     internal
```

These five services (*echo, discard, time, daytime, and chargen*) have no real functions on a production network these days.

The *chargen* service (TCP and UDP port 19) does not accept any data. Instead, it simply spits out an ASCII sequence of characters:

```
$ telnet localhost chargen
Trying 127.0.0.1...
Connected to localhost.
Escape character is '^]'.
123456789:;<=>?@ABCDEFGHIJKLMNOPQRSTUVWXYZ^[
```

Unless you disconnect, this flood of characters will continue indefinitely. For this reason, it is typically turned off, as it can be used to flood other machines off the network or to disrupt network operations.

The *echo* service (on TCP and UDP port 7) responds with whatever was sent to it:

```
$ echo "hello there" | nc localhost 7
hello there
```

You can imagine the security risks of having this port open if an attacker is able to point arbitrary streams of data at it. This service is also typically left turned off.

The *time* and *daytime* services (TCP and UDP ports 37 and 13, respectively) are ways of sending a remote machine the time of day. The *daytime* service replies in a human-readable format, while the *time* service responds in binary:

```
$ telnet localhost daytime
Trying 127.0.0.1...
Connected to localhost.
Escape character is '^]'.
Wed May 28 21:48:29 2003
```

```
Connection closed by foreign host.
$ echo "QUIT" | nc -u localhost 37
$
```

(Here we see how to use *nc*, the *netcat* tool, to connect to a UDP port.) In the presence of the NTP service, these ports are typically no longer used.

Lastly, the *discard* service is exactly what its name implies—a port that silently ignores anything sent to it:

```
$ telnet localhost discard
Trying 127.0.0.1...
Connected to localhost.
Escape character is '^]'.
 Foo Bar!!!
 ^]
telnet> quit
Connection closed.
```

The *discard* service listens on UDP and TCP port 9. It is typically left turned off as it is unused, but can be a convenient way to sink traffic to a legitimate host without affecting its CPU (although the available bandwidth and any interrupt load from excessive packets is affected).

10.10 Kerberos Services

The Kerberos lines in the **inetd.conf** file are used by Kerberos and are discussed in more detail in Chapter 25.

10.11 RPC Services

Any services that use RPC-based communication need the *portmap* service to be running. This service maps RPC port numbers to Internet port numbers.

The five RPC services in the **/etc/inetd.conf** file all require the *portmap* server. Very few people use these services today, so they will not be discussed in this book.

Chapter 11

Other Installed Services

In addition to a vast variety of useful and popular services, OpenBSD provides some services that don't see wide usage. Some of these services are covered in this chapter.

11.1 *tftpd*

The *tftpd* server is a very simple *ftp* server. Its main use is for serving files to simple systems. Because the protocol is simple to implement, it consumes very little space, unlike a normal FTP client. These *tftpd* servers are used by *bootp* servers for diskless systems, for transferring of Cisco IOS to routers, and for other purposes.

The *tftpd* server is a risky program to use. It doesn't rely on the concept of logins, so anyone who can reach the server can get any file offered. The implementation used for OpenBSD does have some features that help in making it more secure. These features can be set by two command-line options:

- **-s** Chroot the program to the directory it was started in. This will restrict users from obtaining files that are outside of the specified folder.

- **-c** By default, the *tftpd* server won't let the remote user create new files, just write to existing files (if the access rights are correct). With the *-c* flag, files can also be created (again, presuming correct folder access rights).

The *tftpd* server can't be controlled by *tcpd* through *inetd* because it uses UDP and not TCP for its communications. You can control connections to it by using the PF system (see Chapter 22).

11.2 *rarpd/bootparamd*

Once upon a time, computers didn't have hard drives on which to store their operating systems. They started up from the network and loaded everything into memory. The clients also NFS-mounted filesystems over the network to provide applications. Although those days are long gone, the services that were used to support this process are still used occasionally.

The first service considered here is the *rarpd* service. The Address Resolution Protocol (ARP) makes Ethernet work. When a host needs to connect to an IP address, it broadcasts an ARP request for the IP address, and the machine with that IP address answers with its MAC address. RARP (reverse ARP—serviced by *rarpd*) does the reverse. When the diskless systems of yore started, they didn't know their IP addresses and "rarped" for them. The *rarpd* service needs the host information to be held in two files:

- **/etc/ethers**   This file has a line for each host containing first a MAC address and then a host name. Entries therefore look like the following:

  ```
  00:05:5d:f2:cb:11 tank
  ```

- **/etc/hosts**   This file contains an IP address and the host name. Entries in this file have a simple structure:

  ```
  10.10.32.1     tank
  ```

Upon receipt of a request, the *rarpd* service looks up the MAC address in the **/etc/ethers** file, gets the hostname, looks up the hostname in the **/etc/hosts** file, and returns the IP address to the host. In this way, reverse ARP mappings are performed.

Another program, *bootparamd*, sends the kernel information to the diskless client. It is used to return the NFS mount points for the clients. NFS, which is also covered in detail in Chapter 23, must be set up to enable support for booting diskless systems.

Because there is no authentication for the whole process, any system relying on this process can be exploited.[1]

The use of these program for booting diskless clients is described in the *diskless(8)* manual page.

11.3 The Remote Shell

The BSD UNIX family introduced the *rsh* command, which allows users to spawn a shell on a remote host. Unlike *telnet*, the *rsh* system does not exert any terminal control.

---

[1]An example: An environment used five mail servers to handle the e-mail load. All of the servers used diskless booting (they were just exploited for processor power) and mounted all the filesystems on a read-write basis from a central server. One of these servers went down once—a fact noticed by a student. The student set his MAC address to that of the downed system and booted as the broken mail server. This user then had access to all the mail on a read-write basis. (This may be an urban legend, but it is a good story all the same.)

The *rsh* commands actually comprise a small set of programs, most of which have been deprecated in favor of *ssh*. The *rsh* family does only weak authentication based on hostnames and does not encrypt authentication or session data. For these reasons, users are discouraged from using *rsh* for any work.

Basic usage of *rsh* is to execute a command on a remote host:

```
$ rsh 10.10.10.23 ls
bin
crimelabs
infobot-0.45.3
math
openssh
$ rsh 10.10.10.23 uname -a
OpenBSD hoover 3.4 GENERIC#9 i386
$ uname -a
OpenBSD tank 3.4 GENERIC#2 i386
```

When executed without a username, *rsh* will assume the current local username. To specify a username, either use *rsh -l username hostname* or use the form *rsh user@hostname*. In the absence of a command to execute, *rsh* will spawn a shell that the user can work with.

The *rsh* facility can perform password-less authentication, as seen in the preceding examples, via the global file **/etc/hosts.equiv** or the per-user file **.rhosts**. The file has a two-column format: The first column is the host name to check and the second column is the username to check. Wildcards can be generated using the "+" character. This is extremely weak authentication and is heavily discouraged.

Users of *rsh* connect to the *rshd* process on the remote host, typically spawned from *inetd*.

Because *rshd* usage is discouraged in the face of its security problems and the widespread adoption of *ssh*, we will not discuss it further.

11.4 Time Services

Getting started with the NTP protocol in OpenBSD is relatively easy, with kernel support no longer required. The NTP suite installs from the ports tree (see Chapter 13) in **net/ntp**, including the two major pieces, *ntpdate* and *tickadj*. NTP works by calculating the difference in time between the client and the NTP server, and then using that skew to adjust the received time on the local machine.

Once installed, NTP services are configured to start at boot time in the start-up scripts *rc.securelevel* and *rc.local*. The *tickadj* program must be started before the kernel's secure level can be changed to adjust the system time backward, an otherwise prevented operation. If the option **ntpd** is set to "Yes" in *rc.conf*, the NTP server will also be started, but after any clients are started.

Configuration of the client is straightforward. Simply choose a small number (2–3) of servers from which to poll for time. Optionally, peers can be configured from the local set of clients to ensure that proper time is kept on the local network. These peers do not need to be OpenBSD or even UNIX systems. The configuration file **/etc/ntp.conf** is used to establish these values:

```
server clock.isc.org
server clock.via.net

peer tank
peer venus
peer scrubby
```

In this file two servers and three peers were specified; the peers are all on the local network. The host will collect time information and synchronize it with the local peers to remain in the proper time spectrum.

Servers come in two main types—primary and secondary servers, also known as Stratum 1 and 2 servers. Both types of servers are open to the public, although some operators may seek to limit bandwidth consumption by limiting the number of clients that use them. If you are in doubt, you should contact the server operator. Additionally, you should always choose a well-connected server near your location. This will minimize the clock skew and the jitter introduced by the network.

A list of servers is found at **http://www.eecis.udel.edu/ mills/ntp/servers.html**, sorted by server type and location. NTP uses UDP port 123, which must be open in a firewall or NAT device for proper operation.

11.5 Mouse Services

One thing that many Linux users complain about when they move to OpenBSD is that you can't use the mouse in console mode. This, however, is not the case. The *wsmoused* daemon will allow you to do all you could in Linux. Simply enable it from **/etc/rc.conf** and restart the computer or run *wsmoused* from the command line. This service supports most mice (now that OpenBSD uses *wsmouse* rather than separate drivers for the mouse).

11.6 Printing

The *lpd* command is the line printer daemon, which provides basic printing services under UNIX. This service uses the file **/etc/printcap** to configure printers, both locally and remotely. Printers are named and become accessible via the *lpr* command.

A typical entry for a local printer looks like the following:

```
lp|local line printer:\
        :lp=/dev/lp:sd=/var/spool/lpd:lf=/var/log/lpd-errs:
```

Here the printer is named "lp" and has several basic parameters associated with it. The *lp* parameter is the device on which the printer is located, *sd* defines a spool directory (where jobs are stored before they are printed), and *lf* specifies a logfile. Larger **printcap** files specify filters to handle special attributes of various filters:

```
hp750|Printer2 auto:\
    :lp=/dev/ptal-printd/mlc_usb_PSC_750:\
    :sd=/var/spool/lpd/hp:\
    :lf=/var/spool/lpd/hp/log:\
    :af=/var/spool/lpd/hp/acct:\
    :mx#0:\
    :sh:
```

Remote printers are very similar to the basic "lp" entry, but use an *rm* entry to specify a remote hostname and an *rp* entry to indicate which printer to use on the receiving end:

```
office-hp|remote line printer:\
    :lp=:rm=hp-lp:rp=hp-4500n:sd=/var/spool/lpd:lf=/var/log/lpd-errs:
```

Here the local spool and logfile are specified, but the printer will actually reside on another host. The *lpd* daemon listens on TCP port 515 for incoming connections, regardless of any printers specified. For this reason it is best to filter IP addresses that can connect to this port.

Printing to the *lpd* system is done via the *lpr* command. The specific instances of printers are combined with the *-P* switch to the command. For example, to print to the remote printer specified above ("office-hp"), we would run the command *lpr -P office-hp*. Note that the *lpd* daemon must run on the local host, even though no printer is attached. This approach is necessary to handle the remote connection and spooling. If there is no *-P* switch, the default printer is used.

Printers have a "queue" associated with them in which jobs are sorted by priority and arrival time. This queue can be examined using the *lpq* tool. For example, to examine the queue on the remote printer that hosts the "office-hp" printer, we would issue the command *lpq -P office-hp*. Its output would tell us the number of jobs that are spooled, their ID numbers, and their statuses. A job can be removed from the queue using the command *lprm*, but only if you are the job's owner.

The *lpr* system is very complex, yet very obtuse. Filters for printers are challenging to develop manually, so they are typically found and installed either from the vendor's recommendations or by searching the Internet.

Two new printing systems hope to address several of the deficiencies of the current *lpd* system. The LPRng project is a modernized and improved version of the *lpd* system and is available in the ports and packages tree. The CUPS printing interface is a complex revision of the entire interface to printing and is significantly less complicated to use. It is not yet available in the ports tree, but should prove easy to install for most administrators.

11.7 *dhcpd*: The DHCP Server

Not only does OpenBSD support DHCP for the client end, but DHCP can also be set up as a DHCP server with the *dhcpd* program. The DHCP server on OpenBSD will work with most clients and has full support for all standard client settings.

Dynamic Host Configuration Protocol (DHCP) is a protocol for the automatic configuration of hosts on a network. At boot time, a DHCP client sends a UDP request from an address-less source to the broadcast address; thus the source is 0.0.0.0 and the destination is 255.255.255.255, using the BOOTP port, 67. This message basically says, "The host at the Ethernet address is looking for a DHCP server." An acknowledgment is sent by the server to the Ethernet address of the client, as the client doesn't yet have an IP address. The client then requests parameters from the server, which are subsequently sent back to the client. At this time the client reads the parameters and the configuration is installed.

11.7.1 Requirements

The DHCP daemon must listen on the broadcast interface, which requires the use of the BPF device. Without kernel support for this option, the *dhcpd* program cannot run. Note that this support is available in the GENERIC kernel configuration file. Likewise, the client program, *dhclient*, requires this kernel option.

11.7.2 Configuration

The DHCP server is configured by the file **/etc/dhcpd.conf**, which contains all of the needed information about the networks served by the *dhcpd* process. This information includes things such as the network served, addresses leased out, length of time for which they're leased, and additional host configuration options. OpenBSD contains a sample configuration file in this location, which can be edited to support a small network in just a few minutes. Typical of configuration files, the # character is used to signify a comment until the newline. The manual page *dhcpd.conf(5)* describes this file.

A simple example serving the 10.252.0.0/16 network is as follows:

```
subnet 10.252.0.0 netmask 255.255.0.0 {
        default-lease-time 3600;
        max-lease-time 7200;
        option domain-name "example.net";
        option domain-name-servers 10.252.1.2, 10.252.1.3;
        option routers 10.252.0.1;
        range 10.252.0.4 10.252.255.6;
}
```

The network specification is provided in the subnet and netmask directive, and then options for this network are given. Lease times are given in seconds. In this example, a one-hour lease is typical, with a two-hour lease being the maximum. The domain name information appears next, including the name of the domain along with two DNS servers. The default router is also provided, plus a valid range for the network to assume in a "high-low" format. Note the trailing semicolons, which signify the end of the option. They can be used to specify long lines, such as a large number of DNS servers.

Lease times and domain name information may also be specified globally, outside of a subnet directive. This choice will affect all subnets configured by the DHCP server.

Additional configuration parameters you may wish to invoke include the following:

- **broadcast-address**   Specifies a broadcast address for the host that may not be easily gleaned from the node address and subnet mask.

- **hardware ethernet**   Specifies an Ethernet address and associated information, tying a host configuration to a MAC address.

- **fixed-address**   Used with **hardware address** to provide an address or host name to the specified host.

- **server-name**   Specifies a name for a particular host when using static configurations.

11.7.3 Starting *dhcpd*

To start the DHCP server daemon process, simply invoke *dhcpd*. If it is presented without any arguments, the server will fork and run in the background and use the default configuration file **/etc/dhcpd.conf**. Note that it will listen on the default port, 67/UDP, and on all available interfaces in the absence of any additional directives. For a multihomed machine (one with more than one network interface), you may wish to specify a limited number of interfaces on which to listen for requests. For example, to listen on the interface **fxp1** only, use the command *dhcpd fxp1*. You can specify more than one interface on the command line.

Other useful arguments include the following:

- **-q**   Start *dhcpd* in quiet mode, not printing out start-up information.
- **-cf**   Specify a configuration file other than the default.
- **-lf**   Specify an alternate file containing leases handed out.
- **-d**   Print debugging information to the standard output—useful for troubleshooting.
- **-p nn**   Specify a port number other than 67/UDP on which to listen.

Automatic start-up of *dhcpd* can be configured in the file **/etc/rc.conf**. Simple edit the arguments to *dhcpd_flags* and change it from *NO* to *-q* (to run in quiet start-up mode). You may wish to use alternate flags, such as a list of interfaces or additional parameters. Remember to use quotes for multiple parameters.

The *dhcpd* server stores its current process ID in the file **/var/run/dhcpd.pid**. You can use this value to recover the PID to kill or restart the process if needed.

11.7.4 DHCP Leases

The DHCP negotiations lead to *leases* from the server to the client. These leases have a limited lifetime, which can be set by the network administrator. Clients will periodically attempt to renew their leases, while maintaining their settings, after the lease passes the one-half mark in its lifetime. The server maintains this database of leases to ensure that duplicate addresses are not handed out before they're available for others to use.

The leases are stored in the file **/var/db/dhcpd.leases**. This file records the IP address assigned to the host, the start and end times of the lease, along with the hardware address, a unique ID assigned by the DHCP server, and any additional information relevant to the host. A typical entry looks like this:

```
lease 10.252.0.23 {
        starts 0 2001/07/15 12:41:21;
        ends 1 2001/07/16 12:41:21;
        hardware ethernet 00:30:65:10:60:23;
        uid 01:00:30:65:10:60:23;
}
```

In this example, the lifetime of addresses has been set to one day. If any additional identifying information from the client, such as a host name, is present, it is also recorded. Periodically, the lease file is backed up to the file **/var/db/dhcpd.leases~**. It allows the server to attempt a graceful recovery should it crash or the database become corrupted.

The DHCP specifications state that a host cannot use an IP address beyond its lease's lifetime. This constraint is imposed to avoid potential conflicts between two (or more) hosts using the same address. If a user manually sets his or her address to one that is assigned by a DHCP server, a conflict will ensue. Tracking this problem down can be a bit difficult. Thus, for the smooth operation of a DHCP-based network, this consideration is important to keep in mind.

11.7.5 Considerations to Note

DHCP can be a great convenience in the management of a large network, and a valuable aid for mobile hosts. However, there are a few considerations to keep in mind if you decide to employ it. This section has focused on IPv4-based DHCP operations. Stateful autoconfiguration of IPv6 hosts is also possible, as discussed in Chapter 28.

Static Hosts

Not all systems should use DHCP, including the DHCP server itself (obviously). Static hosts should be set up using their normal, hard-coded addresses. If you wish to use DHCP clients on these systems, use the *fixed-address* directive in your configuration file and include the Ethernet address of the host there.

11.7.6 BOOTP Support

The *dhcpd* program also supports the **bootp** protocol, which can be used to configure diskless clients. These include terminals and routers as well. The setup is quite easy to perform. See the manual pages *dhcpd.conf(5)* and *bootp(8)* for this information, as well as section 11.1.

DHCP Security

Because the DHCP negotiation is based on unsigned requests and replies, an attacker could potentially insert a rogue DHCP server on the network and maliciously configure hosts. If a client receives a duplicate acknowledgment, only the initial acknowledgment is respected. That is, the client has no mechanism for verifying the messages or their content. To maintain the security of a DHCP-based network, it is wise to periodically check for the presence of rogue DHCP servers. Several consumer devices, such as WAP devices, now come with embedded DHCP servers. If improperly configured, they can interfere with the normal operation of your network.

DHCP traffic bypasses IPsec flows that you may have set up (see Chapter 27), because an address-less client may not know how to communicate with its IPsec peers. As a consequence, IPsec options should be started *after* the clients are configured.

DNS Integration

In a dynamic network, if hostnames are not tied to MAC addresses, you may wish to have dynamic DNS installed on your site. This topic is beyond the scope of this section. Note, however, that this integration of the DHCP and DNS servers can provide for consistent mappings despite changing IP addresses.

DHCP Relaying

Because DHCP uses the broadcast address for its requests, to reach a DHCP server that resides beyond a router, the router must relay these requests to the server. To do so, use *dhcrelay* on an OpenBSD-based router. The *dhcrelay* program listens on the interface that faces the served network and transmits DHCP communications between the client and the server.

Usage of *dhcrelay* is rather straightforward. Simply start it with a list of interfaces and at least one server to forward the requests to. Use the *-i* flag to specify an interface; multiple uses of the *-i* flag are allowed to specify multiple interfaces. For example, the start-up of *dhcrelay* for an OpenBSD router listening on two interfaces, **fxp0** and **fxp1**, to forward to two DHCP servers at 10.10.4.1 and 10.10.4.2 would have the following format:

```
#  dhcrelay -i fxp0 -i fxp1 10.10.4.1 10.10.4.2
```

Additionally, you can specify which UDP port to listen to for requests if this port number differs from the default value of 67/UDP. See the manual page for *dhcrelay(8)* for more information on advanced features in *dhcrelay*.

Chapter 12
Precompiled Third-Party Software: Packages

Most people use Linux with either *.rpm* or *.deb* packages. Many Solaris users are used to packages for installation as well. In contrast, few people are familiar with the process of downloading and compiling applications. OpenBSD relies upon this method, but works through an advanced build system held in the ports tree. The result of the ports tree is packages; precompiled ports.

12.1 An Overview of Packages

Packages are third-party applications that work with the OpenBSD system. Unlike ports, packages are ready to be downloaded from the OpenBSD site, or copied off of the CD, and then installed, leaving them instantly ready to run:

```
#  pkg_add -v despoof-0.9.tgz     the -v option is for verbose
Requested space: 45128 bytes, free space: 943349760 bytes in
    /var/tmp/instmp.cFJOy26260
pkg: Handling dependencies for despoof-0.9
  checking libnet-* (libnet-1.0.2a) -> libnet-1.0.2a
checking net.0.0 found libnet.so.0.0
Package 'despoof-0.9' depends on 'libnet-1.0.2a'
 - 'libnet-1.0.2a' already installed
extract: Package name is despoof-0.9
extract: CWD to /usr/local
extract: /usr/local/bin/despoof
extract: /usr/local/share/doc/despoof/LICENSE
extract: /usr/local/share/doc/despoof/README
extract: CWD to .
Attempting to record package into '/var/db/pkg/despoof-0.9'
```

```
Attempting to record dependency on package 'libnet-1.0.2a'
Package 'despoof-0.9' registered in '/var/db/pkg/despoof-0.9'
```

In this verbose example (*pkd_add* is normally quiet), we can see the program checking for available space, identifying a dependency (*libnet*), and then extracting the package. The package is then recorded, along with the dependency, and all is done. The dependency registering will warn you later if you attempt to remove (via *pkg_delete*) this dependency. Other software will likely break in such an event, so the system warns you about this possibility before you can do any harm. You can, of course, force uninstallation, ignoring this warning.

Packages are nothing more than prebuilt and packaged ports. In fact, all ports are periodically built as packages to ensure that they will work correctly, which is how the release packages are created. Not all packages can go on the CDs due to space and licensing considerations, but most of them are available on the OpenBSD FTP mirrors.

Because OpenBSD is a multiplatform operating system, it is important that you get the right package for your platform. SPARC binaries will not work on a MacPPC machine, for example.

Packages are named after the port to which they correspond, along with the software version number. Any **FLAVOR** of the port, such as **no_x11**, is also used in the name. Packages will have the same requirements as a port's runtime dependencies.

Of course, not all ports are distributed as packages. Licensing issues for some software may prevent a third party from distributing modified files or even any files of the software. Hence, some packages will not be available for some ports. These can still be built as ports, however, and run manually. If you have a large number of systems to install, you can build a package for one platform and distribute it locally to the remaining systems.

12.2 Installation of Packages

The installation of precompiled packages is done with the *pkg_add* command. This tool can install packages and handle dependencies (such as the libraries needed by one application that are available in a separate package). The source of installation can be a local filesystem, a release CD, or an FTP/HTTP mirror.

12.2.1 Local Installation Sources

The easiest way to install a package is to download it from a source and install it from that location. Alternatively, if the package is found on the CD set purchased, it can be installed directly from the installation media. The package is then added with the simple command *pkg_add package.tgz*. Upon its execution, the software will be installed and registered into the database of installed packages.

Dependencies, such as libraries, will be handled by looking in the current directory and any other directories specified in the environmental variable *PKG_PATH*.

12.2.2 Network Installation Sources

As an alternative, packages can be installed via the network. To do so, issue the command with a network source. The command *pkg_add http://server.net/packages/package.tgz* will install the package from the specified server, using the HTTP protocol. The FTP protocol can also be used.

The biggest advantage to this method of package installation is that the space required for the package is minimized and dependencies are handled transparently. The current source directory for the package, a network location, allows it to fetch these dependencies by accessing the network source as well. This approach can save time and effort when you are handling packages with dependencies, as only the final target needs to be specified.

12.2.3 Options for Package Installation

As hinted earlier, several environmental variables control the options for the package system:

- **PKG_PATH**   The locations in which to look for additional packages. For example, if all packages are stored in **/tmp/pkg**, an entry specifying this directory would allow a simpler command to be issued: *pkg_add package.tgz.* The directory would then be searched automatically. The first instance of the package found is used, and the path is searched in order.
- **PKG_DBDIR**   The location of the package database, defaulting to the directory **/var/db/pkg**.
- **PKG_TMPDIR**   The directory used for the temporary staging and preparation before installation, defaulting to **/var/tmp**.

One important caveat applies to these options, however: The directory specified in *PKG_TMPDIR* must be executable. Thus, if the filesystem holding **/var/tmp** is mounted with the *no-exec* option, a package installation that requires the execution of an installation script will fail.

Other options to the command *pkg_add* are as follows:

- **-v**   The installation process is verbose.
- **-I**   The installation process will not run installation scripts contained in the package.
- **-n**   Fake the installation; don't actually perform anything.
- **-R**   Install the package but don't register the action in the database.
- **-f**   Force the installation, ignoring any errors. This option is not recommended.
- **-p**   Specify an extraction directory for staging, defaulting to **/var/tmp**.

For most users the default options will suffice.

If an installation is forced via *pkg_add -f* and files with conflicting names are installed, the previous filename will be moved aside to make way for the new one. The old filename will have an **-0** appended to its name, indicating that it is an old file and preventing it from being run instead of the new file.

12.3 Uninstalling Packages

As mentioned earlier, the *pkg_delete* command is used to remove a package. It is, as you might expect, the opposite of adding a package:

```
#  pkg_delete -v despoof-0.9          the -v flag is for verbose
Change working directory to /usr/local
Delete file /usr/local/bin/despoof
Delete file /usr/local/share/doc/despoof/LICENSE
Delete file /usr/local/share/doc/despoof/README
Delete directory /usr/local/share/doc/despoof
Change working directory to .
Attempting to remove dependency on package 'libnet-1.0.2a'
```

This is a verbose example, using *pkg_delete -v*. In the real world, the command is normally silent in its operations, unless an error is encountered.

12.3.1 Options for Uninstallation

To force the removal of a package, such as one with a dependency, use *pkg_delete -f*. This command will ignore errors and dependency issues. This tactic is, of course, not recommended, as you could break some installed components by removing a library, for example. You might remove a package if you somehow messed up the package installation and needed to override any internal checks. Don't take this step unless it's really needed, however.

Other options for package removal are described below:

- **-d**   Remove empty directories, even if they are not specified in the package's file listing.
- **-n**   Fake the removal process—a useful option for testing the process.
- **-D**   Skip any *DEINSTALL* scripts supplied in the package. This option is the complement to the *-I* option for *pkg_add*.

Again, for most users the default options will suffice.

12.3.2 Upgrading Packages

An astute reader will notice that OpenBSD 3.4 doesn't come with any tool named *pkg_upgrade*. The process of upgrading a package is quite tricky to master manually, and an automated process would be prone to error. Although such a tool is being developed, it has not been released as yet.

The biggest difficulty in upgrading ports relates to handling libraries and version numbers. Library interfaces change, and new behaviors may be incompatible with the behavior of the older version (and the applications that depend on it). It is also impossible to install two versions of the same package without forcing the installation (via *pkg_add -f*).

The recommended procedure, therefore, is to upgrade packages en masse and to coordinate the dependencies and affected ports together. For example, upgrade all packages when a new release becomes available to ensure that they will work correctly.

12.4 Information About Installed Packages

The command *pkg_info* is used to discover information about the packages that have been installed on your system. To get a full listing of the packages and their one-line descriptions, use the command *pkg_info -a*:

```
$ pkg_info -a
gperf-2.7.2      perfect hash functions, to help write parsers
popt-1.5.1       getopt(3)-like library with a number of enhancements
```

```
rpm-3.0.6p1        redhat package manager
...
```

To find detailed information about a specific package, use the package name as the argument to *pkg_info*:

```
$  pkg_info rpm-3.0.6p1
Information for rpm-3.0.6p1:

Comment:
redhat package manager

Description:
RPM is a package management system based on top of cpio.
It supports digital signatures, source and binary packages,
complex dependencies handling, complex installation scripts
and a lot more.

It has its own macro language, and is well-spread in
the Linux world.

The package database is set to /var/db/rpm by default, to conform
with hier(7).

WWW: http://www.rpm.org/
```

Here the comments are shown as well as the full description of the package. To find out which files are in the package, you can use the *pkg_info -L* command:

```
$  pkg_info -L popt-1.5.1
Information for popt-1.5.1:

Files:
/usr/local/include/popt.h
/usr/local/lib/libpopt.a
/usr/local/lib/libpopt.la
/usr/local/lib/libpopt.so.0.1
/usr/local/man/man3/popt.3
```

```
/usr/local/share/locale/sk/LC_MESSAGES/popt.mo
/usr/local/share/locale/ro/LC_MESSAGES/popt.mo
```

There are many other options to use with *pkg_info*, but these are the most commonly encountered. See the manual page *pkg_info(1)* for more information.

12.5 Third-Party Software and Security

Unlike the base system, the OpenBSD ports tree is not rigorously audited for security issues. As a consequence, you can introduce new security holes by adding a new port, such as a network service. While some basic auditing is done to remove obvious holes, such as the `gets()` function, this isn't a rigorous process. In some cases more significant audits have been done, but you should not rely on this in general. Some ports have blatant security holes and may be marked as broken to dissuade you from incorporating them.

Unlike NetBSD and FreeBSD, OpenBSD does not issue security advisories for every port or package. Nevertheless, for the most important problems, and for the more used architectures, *-stable* packages are created to fix a problem in a package shipped with the last release of the OS. Users are expected to keep a watchful eye on **http://www.openbsd.org/pkg-stable.html**, where these patches are announced.

## Chapter 13

The Ports Tree: Third-Party Software from Source

13.1 Ports

A great number of ports (almost 2000 at this writing) are included in the ports tree for the OpenBSD project. A common misperception is that there are few applications ported to OpenBSD—that just isn't true. The ports tree contains the information your system needs to get the source code from the master repository (or a mirror), patch the application to work with the OpenBSD libraries and system, and build and install the application as a registered package. It also does dependency checks to make sure you have all the support applications that are needed. In other words, with a single command, the ports tree will automatically perform the series of things required to do what you want.

One big advantage of using ports versus precompiled packages is that any changes that have been made to your system, such as library updates, are propagated to the newly built software. However, packages can be installed without a compiler present, which can be useful on a low-disk system or a nondevelopment system, like a Web server or firewall.

The result of building something from ports is ultimately the same as installing a package. Both schemes install their components in a directory hierarchy, commonly in **/usr/local**. Things never get installed into **/usr** with the rest of the system, which is an important convention. For more on the filesystem layout, consult the *hier(7)* manual page. The directory **/usr/local/bin** (and, if appropriate for the binaries you need to run, **/usr/local/sbin**) should be in your path to ensure that you have transparent access to the newly installed software.

13.1.1 Getting the Ports Tree

The first requirement with the ports tree is to get a working copy of it. There are two main ways to do so: using the tarball provided with the release or checking out a copy using CVS. The ports tarball is pretty small, but contains countless files and will take a long time to extract. On the OpenBSD CD or from FTP, the file **ports.tar.gz** should be copied to **/usr** and extracted there:

```
#  cd /usr
#  tar vvzxfp ports.tar.gz
```

This will give you all of the applications for your version of OpenBSD. While sometimes you may want to get the current version of the ports tree via CVS, this approch is not recommended and is unsupported, because often parts of the newer ports tree will depend on new features in the base system. As important fixes are also brought to the stable branches, however, it is a good idea to follow *-stable* with CVS; see Appendix A.

13.1.2 The Structure of the Ports Tree

The ports tree is organized to allow for a nearly intuitive perusal. Applications are grouped into their directories on the basis of their type, such as a math application, a security tool, or a productivity tool. A port is commonly referred to by its category and directory name, such as "security/nmap." A few of the directories have subtrees with different versions, such as the Java directory.

If you are unsure of the location of an application, you can use the top-level **Makefile** to search for it:

```
$  cd /usr/ports
$  make search key=apg
Port:   apg-1.2.13
Path:   security/apg
Info:   automated password generator
Maint:  Jose Nazario <jose@crimelabs.net>
Index:  security
L-deps:
B-deps:
R-deps:
Archs:  any
```

The output tells you the version of the package that the port builds, its location as a path, and some brief information about it. Included in this information are any dependencies (e.g., library, build, or runtime dependencies) and any restrictions on the architectures for which it will build packages.

The **INDEX** file at the top-level directory of the ports tree is a condensed repository of information. While not readable by people (it's used by programs to build a directory of information about the ports tree), it can be "grepped" to find the name of a port in a pinch. In fact, the aforementioned "make search" method uses this file.

A number of directories within the ports tree are used by the system and do not contain any ports. Examples include the subdirectories **infrastructure**, **packages**, and **distfiles**. The directory **infrastructure** holds the templates and directions for the ports' **makefiles**. The directory **packages** contains packages for ports that have been built from the ports tree. The directory **distfiles** contains the distribution archives of the ports as they appeared on the archive site.

Within each port directory are several files and directories. A **Makefile** holds it all together. This file uses *include* directives to fill in the rest of the information needed to build the port from a larger template in the **infrastructure** subdirectory. Within any port, the subdirectory **patches** contains any OpenBSD-specific patches needed to build the application, and the subdirectory **pkg** contains accessory files for the package, including the list of files included and the description of the package. The **files** directory sometimes contains files that the port needs to add to the distribution for it to be built properly. The **distinfo** file contains cryptographic checksums of the **distfile**, to ensure that the proper file was downloaded correctly before the package build is attempted.

When the port build is launched, the **distfile** is extracted into a working directory, and the patches are applied. Then the actual build is performed. Next, the installation process uses a fake filesystem to install the newly built package in, to make sure your real filesystem remains clean. The packaging step uses the fake hierarchy to create the actual package, which is later extracted in the proper location at installation time.

13.1.3 The Life Cycle of a Ports Build

When you begin the "make" process in a ports directory, the following sequence of events happens.

First, the system checks whether the source archive exists on the system, typically by looking for the file **DISTNAME.suffix** in the directory **distfiles**. If it doesn't exist, the system consults the site listed in the **Makefile** to retrieve it. This file is then examined to ensure that the checksums from the fetched archive match the checksums in the file **distinfo** (formerly **files/md5**). If they match, the system proceeds with the build process.

The next step is preparation of the source code. The work directory is created and the archive is extracted into this directory. Any patches, which appear in the directory **patches**, are applied to the source code. Any dependencies, such as auxiliary libraries, are also identified at this point; should they need to be obtained, they are fetched, built, and installed before installation of the port can continue.

Now the system begins to build the source code. Depending on what the software build system uses, there may be a configuration step in which the configuration of the source code takes place, much like what one would do when building a piece of software manually by issuing the *./configure* command. Then the software's **Makefile** is used to create the software using the system's compiler.

After the build is complete, the software is installed into a fake root directory, which exists under the working directory. The files specific to the package are built, along with the package information, into a package, which is a compressed archive of the binary software. This package is then copied in the ports system directory **packages**.

Installation takes place using the system's *pkg_add* tool, which acts on the newly built package. It installs and registers the package, leaving you ready to begin using the software.

The time it takes to complete this process depends on the speed of your network link, the need to fetch any of the components, and the speed of your system when compiling the package. This approach is typically much faster, however, than downloading and installing the software by hand, as the person who made the port has checked for any needed patches or dependencies before the port was included in the distribution.

13.1.4 Building a Package from Ports

You are now ready to install any of the applications. This is as simple as changing to the directory of the program you want and doing a *make install*.[1]

The following is a simple walkthrough of the installation of a common application, *nmap*.

```
#  pwd
/usr/ports/net/nmap
#  make install
>> nmap-2.54BETA7.tgz doesn't seem to exist on this system.
>> Attempting to fetch /usr/ports/distfiles/nmap-2.54BETA7.tgz from
http://www.insecure.org/nmap/.
Trying www.insecure.org...
Requesting http://www.insecure.org/nmap//nmap-2.54BETA7.tgz
  0% |                                          |    0       --:-- ETA
100% |*****************************************|   685 KB   00:00
Successfully retrieved file.
>> Checksum OK for nmap-2.54BETA7.tgz. (sha1)
```

---

[1]If you are using the current CVS version of the ports tree, remember that it is a work in progress and there may be a few bumps in the road.

```
===>  nmap-2.54b7 depends on shared library: gtk.1.2 -
    /usr/local/lib/libgtk.so.
1.2 found
===>  Extracting for nmap-2.54b7
tar: End of archive volume 1 reached
===>  Patching for nmap-2.54b7
===>  Configuring for nmap-2.54b7
creating cache ./config.cache
checking for gcc... cc
checking whether the C compiler (cc -O2    -I/usr/local/include
-L/usr/local/li
b) works... yes
checking whether the C compiler (cc -O2    -I/usr/local/include
-L/usr/local/li
b) is a cross-compiler... no
checking whether we are using GNU C... yes
checking whether cc accepts -g... yes
checking host system type... i386-unknown-openbsd2.8
checking for gethostent... yes
checking for setsockopt... yes
checking for nanosleep... yes
checking how to run the C preprocessor... cc -E
checking for pcap.h... yes
...
...
...
cc -O2    -I/usr/local/include -Wall  -Inbase -I/usr/local/include
-I/usr/local/include/glib -I/usr/X11R6/include -I../nbase -DVERSION=
Ö.2.54BETA7" -I.   -L.
./nbase -o nmapfe nmapfe.o nmapfe_sig.o -L/usr/local/lib -L/usr/X11R6/lib
-lgtk -lgdk -lgmodule -lglib -lintl -lXext -lX11 -lm -lnbase

===>  Faking installation for nmap-2.54b7
Compiling libnbase
cd nbase; make
Compiling libnbase
rm -f libnbase.a
ar cr libnbase.a snprintf.o getopt.o getopt1.o nbase_str.o nbase_misc.o
```

```
Compiling nmap
...
...
...
./shtool install -c -m 644 nmap-services /usr/ports/net/nmap/work/
    fake-i386/usr /local/share/nmap/nmap-services
./shtool install -c -m 644 nmap-protocols  /usr/ports/net/nmap/work/
    fake-i386/usr/local/share/nmap/nmap-protocols
./shtool install -c -m 644 nmap-rpc  /usr/ports/net/nmap/work/
    fake-i386/usr/local/share/nmap/nmap-rpc
===>  Building package for nmap-2.54b7
Creating package /usr/ports/packages/i386/All/nmap-2.54b7.tgz
Using SrcDir value of /usr/ports/net/nmap/work/fake-i386/usr/local
Registering depends: gettext-0.10.35 glib-1.2.8 gtk+-1.2.8.
Creating gzip'd tar ball in '/usr/ports/packages/i386/All/
    nmap-2.54b7.tgz'
===>  nmap-2.54b7 depends on shared library: gtk.1.2 - /usr/local/
    lib/libgtk.so.
1.2 found
===>  Installing nmap-2.54b7 from /usr/ports/packages/i386/All/
    nmap-2.54b7.tgz
```

As can be seen here, the system connected to a remote server, downloaded the source file, checked the SHA1 hash for the file, extracted it, applied any necessary patches and built the application. The installation script then created the package and installed it. This package could be moved to another machine with the same OS version and hardware architecture.

We decided we wanted the applications installed, but in other circumstances we might have decided that the package should be installed later. In the installation process, we could have used *make package* so that the package would have been generated without being installed.

Likewise, if we had just wanted to see whether the package would compile, we could have used the *make* command.

OpenBSD also supports the concept of flavors. With a larger package, some options that the user may want may not be enabled by default. For example, *nmap* has a *no_x11* flavor for systems that don't have X installed. To install this version,[2] we would use the

---

[2]If the other version of *nmap* has been installed, the installation script will say so and will not allow the new package to be installed until the old one has been removed.

following command:

```
# env FLAVOR=no_x11 make install
```

The flavor *no_x11* is a common one, useful on systems where no X11 libraries have been installed—many ports provide this flavor. Other flavors may exist for a given port, so check the description to see what's available. Some ports have many flavors: PHP, for example, has support for many external applications.

In general, there are several key targets for the *make* utility when building a port entry, most of which are executed in the general build process. In certain cases, some of them are skipped. The targets are described below:

- *fetch*   Retrieves the **distfile** for the port and any accessory patches. These are placed into the **distfile** directory.
- *extract*   Unpacks the retrieved **distfile** into a working directory in the port directory, typically named **port name-version**, located in the **WRKOBJDIR** directory. This calls the *fetch* target.
- *patch*   Applies all of the patches to the source code already located in the working directory. This depends on the *extract* target.
- *configure*   Usually configures the source code, typically the GNU *configure* utility or any other specified utility. It proceeds only after *patch* has completed.
- *build*   Compiles the source code of the patched and configured port source. Any needed dependencies are built before the port can be compiled.
- *package*   Performs a fake installation into a temporary filesystem hierarchy under the working directory for the port build, then uses this system to create an installable package. It depends on the successful completion of the *build* target.
- *install*   Installs the built package, once it is created.
- *clean*   Removes the working source code directory and any associated subdirectories that live under it, such as the fake installation tree. When used without any options, it cleans only the default flavor and its working directory, so any *FLAVOR* values used will not be cleaned by this method. Furthermore, none of the dependencies built are cleaned, so the sources to their port builds are left behind. By specifying what you want, however, it is possible to control this process. For example, if *CLEANDEPENDS* is set to "YES" in the environment, it will also clean the port's dependencies.
- *distclean*   Removes all traces of the port aside from the installed package, including the working source tree, the fetched archive, and the built package. Note that the installed package is left alone. This is a popular target for saving space.

- *uninstall*   Removes any trace of the built package from the system. This is effectively equivalent to use of the *pkg_delete* utility on the newly built package.

For a complete description of the OpenBSD ports infrastructure, see the manual page for *bsd.port.mk(5)* and the various documentation linked to it.

13.2 Making Many Ports at Once

It is possible to use the build system to build several packages at once. This ability is useful if you wish to quickly bring a new system back up to a previous level. The ports tree has support for bulk port installation, which automatically handles dependencies.

Building multiple ports is quite easy. First, we create a list of ports we wish to install. That is, list the subdirectory of the ports entry along with its name. Also, list any flavors you wish to install. Use one entry per line.

```
graphics/imlib
math/graphviz
mail/procmail
...
```

It isn't necessary to attempt to satisfy dependencies at this stage—the ports tree will handle this task for you. Flavors are specified specially:

```
graphics/gdk-pixbuf,no_gnome
security/dsniff,no_x11
x11/qt3,no_mysql,no_postgresql,-examples,-html
```

Multiple flavors can also be specified per line. Place this information in a file, such as **/usr/ports/mypackages**.

The next step is to activate the build process and tell it to use this file as its package list:

```
#  cd /usr/ports
#  make BUILD=Yes SUBDIRLIST=/usr/ports/mypackages install
```

The system will begin fetching **distfiles** as needed, satisfying dependencies, and installing all packages. You can clean up after this process by specifying the *clean* target for *make* in the last command above.

13.3 Updating Specific Ports

Sometimes you will want to upgrade only one port at a time—for example, when new features become available. This process is not gracefully handled by the OpenBSD ports tree, but can be done manually.

The tool *out-of-date* can be used to identify which ports are lagging behind their counterparts in the CVS version of the ports tree. The first step is to use *cvs* to update the ports tree, including the index file. Then use the *out-of-date* tool to examine it and compare the installed packages with the versions in CVS:

```
$  cd /usr/ports
$  ./infrastructure/build/out-of-date
>>> Is /usr/ports/INDEX up-to-date ?
>>> Otherwise, this script will find out outdated flavors of packages
>>> compared to your installed packages...
Update gaim-0.59.7 to one of gaim-0.59.8 gaim-0.59.8-esd
Update xpdf-1.01p1 to xpdf-2.01
Update libdnet-1.4 to libdnet-1.5
Update metaauto-0.1 to metaauto-0.0
Update gd-1.8.1 to gd-1.8.3
```

The output lists which ports need to be updated for the local system.

The next step is to take this list and identify which other ports and packages depend on this version of the package. It is very important to keep the dependencies up to date, but even more important to keep the packages that depend on others in sync with the new versions. If a package is linked to an older library, implementing the newer version will typically cause failures.

This requirement is analyzed using the *pkg_info -R* command. To see which packages require **gd-1.8.1**, for example, we would use this command:

```
$  pkg_info -R gd-1.8.1
Information for gd-1.8.1:

Required by:
p5-GD-1.41
```

This output reveals that any updates to **gd-1.8.1** will also require an update to the port for **p5-GD-1.41**. Repeat this step for the ports that require this entry until no additional requirements are found. These two lists will comprise the ports to upgrade.

The next step is to uninstall the older packages using *pkg_delete* and to ensure that no stale versions exist.

Finally, begin building the new ports from the ports tree by using the *make* and *make install* cycle, or by installing the new packages via *pkg_add*.

It is typically best to upgrade an entire ports tree and all of the installed packages at once, to ensure smooth operation of the system.

13.4 Troubleshooting

1. I get errors stating that patches are not being applied cleanly.

   This problem can happen if you upgrade your ports tree incorrectly, probably using CVS. Clean the directory and refetch it, and it should work.

2. The software just doesn't work.

   First, make sure the ports tree you are using and the release software you are building it on match. You can't run the "current" ports tree on the "release" software. Make sure these versions match before you state with certainty that software doesn't work. Second, watch the build process, making sure that no strange errors appear. Third, uninstall the port, clean up your ports tree, and rebuild it. Make sure that dependencies are up to date. If this effort fails, contact the port's maintainer for assistance.

3. I get a message that *"portname* is marked as broken." Why?

   Simply put, it's broken and it doesn't work correctly for the reason specified. If you feel up to it, contact the maintainer of the port and offer any assistance that you can. If you can help get it working, that's a good thing. However, ports are usually marked as broken because there is a fundamental problem with them. If you want to ignore this problem, comment out the line that reads "BROKEN."

4. I get a message that *"portname* comes with OpenBSD." What gives?

   The software supplied by the port has been integrated into the base system, and the port is no longer relevant. In this case, you have no need for the port—use what comes with the base system.

## Chapter 14

Disks and Filesystems

Disks and filesystems form one of the main components of any computer system. The files you create and work with are stored on disks, and the operating system itself is stored on the hard disk. Support for various disk types and arrangements in OpenBSD is enabled by default and typically is quite easily configured.

SCSI and IDE disks are handled in much the same way by the system. Support for them is enabled in the kernel in the configuration file. For an i386 system, the configuration setup in the GENERIC kernel looks like the following:

```
sd*       at scsibus? target ? lun ?        # SCSI disk drives
fd*       at fdc? drive ? flags 0x00
wd*       at pciide? channel ? drive ? flags 0x0000
```

The first entry is for SCSI disks, which attach to the SCSI bus (typically attached to the PCI bus on i386 hardware). The second entry is for a typical floppy disk device attached to a floppy drive controller. The last entry is for IDE devices. Most controllers for common SCSI and IDE disks are available in the GENERIC kernel.

14.1 Disk Devices

On an OpenBSD system, disks are identified by their type. For example, an IDE disk would be **/dev/wd*** and a SCSI disk would be **/dev/sd***. If the drives were attached as part of a RAID array, they would have other identifications. When the system boots, *dmesg* will show which disks are found and how they are identified. One point that new users to OpenBSD will notice is that disks are numbered based on their identification order. For example, if the system had three IDE drives, they would be **/dev/wd0***, **/dev/wd1***, and **/dev/wd2***. Their locations on the IDE bus aren't important. The first disk found is always called **wd0**, and so on. On a Linux system, in contrast, disks are named by their locations.

The primary disk on the first IDE bus would be **/dev/hda1***, for example. On a Solaris system, the disks are named based on exactly where they are connected to the SCSI or IDE bus—for example, **/dev/dsk/c0t0d1s1**. SCSI disks follow the same naming scheme, based on the order in which they are detected, not the SCSI ID. The user must keep this nomenclature in mind when changing drive settings on a system. If one IDE disk acted as the primary disk on each controller, and a second disk was then added to the first controller, it would become **/dev/wd1** and the old **/dev/wd1** would become **/dev/wd2**. That name change would break any filesystem mounts that were done from these disks.

14.1.1 The Concatenated Disk Driver and RAIDFrame

OpenBSD supports two very powerful systems for building flexible filesystems: the Concatenated Disk Driver (CCD) and RAIDFrame. CCD allows for the creation of filesystems from partitions on the disk. These systems don't need to be the same size and can span multiple disks. Mirroring and interleaving are both supported. RAIDFrame allows for the creation of software RAID 0, 1, 4, and 5 filesystems. It is far more flexible than CCD and offers many more features. It also has the advantage of being able to support RAID for the root filesystems.

CCD

CCD is best used for creating massive filesystems from multiple disks. If you need to store a large amount of data, but don't care about maintaining the integrity of that data, CCD is a great option. Because it doesn't support the concept of RAID 5 or parity, a loss of one disk or partition in the set would cause the partition to become corrupt (and it would need to be created anew). CCD does support RAID 1, the creation of mirrored pairs, but RAIDFrame is a better tool for meeting that need.

To use CCD, the user must add support for it in the kernel. The GENERIC kernel doesn't have precompiled support for CCD. Thus the following line needs to be added to the kernel configuration:

```
pseudo-device   ccd   4
```

This will create four CCD devices that the system can use. These will appear as **/dev/ccd0** through **/dev/ccd3** if only four are created.

Once the new kernel has been installed, the new filesystems can be created. In our example, we have two partitions, **/dev/wd0e** and **/dev/sd2b**,[1] and will be creating **/dev/ccd1**.

---

[1] We are able to create a filesystem over not only two disks, but also two different types of disks! There may, however, be massive performance problems with this setup.

Configuration information for the CCD filesystem is contained in **/etc/ ccd.conf** and will be loaded if it exists as the system boots.

```
ccd1 32 none /dev/wd0e /dev/sc2b
```

This line in our configuration file says to create the CCD filesystem **/dev/ccd1** with an interleave of 32 blocks.[2] The number choosen depends on the hardware in question and the application being used. Testing needs to be done to find the best solution. If the interleave is set to zero, we get a serial filesystem and the second disk is never used until the first disk is full. Here we have set the flags to *none*, but two settings may be worth considering. The first, 0×02, will set the interleave to be uniform over the disks (the relative amount written to each disk depends on the geometry of the disk). The second, 0×04, enables mirroring. With this setting, we need to have two partitions that are the same size. Once the filesystem is created, every block is written to both disks. This allows for one disk to fail and the other to recover. RAIDFrame supports this concept much better, and the use of mirroring with CCD should be avoided. The last two items in the preceding command are the disks we are using.

Once the CCD filesystem has been created, it can't be changed without being recreated.

RAIDFrame

OpenBSD has full support for RAIDFrame from CMU[3] and allows for the creation of software RAID file systems. As mentioned before, it also permits the use of RAID for the root filesystem. Like CCD, RAIDFrame needs options added to the kernel and the kernel needs to be reinstalled:

```
pseudo-device   raid   4
options      RAID_AUTOCONFIG
```

We will show two examples: a RAID 5 filesystem with a spare[4] disk and a simple RAID 1 set. RAIDFrame has many options and functions that won't be covered in this book but are fully explained in the manual page, *raidctl(8)*. The configuration file for the filesystem

---

[2] The interleave is how many blocks are written to each partition. If 100 blocks were to be written, the first 32 would go to **wd0e**, then the next 32 to **sd2b**, and so on.

[3] **http://www.cmu.edu**.

[4] If a disk in a RAID 5 set fails, the array can still operate, but it will be suboptimal. If a spare disk is used, the parity information will be used to rebuild the set on the spare disk and the array will return to its optimal state.

is stored in **/etc** and named **raid?.conf**. For example, **/etc/raid0.conf** is the configuration file for the RAID filesystem **/dev/raid0**.

```
START array
1 3 0

START disks
/dev/sd0e
/dev/sd1e
/dev/sd2e

START spare
/dev/sd3e

START layout
# sectPerSU SUsPerParityUnit SUsPerReconUnit RAID_level
32 1 1 5

START queue
fifo 100
```

This first example creates a RAID 5 array with three disks and a backup disk. The first command specifies the array dimensions. This array has one row and three columns.[5] It also has one spare disk. The second command specifies that the array has three partitions. We are using a spare disk as specified in the third section. This section is not mandatory, and is used only for RAID 4 and RAID 5 arrays at this time. The layout specifies how many blocks are written to each disk and which RAID level we are using. The middle two options are almost always set to 1. The last section indicates how the queue is used. These are the default settings. The manual page should be consulted for more information; see *raidctl(8)*.

```
START array
# numRow numCol numSpare
1 2 0

START disks
```

---

[5] Although you can specify more than row, such a scheme is not really supported.

```
/dev/sd20e
/dev/sd21e

START layout
# sectPerSU SUsPerParityUnit SUsPerReconUnit RAID_level_1
128 1 1 1

START queue
fifo 100
```

This array is for a pair of mirrored disks with no spare disk. We are using a write set size of 128 blocks and have specified RAID 1.

For arrays that are supported by RAIDFrame, all partitions need to be the same size. CCD can be used to create different-size disks if necessary.

14.2 Filesystems

When taken fresh out of a box, a hard drive needs to go through several steps before it can hold a filesystem, a place where files can be placed and viewed. The first step is to have the disk recognized by the OS. From there, you can make partitions on the disk. On an OpenBSD system, a BSD style is used for disks where the entire disk is partition c.

```
16 partitions:
#        size   offset    fstype [fsize bsize   cpg]
 a:    524097       63    4.2BSD   1024  8192  16 # (Cyl.     0*- 519)
 b:    524160   524160      swap              # (Cyl.   520 - 1039)
 c:  78140160        0    unused      0     0  # (Cyl.     0 - 77519)
 d:    262080  1048320    4.2BSD   1024  8192  16 # (Cyl.  1040 - 1299)
 e:    524160  1310400    4.2BSD   1024  8192  16 # (Cyl.  1300 - 1819)
 f:  28165441  1834560    4.2BSD   1024  8192  16 # (Cyl.  1820 - 29761*)
 i:  48140159 30000001   unknown              # (Cyl. 29761*- 77519)
```

As can be seen here, the whole disk is occupied by partition c. We have then created a root filesystem as partition a, a swap as partition b, and so on. Once the disk has been partitioned, those partitions can either be formatted or used by systems like CCD or RAIDFrame.

14.2.1 New Filesystems

By default, OpenBSD uses a slight variant of the BSD fast filesystem (FFS). In *disklabel* this shows up as the **4.2BSD** filesystem. Once these partitions have been created, new filesystems can be made using the *newfs* command:

```
#  newfs /dev/wd0d
newfs: /dev/wd0d: not a character-special device
/dev/wd0d:       262080 sectors in 260 cylinders of 16 tracks,
    63 sectors
        128.0MB in 17 cyl groups (16 c/g, 7.88MB/g, 1920 i/g)
super-block backups (for fsck -b #) at:
 32, 16224, 32416, 48608, 64800, 80992, 97184, 113376, 129568,
 145760, 161952, 178144, 194336, 210528, 226720, 242912, 258080,
```

This will create the default OpenBSD filesystem type of the **sd0** disk—a partition. The raw device (notice that the device name is prepended with an "r") is used rather than the normal device. If the drive geometry doesn't match the BIOS-reported geometry, you can specify additional parameters to *newfs*:

- -S *bytessector* to specify the bytes per sector
- -u *sectorstrack* to specify the number of sectors per track
- -z *trackscyl* to specify the number of tracks per cylinder

These values are available through the *disklabel* command. By default, *newfs* will store backup superblocks on the filesystem. They become important if the *fsck* command fails to find a usable superblock.

Once a disk is labeled and formatted with a filesystem, it can be mounted. For permanent mounts, create an entry in the **fstab** file as described later in this chapter.

14.2.2 Other Common Filesystems: ext2, msdos, iso9660

OpenBSD cannot create either ext2 or iso9660 filesystems using the *newfs* command. To create an MS-DOS filesystem, however, you can use the command *newfs -t msdos* on the filesystem. This will create an older, FAT16-style partition that can be shared between Windows and OpenBSD systems on the same host—for example, on a dual-boot machine.

OpenBSD can mount filesystems of types msdos, ext2, and iso9660 using the *mount -t type* command. The *type* argument is one of these three filesystem types.

OpenBSD can also *fsck* msdos and ext2 filesystems, also using the *fsck -t type* command.

14.2.3 Disk Quotas

OpenBSD supports disk quotas for users and groups by default. Disk quotas enforce policies of disk usage, allowing the administrator to control the amount of space used by users. Quotas are an option configured as a mount option. Kernel support is also required:

```
option          QUOTA          # UFS quotas
```

The GENERIC kernel has this option enabled by default. Only the default filesystem, FFS, supports quotas.

If the filesystem is mounted with quota support, the system's start-up scripts check for any quota filesystems and enable quotas for them. Changing the options for the **/home** filesystem in the **/etc/fstab** file will give both group and user quotas:

```
/dev/wd0g /home ffs rw,userquota,groupquota 1 2
```

Once quota support is enabled for the filesystem, the respective quota files need to be created. For the **/home** filesystem, the files exist in the top of the mount point.

```
#  touch /home/quota.user
#  touch /home/quota.group
```

If these files are empty, any user can use any amount of space.

Editing the quota for the user lets you set four limits. The first, set to 10,000 blocks (presumable 1024 bytes per block), is the soft space use restriction. When the user uses more than this amount of space, the system will start to issue a warning about space use. When the next number, 15,000 blocks is hit, the user will not be able to create any more files. This is a hard restriction. The inode use restrictions work the same way but limit the number of files that a user is allowed to have.

```
#  edquota bpalmer
Quotas for user bpalmer:
/home: blocks in use: 0, limits (soft = 10000, hard = 15000)
       inodes in use: 0, limits (soft = 1000, hard = 1200)
```

If we had a group called *webmasters*, we could set limits on the group as well. In this example, the group is restricted to 100,000 blocks soft and 120,000 blocks hard. The 0 for the inode restriction means that there is no limit on the number of files.

```
#  edquota -g webmasters
Quotas for group webmasters:
/home: blocks in use: 0, limits (soft = 100000, hard = 120000)
        inodes in use: 0, limits (soft = 0, hard = 0)
```

Setting restrictions for a large number of users would be a great deal of work, so tools are available that allow a prototype user to set other accounts' restrictions:

```
#  edquota -p bpalmer user1 user2 user3
```

This command will set quota restrictions for *user1*, *user2*, and *user3* to be the same as the quotas for *bpalmer*.

To check the status of a user's space consumption against the specified limits, use the *quota* command:

```
$  quota bpalmer
Disk quotas for user bpalmer (uid 1000): soft = 10000, hard = 15000
$  quota  -g wheel
Disk quotas for group wheel (gid 0): none
```

Only the superuser may check quotas for users or groups to which the user does not belong.

A good tool to show the quotas placed on a system is *repquota*. The most common practice is just to show all usage on one filesystem or on all file-systems with quotas enabled.

```
#  repquota /tmp
                        Block limits              File limits
User           used    soft    hard  grace   used  soft  hard  grace
root     --       9       0       0            3     0     0
bpalmer +-     704     100     110  none      89     0     0
#  repquota -a
                        Block limits              File limits
User           used    soft    hard  grace   used  soft  hard  grace
wheel    --     705       0       0           91     0     0
```

```
operator--      8       0       0          1       0       0
                        Block limits               File limits
User            used    soft    hard grace used  soft    hard grace
root     --     9       0       0           3      0       0
bpalmer +-      704     100     110  none   89     0       0
```

If necessary, calling *repquota* from *cron* can generate daily information and send it to the system administrators.

14.3 Soft Updates

For several years, the BSD world has been developing a robust addition to the filesystem code called "soft updates." Developed primarily by Kirk McKusick, soft updates offer a way to greatly improve the disk access performance of a running filesystem. They rely in part on buffering and ordering the disk operations in the writing phases.

Enabling soft updates is easy to do. The option **FFS_SOFTUPDATES** must be enabled in the running kernel (it is available in the GENERIC kernel), and the option must be used on an FFS partition. This does not work for other filesystem types.

The *softdep* option can be specified either when the filesystem is mounted or in the configuration file for the filesystem. To mount a filesystem using soft updates a single time, a command like the following would be used:

```
# mount -o softdep /dev/wd1a /data
```

This will mount the partition on **/dev/wd1a** on the mount point **/data** with soft updates enabled. To make this change permanent, edit the file **/etc/fstab** as follows:

```
# cat /etc/fstab
/dev/wd0a / ffs rw 1 1
/dev/wd0e /home ffs rw 1 2
/dev/wd0d /usr ffs rw 1 2
/dev/wd1a /data ffs rw,softdep 1 2
```

Now the system will mount this filesystem using soft updates every time. This behavior can be overridden on the command line by remounting the filesystem with this option disabled. All filesystems can be mounted using this option, including the root filesystem.

If the system crashes, the *fsck* process will still have to be run on all filesystems, including those mounted with soft updates enabled.

14.3.1 Other Tricks to Speed Up Access

On some systems, disk access is a noticeable performance bottleneck. Vulnerable systems may include busy systems or hosts with constrained disk bandwidth, such as older systems. Under many circumstances, the option *noatime* can be used without peril to greatly improve read and write access to a filesystem. It turns off the calculation and recording of the access times for files on the system.

A dangerous option is *async*, which mounts filesystems asynchronously. While a significant performance increase can result, it comes with the risk of losing significant portions of data. An asynchronous mount will not commit changes to the disk unless the buffer is full or a significant lull in activity occurs. If a crash occurs before this happens, data loss is inevitable. Use of this option is discouraged. All OpenBSD filesystems are mounted synchronously (*mount -o sync*) by default.

14.4 Disklabels

BSD and BSD-derived systems store their drive geometry, configurations, and partitions in a *disklabel*. The *disklabel* command can be used to view and manipulate this information. With this tool, drives can be partitioned and prepared for use in an OpenBSD system. The *disklabel* command can specify a raw device (e.g., **/dev/rwd0c**) or just the device name (e.g., **wd0**).

Viewing the default disklabel (*-d*) for the device **wd0** illustrates a typical case:

```
$  sudo disklabel -d wd0
Password:
# using MBR partition 3: type A6 off 63 (0x3f) size 11717937
  (0xb2cd31)
# /dev/rwd0c:
type: ESDI
disk: ESDI/IDE disk
label: FUJITSU MHK2060A
flags:
bytes/sector: 512
sectors/track: 63
tracks/cylinder: 15
sectors/cylinder: 945
cylinders: 12416
total sectors: 11733120
```

```
rpm: 3600
interleave: 1
trackskew: 0
cylinderskew: 0
headswitch: 0              # microseconds
track-to-track seek: 0  # microseconds
drivedata: 0

16 partitions:
#        size offset   fstype  [fsize bsize  cpg]
  a: 11717937     63   unused       0     0          # (Cyl.    0*- 12399)
  c: 11733120      0   unused       0     0          # (Cyl.    0 - 12415)
```

(Note that the RPM entry of 3600 is incorrect and has been fixed in post-3.3 releases of OpenBSD for SCSI disks.) This default differs from the actual disklabel, however (the same header applies to both and is omitted here for space-related reasons):

```
16 partitions:
#         size    offset    fstype  [fsize bsize cpg]
  a:   2096892        63    4.2BSD   1024  8192  16 # (Cyl.    0*- 2218)
  b:    261765   2096955      swap                  # (Cyl. 2219 - 2495)
  c: 11733120         0    unused      0     0     # (Cyl.    0 - 12415)
  d:   6340950   2358720    4.2BSD   1024  8192  16 # (Cyl. 2496 - 9205)
  e:   3033450   8699670    4.2BSD   1024  8192  16 # (Cyl. 9206 - 12415)
```

The partitions and geometry of the drive are clearly shown for the system.

Editing a disklabel is done via the *-e* option to *disklabel*:

```
#  disklabel -e wd0
```

An editor is invoked (specified in the shell variable *EDITOR*) to allow you to edit this label. If no errors are present, the label is returned to the disk and the kernel is updated.

The system can store disklabels for a variety of disks, holding them in the file **/etc/disktabs**. The basic installation comes with popular entries already present. New entries can be generated automatically and formatted using the *-t* option to *disklabel*:

```
$  sudo disklabel -t wd0
# using MBR partition 3: type A6 off 63 (0x3f) size 11717937
```

```
# (0xb2cd31)
FUJITSU MHK2060A|ESDI/IDE disk|Automatically generated label:\
        :dt=ESDI:se#512:ns#63:nt#15:nc#12416:sc#945:su#11733120:\
        :pa#2096892:oa#63:ta=4.2BSD:ba#8192:fa#1024:\
        :pb#261765:ob#2096955:tb=swap:\
        :pc#11733120:oc#0:\
        :pd#6340950:od#2358720:td=4.2BSD:bd#8192:fd#1024:\
        :pe#3033450:oe#8699670:te=4.2BSD:be#8192:fe#1024:
```

This creates an entry for the disk **FUJITSU**. The fields specify the drive's type and geometry, as well as characteristics for each partition.

Once entries are populated, the command *disklabel -w entry* can be used for writing a disklabel:

```
#  disklabel -w wd0 FUJITSU
```

The *disklabel* command can also be used to install a boot sector:

```
#  dislabel -w -B /dev/rwd0c -b boot FUJITSU
```

This command installs the boot section (*-B*) on the raw **wd0** device along with the second-stage boot loader (*-b*) **boot**. Note that the disklabel entry is still the last argument on the line.

14.5 Mounting Filesystems

Once filesystems have been created and formated, we need to mount them and put them to use. The name of the tool employed, very appropriately, is *mount*. The reciprocal tool, *umount*, unmounts filesystems:

```
#  umount /tmp
#  mount /dev/wd0d /tmp
```

Most people won't use *mount* and *umount* very often, as they have little need to worry about their filesystems. The OS takes care of mounting and unmounting on start-up and shutdown. That said, there are a few flags that may be used from time to time.

mount

- **-A**   Mount all filesystems in the **/etc/fstab** file.
- **-a**   Mount all filesystems in the **/etc/fstab** file that aren't mounted.
- **-o** *   Filesystems can be mounted with options such as *noexec* and *nosuid*.
- **-r / -w**   Mount the filesystem in read-only or read-write mode, respectively.

umount

- **-a**   Unmount all filesystems in the **/etc/fstab** file.
- **-f**   Force a filesystem to be unmounted. Normally, a filesystem can't be unmounted unless there are no open file descriptors on the filesystem. A tool like *fstat* can be used to find which files are open or the *-f* flag can be set to kill the open files and unmount the system. Usually it is enough to just stop any processes (such as an open shell) that have the mounted filesystem as their working directory.

OpenBSD supports the use of union filesystems. With this capability, the user can mount any folder anywhere else on the system. This can be especially useful in chroot environments.

```
# mount_union -o rdonly /mnt/cvs /var/www/htdocs/cvs
```

In this example, **/mnt/cvs** is mounted in the directory for the Apache Web server to see. It's mounted in read-only mode (all *-o* flags from *mount* are available for *mount_union*). Without such an application, access to files outside chroot would not be available.

Also supported in OpenBSD is the memory filesystem (mfs). This virtual filesystem allows for a portion of the system RAM to be treated as a filesystem. It is often used in embedded systems where no writable disk is available. The most common option given to the command *mount_mfs* is *-s*, which specifies the filesystem size in 0.5K increments. For example, to mount a 10MB memory filesystem on **/mnt**, the following command would be issued:

```
# mount.mfs -s 5120 swap /mnt
```

This filesystem is now visible to the system and is available for use for storage. The output of the *df* command shows that it is ready for use and indicates how much space remains:

```
# df
Filesystem   512-blocks      Used     Avail Capacity  Mounted on
/dev/wd0a      2030134    404702   1523926    21%     /
/dev/wd0d      6139304   4885572    946768    84%     /usr
/dev/wd0e      2936930   2550654    239430    91%     /home
mfs:28551         4574         2      4344     0%     /mnt
```

This filesystem can be used like any other filesystem, but all contents will be lost when it is unmounted or the system is rebooted. Also, with a memory filesystem, more storage space comes with a tradeoff of less working RAM space.

OpenBSD can also support mounting of filesystems over the network using *nfs*. This approach is discussed in Chapter 23.

14.6 Pseudo-Disks with *vnconfig*

You can create a virtual disk for use by the system. This simple file is actually a filesystem image. You can use this driver to mount a filesystem you have received (e.g., the output of a command such as *dd if=/dev/fd0a of=/tmp/floppy.fs*) or a newly created file. If you need to create this file, you can do so using the *dd* command, with the **/dev/zero** device as a source:

```
$  dd if=/dev/zero of=new.img bs=512k count=128
128+0 records in
128+0 records out
67108864 bytes transferred in 4.616 secs (14538243 bytes/sec)
$  ls -l
total 131160
-rw-r--r--  1 jose  wheel  67108864 Apr 24 22:16 new.img
```

Now we have an empty file that we can fill out. Of course, you don't need to take this step if you have an existing filesystem image to mount.

Our next step is to use *vnconfig* to associate the image with a device so we can work with it:

```
$  sudo vnconfig svnd0 new.img
```

Now we need to create a partition table for this device, just as we would for a new disk. We can do so using *disklabel*:

```
$  sudo disklabel -E vnd0
disklabel: Can't get bios geometry: Device not configured
Initial label editor (enter '?' for help at any prompt)
>  a
partition: [a]  a
offset: [0]  enter
size: [131072]  enter
FS type: [4.2BSD]  enter
>  p
16 partitions:
#     size  offset  fstype  [fsize bsize  cpg]
 a: 131072       0  4.2BSD    1024  8192   16   # (Cyl.    0 - 1310*)
 c: 131072       0  unused       0     0        # (Cyl.    0 - 1310*)
>  w
>  q
No label changes.
```

This is then formatted with *newfs*, just as we would for a disk device:

```
$  sudo newfs /dev/svnd0a
newfs: /dev/svnd0a: not a character-special device
Warning: 28 sector(s) in last cylinder unallocated
/dev/svnd0a: 131072 sectors in 1311 cylinders of 1 tracks,100 sectors
        64.0MB in 82 cyl groups (16 c/g, 0.78MB/g, 192 i/g)
super-block backups (for fsck -b #) at:
 32, 1632, 3232, 4832, 6432, 8032, 9632, 11232, 12832, 14432, 16032,
 ...
```

The next steps work for the newly created device as well as any disk images already found in files (such as a floppy image). You can mount the device as you would any other disk device:

```
$  sudo mount /dev/svnd0a /mnt/
$  mount
/dev/wd0a on / type ffs (local)
/dev/wd0d on /usr type ffs (local)
/dev/wd0e on /home type ffs (local)
/dev/svnd0a on /mnt type ffs (local)
```

The filesystem on **/mnt** is now available for use just like any other filesystem. You can even share it using NFS. The size of the filesystem is what you specified when you created the file.

To unconfigure a virtual disk device, use the *vnconfig -u* command on the device. After the disk in unmounted, you can clear out the configuration:

```
# vnconfig -u svnd0
```

Now the only remnant is a file, which you can delete or store someplace else.

14.7 Caring for Filesystems

Modern UNIX filesystems are well designed and recover from crashes effectively, but occasionally manual recovery becomes necessary. The most popular tool for this purpose is *fsck*. Most people will use *fsck* only during start-up if a filesystem is really trashed. When a filesystem isn't unmounted cleanly, *fsck* can be used to clean up. Keep in mind, however, that there are filesystem problems in these circumstances, so files may be lost or corrupted even with *fsck* trying to recover them. If necessary, you can use the following flags:

- **-f**   Force a check even if the filesystem is mounted. This can be dangerous if there are open files and should only be used with discretion.

- **-n / -y**   Answer "no" or "yes" to all repair questions. These flags can save a great deal of time if there are a large number of errors or a large number of file systems to be checked.

14.8 The Last Resort for Mistakes: *scan_ffs*

Sometimes you may make a mistake and accidentally start to wipe out a filesystem. One way to try and recover the partition table for an OpenBSD FFS partition is via the *scan_ffs* tool. It is run on a drive and attempts to list the partitions it can identify by walking through the data:

```
# scan_ffs wd1
ffs at 0 size 6800048128 mount /data time Sun Aug 18 10:12:17 2003
scan_ffs: read: Input/output error
```

The error at the end of the scan is normal and typically arises when the tool hits the end of a disk. Here *scan_ffs* found one parititon on the disk, **/data**, and identified its size and creation time. Because *scan_ffs* slowly walks through the filesystem, you may wish to speed it up via *scan_ffs -s*. A more condensed output format, which can also be used with *disklabel*, can be obtained by using *scan_ffs -l*:

```
#  scan_ffs -ls wd1
X: 13281344 0 4.2BSD 1024 8192 16 # /data
```

Here the total size of the disk, the filesystem, fragment size, block size, number of cylinders per group, and last mount point are listed.

While *scan_ffs* can't solve all of the problems associated with a trashed FFS partition map, it can help reduce the time needed to fix many of them.

14.9 Listing Open Files and Devices

When a device is to be disconnected, you may find an error when trying to ungracefully unhook it:

```
#  umount /home/
umount: /home: Device busy
```

Here the **/home** filesystem cannot be unmounted because it is currently in use. To see what processes, users, and files are open on this filesystem, use the *fstat* command.

The *fstat* command shows the status of open files, file descriptors, devices, and the filesystem on a running system. (You can also look at a kernel crash dump using *fstat* and observe which files were open, but that application is not described here.) The information about the context of the device status is easily displayed using this command. Note that only root can execute this command due to the sensitive nature of the memory areas being queried.

To see which process or user is using a device, *fstat* can be used to peer into the device tree. For example, we can observe which process is using the first BPF device:

```
#  fstat /dev/bpf0
USER    CMD       PID  FD MOUNT    INUM  MODE       R/W  DV|SZ NAME
root    pflogd 27139   3  /        42252 crw-------  rw  bpf0 /dev/bpf0
```

Here the PF logging daemon is listening on the first BPF device. Notice how the information needed to understand the process and its context is displayed, including the username, command, process ID, associated filedescriptor for the process, mountpoint, inode number, file mode, and read-write status, along with the device file itself.

To see which open file descriptors a user is using, you can specify the *-u* option. Here we can see some of what the root user is doing on a small system:

```
#  fstat -u root
USER    CMD           PID   FD MOUNT       INUM MODE        R/W      DV|SZ
root    syslogd     11213   17 /         189958 -rw-r--r--    w        135
root    cardslot1      11   wd /              2 drwxr-xr-x    r        512
root    cardslot0      10   wd /              2 drwxr-xr-x    r        512
root    usb0            9   wd /              2 drwxr-xr-x    r        512
root    apm0            8   wd /              2 drwxr-xr-x    r        512
...
```

This output is obviously truncated to save space but shows the commands and associated open file handles.

The *fstat* command can also show open files and devices used by any process number. The *-p* option can be used in this case:

```
#  ps -ax |  grep 31181
  PID TT    STAT       TIME COMMAND
31181 ??  Is       0:02.55 ssh-agent -s
#  fstat -p 31181
USER    CMD           PID   FD MOUNT       INUM MODE        R/W      DV|SZ
jose    ssh-agent   31181   wd /              2 drwxr-xr-x    r        512
jose    ssh-agent   31181    3 /          42220 crw-rw-rw-   rw      crypto
jose    ssh-agent   31181    4* unix stream 0xd0a71e00
```

Here the *ssh-agent* process has an open file descriptor in the root filesystem, an open socket to the crypto device, and an open UNIX domain socket.

Chapter 15

Backup Utilities

15.1 Introduction

A safe system can protect its data through a variety of means. Only a fool would expect his or her system to never suffer unexpected failures leading to data loss. Backups can help prevent such events from creating large-scale problems and assist in minimizing the damage.

Discussing backup strategies and media in their entirety is not possible in a single chapter and would most certainly be beyond the scope of this book. Indeed, whole books covering these topics have been written. Instead, we will discuss backup methods using the tools provided in the base installation of OpenBSD and in the ports tree 13.

15.2 Devices

OpenBSD supports a vast variety of backup media, from CDR and CDRW drives to SCSI tapes and tape changers. Given that hardware support is a moving target, you should consider finding out what is supported for your platform at the OpenBSD Web site (**http://www.openbsd.org/plat.html**).

What type of backup medium you choose entirely depends on your budget and your needs. Obviously, the typical home user does not need a hot standby server in a remote location that is packed with disks and can take over the function of the primary server in a snippet of a second.

The most widely used backup medium today is probably CDR, with factors driving its popularity including its low cost and ease of use. Also very common are dedicated file servers that have built-in RAID arrays. Such servers provide the space needed for a backup plus the redundancy of a RAID 5 setup and real-time access to data. However, cost can be a major issue for most users.

15.3 Preliminaries

Regardless of the backup strategy chosen, there are some important things to keep in mind.

- **Document**   Document your backup procedure. This step is very important in a setting were other people (e.g., fellow administrators) might need access to backups to recover the system.
- **Label**   Label your backups. You do not want to be searching for the CDR on which you put your thesis just before your hard drive decided to give up.
- **Verify**   Take the extra time that verifying each backup costs. Automating this step and having the results mailed to you daily is easy.
- **Test**   Test your backup procedure. Does it really back up what you want it to back up?
- **Test again**   So how does recovering the file **corp-tax-all-employees.doc** from last Friday really work?
- **Be pessimistic**   Disasters happen, and when they strike they will inevitably catch you on the wrong foot.

To back up all or not to back up all—that is the question!

Picture this: Your main hard drive decided it's a bad day and died. Can you spend the time needed to reinstall the OS or can't you? This is exactly the question you have to ask yourself when it's time to decide whether to back up everything or to omit things because of space constrictions. Typically, it suffices to back up your data and the system configuration files.

Plan for the future. Can you live with burning another CDR when you have even more data than you have now?

Plan in advance. If you have a lot of data, the cheapest backup strategy (short of buying a huge tape drive) is setting up a dedicated host with a big disk that can handle all of your data and then some. Imagine what would happen if the drive in your desktop computer dies when your old backup on the backup host has just been deleted to make space for the new backup you were trying to do when your desktop decided to keel over dead.

15.4 Backup Strategies

In this section we define different levels of backups analogous to those defined by *dump* (*man 8 dump*) to simplify the concepts. In particular, one has to distinguish between full, incremental, and differential backups. A full backup (level 0) backs up all data on the given partition/system. An incremental backup (levels 1–9) backs up the changes made since the last backup. A differential backup catches the changes that have occurred between incremental backups. To summarize:

- **Level 0**   Full backup.
- **Levels 1–9**   Level 1 backs up changes that have taken place since the last level 0 backup. Level n backs up changes that occurred after the level $n - 1$ backup, or after the level $n - x$ backup if there was no level $n - 1$ backup.

Father-Son

The Father-Son strategy is based on using incremental backups every day Monday through Thursday and a full backup each Friday. A standard procedure would use six tapes, alternating the full backup tape every two weeks:

Mon	Tue	Wed	Thu	Fri (1)	Mon	Tue	Wed	Thu	Fri (2)
1	2	3	4	5	1	2	3	4	6

This strategy puts your weekday tapes under great strain and limits your recovery to the last six days, although you can recover quickly and easily. A better approach is to use 10 tapes, thus increasing your recovery time frame to 10 days and decreasing the wear on your daily tapes:

Mon	Tue	Wed	Thu	Fri	Mon	Tue	Wed	Thu	Fri
0	1	2	3	4	5	6	7	8	9

Grandfather-Father-Son

Another popular method is the Grandfather-Father-Son strategy. It also relies on daily incremental backups and weekly full backups but incorporates monthly backups (the so-called Grandfather). This method, using only 10 tapes, extends your maximum recovery time frame to 90 days, although it limits your daily recovery ability to only 6 days. Increasing the number of tapes in this case can decrease tape wear and increase your maximum recovery time frame.

Towers of Hanoi

The most highly recommended backup strategy, the Towers of Hanoi method is derived from the age-old mathematical game. This strategy seems rather complicated at first glance but shows its beauty after some thought:

Mon	Tue	Wed	Thu	Fri	Mon	Tue	Wed	Thu	Fri
0	2	1	4	3	6	5	8	7	9

The first day, Monday, a level 0 backup is taken. It backs up everything.

On Tuesday, a level 2 backup is performed (everything since level 0). On Wednesday, a level 1 backup is performed (everything since level 0). On Thursday, a level 4 backup is performed (everything since level 2). On Friday, a level 3 backup is performed (everything since level 2). And so it continues. The pattern here seeks to strike a balance between recovery time and data redundancy. A level 0 backup is performed to back everything up, then two backups of Monday's changes are kept, in the level 2 and 1 tapes. Two copies of Tuesday's changes are kept, in the level 1 and 4 tapes. This pattern continues, with each changed file being backed up twice in a two-week rotation.

Modified Towers of Hanoi

As the *dump* manual page suggests, there are several ways to improvise based on the Towers of Hanoi strategy. One method is presented here.

Every month or two, a level 0 backup is performed. These tapes are "kept forever." Every week, on Monday, a level 1 backup is done:

Sun	Mon	Tue	Wed	Thu	Fri	Sat
1	3	2	5	4	7	6

This strategy provides monthly backups, with weekly "nearly full" backups, and uses the Towers of Hanoi approach for the incremental and differential backups.

These are just a few examples of possible backup strategies using the *dump* program. A customized strategy might potentially be most useful for you.

15.4.1 Data-Specific Options

Your backup strategy should match the data being backed up, allowing for both flexibility and strength. Electronic mail, for example, is traditionally stored in the *mbox* format, which yields a flat text file. Users have a central mail spool and possibly, depending on the mail client they use, one or more spools in their home directories. An alternative mail spool format is the **maildirs** format, where each message constitutes a single file. It allows for greater granularity in the backup of mail messages. Note that not all software supports this mail spool format.

Obviously volatile data, such as home directories and generated data, have different requirements for preservation in the event of system failure than does system software. The system is usually installed from a central source or local, read-only media, such as a CD-ROM. It is often easier to reinstall this portion of he system than to restore it. Configuration files, however, can be backed up and stored, and later quickly recovered due to their small size.

Lastly, it is important to invest a reasonable amount of effort in, and pay attention to, back ups with respect to the data's value. For many home users it may be worthwhile to back up data only to another machine, rather than investing in a tape drive and other media. The chance that both drives will fail simultaneously is low enough given the value of the data for many users. In contrast, an ISP with paying customers needs to ensure the reliability of its data, along with the timeliness of restoring the data. As such, a backup solution that matches the value of the data is wise to consider.

15.4.2 Authentication

Sometimes, it is desirable to have a central backup server connect to remote machines and back up the filesystems using the *dump* program.

SSH Public Key Authentication

A basic setup would be to issue the following command on the central backup server:

```
level=0
fs=/var/www/users
host=client_hostname
fsname=var_www_users
ssh -l backup -c blowfish $host dump -$levelau -f - $fs |
        gzip -9 > $host-$level-$fsname.dmp.gz
```

This works well, if an administrator is on hand to type the password for the "backup" user for each client for each filesystem. Most people don't have this patience, however. Instead, they would generally prefer to generate an *ssh* public/private key pair on the server:

```
$  ssh-keygen -t rsa
Generating public/private rsa key pair.
Enter file in which to save the key(id_rsa): enter
Enter passphrase (empty for no passphrase):  enter
Enter same passphrase again:  enter
Your identification has been saved in /tmp/abc.
Your public key has been saved in /tmp/abc.pub.
The key fingerprint is:
    5f:1a:c7:79:bc:31:c8:ee:39:ab:a3:55:f3:86:c1
        backups@hostname.net
```

Pressing *enter* for the passphrase enables this backup to occur within a *cron* job.

The following script, developed by Todd T. Fries,[1] uses the *dump* command to make filesystem backups using this Towers of Hanoi strategy and *ssh* via key-based authentication that seeks to contact remote systems and build their filesystem backups.

```sh
#!/bin/sh

# script contributed by todd fries.

# 1st try
# 0 5 3 7 4 9 8

# Tower of Hanoi
# 0 3 2 5 4 7 6 9 8 9 9
# 0 2 1 4 3 6 5 8 7 8 9 <-- using this (starting 9/3/2002)

# 0 1 2 3 4 5 6
# 1 2 3 4 5 6 7

if ! ssh-add -l > /dev/null 2>&1 ; then
    echo "cannot contact ssh-agent via $SSH_AUTH_SOCK. Exiting."
    exit 1
fi

if ! [ "${exec_success_dobackup}" = "true" ]; then
    export exec_success_dobackup=true
    td=$(mktemp -d /tmp/dobackup.XXXXXXXXXXXX)
    cp $0 $td/backup
    exec $td/backup "$@"
    echo "SHOULD NOT BE HERE SOMETHING WENT WRONG"
    exit 1
fi
echo "Starting $0.."

dayofweek=$(date +%w)
```

---

[1]This program is available at **http://www.crimelabs.net/openbsdbook**.

```
level=$(( $dayofweek ))

hn=$(hostname)
thishost=${hn%%.*}

dormt() {
    dossh -2 -c blowfish $1 sh | gzip -d
    return $?
}

dossh() {
    err=255
    while [ $err -ne 0 ]
        do
        #echo ssh "$@" > /dev/tty
        ssh "$@"
        err=$?
    done
    return $err
}

[ "$1" ] || {
    echo "No host specified on cmdline, please specify at least one"
    exit 1
}

while [ "$1" ]
do
    host="$1"

    # If we can't reach it, dont try
    if ! ping -c 3 $host > /dev/null 2>&1 ; then
        if ! ping6 -c 3 $host; then
            shift
            continue
        fi
    fi
```

```
shift

[ -f $host/list ] || {
    # create the list of filesystems to dump
    mkdir -p $host
    ssh $host df -Pt ffs | awk '/^F/{next} {print $6}' > \
        $host/tmplist
    egrep -v "^/usr/obj|^/tmp|^/var/tmp|^/sw/loc" \
        $host/tmplist > $host/list
    rm -f $host/tmplist

}

# This assumes we dont try to backup a machine with non ffs root fs,
# aka if $host/list contains '/' and it is not ffs, we will always
# take level 0's

[ -f ${host}/${host}_-0.dmp.bz2 ] || {
    # First time we do a level 0, regardless of the day
    level=0
}

while read line
do
    fn=${host}$(echo $line | sed 's/\//_/g')-${level}.dmp.bz2
    echo $fn

    case $host in
    $thishost)
        dump -${level}au -f - $line
        ret=$?
        ;;
    *)
        echo "dump -${level}au -f - $line|gzip -1"|dormt $host
        ret=$?
        ;;
        esac | bzip2 -9 > $host/.$fn
```

```
            echo return is: $ret
            #[ $ret ] && mv $host/.$fn $host/$fn
            mv $host/.$fn $host/$fn
    done < $host/list 2>&1 | tee -a $host.log
done
```

The choice of using the script is left up to the user, but it does demonstrate how a powerful shell script can facilitate automated backups of machines. This simplifies management and overall network operations. The script's length is partly due to the number of options available and logging performed, and partly due to how gracefully it attempts to handle errors. With minor modifications, it could easily serve for a heterogeneous environment as well.

15.5 Available Tools

This section gives an overview of the tools available in the base system and their use for backups. Not all of these tools are useful for all environments, but overall they work well for a variety of systems.

15.5.1 *cpio*

The *cpio* command accepts input in the form of a list of files, one per line, from standard input. It is predestined to be used in conjunction with *find* and some piping for good measure. The command-line argument -*o* tells *cpio* to create a new archive (-*A appends*). You can write your backup either to a file (-*F*) or to a device. In addition, *cpio* supports compression with *gzip 1* (-*z*) or *compress 1* (-*Z*). The argument -*i* tells *cpio* to restore an archive. The problem with *cpio* can be that the user has to explicitly provide a list of files that should be included in a backup. The concept of explicit exclusion is, however, more suitable for backup procedures. Imagine you have a new directory and forget to add it to your file list—you might be relying on *cpio* to archive just that directory.

15.5.2 *pax*

The *pax* command works much like *tar*, with a few key differences. Like *tar, pax* rolls multiple files into a single archive that can be compressed. The compression action is separated from the bundling. Unlike *tar*, however, *pax* sends its output to the standard output device by default. To create a simple *pax* archive from a directory, the command *pax -wf* is used to write the archive to a file:

```
$  pax -wf recipes.pax recipes/
```

Notice that *pax* is not verbose by default—another feature it shares with *tar*. Use the command *pax -v* to have verbose output as each file is added and to obtain a final summary of statistics. In fact, the archive will even look like a *tar* archive to the system:

```
$  file recipes.pax
recipes.pax: POSIX tar archive
$  pax -f recipes.pax
recipes
recipes/arroz-con-pollo
recipes/flan
```

Appending to an existing *pax* archive is done with the *pax -a* command. Compressed *pax* archives can be made using the *pax -z* command, but only in new archive creation mode. To read from an archive and unpackage it, use the *pax -r* command (again, in conjunction with *-f*):

```
$  cd /tmp
$  pax -vrf /home/jose/recipes.pax
recipes
recipes/flan
recipes/arroz-con-pollo
notes
rssfeeds
pax: ustar vol 1, 5 files, 10240 bytes read, 0 bytes written.
```

The files and directory structure are unpacked in the same order as they were written. At this point *pax* becomes a simple-to-use packaging system.

What makes *pax* so interesting is that it understands devices and how to handle them when they are full:

```
#  pax -wvf /dev/sd0a openbsd/www/
openbsd/www
openbsd/www/CVS
```

```
openbsd/www/CVS/Root
...
openbsd/www/pkg-stable31.html
pax: Failed write to archive volume: 1 <Invalid argument>
pax: ustar vol 1, 117 files, 0 bytes read, 0 bytes written.

ATTENTION! pax archive volume change required.
/dev/sd0a ready for archive volume: 2
Load the NEXT STORAGE MEDIA (if required) and make sure
it is WRITE ENABLED. Type "y" to continue, "." to quit pax,
or "s" to switch to new device.
If you cannot change storage media, type "s"
Is the device ready and online? >
```

At this point you can replace the existing media with a new, empty volume, and then point the new volume at a new device or simply quit *pax*.

Like *tar*, *pax* can preserve various file and directory attributes, such as ownerships, modification times, permissions, and the like. But unlike *tar*, the *pax* command can create archives fully compatible with other archives. Using the command *pax -x*, file formats compatible with *cpio* (and various versions and flavors of it) and *tar* formats can be written. This makes *pax* a very full-featured tool.

Other advanced features of *pax* are discussed in detail in its manual page.

15.5.3 *dump* and *restore*

The *dump* and *restore* tools have been around as long as almost any other commands to be found under UNIX. The *dump* command backs up files or partitions directly to the back volume. It is aware of the limitations of the backup drives and knows where the backup volume ends. It can be used to back up more data than will fit onto one volume and will prompt the user when the volume needs to be switched.

```
#  dump -0ua -f /dev/sd0c /mnt/master/cvs
  DUMP: Ignoring u flag for subdir dump
  DUMP: Dumping sub files/directories from /mnt/master
  DUMP: Dumping file/directory /mnt/master/cvs
  DUMP: Date of this level 0 dump: Mon Jun  2 22:28:10 2003
  DUMP: Date of last level 0 dump: the epoch
  DUMP: Dumping /dev/rwd1a (/mnt/master) to /dev/sd0c
```

```
DUMP: mapping (Pass I) [regular files]
DUMP: mapping (Pass II) [directories]
DUMP: estimated 54987 tape blocks.
DUMP: Volume 1 started at: Mon Jun  2 22:28:11 2003
DUMP: dumping (Pass III) [directories]
DUMP: dumping (Pass IV) [regular files]
DUMP: 51151 tape blocks on 1 volume
DUMP: Volume 1 completed at: Mon Jun  2 22:29:39 2003
DUMP: Volume 1 took 0:01:28
DUMP: Volume 1 transfer rate: 581 KB/s
DUMP: Date of this level 0 dump: Mon Jun  2 22:28:10 2003
DUMP: Date this dump completed:  Mon Jun  2 22:29:39 2003
DUMP: Average transfer rate: 581 KB/s
DUMP: Closing /dev/sd0c
DUMP: DUMP IS DONE
```

In the preceding example, a level 0 (full) backup of **/mnt/master/cvs** is being done to a Zip drive, **/dev/sd0c**. The *-u* flag tells *dump* to update the **/etc/dumpdates** file, and the *-a* flag says to write until the end of tape marker is reached. We can see that 51,151 blocks were backed up in about 1.5 minutes at a rate of almost 600 kilobits/second. In this case, the block size on the Zip drive is 1KB which means about 51MB of data was backed up.

The *dump* utility supports the concept of dump levels for doing non-full backups. Backup levels were discussed earlier in this chapter. When a backup is done of a filesystem, rather than a folder, the backup level information is saved in the **/etc/dumpdates** file. This file contains the name of the filesystem, the most recent backup level, and the date on which the backup was performed.

```
# cat /etc/dumpdates
/dev/rwd0a      0 Mon Jun  2 22:35:01 2003
```

Similar backup plans and scripts should be used for *dump* as for the other tools documented earlier in this chapter.

Just as *dump* can be used to back up files, so *restore* can be used to restore the files from the backup media. It has two main modes of operation: interactive and full restoration. The interactive mode reads off the backup media and allows the user to walk through the contents of the backup volume, much like an *ftp* server. The following example shows the process for restoring just the **OpenBSD-book** folder from the volume:

```
#  restore -i -f /dev/sd0c
restore >  ls
.:
cvs/

restore >  cd cvs
restore >  ls
./cvs:
CVSROOT/      OpenBSD-book/ cvslock/

restore >  add OpenBSD-book
restore >  extract
You have not read any tapes yet.
Unless you know which volume your file(s) are on you should start
with the last volume and work towards the first.
Specify next volume #:  1
set owner/mode for '.'? [yn]  y
restore >  quit
#  ls
cvs
#  ls cvs/OpenBSD-book/
Attic                 copyright.tex,v
fdisk.tex,v           ipv6.tex,v
performance.tex,v
CVS                   core_files.tex,v        future.tex,v
kerberos.tex,v        pf.tex,v
...
...
...
```

In this example, the folder **OpenBSD-book** was added to the files to be restored, and then the *extract* command was used to start the restoration process. The restoration was done to the current working directory and included a re-creation of all of the path information from the original backup. The restoration process will overwrite any existing files that get in the way.

In full restoration mode, all files from the media are retrieved. If the full path for a folder were known, it could be extracted. Without any files or folders specified, the entire volume is restored.

```
#  restore -x -f /dev/sd0c cvs/OpenBSD-book
You have not read any tapes yet.
Unless you know which volume your file(s) are on you should start
with the last volume and work towards the first.
Specify next volume #:  1
set owner/mode for '.'? [yn]  y

#  restore -x -f /dev/sd0c
You have not read any tapes yet.
Unless you know which volume your file(s) are on you should start
with the last volume and work towards the first.
Specify next volume #:  1
```

The first example extracted the known folder, while the second extracted just the backup volume. Any of these *restore* commands can use the *-v* option, which will display large amounts of output when *restore* is running. When *restore* asks for the volume number, 1 is used since everything fits onto one volume.

15.5.4 *tar*

The *tar* command is a hard link to *pax* and represents another personality for this utility. In *tar* mode, the utility behaves as POSIX dictates. In general, you may back up data by specifying one or more files, one or more directories, or both. Any directory listed is traversed recursively.

An example follows:

```
$  ls -ld testdir
drwxr-xr-x  2 todd  wheel   512 Feb 24 12:38 testdir/
$  ls -l testdir
total 5648
-rw-r--r--  1 todd  wheel    131072 Feb 24 12:38 testfile-1
-rw-r--r--  1 todd  wheel   2736283 Feb 24 12:38 testfile-2
$  tar cvf backup.tar testdir
testdir
testdir/testfile-1
testdir/testfile-2
$  tar cvf backup.tar testdir/testfile-1        testdir/testfile-2
testdir/testfile-1
testdir/testfile-2
$
```

The *tar* has three main modes of operation:

- Creation of an archive
- Testing of an archive
- Extraction of an archive

These three modes are designated by *c, t,* and *x,* respectively.

In the preceding example, *c* is the first character after the *tar* command. It "creates" the archive.

To verify that the archive in the example is readable, you could use *tar tvf backup.tar.* In that case, no files will be extracted, but a list of files included will be listed.

To "extract" the example archive, you could use *tar xvf backup.tar.*

One additional option, present in all of the preceding examples, is *v.* Omitting it changes only the presence of the file listing. Without it, *tar* is silent, except regarding errors.

A final option, not seen in the preceding examples, is *z.* It will create, test, and extract compressed archives using the *gzip(1)* command.

15.6 Additional Tools from Ports and Packages

More serious backup tools exist for larger installations. The *amanda* tool, for example, helps with large backups' rotation in a convenient manner. A simple backup solution using *rsync* is also described in this section.

15.6.1 Amanda

Amanda stands for Advanced Maryland Automatic Network Disk Archiver. This highly automated backup solution is appropriate for any size of site, provided its e-mail output is read for potential problem notifications.

From the package description:

```
Amanda is a backup system designed to archive many computers on a network
to a single large-capacity tape drive.  It is built on top of standard
backup software: UNIX dump/restore, GNU Tar and others, so it possible to
restore from a backup tape even if Amanda is not installed.

Amanda requires a host that is mostly idle during the time backups are
done, with a large capacity tape drive (e.g., an EXABYTE, DAT or DLT tape).
This becomes the "tape server host." All the computers you are going to dump
are the "backup client hosts." The server host can also be a client host.
```

More detailed instructions can be found in **/usr/local/share/doc/amanda/INSTALL** after installing the package (starting with item 2). We will attempt to summarize those instructions here.

After installing the *amanda-2.4.2.2.tgz* package, follow the message that explains how to add **/etc/inetd.conf** lines for the *amanda* package, and permissions for an operator **/operator/.amandahosts** file:

```
**
** In order to update /etc/services and /etc/inetd.conf, run
**
**    /usr/local/libexec/amanda/patch-system --enable-index
**       --enable-tape
**
** You should check both of these files, verifying proper
** installation. Once verified issue the command:
**
**    kill -HUP `cat /var/run/inetd.pid`
**
** You also need to create /operator/.amandahosts, which will
** contain the FQDN of the tape server.  The contents should look
** like this:
**
**    backup.openbsd.org amanda
**
** The permissions of /operator/.amandahosts must be restricted:
**
**    chmod u=rw /operator/.amandahosts
**    chown operator.operator /operator/.amandahosts
**
```

Now several pieces of information need to be gathered. You must select a server, "name" your backup set(s), specify the frequency of backup, and indicate the number of tapes you have.

An example backup set named *csd* is provied in **/etc/amanda/csd.** On your backup server, copy this to your own backup set name. For this example, we will use *corenet*. We will also leave most of the defaults in place. In the real world, you will likely find it useful to customize them to your own needs.

Inside **/etc/amanda/corenet** you will find **amanda.conf** and **disklist**. Both require editing.

By default, the *operator* user is e-mailed for notifications. If this should change, modify the "mailto" line. The "tapecycle 25 tapes" instruction means there are 25 tapes used during the backup rotation. Amanda will ask for each as it becomes necessary. Other parameters are documented in this file as well. More example files exist in **/usr/local/share/examples/amanda**. The name of the default tape set is *DailySet1xx*, where *xx* are numbers 0–9. Edit "labelstr" and "org" if you have other preferences.

Create the **/var/amanda/DailySet1** directory, and make sure the backup user has the ability to write to this directory.

The **amanda.conf** file describes the methods of backups available. They include strategies that limit the network bandwidth used, establish concurrent network connections, and choose whether the server or the client compresses the data.

In the end, you edit **disklist** For each uncommented, nonblank line, you should list "machine diskdevice backupmethod." A number of examples are provided that use a variety of backup methods. Compare the backup methods here with the **amanda.conf** file to determine precisely what they mean.

Once you have taken these steps on the server, you should install the *amanda-client-2.4.2.2.tgz* package on the clients. Note that the server already has the client binaries installed.

Once everything is in place, it is time to run your first "check." This is bound to find some errors. Simply correct the problems and rerun the check:

```
$ su -m operator -c "/usr/local/sbin/amcheck -m corenet"
```

Once you are comfortable that things are ready to run, place the following in root's *crontab*:

```
0 16 * * * su -m operator -c "/usr/local/sbin/amcheck -m corenet"
45 4 * * * su -m operator -c "/usr/local/sbin/amdump corenet"
```

You should get e-mails every morning and afternoon, informing you of completed backups and tape(s) needed, any hosts that are unreachable, and other informational bits.

15.6.2 GNU *tar* for Backups

The GNU development team has made a significant number of enhancements to the *tar* command. GNU *tar*, commonly referred to as *gtar*, is available in the ports tree in **archivers/gtar/**. Like *tar*, it can use tape devices or other media. Unlike the built-in version of *tar*, it can link to arbitrary compression algorithms, such as *bzip2*, and not just *gzip*. Most of the other options used in *tar* can be found in *gtar*.

15.6.3 Backup Using *rsync*

The *rsync* utility, listed as a "fast, flexible replacement for *rcp*," is a protocol similar to CVS for remote file synchronization (hence the name *rsync*), but much simpler to set up and use. In fact, *rsync* can behave very similarly to *cvs* and *gtar* in terms of the files it handles. Its strength is its ability to use an intelligent algorithm to transfer only the *differences* between files, rather than the files themselves (be sure to use the *–partial* option, which is not enabled by default). The intelligence arises from the way it detects the differences in the files and handles these updates.

Using *rsync* as a backup strategy is simple. It is best done on a remote disk system, rather than a device such as a tape drive, due to the way the files are kept on either end. Indeed, one of the authors uses *rsync* to keep one of his laptops backed up to a central file server. A remote shell utility, such as *rsh* or *ssh*, is used for communications. Alternatively, a network *rsync* protocol can be used over the default TCP port, 873.

To install *rsync*, use the ports entry in **net/rsync** as described in Chapter 13. The *rsync* utility is used by many people, so it's often updated and kept working smoothly. Many sites use it to distribute updates to their software, including several large Linux mirrors. There *rsync* is not used as a backup tool but rather as a file distribution method, which is an alternate use for this utility. Note that both ends of the setup must have *rsync* available.

Setup of *rsync* is also rather straightforward. If you are not using this protocol, but rather *rsh* or *ssh*, there is no need for any setup. Unlike in CVS, no special file entries are required to keep files and directories backed up. Instead, simply run *rsync* with the proper set of arguments and any files or directories can be backed up.

To set up *rsync* to use its own protocol, insert a line such as the following in your **/etc/inetd.conf** or similar file:

```
rsync   stream  tcp     nowait  root    /usr/local/bin/rsync  \
    rsyncd --daemon
```

You will also need to create a configuration file for the daemon, **/etc/rsyncd.conf**. A minimal configuration for the module *www* follows:

```
[www]
      path = /var/www/htdocs
      read only = yes
```

This file provides read-only access to retrieve the **htdocs** subdir of the *www* server. Any *rsync* clients that connect to the server can access a read-only copy of the module *www*.

Once you restart *inetd*, a new TCP socket will be listening, which you can verify using *netstat -na*:

```
tcp  0  0 0.0.0.0:873   0.0.0.0:*    LISTEN
```

This machine is now an *rsync* server, and the use of *rsh* or *ssh* as a transport protocol is no longer needed. To connect to an *rsync* server, the hostname and the storage location are separated by *two* colons, "::", rather than one. Furthermore, anonymous shares or password-protected shares may be set up using the **rsyncd.conf** file. In this sense, the *rsync* server is similar to the CVS pserver. See the manual page for **rsyncd.conf** for more information on how to use this capability.

You can also run *rsync* as a "stand-alone" daemon by issuing *rsync –daemon* on the command line as root. If this method is used, adding a few lines to **/etc/rc.local** is an appropriate way to restart this daemon when the system restarts.

An example *rsync* session is shown below, with some parts omitted for brevity. Here the home directory is backed up to a remote server, with the **music/** subdirectory being omitted. The remote server, 192.168.0.11, has a subdirectory, **rsync/tank**, for the machine, a laptop named *tank*.

```
$  export RSYNC_RSH=/usr/bin/ssh
$  rsync -avz ~/* --exclude music/ \
     jose@192.168.0.11:~/rsync/tank/
building file list ...
done
software/
software/bind-9.1.3/
software/bind-9.1.3/Makefile
 omitted
wrote 333069 bytes  read 20 bytes  11291.15 bytes/sec
total size is 486453218  speedup is 1460.43
```

After setting up *ssh* for use with the transport layer, the *rsync* command is used to **archive** all files (*-a*) listed using **compression** (*-z*), and to be **verbose** in its operations (*-v*), which is why we have the files listed when *rsync* runs—a nice diagnostic. Newer versions of OpenBSD modify the *rsync* package to use *ssh* by default, so you can omit this step.

Recovery of files from a remote *rsync* server is straightforward: You simply reverse the options to *rsync* that you used to create the backup. For example, to retrieve a specific subdirectory of an archive, **software/bind-9.1.3**, the following command would be used:

```
$  rsync -avz jose@192.168.0.11:~/rsync/tank/software/bind-9.1.3 \
   ~/software
receiving file list ... done
bind-9.1.3/
bind-9.1.3/bin/
bind-9.1.3/bin/check/
 omitted
wrote 30288 bytes  read 28703896 bytes  88549.10 bytes/sec
total size is 97056215  speedup is 3.38
```

This would bring the subdirectory **software/bind-9.1.3** to the software directory (**/software**) on the local machine. Notice the lack of the trailing slash on the source location. With the trailing slash the contents of the directory are copied but the structure of the directory is not honored. This is an important distinction to remember, although a bit counterintuitive.

For more documentation on *rsync*, see the manual page once the tool is installed. It includes several real-world examples of setups and arguments to the tool for backup and file distribution strategies.

Chapter 16

Housekeeping

16.1 What Is Housekeeping?

UNIX systems tend to generate a lot of data when they run, all of which must be managed. Such data include temporary files, changes to the filesystem that require updates to file content databases, and much more. This chapter covers the built-in housekeeping performed by the system, which includes daily and weekly scripts, as well as logfile rotation duties. Also, the schedulers *cron* and *at* are discussed; they can be used to schedule additional activities.

16.2 Regular System Scripts

OpenBSD systems run scripts on daily, weekly, and monthly bases to do some general health checks and clean up after themselves. These scripts are scheduled through *cron* and mail sent to root upon completion.

16.2.1 Daily Checks

The first check that is run is the **/etc/daily** script. It is run at 1:30 in the morning every day. The script performs the following tasks:

- If there is an **/etc/daily.local** script, run it. This is where local housekeeping duties are performed. Note that this script runs before any of the system duties are handled.
- Clean up files in **/tmp, /var/tmp, /var/preserve**, and **/var/rwho**; core dumps; and system messages in **/var/msgs** that are older than three weeks.
- Clean up NNTP expirations using **/etc/news.expire**.
- Clean up process accounting logs in **/var/account/*** and process accounting information.

- Back up the root filesystem if *ROOTBACKUP* is set to *1.*
- Report on drive space usage.
- Show the last system dumps (backups) using *dump W.*
- Display the system's mail queue.
- Report on interface settings using *netstat.*
- If the *rwho* tools are in use, provide a list of users, along with remote system uptime information.
- Send reminders using the *calendar* facility if *CALENDAR* is set to *1.*
- If the environmental variable *CHECKFILESYSTEMS* is set to *1,* check the system disks using *fsck -n.*
- If the *rdist* facility is in use with the file **/etc/Distfile,** back up system files using *rdist -f /etc/Distfile.*

The **/etc/daily** script then calls another lengthy security script, **/etc/security,** which does the following:

- The integrity of the file **/etc/master.passwd** is verified.
- A backup of **/etc/master.passwd** is made to **/var/backups.**
- The syntax of the file **/etc/group** is verified.
- Root's **umask** is checked for group or other writable settings, as is root's *PATH.*
- The security of the FTP daemon is checked in the file **/etc/ftpusers.**
- The security of the **/etc/mail/aliases** file is checked.
- The existence of **.rhosts** and **.shosts** file is confirmed.
- The security of home directories and mailboxes is verified, as well as some files in their directories.
- NFS exports are checked for basic security.
- The **setuid** and **setgid** files are verified for basic security and integrity.
- The itemSystem block devices are checked for group or world writability or changes.
- A basic *mtree* check is done on the system.
- File backups are listed.

The output is mailed to the root address at the local system, which can be set in the aliases database as described in Chapter 17.

The daily routine is a perfect place to do an incremental backup of the system. Simply keep a tape or other storage device ready and, when the process is begun, a backup of the system is made.

16.2.2 Weekly Checks

The system runs the weekly check script, **/etc/weekly**, every Saturday at 3:30 in the morning. The script performs the following actions:

- If the script **/etc/weekly.local** exists, execute it. This allows for local weekly activities to be scheduled.
- Rebuild the database for the *locate* command.
- Rebuild the *whatis* database used by the manual subsystem.

The local weekly check script is an ideal place to do full system backups. Because the jobs run at relatively idle times on a typical system, they should not interfere with normal operations.

16.2.3 Monthly Checks

The system runs its monthly check script, **/etc/monthly**, on the first day of every month at 5:30 in the morning. This script simply runs the **/etc/monthly.local** script if it exists. In this script you can insert commands for the local system to run.

16.3 Logfile Rotation

One of the main problems that would occur if a system was left running without house-keeping in place would be the massive growth of logfiles. OpenBSD deals with this problem by using *newsyslog*. Based on the configuration of the **/etc/newsyslog.conf** file, this program will take a logfile, archive it, and delete the contents of the original logfile. The new archive file's name will be the original filename followed by a number, up to the maximum number specified in the configuration.

```
# logfilename          owner:group      mode ngen size time [ZB]
/var/cron/log          root:wheel       600  3    10   *    Z
/var/log/aculog        uucp:dialer      660  7    *    24   Z
/var/log/authlog       root:wheel       640  7    *    168  Z
/var/log/daemon                         640  5    30   *    Z
```

```
/var/log/lpd-errs                        640  7   10   *    Z
/var/log/maillog                         600  7   *    24   Z
...
...
```

These lines in the configuration file show us which files to process and how to process each file.

The first field gives the name of the file to be processed. The second field identifies the owner and group of the new archive file. The third field lists the permission setting of the new archive file. The count, the fourth field, specifies how many archive logs to keep. The fifth field tells *newsyslog* to archive a logfile when its size reaches this limit number. For example, the **/var/log/daemon** file is archived when it reaches 30K in size. If the size is an asterisk ("*"), the file isn't rotated based on size, but rather on time, the next field. In this example, the **/var/log/maillog** file is archived every 24 hours. The last field shown here holds flags. The most common one used is Z, which tells *newsyslog* to compress the file.

The *newsyslog* command will send an HUP signal to the program that generates the log. This signal is commonly used to reinitialize a program. However, not all programs will treat the HUP signal in this way, so alternative signals may be specified. Proper care must be taken to ensure that the new logfiles are found and attached to; otherwise, logging will cease for the affected program.

More options for this command are documented on the *newsyslog(8)* manual page.

16.4 Scheduling Facilities

UNIX systems and OpenBSD come with two main execution scheduling facilities. The first, *cron*, is intended for actions that need to be performed at regular times. Examples would include nightly backups or housekeeping duties (the subject of this chapter). The second facility, the *at* system, is intended for one-time scheduling.

Each system maintains a separate scheduling facility for each user. This allows actions to be performed in the context of one level of a user as opposed to another. You can control access to these facilities to enhance system security—for example, allowing only trusted users to perform actions.

16.4.1 The *cron* System

The *cron* system is used to schedule routine and recurring tasks. Most of the time *cron* is used by system administrators, but regular user accounts can also schedule jobs for themselves. Jobs can be scheduled at specific times and dates, and can be repeated as necessary.

Access to the *cron* system is controlled via two configuration files: **/var/cron/allow** and **/var/cron/deny**. The two files have somewhat different default behaviors. If the file **/var/cron/allow** exists, to use *cron* a user's name must appear in that file, with the default action being to deny access to *cron*. The file **/var/cron/deny**, in contrast, specifies only users who *cannot* use the *cron* system. If a user's name appears on that list, then the use of *cron* is prohibited; if the name is absent, then the user is allowed to use the *cron* facility.

Files are stored for each user independently and can be viewed or edited only by the owner of the files. The per-user files are stored in **/var/cron/tabs**. Only root can see and edit all the files.

While a *crontab* for a user can be viewed by editing the file in **/var/cron**, the proper way is to use the *crontab -l* command. This will display all tasks for the user running the command. Only the root user can specify a user's *crontab* to view:

```
#  crontab -u bpalmer -l
```

Note that regular users can view only their own *crontab* files.

Even though a *crontab* file could be edited by hand, any errors in the file will cause problems for *cron* and break all scheduled jobs. To edit the files, use the *crontab -e* command. It will run whatever program you have set in the *EDITOR* or *VISUAL* variable. Although some other systems default the editor to be *ed*, OpenBSD defaults to *vi*. Other editors can be installed from the third-party ports and packages system.

On root's *crontab*, the following information is seen:

```
# rotate log files every hour, if necessary
0       *       *       *       *         /usr/bin/newsyslog
```

The first line is a comment; in fact, any line that starts with the **#** character is a comment. The next line is the command. The first five parameters specify the time and date on which to run commands:

- *minute*   Minute of the hour (0–59)
- *hour*   Hour of the day in military notation (0–23)
- *mday*   Numerical day of the month (1–31)
- *month*   Month (1–12)
- *wday*   Day of the week (0–7 where 0 and 7 are Sunday)

The remainder of the line (the sixth field) gives the command to run with any optional arguments. Commands are passed to the */bin/sh* shell for processing, allowing simple shell scripts to be listed in this file.

In the preceding example, the *newsyslog* command is scheduled to be run on minute 0 of every hour, of every day, of every month, on any day of the week.

The *cron* system also allows you to specify different patterns. To specify a program to run every 20 minutes, we could use either of the following commands:

```
0,20,40   *   *   *   *   /bin/program
*/20   *   *   *   *   /bin/program
```

Which one is used depends on the particular situation at hand.

If the *MAILTO* variable is set in the *crontab* file, the user specified is mailed with the results of the command when it is run. If the variable is not specified, then the owner of the crontab is mailed with the output.

16.4.2   *at*

The *at* command is a resource used to schedule one-time jobs for execution (although the jobs can cleverly reschedule themselves by calling *at* as they end). Using this system, nonperiodic command execution can be performed by the system administrator or regular users. This method is useful for mundane things such as appointment reminders, or important tasks such as critical system backups.

Using the *at* command is relatively easy. First you to set the time and then the command to execute:

```
$  at -t 200306022127
 echo hi!
^D
commands will be executed using /bin/ksh
job 1054603620.c at Mon Jun  2 21:27:00 2003
```

At this point, the *at* command will create a script that mimics the current environment of the shell, including the working directory. The commands fed to the *at* command are processed using the system's shell *sh* by default. An *at* job viewed with the command *at -c username* would look like the following:

```
$  at -c jose
#!/bin/sh
# atrun uid=1000 gid=1000
# mail                          jose 0
umask 22
```

```
PATH=/home/jose/bin:/bin:/sbin:/usr/bin:/usr/sbin:/usr/local/bin:
 /usr/local/sbin:/usr/games:/usr/X11R6/bin:.; export PATH
CVSROOT=jose@192.168.0.11:/home/jose/cvs; export CVSROOT
USER=jose; export USER
HOME=/home/jose; export HOME
XAUTHORITY=/home/jose/.Xauthority; export XAUTHORITY
WINDOWID=10485774; export WINDOWID
CVS_RSH=/usr/bin/ssh; export CVS_RSH
LOGNAME=jose; export LOGNAME
cd /home/jose/ ||
        echo 'Execution directory inaccessible' >&2
        exit 1


/bin/ksh << '_END_OF_AT_JOB'
echo "hello jose"


_END_OF_AT_JOB
```

This script is run by a simple shell, allowing for a complex environment to be established in the shell that launches the job, including the path and any shell variables. The X11 environment, in contrast, is not propagated automatically, meaning that processes will fail to open the display. The above job has its output captured and sent via e-mail to the user's account:

```
From jose@tank Mon Jun  2 21:31:01 2003
From: jose@tank (Atrun Service)
To: jose@tank
Subject: Output from "at" job

Your "at" job on tank
"/var/cron/atjobs/1054603860.c"

produced the following output:

hello jose
```

Now all standard out and error output from the job will be captured and e-mailed. As a consequence, the *at* facility works best for background jobs.

Jobs can be viewed by any user via the command *at -c username*; the superuser can view the jobs of any user. The queue of submitted jobs can be viewed using the *atq* command:

```
$ atq
  Rank    Execution Date    Owner        Job        Queue
  1st   Jun  2, 2003 21:41   jose      1054604460.c   c
```

On larger systems where many users use the *at* queue, a user name may be specified to limit the view of the queue.

To remove jobs from the queue, use the *atrm* command. A user may remove any or all of his or her jobs by job ID (such as 1054604460.c in the preceding *atq* example). Users can remove all of their jobs by specifying the command *atrm -a* or *atrm username*.

```
$ atrm jose
1054604700.c removed
1054604760.c removed
```

Only the superuser may remove others' *at* jobs from the queue. Jobs are stored in the directory **/var/cron/atjobs** until their completion.

16.4.3 Controlling Execution of *at* Jobs

The file **/var/cron/at.allow** lists those users who are allowed to execute jobs using the *at* facility. Only users who are specified here are allowed to use *at*. If this file doesn't exist, only the file **/var/cron/at.deny** is checked, and any users who are not listed there can run *at*.

This control strategy may be desirable for those administrators who do not trust their user base, such as for shell machines at ISP. The *at* tool is sometimes used to abuse systems or to ensure that a backdoor is present. If you are unsure of your setup, it may be wise to control execution by the *at* facility.

Furthermore, *at* jobs may be submitted using the *batch* facility, which will attempt to delay the execution of jobs until a lull in system activity occurs. If a job is submitted using the command *at -b*, the batch facility will be used. This is especially helpful on busy systems where the submission of a time- and resource-consuming job could negatively affect performance.

## Chapter 17

Mail Server Operations

17.1 Introduction to Electronic Mail

Electronic mail operates on a few basic principles, similar to the TCP/IP networking stack. It combines the DNS system with various protocols, including SMTP, POP, and IMAP (typically), to send and receive mail from the desktop to the recipient's desktop.

DNS operations for electronic mail rely primarily on the MX record for a domain or subdomain. Unlike the A record, the MX record covers a group of host names as their primary mail server. This is because not all hosts in the database that have A records can receive mail; instead, they rely on a central mail server. For example, while the host *tank.crimelabs.net* exists, it does not receive mail. Instead, the domain *crimelabs.net* has an MX record that points to its mail server:

```
crimelabs.net.        600     IN      MX      5 mail.crimelabs.net.
crimelabs.net.        600     IN      MX      10 mail2.crimelabs.net.
```

Additionally, MX records have a preference number associated with them. This allows for multiple MX hosts to be established for a network, with each one being tried in turn should any of them fail. MX records with the same preference value will operate in a round-robin fashion.

Electronic mail routing employs a series of lookups. The first operation looks for the MX record of the recipient's domain and contacts the mail servers specified in that entry. If this attempt fails, the A record for the host will be used. The second lookup occurs on the receiving server, where the username is tested for validity. If it is valid, it is routed to. This username can be an alias, a list of addresses, or even a default address. Once it is looked up, mail is delivered to the mailbox (or mailboxes) specified.

Mail software consists of three major parts. The mail transfer agent (MTA) is the server component that speaks the SMTP protocol to another MTA system, typically a remote system. The mail user agent (MUA) is the piece of software that the user uses on his or her system to read and send mail. The mail delivery agent (MDA) is the component that transfers the mail from the MTA to the user's mailbox.

OpenBSD uses two pieces of software to run all three pieces. The *sendmail* program acts as the MTA and MDA component. (The MUA component defaults to the *mail* command, a simple command-line mail reader and composition tool.) The second component is installed by default—*popa3d*, a POP3 daemon. It is used for desktop clients to fetch and receive their mail using the POP3 protocol.

17.2 Overview of Electronic Mail in OpenBSD

OpenBSD uses a transparent system to handle the actual mail server software. This setup allows for a transparent replacement of any or all of the components for migrating to a different mail server system.

All mail operations are transparently handled by the *mailwrapper* command, which is linked to the binaries by name. This approach allows a single program to pass the arguments to the correct binary. In the default case, *mailwrapper* acts as a link between the command */usr/sbin/sendmail* and the actual binary */usr/libexec/sendmail/sendmail*:

```
lrwxr-xr-x  1 root  wheel  21 Feb 23 15:06 /usr/sbin/sendmail ->
    /usr/sbin/mailwrapper
```

These mappings are controlled by the file **/etc/mailer.conf**, which establishes pairings between commands and the actual binaries used to run them:

```
sendmail        /usr/libexec/sendmail/sendmail
send-mail       /usr/libexec/sendmail/sendmail
mailq           /usr/libexec/sendmail/sendmail
```

When *mailwrapper* is invoked as *mailq*, it transparently calls the real *sendmail* binary.

The strength of this approach becomes apparent in the ports system. This relationship determines how the system handles a migration to a different MTA, such as Exim, Postfix, or the like. New binaries are installed but the old *sendmail* aliases are preserved via this mapping. The new aliases point to the new binary locations and translate options as needed. Thus software that has hard-coded calls to *sendmail* can continue to operate smoothly.

17.3 *sendmail*

Most people are shocked when they first learn that OpenBSD has *sendmail* running by default. Although *sendmail* has had many problems in the past, it has gotten much better in recent years. By default, *sendmail* runs in sending-only mode; the settings need to be changed to allow the system to receive mail. In the **/etc/rc.conf** file, the default *sendmail* setting is *-q30m*. If you wanted the machine to also receive mail, you would change the setting to *-bd -q30m*. The *-bd* option causes *sendmail* to begin listening as a background daemon process and to continue to flush its queue every 30 minutes.

Configuration for *sendmail* is done in the **/etc/mail/sendmail.cf** file. The **.cf** files are well known to be nasty for normal people to configure but making simple changes in these files can be done without too much difficulty. If the *sendmail* installation is complicated, the use of *m4* helps to generate the **.cf** files. More information can be found at the **http://www.sendmail.org** Web site.

The *sendmail* configuration file, **sendmail.cf**, is built from a much simpler file with the suffix **.mc**. In the directory **/usr/share/sendmail/cf**, various example **.mc** files are provided. Many of these come from the *sendmail* distribution itself, but others are specific to the OpenBSD system. These can be edited to suit local values and used as templates. To process an **.mc** file into a **.cf** file, simply update the file and run *make* in this directory. Editing and storing the configuration file in this way helps to increase the readability and portability of the configuration file, thereby making your sendmail installation easier to maintain over its lifetime.

For most people, four main changes need to be made to the **.cf** file. The first is to set the domain names served by the machine. The second is to set who is allowed to relay mail through the server. Setting up the machine's name and setting up smart hosts are the last two changes. After making any changes to the configuration file, *sendmail* must be restarted.

- *The host can be set up to receive mail for* particular users. In the **sendmail.cf** file, the *Cw* setting is used for this purpose. By default, it will accept mail only for the local hostname. If we wanted to add an additional name, such as **mail.crimelabs.net**, we would add the following line:

```
Cwmail.crimelabs.net
```

As many of these lines as needed can be added to the configuration file.

- *By default, the mail server will allow mail to be sent only if it matches one of the two following conditions:* If the mail is from anywhere to a user on the machine or if the mail is from the machine to anyone. If a remote host tries to send mail to another remote host using the mail server, this operation is considered relaying and is denied. For a mail server to be useful, however, we need to specify other hosts that are allowed to send mail through it. This is done by adding entries to the **/etc/mail/relay-domains** file. If we wanted any host in our network to send mail, we would simply put the host in the file (which does not exist by default and needs to be created first):

```
192.168.1.0
```

Additional IP addresses and networks can be added, one per line.

- *It is often desirable to change what* sendmail *thinks is the name of the server.* Most of the time, this is done by changing the SMTP header that the server gives out when people connect to it. The system also can rewrite the envelope of the message to make it appear to come from somewhere else (to allow for smarter mail routing). This can be done with the *Dj* setting:

```
Djmail.crimelabs.net
```

- *Most hosts in a network don't need to run full-fledged mail servers.* A smarter idea is to relay mail to another server on the network intended just for mail. This can be done my using the *DS* setting. If we wanted to send all mail to a machine named **mailgw.crimelabs.net**, for example, we would use the following:

```
DSmailgw.crimelabs.net
```

All mail to be delivered that isn't local will then be sent to this smart host.

There are many other settings for *sendmail*. Good configuration information can be found at **http://www.sendmail.org**. The Sendmail FAQ (at **http://www.sendmail.org/faq/**) is especially useful.

One simple task that needs to be done on any OpenBSD system is to configure where mail for root goes. This is done by editing the **/etc/mail/aliases** file. It has a very simple format:

```
bin:    root
```

The first column is the account name, followed by a colon. The second column indicates where mail for the account should be sent. This example sends all mail for *bin* to *root*.

Note that the first account doesn't have to exist to be able to receive mail—only the second account.

```
# root:
```

By default, mail for the root account doesn't go anywhere. This destination needs to be set if you wish to receive the mail that the system sends every night.

```
root:    bpalmer@crimelabs.net, rootmail@crimelabs.net
```

Here, all mail from root on the author's system is mailed to his account and to a second account to be archived. After any changes to the **aliases** file are made, the command *newaliases* needs to be run (as root) to build the **.db** file that *sendmail* expects to read.

17.4 Virtual Hosting

The *sendmail* server can also act as a virtual server for various additional domains that do not share its native hostname. This operation is similar to virtual hosting under Apache. It can be useful for an ISP or similar hosting architecture, or if your domain has multiple domain names (such as the **.com, .org,** and **.net** instances).

Virtual hosting is done by adding a feature to the **.mc** file for your *sendmail* configuration. These files hold the source code of the **.cf** configuration files for *sendmail*. To add this feature, a line like the following is used:

```
FEATURE('virtusertable', 'dbm /etc/mail/virtusertable')dnl
```

This is already done for you in several prototype configuration source files found in the directory **/usr/share/sendmail/cf**. The example files **courtesan.mc**, **openbsd-bulk.mc**, **openbsd-lists.mc**, and **knecht.mc** all have the *virtusertable* option built in (among others). You can edit these files for your needs, run *make* in this directory, and generate a configuration file to use for your *sendmail* server.

Once you have done that, you can create the file **/etc/mail/virtusertable.txt**. This file contains the mappings between the virtual domains and usernames you wish to host on the left-hand side and the real mail addresses on the right-hand side.

```
jose@example-domain.com      jose
bpalmer@mydomain.com         bpalmer@crimelabs.com
@mydomain.com                jose@crimelabs.com
@example-domain.com          error: no such user
```

Only one entry can be used on the right-hand side, so you must use the **aliases** file if you want to expand one address into multiple addresses. Notice that the third entry acts as a catch-all for the domain *mydomain.com*, routing all mail to *jose@crimelabs.com*. The fourth entry catches all remaining entries in *example-domain.com* and generates an error.

Once this file is built, you need to create the actual map in the file **/etc/mail/virtusertable**. This is done with the command *makemap dbm /etc/mail/virtusertable < virtusertable.txt*, which creates a Berkeley-style database from the text file you created.

Next, make sure that the configuration file **/etc/mail/sendmail.cf** has the domains configured in the *Cw* (or *Fw*) directive to tell the server for which entity it is hosting mail:

```
Cw localhost mail.crimelabs.net mail.example-domain.com
```

Finally, you need to tell *sendmail* to reread its configuration process. This is done by sending a HUP signal to the process, via the command *kill -HUP sendmail process*. You will not need to take this step when you edit the virtual user table—only if you edit the mail configuration file again.

17.5 Security with STARTTLS

The *sendmail* service installed by OpenBSD supports encryption and authentication using TLS via the STARTTLS facility by default (see RFC 2487). Using this feature, your *sendmail* server can provide authentication (or remote servers or SMTP clients, such as mobile users), confidentiality, and integrity assurance. The default configuration file does not support STARTTLS directly, but can be adjusted to do so via a few key steps.

The first steps are to create the PEM-encoded certificates for the server. We will be storing these in the directory **/etc/mail/certs**. Next, we will generate a 1024-bit DSA key pair:

```
#  openssl dsaparam 1024 -out dsa1024.pem
#  openssl req -x509 -nodes -days 365 -newkey dsa:dsa1024.pem
  -out /etc/mail/certs/mycert.pem -keyout /etc/mail/certs/mykey.pem
#  rm dsa1024.pem
```

Two options are important on the second command line. The first option is the lifetime of the key, specified in days. The command above will create a key valid for one year, but longer (or shorter) keys can be used as well. The second option is *-nodes*, which tells the *openssl* command to not encrypt the key. If the key is encrypted, the server cannot begin using it as there is nowhere to enter a password at start-up.

Next, we want to clear the bits that allow others to view this directory:

```
# chmod -R go-rwx /etc/mail/certs
```

The keys must be kept from others' eyes.

Now a *sendmail* configuration file must be generated that can utilize these keys. An example configuration appears in the file **knecht.mc**. The following options will tell the *sendmail* configuration file to point the server at the new keys we have generated:

```
define('CERT_DIR',         'MAIL_SETTINGS_DIR''certs')
define('confCACERT_PATH', 'CERT_DIR')
define('confCACERT',       'CERT_DIR/CAcert.pem')
define('confSERVER_CERT', 'CERT_DIR/mycert.pem')
define('confSERVER_KEY',  'CERT_DIR/mykey.pem')
define('confCLIENT_CERT', 'CERT_DIR/mycert.pem')
define('confCLIENT_KEY',  'CERT_DIR/mykey.pem')
```

Next, rebuild the **.cf** file from the **.mc** file and install it as the configuration file in **/etc/mail**. Restarting the *sendmail* process will cause it to reload this configuration file.

The *sendmail* server can now access the file **/etc/mail/access** for instructions on how to use the STARTTLS option for SMTP transactions. Two options are used: *VERIFY* and *ENCR*. The *VERIFY* option mandates that the host must verify itself to the local *sendmail* server:

```
client.crimelabs.net     VERIFY:80
```

This line specifies that the system must verify to at least 80 bits of encryption. By prepending the term *TLS_Clt*, this restriction can be forced for TLS clients and not servers. To force a minimum amount of encryption to be used, a configuration line like the following would be used:

```
mail.crimelabs.net       ENCR
```

This will force encrypted communications (at a minimum bit length to which both servers agree) between the local server and the indicated server.

Additional documentation appears in the manual page *starttls(8)*.

17.6 Upgrading

While many people will happily continue to use the OpenBSD *sendmail* server, others will want to replace this software. Two major systems are available in the ports and packages system, and a third is available outside of the official system. The installation and configuration of these systems will not be discussed here.

The Postfix mail server, a highly modular replacement for *sendmail*, is easily installable via the ports and packages system. Postfix comes in a variety of flavors, including a TLS-enabled version, an LDAP-enabled version, and a MySQL-linked version. It transparently replaces *sendmail* on the system. Many people prefer the Postfix model of security as well as its greater ease of configuration relative to *sendmail* making it popular.

The Exim mail server, also available via ports and packages, provides another simple and easy-to-use mail server. The version available in OpenBSD offers various flavors, including an LDAP-linked version, one linked against the MySQL or PostgreSQL database, and a TLS-enabled version. Like Postfix, Exim is a transparent replacement for *sendmail* that works via the **mailer.conf** system.

Another mail system is Qmail, which resembles Postfix in its modularity and rivals its popularity among security-conscious mail server administrators. Note, however, that it has been removed from the ports and packages system due to licensing issues. Several other unofficial ports and packages are maintained by users of the system, but can be built without issue on an OpenBSD system.

17.7 POP Server Administration

The *popa3d* daemon provides POP3 services for native OpenBSD systems. It is a secure implementation of the POP3 protocol, which itself is insecure. Both the authentication credentials (username and password) and the mail messages are transferred between the server and the client in plain text.

The *popa3d* system can be run in two ways: from *inetd* or as a stand-alone daemon. It is not started by default. To run it from the *inetd* superserver, edit the file **/etc/inetd.conf** by adding this line:

```
pop3 stream tcp nowait root /usr/sbin/popa3d popa3d
```

After the system is restarted or a HUP signal is sent to the *inetd* process, the *popa3d* server will listen on TCP port 110. To enable security checks with the TCP wrappers system, the following line is used:

```
pop3 stream tcp nowait root /usr/libexec/tcpd /usr/sbin/popa3d
```

Now *popa3d* can use the TCP wrappers control files to provide access control to the daemon.

To start *popa3d* in stand-alone daemon mode, use the command *popa3d -D* as root. The resulting root-owned parent will spawn children for the incoming connections. In this mode the daemon can also access the TCP wrappers control files and limit the connection rate.

With the *popa3d* daemon running, users can use their POP3 client software systems to retrieve their mail from an OpenBSD mail server.

17.8 IMAP Server Administration

While the base OpenBSD system comes with a ready-to-use POP3 server, the ports and packages system also provides IMAP server software. The major classes of IMAP systems were developed by Courier and the University of Washington (UW). The Courier package supports a number of back-end systems, including, LDAP and various SQL databases, but can be more difficult to set up. UW's IMAP tools have a notorious security track record and are sometimes frowned upon by administrators.

Both IMAP systems are easily installed from the third-party packages system and are not covered here.

17.9 Mailing List Software

OpenBSD can act as an efficient and simple-to-configure mailing list server. This feature is useful for groups of users who want to join a list for discussions or announcements. Static lists can be built by using the **aliases** file, whereas dynamic lists can be run using third-party packages.

The *majordomo* and *mailman* packages, available for OpenBSD systems via the ports tree or as precompiled packages, provide dynamic mailing lists. Their installation is simple and not covered here. Each package has its own merits and drawbacks, but both are popular to a similar degree. The *mailman* package has a Web interface and can tie into the Postfix system natively; *majordomo* works just as well with Postfix.

17.10 E-mail Security

Electronic mail conveys many organizations' biggest secrets, or even personal information. Typical SMTP transactions are carried out in plain text, meaning that anyone who can observe the connection can read the data without any difficulty. Additionally, the system relies on DNS verification, which is easy to forge. Lastly, spammers and various mail-based attacks can take advantage of poorly configured servers to cause havoc and eventually disable your server.

17.10.1 MTA Security

By far, the biggest threat to any mail server is a misconfiguration that renders it an open relay. Mail relaying entails the use of a mail server to relay a message to another server. Typically, this process is tightly controlled and occurs only for authorized systems. In an open relay, however, the system will resend mail for anyone, regardless of that entity's address or connection status. This ability obviously represents a potential tool for a spammer or someone carrying out a mail-based attack, such as injecting viruses into a system. Care should be taken to ensure that the system is relaying mail only for the network that it is intended to serve and no others. A variety of systems on the Internet will assist you in testing your server for conformance to this configuration policy. Several others will list your server's address and assist others in rejecting mail traffic from you if your system is thought to be carrying spam.

Another common threat to an organization posed by the MTA system relates to information leaks. Because mail servers must validate an account before they can accept mail, they can potentially be used to enumerate accounts. This vulnerability can be exploited by an attacker to mine your network for information.

Lastly, because a mail server is exposed to the outside Internet, it can become a target for an attacker who seeks to gain entry to your network. For this reason, it is important to ensure that your installation has up-to-date patches and is reasonably well configured.

17.10.2 POP Security

OpenBSD includes a POP3 server in its base system via *popa3d*, but the POP3 protocol itself is insecure. That is, it exposes all username and password information in clear text, as well as all messages. Stronger authentication measures, such as APOP and KPOP (Kerberized POP), can be used to defend against password theft, but they still transmit mail in the clear.

POP (or IMAP) over SSL is the preferred method of securing a POP server. Not all clients support this method for communications, but for sites that use compliant clients it is the best method to secure a POP server. Using the *stunnel* tool (available in the ports and packages system), the *popa3d* daemon can be wrapped in SSL without any modification of the binary itself.

17.10.3 Message Security

Messages themselves are not secure if they can be stolen from the mail spool or even the client machine. Encrypted mail, via PGP or S/MIME, is the best solution to this problem. GnuPG, the older MIT version of PGP (2.6), and the NAI version of PGP (PGP 5) are all available in the ports and packages system. These tools can be used to encrypt and authenticate messages between recipients, but have difficulty in scaling to large networks that lack a common key distribution center.

Chapter 18

The Domain Name Services

18.1 Introduction to DNS

DNS is the lifeblood of the Internet. It converts hostnames (such as *tank.crimelabs.net*) to IP addresses, suitable for use by machines. This conversion is accomplished via a name server. This server runs software that listens for requests on TCP and UDP port 53 and sends the appropriate reply.

Queries come in a simple format, with a particular type of query asking for a piece of information. Several forms of records exist. The major types are A records, which map hostnames to IP addresses; NS records, which identify a domain's nameserver; PTR records, which convert IP addresses to hostnames (the opposite of A records); CNAME entries, which are aliases to hostnames; and MX records, which provide information about the mail exchange host for a domain.

The default server software that runs on an OpenBSD name server is *named*, which is part of the BIND package. It also includes several auxiliary components, such as a resolver library (which enables applications to access DNS data) and client tools like the *nslookup, dig,* and *host* commands.

This chapter explains how to set up a primary server and a caching-only name server using BIND 9.2.2 from the base OpenBSD 3.3 installation.

18.2 Configuring the Resolver

The base resolver, which is used via library routines in the system, is configured by the **/etc/resolv.conf** file. A simple file will state the domain to search and up to three nameservers to contact:

```
search crimelabs.net
nameserver 10.10.10.23
```

227

```
nameserver 12.100.16.98
nameserver 144.228.255.10
```

The system will attempt to contact these DNS servers for replies in order. If no fully qualified domain name is provided, the domain "crimelabs.net" will be searched. The *search* keyword is similar to the *domain* keyword in the **resolv.conf** file, which specifies one or more domain names to try. The *domain* keyword provides a default domain name for non–fully qualified hostnames to resolve.

A commonly used line specifies the order in which to attempt name resolution. The *lookup* directive can specify the order in which to search for answers for resolving hostnames:

```
lookup file bind
```

This configuration will first attempt to find an answer in the file **/etc/hosts** before trying the nameservers listed. In the absence of this directive, the default order is "bind file."

18.3   The DNS Server *named*

OpenBSD ships with the BIND DNS server, *named* version 9.2.2, which was installed as of release 3.3. The version in OpenBSD has been audited, so it has some patches beyond the base ISC BIND-9.2.2 package.

The *named* service expects to find its configuration file in **/var/named/etc/named.conf**. Note that *named* is the binary file for BIND. Some people may wish to use BIND8 for their own reasons; this server works with OpenBSD and is available from the ports tree. Also, some ports applications require pieces of BIND9 that are not installed in the base system, but that are available in the ports tree.

A DNS server can serve three functions:

- Primary server for a zone
- Secondary server for a zone
- Forwarding server (all other zones)

A primary server is authoritative for its DNS zone, which consists of one or more domain names. Edits to this zone file will propagate to all other DNS servers. Secondary servers read the information from the primary server when it changes and update their tables accordingly. Forwarding servers merely proxy DNS requests and cache the information they receive. They must consult other servers for information they do not have.

The first file that we need to look at when setting up DNS is **/var/named/etc/ named.conf**. It tells the server where the zone files live, what primary zones exist, what secondary zones exist, and what forwarding it will do. Because *named* normally relocates its root directory in **/var/named**, all paths are specified relative to this path. Thus the configuration file that *named* sees is **/etc/named.conf**.

Here is a sample configuration file, specifying how to handle a primary network, a secondary network, and caching options:[1]

```
acl clients {
        localnets;
};

options {
        version ""; // remove this to allow version queries
        allow-recursion { clients; };
};

zone "." {
        type hint;
        file "standard/root.hint";
};

zone "localhost" {
        type master;
        file "standard/localhost";
        allow-transfer { localhost; };
};

zone "127.in-addr.arpa" {
        type master;
        file "standard/loopback";
        allow-transfer { localhost; };
};

zone "0.0.0.0.0.0.0.0.0.0.0.0.0.0.0.0.0.0.0.0.0.0.0.0.0.0.0.0.0.\
   0.0.0.ip6.arpa" {
```

---

[1]For printing, the *zone* lines of the reverse IPv6 zones had to be broken over two lines.

```
            type master;
            file "standard/loopback6.arpa";
            allow-transfer { localhost; };
};

zone "0.0.0.0.0.0.0.0.0.0.0.0.0.0.0.0.0.0.0.0.0.0.0.0.0.0.0.0.0.0.\
    0.0.0.ip6.int" {
            type master;
            file "standard/loopback6.int";
            allow-transfer { localhost; };
};

acl crimelabs-slaves {
            ns.qsec.com;
};

zone "crimelabs.net" {
            type master;
            file "master/crimelabs.net";
            allow-transfer { localhost; crimelabs-slaves; };
};

zone "1.168.192.in-addr.arpa" {
            type master;
            file "master/1.168.192-rev";
            allow-transfer { localhost; };
};

zone "crimelabs.com" {
            type slave;
            file "slave/crimelabs.com";
            masters { 192.168.1.2; };
};
```

This example shows the default configuration file installed on OpenBSD, plus a few Crimelabs.com-specific additions.

The first group, *acl*, defines a *clients* ACL that includes local networks—namely, any IPv4 networks for which the system has an interface. The *options* sets global options for all other zones. The *zone "."* tells the DNS server that if it doesn't know the answer to ask the root servers (listed in the **root.hint** file). We then have six primary zones. The second, third, fourth, and sixth primary zones are for the reverse DNS lookup. The names of the zones are reversed (i.e., 192.168.1.0/24 becomes 1.168.192.in-addr.arpa for IPv4, and 0:0:0:0:0:0:0:0 becomes 0.0.0.0....ip6.arpa for ipv6) and have the additional *arpa* suffix added. The details of the **ip6.int** versus **ip6.arpa** battle are outside the scope of this book; suffice it to say that one should serve data for both and expect **ip6.int** to go away in the short term. OpenBSD's *libc* resolver routines search first for **ip6.arpa**, then for **ip6.int**, when reverse-resolving an IPv6 IP address.

The names for the files containing the zone information are completely arbitrary, but the following format is followed by most: Reverse zones are the reverse IP of the zone and can be placed in the **master** directory and typically end in *-rev*. Secondary zones are placed in the **slave** directory. The secondary zone serves the **crimelabs.com** domain from the server 192.168.1.2 and saves the information in **slave/crimelabs.com**.

18.3.1 A Simple Caching-Only Nameserver

A very simple nameserver merely makes queries on behalf of its clients and is not authoritative for any networks (aside from its own localhost entry). The file below applies to such a caching-only DNS server. It will receive queries from clients and, if it has the response, will send back the proper reply. If it doesn't have the information, the server will fetch the data from the right location and store the data after making a reply.

The file is very simple, with the only addition being a local ACL for the internal network it serves:

```
acl "internal" {10.10.0.0/16; };
options {
        pid-file "named.pid";
        allow-query  "internal"; ;
};


zone "." {
        type hint;
        file "db.cache";
};


zone "0.0.127.in-addr.arpa" {
        type master;
```

```
        file "db.127.0.0";
        allow-update none;;
};
```

The file **db.cache** contains addresses of other nameservers that this DNS server can contact for additional information. A simple way to get this information is to issue a *dig* query for the root nameservers and their associated A records:

```
#  dig @A.ROOT-SERVERS.NET > /var/named/db.cache
```

Now *named* can operate as a caching-only server for the local network, making requests to the root servers when it needs additional information.

18.4 DNS Security Issues

Running a publicly accessible DNS server carries many inherent security risks. While it is audited to a certain degree, the BIND9 installation in OpenBSD is built on an ISC source, which has a long history of security problems. While the server runs as a non-root user and in a chroot() jail, which mitigates the effects of successful attacks, it does not stop all attacks.

Other noteworthy security issues include zone transfers, which would allow an attack full access to both external and internal data, and zone poisoning. Zone poisoning occurs when false information is injected, typically via an update or a reply, causing the name server to poison its information for its clients. This can create an effective denial-of-service attack or a redirection attack. For example, if the information for the Hotmail service were directed at an attacker's site, sensitive information could be obtained.

Both types of attacks are also mitigated in BIND9, through the use of ACL statements and fine-grained zone handling.

18.4.1 Firewall Rules for DNS

It is tempting to think that a simple PF ruleset will provide adequate protection for a DNS server. A ruleset for a DNS-only server may look like the following:

```
block in all
block out all
pass in all quick from any to any inet proto tcp port 53 keep state
pass out all quick from any to any inet proto tcp port 53 keep state
```

```
pass in all quick from any to any inet proto udp port 53 keep state
pass out all quick from any to any inet proto udp port 53 keep state
```

Here we can send and receive DNS requests on TCP and UDP port 53.

In reality, this ruleset will not prevent an attacker from reaching the local network and compromising the local DNS server. Here the ACL statements in the **named.conf** file are especially important. The statement *allow-update*, which controls which systems can send updates to the stored zone files, can help prevent poison updates from being inserted. The *allow-recursion* option can help prevent resource attacks against a DNS server and attacks that require recursive queries. Lastly, the *allow-transfer* option can control which hosts are permitted to perform a zone transfer, which would allow them to have a full view of the DNS information. This command can hide internal data, for example.

BIND9's capabilities for fine-grained ACL support are as good as they have ever been, although the system remains very complex. Interested readers are directed to the BIND9 manual for full information.

18.5 Upgrading *named*

While the BIND9 installation in the base OpenBSD system suits most users, some needs are not met by this installation but can be met by other DNS servers.

18.5.1 BIND8 and BIND9

A full BIND9 port exists that fully supports IPv6 DNS, the security extensions in DNSSec, and much more. This port has been disabled in the base system. DNSSec, for example, can allow for enforced and signed updates to zones and zone transfers, giving even more security to this operation. The full BIND9 port exists in the ports and packages tree, and is installed with a script that enables its use in the base system.

Many users continue to use the older BIND8 codebase due to migration issues. While a port no longer exists in OpenBSD 3.4, BIND8 should build from the base system. ISC provides only marginal support for this release of BIND, and users are encouraged to upgrade from it.

18.5.2 DJBDNS

The DJBDNS system is much like the Qmail system, a highly modular and easy-to-configure DNS server. For this reason, it is popular with many OpenBSD users and site administrators. However, due to licensing issues, the port was removed from the ports system. Unofficial ports of the current codebase can be found at various sites around the Internet, and they should build on a base system without raising too many issues.

Most users of DJBDNS are attracted by its attention to security and modular nature. For these reasons, it is widely considered to be the best alternative to ISC BIND available at this time.

18.6 DNS Tools

As mentioned in the introduction to this chapter, the BIND package includes several client-oriented tools. These are useful for gathering information on the command line or performing diagnostics.

18.6.1 *dig*

The *dig* command is a raw interface to a DNS server that returns records in a format suitable for use in a nameserver. Its major options are @*hostname*, which specifies a nameserver to use (otherwise the default servers in **/etc/resolv.conf** are used); *-t*, which specifies a request type; and the query material itself.

The following example shows the command to get any DNS information about the **openbsd.org** domain from the nameserver **ns.crimelabs.net** and the resulting output:

```
$ dig @ns.crimelabs.net openbsd.org -t any

; <<>> DiG 9.2.2rc1 <<>> @ns.crimelabs.net openbsd.org -t any
;; global options:  printcmd
;; Got answer:
;; ->>HEADER<<- opcode: QUERY, status: NOERROR, id: 61203
;; flags: qr rd ra; QUERY: 1, ANSWER: 9, AUTHORITY: 6, ADDITIONAL: 5

;; QUESTION SECTION:
;openbsd.org.                   IN      ANY

;; ANSWER SECTION:
openbsd.org.            58074   IN      A       199.185.137.3
openbsd.org.            23369   IN      MX      7 openbsd.cs.colorado.edu.
openbsd.org.            23369   IN      MX      10 cvs.openbsd.org.
openbsd.org.            58074   IN      NS      zeus.theos.com.
```

```
openbsd.org.                   58074    IN        NS      cs.colorado.edu.
openbsd.org.                   58074    IN        NS      ns.appli.se.
openbsd.org.                   58074    IN        NS      ns.sigmasoft.com.
openbsd.org.                   58074    IN        NS      cvs.openbsd.org.
openbsd.org.                   58074    IN        NS      citi.umich.edu.

;; AUTHORITY SECTION:
openbsd.org.                   58074    IN        NS      zeus.theos.com.
openbsd.org.                   58074    IN        NS      cs.colorado.edu.
openbsd.org.                   58074    IN        NS      ns.appli.se.
openbsd.org.                   58074    IN        NS      ns.sigmasoft.com.
openbsd.org.                   58074    IN        NS      cvs.openbsd.org.
openbsd.org.                   58074    IN        NS      citi.umich.edu.

;; ADDITIONAL SECTION:
openbsd.cs.colorado.edu. 4825           IN        A       128.138.192.83
cvs.openbsd.org.               144474   IN        A       199.185.137.3
ns.sigmasoft.com.              86400    IN        A       24.172.18.163
citi.umich.edu.                42811    IN        A       141.211.92.141
citi.umich.edu.                42811    IN        A       141.211.133.111

;; Query time: 213 msec
;; SERVER: 3ffe:b00:4004:1::1:0#53(fries.net)
;; WHEN: Tue Feb 25 07:37:03 2003
;; MSG SIZE  rcvd: 401


$
```

This command returns a sizable amount of information, which is useful for debugging the status of a domain's DNS service. This can, of course, be limited to a hostname:

```
$ dig @ns.crimelabs.net www.openbsd.org -t any

; <<>> DiG 9.2.2rc1 <<>> @ns.crimelabs.net www.openbsd.org -t any
;; global options:  printcmd
;; Got answer:
;; ->>HEADER<<- opcode: QUERY, status: NOERROR, id: 15130
;; flags: qr rd ra; QUERY: 1, ANSWER: 1, AUTHORITY: 6, ADDITIONAL: 4
```

```
;; QUESTION SECTION:
;www.openbsd.org.                    IN      ANY

;; ANSWER SECTION:
www.openbsd.org.        15056   IN      A       129.128.5.191

;; AUTHORITY SECTION:
openbsd.org.            58022   IN      NS      citi.umich.edu.
openbsd.org.            58022   IN      NS      zeus.theos.com.
openbsd.org.            58022   IN      NS      cs.colorado.edu.
openbsd.org.            58022   IN      NS      ns.appli.se.
openbsd.org.            58022   IN      NS      ns.sigmasoft.com.
openbsd.org.            58022   IN      NS      cvs.openbsd.org.

;; ADDITIONAL SECTION:
ns.sigmasoft.com.       86400   IN      A       24.172.18.163
cvs.openbsd.org.        144422  IN      A       199.185.137.3
citi.umich.edu.         42759   IN      A       141.211.133.111
citi.umich.edu.         42759   IN      A       141.211.92.141

;; Query time: 40 msec
;; SERVER: 3ffe:b00:4004:1::1:0#53(fries.net)
;; WHEN: Tue Feb 25 07:37:55 2003
;; MSG SIZE  rcvd: 265


$
```

As you can see, *dig* is a powerful but raw command to identify the information stored in a nameserver about a domain or a hostname.

18.6.2 *host*

The *host* command is used to make standard inquiries to name servers. You can look up the information about a hostname to resolve the IP address or work in the reverse, by mapping an address to a hostname. Here is a simple example:

```
$  host www.openbsd.org
www.openbsd.org has address 129.128.5.191
```

```
$  host 128.138.192.83
83.192.138.128.in-addr.arpa domain name pointer
    openbsd.cs.colorado.edu.
$
```

The first query returns the A record of the hostname *www.openbsd.org*. The second query shows the reverse process, mapping an IP address to an address. Notice that the output is different for the two directions. **CNAME records** are also displayed by *host*, resolving both the hostname and then the real **A record** of the hostname:

```
$  host mail.openbsd.org
mail.openbsd.org is an alias for openbsd.cs.colorado.edu.
openbsd.cs.colorado.edu has address 128.138.192.83
```

The *host* command is a succinct and easy-to-use interface for querying for DNS information. As with *dig*, the *host -t* command can be used to specify a query type:

```
$  host -t mx openbsd.org
openbsd.org mail is handled by 10 cvs.openbsd.org.
openbsd.org mail is handled by 7 openbsd.cs.colorado.edu.
```

Here we can see the information about the MX records for the **openbsd.org** domain in a friendly format.

18.6.3 *nslookup*

The *nslookup* command works in much the same way as the *host* command. It can be run either interactively or on a single command line. Again, simple usage is to query a single address in one command:

```
$  nslookup www.openbsd.org
Server:         12.100.16.98
Address:        12.100.16.98#53

Non-authoritative answer:
Name:   www.openbsd.org
Address: 129.128.5.191
```

An optional second argument to *nslookup* specifies the DNS server to use. In the absence of this option, the default nameservers in **/etc/resolv.conf** are used.

```
#  nslookup www.openbsd.org 10.10.10.23
Server:         10.10.10.23
Address:        10.10.10.23#53

Non-authoritative answer:
Name:   www.openbsd.org
Address: 129.128.5.191
```

The *nslookup* command can also be run interactively. When it is used with no arguments, you are dropped to an interactive session, where you can adjust parameters to search for information:

```
$  nslookup
>  www.openbsd.org
Server:  ns.crimelabs.net
Address:  204.181.64.10

Non-authoritative answer:
Name:   www.openbsd.org
Address: 129.128.5.191
```

You can also identify special types of information to return using *nslookup*. Here we look up the information on the mail exchange host for the **openbsd.org** domain:

```
>  set type=mx
>  openbsd.org
Server:  ns.crimelabs.net
Address:  204.181.64.10

Non-authoritative answer:
openbsd.org     mail exchanger = 10 cvs.openbsd.org.
openbsd.org     mail exchanger = 7 openbsd.cs.colorado.edu.

Authoritative answers can be found from:
openbsd.org     nameserver = cs.colorado.edu.
```

```
openbsd.org        nameserver = ns.appli.se.
openbsd.org        nameserver = ns.sigmasoft.com.
openbsd.org        nameserver = cvs.openbsd.org.
openbsd.org        nameserver = citi.umich.edu.
openbsd.org        nameserver = zeus.theos.com.
openbsd.cs.colorado.edu internet address = 128.138.192.83
cvs.openbsd.org internet address = 199.185.137.3
ns.sigmasoft.com        internet address = 24.172.18.163
citi.umich.edu   internet address = 141.211.92.141
citi.umich.edu   internet address = 141.211.133.111
```

Query types can also be set on the command line. For example, the same information as was returned above could have been returned non-interactively using the command *nslookup -query=mx openbsd.org*.

18.6.4 *nslint*

While not part of the base installation, the tool *nslint*, available in the ports and packages tree, is especially useful for debugging errors in DNS servers. To run it, point the command at a **named.conf** file and have it check for errors:

```
#  nslint -db named.conf
nslint: 0/131072 items used, 0 errors
```

Here the debugging output shows that zero errors were found. Without it, *nslint* returns without any output.

18.7 Resources

Running a DNS server can be significantly more complex than demonstrated by the examples in this chapter. This book does not have enough space to go into the details of running a complex setup for DNS operations. Readers are encouraged to seek additional information at the ISC Website for BIND at **http://www.isc.org/products/BIND/** and to see the *BIND9 Administrator's Reference Manual* at

http://www.nominum.com/content/documents/bind9arm.pdf.

18.8 Troubleshooting

1. I can't seem to reach hosts by name, in any service (e.g., Web surfing, *telnet*, *ssh*).

   One easy way to diagnose this situation as a DNS problem is to reach hosts using IP addresses. If this is possible, there is probably a DNS problem on the client system. First, check the file **/etc/resolv.conf** for a correct setup. Second, check the reachability of the specified nameservers, including your routing tables and the intermittent path. Third, make sure the server is responding correctly, using a tool like *dig* or *nsloookup* to verify the replies from the server.

2. I am not in control of nameservers on the Internet. How do I know when they will next retrieve information from me?

   Use *dig* to query for information about your zone. Perhaps you have changed the IP address of your Web server, but some people are still going to the old address. Doing multiple queries with *dig @their.dns.server -t any www.crimelabs.net* will show a "countdown" in seconds of the cache before it retries the server.

3. I want to know who is "in charge" of a particular zone.

   Use the *whois* command to see the domain registry information for a particular zone. Zone information databases are handled by various network organizations around the world. By default, the *whois* command will contact the right domain. For example:

```
$  whois crimelabs.net
[..]
   Domain Name: CRIMELABS.NET
   Registrar: TUCOWS, INC.
   Whois Server: whois.opensrs.net
   Referral URL: http://www.opensrs.org
   Name Server: NS.CRIMELABS.NET
   Name Server: NS.QSEC.COM
   Status: ACTIVE
   Updated Date: 28-dec-2002
   Creation Date: 19-feb-2000
   Expiration Date: 19-feb-2006
[..]
Registrant:
 crimelabs.net
```

```
1 No Street
New York, NY 10010
US


Domain name: CRIMELABS.NET

Administrative Contact:
    Palmer, B  spam@crimelabs.net
    1 No Street
    New York, NY 10010
    US
    212-555-1234
Technical Contact:
    Palmer, B  spam@crimelabs.net
    1 No Street
    New York, NY 10010
    US
    212-555-1234



Registrar of Record: TUCOWS, INC.
Record last updated on 28-Dec-2002.
Record expires on 19-Feb-2006.
Record Created on 19-Feb-2000.

Domain servers in listed order:
    NS.CRIMELABS.NET    64.94.171.112
    NS2.CRIMELABS.COM   64.94.171.114
[..]
```

Chapter 19
Web Servers with Apache

19.1 Apache

A very common role played by an OpenBSD system is that of a Web server. With so many attacks being launched against Web servers, and the fact that the Web server is the tier that faces the attacks on the Internet most often (rather than database servers, for example), it is vital to have a secure Web server. OpenBSD uses the industry-standard Apache Web server, which has passed through the OpenBSD code audit process. Apache is very powerful software with many features and options, but this text will not attempt to cover all of them. Instead, this chapter gives a quick overview of some of the most common Apache settings that OpenBSD users will change and highlights the main differences between Apache on OpenBSD and Apache on most other operating systems.

19.1.1 Quick Overview

The first thing to note about Apache on OpenBSD is that the files are stored in a different location than they are on many other installations. For OpenBSD, everything is stored under the **/var/www** hierarchy. Not only does this allow for a central storage location, but it also permits use of the *chroot* procedure to enhance Apache security as described later in this chapter.

The root folder of **/var/www** contains six default folders:

- **cgi-bin**   This folder contains any CGI files that are used by the system. By default, it contains only two scripts. The first, **printenv**, shows all of the variables for the user running Apache (*www* in the case of OpenBSD). The second, **test-cgi**, prints out several remote client variables. Neither of these scripts is readable or executable unless the bits are changed by root.

- **conf**   This folder contains the configuration files for *httpd*, the Apache binary. The main file that is read is the **httpd.conf** file. It contains the main configuration settings.

- **htdocs**   This is the default document root. The default page is a simple "It Worked!" page accompanied by all of the Apache documentation.

- **icons**   Icons that are used by the files under **htdocs/** are stored in this folder.

- **logs**   By default, *httpd* logs to this folder. Moving logs outside of this folder would break the *chroot* process.

- **users**   Given that Apache runs in *chroot*, using folders in the user's home directory to hold user Web pages can no longer work. User directories must now be created in a folder like this one within the new *chroot* directory

Apache Configuration

For most users, the default configuration will work well without any changes. A few of the more common changes that can be made are described below:

- **ServerRoot**   This variable indicates where the Apache server will *chroot* to. Changing it means that all files in **/var/www** should be moved to the new location. Note, however, that Apache will still look for the default configuration file in **/var/www/conf/httpd.conf**, so it can't be moved unless the new configuration file location is specified on start-up (the path is set at compile time to this default).

- **Listen**   Most servers will listen only on the host's IP address and on port 80, but that behavior can be changed with this variable.

- **LoadModule**   Modules can be used when adding packages like PHP, as discussed later in this chapter.

- **ServerAdmin**   The server administrator's address should be set to reflect who should get administrative e-mails.

- **ServerName**   The server name should be set to the fully qualified host name for the system, if one exists.

- **DirectoryIndex**   If modules (e.g., PHP) are loaded, additional entries for them can be added here. This variable tells Apache which file to look for if none is specified. For PHP, for example, we would add **index.php**.

- **HostnameLookups**   Apache logs only IP addresses of clients, but with this variable set, it will also resolve and save host names.

- **AddType**   This setting is associated with modules like PHP. It must be set if you wish to use some modules.

19.1.2 *chroot*

One of the most significant differences between Apache as it runs on OpenBSD and Apache on most other operating systems is that the former version is configured to run in *chroot* mode by default. With this in place, the Apache daemon can access only files that reside within this new root. The default *chroot* is **/var/www**. Thus any files that will be used by Apache, like the logfiles, HTTP files, or any configuration files and modules, must be contained in this new root. The main thing that is gained from this approach is that Apache becomes contained to only a small section of the filesystem. Any exploitation of either Apache or any of the scripts that are developed can, therefore, affect only the new root. Other files don't exist as far as Apache can tell. This also has the effect of breaking some software that is not configured properly. For example, many Web logging software applications are installed outside of **/var/www**. Under the *chroot* procedure, such software cannot be accessed by Apache because it resides outsides of the root.

The *chroot* used by Apache is whatever the *ServerRoot* variable is set to in the **/var/www/httpd.conf** file.

```
ServerRoot "/var/www"
```

Because this new *chroot* process can break a lot of applications, there is an option to disable it. The best place to specify this setting would be in the **/etc/rc.conf** file:

```
httpd_flags="-u"
```

19.1.3 SSL

Another benefit of Apache on OpenBSD is that it is compiled to support SSL by default. Although the server and the configuration file are able to use SSL, keys need to be generated and the server needs to be started in a different way.

Generation of the SSL keys for the server is done in three steps. The first step is the creation of the private key for the server.

```
#  openssl genrsa -out /etc/ssl/private/server.key 1024
Generating RSA private key, 1024 bit long modulus
...++++++
.........................................++++++
e is 65537 (0x10001)
```

Because this is a private key, it can be protected with a password to make it more secure. The drawback is that this password or passphrase must be entered each time the server is stated.

```
# openssl genrsa -des3 -out /etc/ssl/private/server.key 1024
Generating RSA private key, 1024 bit long modulus
.....++++++
.............................++++++
e is 65537 (0x10001)
Enter PEM pass phrase: enter a passphrase
Verifying password - Enter PEM pass phrase: enter a passphrase
```

The next step is to create the certificate request key. Information about the site that this key will be protecting must be entered.

```
# openssl req -new -key /etc/ssl/private/server.key \
  -out /etc/ssl/private/server.csr
Using configuration from /etc/ssl/openssl.cnf
You are about to be asked to enter information that will be
incorporated into your certificate request. What you are about to
enter is what is called a Distinguished Name or a DN. There are quite
a few fields but you can leave some blank For some fields there will
be a default value, If you enter '.', the field will be left blank.
-----
Country Name (2 letter code) []: US
State or Province Name (full name) []:  New York
Locality Name (eg, city) []: New York
Organization Name (eg, company) []: My Company
Organizational Unit Name (eg, section) []: enter
Common Name (eg, fully qualified host name) []: www.mycompany.com
Email Address []: webmaster@mycompany.com

Please enter the following 'extra' attributes
to be sent with your certificate request
A challenge password []: optional passphrase
An optional company name []: optional passphrase
```

The security behind SSL assumes that a trusted third party will sign the key. The best known of these entities is Verisign. If the Web server is to be used by the general public, a key should be purchased from Verisign or another major certificate authority (CA). Verisign would need the certificate request key to create the valid certificate.

Most people don't plan to use their servers in such a way that would require a trusted key. As an alternative, the *openssl* tool, which is used to create the other keys, can allow the user to sign the key rather than having a public company sign it. Although this key can't be verified as belonging to the company presenting it, it is good enough for the needs of most people.

```
#  openssl x509 -req -days 365 -in /etc/ssl/private/server.csr \
  -signkey /etc/ssl/private/server.key -out /etc/ssl/server.cr
Signature ok
subject=/C=US/ST=New York/L=New York/O=Crimelabs.net/CN=\
    www.crimelabs.net/Email=webmaster@crimelabs.net
Getting Private key
```

Once these keys have been created, the start-up file, **/etc/rc.conf**, must be modified to start Apache with SSL enabled. This file needs to be changed as follows:

```
#httpd_flags=NO
httpd_flags="-DSSL"
```

Once the server has been restarted, people can connect to it using SSL.

19.2 Using Dynamic Content in the *chroot* Environment

With the shift to a *chroot* environment for the Web server, Apache on OpenBSD now requires some additional setup to accommodate content that uses external programs. One solution is to run Apache in its insecure mode (as *httpd -u*). A more useful, and security-conscious, solution is to import the needed tools into the Web server root.[1]

To make CVSweb operate in a *chroot* environment, it is necessary to copy all of the relevant tools, libraries, and Perl modules that CVSweb employs into **/var/www**.

First, create the basic directory structure:

```
$  cd /var/www
#  mkdir tmp usr          creates both directories
#  chown www:www tmp      needs to be writeable for
                          the www user
```

---

[1]This section is based on notes and instructions from Jolan Luff.

Next, set up the Perl directory structure:

```
$  cd /var/www/usr
#  mkdir -p bin lib libdata/perl5 libexec
$  cd /var/www/usr/libdata/perl5
#  mkdir -p File IPC Time warnings `machine`-openbsd/5.8.0
```

Now, copy the required binaries:

```
$  cd /var/www/usr/bin{co,cvs,diff,perl,rcsdiff,rlog,uname} .
                  copy all of these individually
```

Copy the libraries to which the binaries are linked. Wildcards will, of course, copy any old, unused libraries that are lurking around (for example, from an upgrade).

```
$  cd /var/www/usr/lib
#  cp -p /usr/lib/lib{asn1,c,crypto,des,gssapi,kafs,krb,krb5}.so* .
#  cp -p /usr/lib/lib{m,perl,util,z}.so* .
```

Copy the runtime link editor:

```
$  cd /var/www/usr/libexec
#  cp -p /usr/libexec/ld.so .
```

Copy the needed Perl modules:

```
$  cd /var/www/usr/libdata/perl5
#  cp -p /usr/libdata/perl5/{Carp,Exporter,Symbol,base,integer}.pm .
#  cp -p /usr/libdata/perl5/{strict,warnings,vars}.pm .
#  cp -p /usr/libdata/perl5/File/Basename.pm ./File/
#  cp -p /usr/libdata/perl5/IPC/Open{2,3}.pm ./IPC/
#  cp -p /usr/libdata/perl5/Time/Local.pm ./Time/
#  cp -p /usr/libdata/perl5/warnings/register.pm ./warnings/

$  cd /var/www/usr/libdata/perl5/`machine`-openbsd/5.8.0
#  cp -p \
   /usr/libdata/perl5/`machine`-openbsd/5.8.0/{Config,Cwd}.pm .
```

This will create the environment needed by Perl so that it can access its libraries, the interpreter, and its modules as needed. These modules were chosen for the example application here, *cvsweb*. This application gives Web users access to the CVS repository of a site, allowing them to browse the files and view their histories.

The *cvsweb* program itself and **cvsweb.conf** both assume that Apache is not running in a *chroot* environment, so we need to change some default paths so they are relative to **/var/www**.

In **/var/www/cgi-bin/cvsweb**, change the base path to remove the Web server root:

```
for ("$mydir/cvsweb.conf",'/var/www/conf/cvsweb/cvsweb.conf')   default
for ("$mydir/cvsweb.conf",'/conf/cvsweb/cvsweb.conf')
```

In **/var/www/conf/cvsweb/cvsweb.conf**, change **CVSrepositories** to reflect the location of the directories that contain *CVSROOT*. This example shows a local repository NFS-mounted over a loopback into **/var/www/cvs**. The directory must be relative to **/var/www**, so we use **/cvs**:

```
@CVSrepositories = (
'local'   => ['Local Repository', '/home/cvs'],default
'local'   => ['Local Repository', '/cvs'],
```

We rely on the same idea for **$mimetypes**:

```
$mime_types = '/var/www/conf/mime.types';   default
$mime_types = '/conf/mime.types';
```

19.3 Modules for Apache

While Apache is wonderful software for serving flat Web pages, it doesn't have native support for dynamic Web pages. Using the ports tree, support for an array of dynamic and robust features can be added to your Apache system.

The following are popular modules found in the OpenBSD ports tree:

- **mod_perl**   This module is useful if you will be developing additional module functionality in Perl. Furthermore, it carries less overhead than calling the Perl interpreter for dynamic pages or content.
- **php**   PHP is a robust, object-oriented scripting language that produces HTML output. It has a large number of flavors to accommodate the variety of features available in PHP, including database connectivity, mail integration, and the like.
- **mod_dav**   The DAV (distributed authoring and versioning) standard has been implemented as *mod_dav* for Apache. It allows your Apache server to provide a

Web-based filesystem to a variety of clients, including UNIX, Windows, and Macintosh (OS X and 9) systems. When mixed with strong authentication and encryption, a simple-to-use network filesystem can be built.

- **mod_frontpage**   Microsoft Frontpage features and extensions can be accessed through *mod_frontpage*. It can help Web clients who use FrontPage authoring tools to make the transition to an OpenBSD and Apache system.

19.4 Other Web Servers

While the Apache 1.3 series server is directly integrated with OpenBSD and has been audited for vulnerabilities, it is not the only Web server available for your OpenBSD installation. Depending on your needs, another server may be more appropriate.

19.4.1 Apache 2.0.x

Along with the current 1.3.x version of Apache, there is a 2.0.x version that boasts many new features. While certain features, like support for IPv6, are useful to some users, v2.0.x breaks many software packages that used v1.3.x. Apache 2.0.x isn't in the ports tree (it has yet to be cleanly integrated) and would have to be compiled manually to be used. Fortunately, OpenBSD is a supported platform, meaning that Apache 2.0 systems are built without problems. Configure the build process to use a different directory for the files, such as **/usr/local/var/www**. This will keep the new system from interfering with the old one.

Apache 2.0 has a few advantages over the 1.3 series that is in the tree. First, it offers native IPv6 support, meaning your OpenBSD Web server can operate in the growing IPv6 world. Second, it brings a slightly higher average performance than does Apache 1.3.

Naturally, there are a few disadvantages to migrating to Apache 2.0 at this time. The first relates to module support, which is steadily improving. The second comprises a lack of support from much of the OpenBSD community with specific issues. While you don't typically have many problems, for some new website maintainers this shortcoming could be a problem. However, Apache has a large and helpful userbase, so you should eventually be able to find useful information about your Apache 2.0 installation from the community.

19.4.2 *thttpd*

Although Apache is a great Web server, it can be overkill for some environments. If a simple, lightweight, and fast Web server is needed to serve static Web content, *thttpd* is a great solution. It fills all of these needs and even supports IPv6. Configuration is easy, and its simple design leads to good security. This port can be found in **/usr/ports/www/thhtpd**.

19.5 Miscellaneous Web Server Tools

Not all Web server features are restricted to the server and its built-in modules. Several external tools can be useful in maintaining a Website and assist you in Web content authoring. These tools are available in the ports tree or as packages.

19.5.1 Squid

Squid is one of the most commonly used proxy servers on the Internet. It makes a great proxy for different environments—from home users to large corporate networks. Using a proxy can facilitate content screening (to mitigate attacks), alleviate some of the demands on your bandwidth by caching the content, and facilitate authenticated access to subscription Websites.

19.5.2 *mod_load*

Once a Web server is set up, it's important to tune it to get the best performance. One good tool to for this purpose is *httpd_load*. Made by the same folks who developed *thttpd*, this tool simulates clients and makes requests of a server. When this process is complete, the tool outputs a good deal of timing information. This port can be found in **/usr/ports/www/http_load**.

19.5.3 *weblint*

The *weblint* tool is a syntax and style checker for HTML. It can be useful for validating the correctness of your Web page source code. It may not suffice for some more complex pages, however.

   An additional tool to look at is the HTML validatory, available in the ports tree as **textproc/validate**. It can be used as an offline WDG HTML validatory to check the correctness of your HTML source.

19.5.4 *analog*

The *analog* tool is used to analyze your Apache logs and produce site summaries. It can be useful in examining the content access and sources of hits, referers, search engine terms that were used to access your site, and much more. One of the most popular logfile analyzers, *analog* produces easy-to-navigate reports.

Chapter 20
OpenSSH

One of the greatest tools that has come out of the OpenBSD project has been OpenSSH. OpenSSH's origins start with SSH. The original SSH was developed to be a replacement for less secure methods of login such as *telnet, rsh*, and *rlogin*. Although these tools worked well for many years to allow users to login to remove systems and copy files, they were completely insecure in nature. No encryption was done anywhere and anyone who was listening to network traffic could easily see not only the login and password, but also all data in the session. The original SSH was a great tool, but the licensing in the product soon became a limitation for most users. The OpenSSH project stemmed from earlier, less restrictive SSH code and was officially released with OpenBSD 2.6.

The most common use of OpenSSH is for connecting to remote hosts. The general format that was used for *rsh* is used for *ssh* as well:

```
user@client:/home/user$  ssh user@remoteserver
user@remoteserver's password:  enter password
Last login: Tue Feb 18 21:45:44 2003 from client
OpenBSD 3.4 (server) #0: Wed May 29 22:42:53 EDT 2003

Terminal type? [xterm]  enter
user@server:/home/user$
```

Another main use of OpenSSH is *scp* (from Secure CoPy). It is used to move files from one host to another.

```
user@client:/home/user/code$  scp root@server:/root/floppy34.fs
    /home/user/images/
root@server's password:
floppy34.fs   100% |*******************************| 1440 KB 00:03
```

There are many options for all of the tools in the OpenSSH package that will be covered later in this chapter.

Note that the *ssh* tool suite is a complex and rich set of tools. Only commonly used command-line options are described here.

20.1 Command-Line Use

Three main end-user programs are used to complete most tasks. The first is the *ssh* client tool. This tool's main use is to connect users to remote servers as seen above. The second program, *scp*, allows files to be moved from one host to another. The third piece, the *sshd* daemon, needs to be running on whatever server is being used.

20.1.1 *ssh*

Most often, the *ssh* command is used on the command line with the server as the only argument:

```
$   ssh server.example.com
```

At other times, the established options for the client do not suffice—for example, when specifying the protocol for a session or an identity file you wish to use. Many of the configuration options can be permanently set in the client configuration file, as described later in this chapter.

The actual SSH protocol has changed over the years, evolving to handle new threats and features. The two most widely deployed protocol versions are SSH 1.5 and 2.0. The 2.0 version of the protocol is not backward computable with SSH-1.5, however, so the client has to detect and negotiate the right version of the protocol. The order of negotiation is flexible and can be specified on the command line. Simply include the *-1* and *-2* command-line arguments to force SSH-1.5 or SSH-2.0, respectively.

The next major option used with *ssh* is the port option, which is useful for reaching servers on nonstandard ports. While the default is 22/TCP, other TCP ports can be used with the *-p* option:

```
$   ssh -p 2222 server.example.com
```

This will reach the server on TCP port 2222 at **server.example.com**.

The *ssh* command can be forced to use a specific identity file to authenticate to a system that may not be the default file or may not be stored in the *ssh-agent* session.

The identity file contains the local hostname and key used to identify the local user and the system from which he or she is authenticating. You can use an identity file from one machine on another machine, or have multiple identities for yourself. This can be useful to limit a key's utility to a secure system, for example, and to a default key for all other systems you use. Simply specify *-i* to point to the identity file:

```
$ ssh -i new-identity server.my.com
```

This will use the private identity key in the file **new-identity** when the user authenticates to the system **server.my.com**. This ability can be useful when working with a key in testing or for automated tasks.

Commands can also be specified on the command line to be executed on the target system. For example, to start up a process securely on a remote system, *ssh* may be combined with key-based authentication as follows:

```
$ ssh server.my.com analyze_logfiles
```

This will execute the command *analyze_logfiles* on the system **server.my.com**. Programs that require *tty* interaction do not work well with this approach, however, as *ssh* doesn't allocated a *tty* in this mode.

By default, the *ssh* command will not attempt to establish X11 forwarding. To enable this on the command line, use the command *ssh -X*.

20.1.2 *scp*

A complementary command to the *rcp* command, used to remotely copy files between computers, is *scp*. Much of the same operational principle has been preserved in *scp*, but several new features have been integrated to accommodate new protocols, encryption, and several niceties.

The simplest usage of *scp* is to copy a file from one computer to another. The basic usage of the command is *scp source destination*, with *source* or *destination* being a remote system. This remote location is specified in two parts, a hostname and a file path, separated by a colon. If no account name is specified, the current account name is assumed. Here, a file is copied to a remote location:

```
$ scp file serverone:/home/jose/file
file                           100%   67KB 785.1KB/s   00:00
```

The reverse operation would be to copy the file to the local machine from the remote system, which could be done using the command *scp serverone:/home/jose/file file*. If no colon is included, the destination is a filename. Relative paths are allowed, starting at the home directory of the remote account. The progress bar indicates how far the copy has gone in terms of percentage and bytes, how fast it is moving between systems, and how much time remains.

The *scp* command can also work with different port numbers by using the option *scp -P*. Here, a file is transferred to a system on TCP destination port 2222:

```
$  scp -P 2222 file serverone:/home/jose/file
file                             100%   67KB 785.1KB/s   00:00
```

This is sometimes confusing, as *scp* uses *-P* and *ssh* uses *-p* to specify the port number.

Recursive copies can also be made, allowing for the copying of entire directory trees. The *scp -r* command is used for this purpose. Here, a local directory (**files/**) is transferred to the remote system *serverone*:

```
$  scp -r files/ serverone:/home/jose
manuscript.txt                        100%  347     10.7KB/s   00:00
application                           100%   74     10.9KB/s   00:00
textfile                              100%   68      6.7KB/s   00:00
picture                               100%  192    145.4KB/s   00:00
something                             100%  95KB   677.4KB/s   00:00
```

Each file is listed as it is copied to the remote system. A really interesting feature of *scp* is the ability to copy between two remote systems without using the local system as a staging platform. Simply make the two endpoints be the two remote systems as the source and the destination:

```
$  scp serverone:somefile me@servertwo:samefile
somefile                         100%   67KB 785.1KB/s   00:00
```

Obviously, authentication must be accomplished on both systems, but this ability can be useful if the two systems are on high-speed links and the local system is on a slower link. The middle system is not used, so no slowdown is incurred through its interference.

Several other flags are useful in *scp*. The *-l* flag can be used to limit the amount of bandwidth used by the copy. For example, use *scp -l 10* to specify a maximum of 10 kilobits/second of bandwidth used. For backups, you may wish to preserve the original attributes of the file by using *scp -p* to preserve the modification times, access times, and mode attributes of the original file. To disable the printing of the progress bar, the *scp -q* option can be used to force *scp* to be quiet. This option is useful in scripts, where output can be suppressed to make it prettier or, in the case of *cron* jobs, to disable any erroneous output.

20.1.3 *ssh-keygen*

The *ssh* command and its relatives all use public key pairs for authentication both at the client level and the server level. These keys are created using the *ssh-keygen* utility. The *ssh-keygen* command can be used for key maintenance as well.

Using *ssh-keygen* for creating keys is simple. The *-t* option is required to specify a type, either "rsa1" to generate an SSH-1.5-compatible RSA key pair or "rsa" or "dsa" for an SSH-2 RSA or DSA key pair, respectively. To generate a 1024-bit DSA SSH 2 key pair, execute this simple command and answer a few easy questions:

```
$  ssh-keygen -t dsa
Generating public/private dsa key pair.
Enter file in which to save the key (/home/jose/.ssh/id_dsa)  id.dsa
Enter passphrase (empty for no passphrase):  fOoey
Enter same passphrase again:  fOoey
Your identification has been saved in id_dsa.
Your public key has been saved in id_dsa.pub.
The key fingerprint is:
eb:3d:6b:99:ec:e9:95:f6:8d:2d:99:89:f3:d6:92:3e jose@tank
```

Here the key pair is saved in the default location and with the default hostnames.

Key management can also be performed using the *ssh-keygen* command, including activities like changing passwords, removing passwords, and editing comments of SSH-1.5 RSA keypairs. To edit the comment in an **rsa1** key pair, use the command *ssh-keygen* *-c* and specify the filename:

```
$  ssh-keygen -c -f .ssh/identity
Key now has comment 'jose@tank'
Enter new comment:  this is a test key
The comment in your key file has been changed.
```

Comments are not supported in the key types used in SSH-2.

To edit the password of a key pair (or to remote it altogether), use the *ssh-keygen -p* command on the key:

```
$  ssh-keygen -p -f .ssh/id.dsa
Enter new passphrase (empty for no passphrase):  new passphrase
Enter same passphrase again:  new passphrase
Your identification has been saved with the new passphrase.
```

This option can be useful in updating keys to new passphrases (or much stronger ones that were previously used) or even removing passphrases for some tasks. Note that the use of a key without any passphrase can allow an attacker access to any of your accounts that use this key without a passphrase.

To generate a new key pair for the systemwide *sshd* server, the following command can be used. It is the same command as is used by the boot scripts to generate keys the first time they are needed:

```
/usr/bin/ssh-keygen -q -t dsa -f /etc/ssh/ssh_host_dsa_key -N ''
```

This will create a password-less DSA key available that the system can use for the daemon. This key is not readable by any nonroot users on the system.

20.1.4 *ssh-agent* and *ssh-add*

Management of your keychain for authentication and use is performed by the *ssh-agent* tool. The agent remains in the background and intercepts requests for key-based authentication, at which time it presents the appropriate key for authentication. The agent is started in a shell (typically a parent shell) or by an external program (such as at the beginning of an X session). All child shells will receive the environmental variables used by the agent to notify the *ssh* client program how to communicate with the agent.

To start a shell that is aware of the agent, use the agent to launch the shell via the command *ssh-agent ksh*. This will invoke a new shell with two new environmental variables set:

```
SSH_AUTH_SOCK=/tmp/ssh-CqrX9164/agent.9164
SSH_AGENT_PID=21554
```

(The exact file of the socket and the process ID of the agent will differ for your system.) Client *ssh* programs, including *scp*, will attempt to use the keys held by the agent for authentication.

Keys are added to the agent with the *ssh-add* command. With no additional arguments, it will assume the default key locations in **.ssh/**. Specific files can be used as well:

```
$  ssh-add /home/jose/.ssh/openbsd_dsa
Enter passphrase for /home/jose/.ssh/openbsd_dsa:  enter passphrase
Identity added: /home/jose/.ssh/openbsd_dsa \
   (/home/jose/.ssh/openbsd_dsa)
```

Notice that the *ssh-agent* program uses the private key file and the password for that file, not the public key file.

To list all of the keys held by the agent, use *ssh-add -l*:

```
$  ssh-add -L
1024 35 15357569... jose@tank
ssh-dss AAAAB3NzaC... /home/jose/.ssh/id_dsa
ssh-dss AAAAB3Nz...   /home/jose/.ssh/openbsd_dsa
```

These keys can now be automatically handled by the agent to authenticate the user to another account.

There is an important security issue to note with *ssh-agent*, however. Suppose the cache is loaded and you have authenticated yourself to use your private keys. The keys are then kept in memory. If you walk away from your workstation, anyone would have access to your hosts that let you authenticate using these keys.

That said, you can unload specific keys by using *ssh-add -d*, or you can unload all keys by using the *-D* flag:

```
$  ssh-add -D
All identities removed.
```

This is a good thing to do when you walk away from your workstation.

20.1.5 *sshd*

The *sshd* process is the server process with which *ssh* clients connect. By default, it will listen on TCP port 22 and accept connections from any *ssh* client. Furthermore, the default configuration will accept both SSH-2 and SSH 1.5 clients, in that order.

Typically started at boot time with the simple invocation of *sshd*, this process forks and runs in the background. It logs to **/var/log/authlog**:

```
Apr 29 22:00:55 tank sshd[26412]: Server listening on :: port 22
Apr 29 22:00:55 tank sshd[26412]: Server listening on 0.0.0.0 port 22
```

The logging records the username, the success (or failure) of the connection's authentication, and the IP address and source port:

```
Apr 27 20:28:52 hoover sshd[26625]: Accepted password for jose from
    10.10.32.1 port 11561 ssh2
Apr 27 23:27:16 hoover sshd[740]: Failed password for jose from
    10.10.32.1 port 24917 ssh2
```

One interesting command-line feature is *sshd -u*, which can be used to control the allocated hostname size to record in the **utmp** entry. Some names may resolve to being longer than the default of 40 characters. Specifying *sshd -u0* turns off DNS loookups by the *sshd* process, leaving such entries in the **utmp** file:

```
jose   ttyp0  10.10.32.1            Tue Apr 29 08:00 - 08:04  (00:03)
```

Furthermore, because of a lack of DNS requests, methods for authentication or access control that use DNS information will fail to be applied correctly.

Another option is *sshd -d*, which keeps the daemon from forking into the background and causes all error messages to be printed to the standard error descriptor. It is useful when you need to debug an error with the *sshd* server.

While it is unwise to use *inetd* to launch *sshd* due to the overhead associated with generating new keys at each invocation, users who wish to do so this should invoke *sshd -i*. This option tells the *sshd* process that it is running from *inetd*, which adjusts its behavior accordingly.

Multiple *sshd* processes can be started on the same machine using two techniques. The first method is to start *sshd* on ports other than ones that are currently in use. For example, to start *sshd* on TCP port 2222, use the command *sshd -p 2222*.

The second method works on hosts that have more than one IP address assigned to them (they are multihomed). Here, the *ListenAddress* configuration directive is used to specify a particular address to listen on. For example, if a host has the addresses 10.1.1.1 and 192.168.3.4, two *sshd* processes can be started, one for each IP address. In one configuration file for the daemon, the line *ListenAddress 10.1.1.1* would be used, and in another configuration file the line *ListenAddress 192.168.3.4* would be used. Use the command *sshd -f sshd_config_1* for the first configuration file and *sshd* process, and *sshd -f sshd_config_2* for the second configuration file and *sshd* listener.

20.2 Configuration

The *ssh* set of tools is controlled by two sets of files. The global set of files in **/etc/ssh** controls the default behaviors of the client and the server. The configuration files in **HOME/.ssh** control the user's *ssh* client behavior.

20.2.1 Client Options

Systemwide configuration options are controlled in the file **/etc/ssh/ssh_config**, or on a per-account basis with the file **.ssh/config**. Here options for the client can be established on a host-level basis, such as ciphers, protocols, and X11 forwarding.

An illustrative example is the control of the SSH protocol version to use for a connection. The declaration in the configuration file **/etc/ssh/ssh_config** for all hosts to first attempt an SSH 2 session and then to fall back to SSH-1.5 would be as follows:

```
Host *
    Protocol 2,1
```

This option can also be specified to always force one version by omitting the other. In this way your client cannot be fooled into using the weaker SSH-1.5 protocol when it should be using SSH-2.0.

Parameters can also be controlled on a host-level basis by specifying the name to match for each subsection. It is important to recognize that this name will be the name of the server as passed on the command line, not the name normalized by the resolver. Hence, **Host tank** is different than **Host tank.crimelabs.net**. To force the use of Blowfish cipher for the server **tank.crimelabs.net**, for example, an entry like the following would be used:

```
Host tank.crimelabs.net
    Cipher blowfish
```

20.2.2 Server Configuration Options

The server configuration file resides in **/etc/ssh/sshd_config** by default. This file controls the global *sshd* options. These options can be overridden with command-line controls, however.

Just as for the client configuration, the *Protocol* directive in the server configuration controls which protocols (SSH-1.5 or SSH-2) will be tried and in what order. For a server that can use both SSH 1.5 and SSH 2, it will advertise the protocol string 1.99. To specify a server to use both protocols, but to apply SSH-1.5 first, the configuration string would be as follows:

```
Protocol 1,2
```

The default is to support both protocols 1.5 and 2, but to use 2 first.

The *Port* option is a global option for the server to use when it listens for inbound connections. The default is to use TCP port 22. As noted above, the *ListenAddress* directive is used to control which IP addresses the server listens to. By default, the all-zero address (0.0.0.0 in IPv4, :: in IPv6) is used, meaning any available address is used by the daemon. Multiple *ListenAddress* directives are allowed. Additionally, a colon separating the address and the port can be used to exert more fine-grained control than is possible with the *Port* keyword:

```
ListenAddress 192.168.1.1:22
ListenAddress [3ffe:501:ffff:0:205:5dff:fef2:fb11]:2222
```

Notice that IPv6 numerical addresses are enclosed in square brackets. *Port* options must come before *ListenAddress* directives for the default to be overridden.

X11 forwarding, performed to give X11 applications a secure channel by using the *ssh* session, is controlled by the options *X11Forwarding*, *X11DisplayOffset*, and *X11UseLocalhost*. The first, *X11Forwarding*, is set to either "yes" or "no" to indicate whether any X11 forwarding will be done, using the port offset listed in **X11DisplayOffset** and listening to either the loopback address (127.0.0.1, controlled by **X11UseLocalhost**) or another external address. The default is to disable X11 forwarding, but to use an offset of 10 when it is enabled (meaning the daemon will listen on port 6010 for the first X11 forwarding session, 6011 for the second, and so on).

20.3 Use in Other Packages

One of the design goals of *ssh* was for it to serve as a drop-in replacement for *rsh*. The major advantages of *ssh* over *ssh* derive from its stronger authentication and encrypted channel, but other advantages include arbitrary port forwarding (allowing you to traverse a firewall while remaining secure) and channel compression. To that end, *ssh* has become a popular replacement for two major network systems that use *rsh:* CVS and *rsync*.

CVS, the concurrent version system, is a network-aware application that allows for the versioning and control of documents. Used by OpenBSD and many other projects, it easily adapts to the use of *ssh* over *rsh*. Just edit the environmental variable *CVS_RSH* to point to *ssh* rather than *rsh:*

```
$  export CVS_RSH=/usr/bin/ssh
```

Now CVS sessions will use *ssh* rather than *rsh*. Users of *ksh* can make this change permanent by adding that command to their **.profile** file in their home directory. No changes are needed on the server to handle an *ssh* connection; the commands are transparent at the shell level to the server, regardless of network protocol.

The *rsync* program, which allows for the remote synchronization of directory trees, can also use *ssh* in much the same way. The environmental variable *RSYNC_RSH* should point to *ssh* rather than *rsh:*

```
$  export RSYNC_RSH=/usr/bin/ssh
```

Again, *ksh* users who wish to make this change permanent can edit their **.profile** file to add this line. Now *rsync* sessions will use *ssh* instead of *rsh* for network communications. No changes are needed on the server to adopt this change.

Most other network programs that call *rsh* should be able to handle *ssh* integration just as smoothly, via either an environmental variable or a configuration setting.

20.4 Command Line

Several other command-line switches to OpenSSH are frequently encountered. They are listed here, along with their limitations.

OpenSSH supports compression of the tunnel on the command line, using a sliding window for its targets. This feature can be helpful over a low-bandwidth link, but at the cost of additional CPU time, making it feasible only for reasonably modern systems. On high-speed networks (such as a typical LAN), this will actually make the connection slower. To enable compression, use the command *ssh -C*. The option *CompressionLevel* controls how aggressive the compression will attempt to be, by trading CPU time for bandwidth. The compression used by OpenSSH is the same as that employed in the *gzip* program.

If you want to specify an alternative key to use on the command line and not in the configuration file (or a key that is stored in the *ssh-agent*), include the command *ssh -i* to indicate which identity file should be used. This command can be useful for selecting a key with a nondefault name or for testing a key without loading it into an agent.

A quick and easy way to verify the fingerprint of a remote server is to temporarily use a different known hosts cache, such as the **/dev/null** device:

```
$ ssh -oUserKnownHostsFile=/dev/null 10.10.10.23
The authenticity of host '10.10.10.23 (10.10.10.23)' can't be
established. RSA key fingerprint is
00:a9:65:72:d9:95:bb:ca:64:98:a3:89:a4:3a:a7:7c. Are you sure you
want to continue connecting (yes/no)? no
Host key verification failed.
```

The key fingerprint can then be compared with an advertised hash of the key, ensuring that it was used correctly. Connecting again without this option set can be used to verify that the key is authentic. If it is in the cache correctly, the daemon will not present an error message when connecting to the remote system. If an error does occur, the key is incorrect and one of the two entities is to blame. The fingerprint will make it easier to compare the candidate key against a known good copy of the key.

20.5 Privilege Separation

An additional feature of the OpenSSH daemon is the use of privilege separation, as controlled by the *UsePrivilegeSeparation* option in the daemon configuration file. With privilege separation activated, the daemon will spawn two copies of itself when it begins. The first copy runs as root, but uses only a small portion of the code for authentication. The second copy handles the inbound connections and makes requests of the root parent. Furthermore, the child is jailed to an empty directory under **/var/empty**. This second process runs as the user *sshd*.

  The goal of this feature is to mitigate any attacks on the daemon, granting the attacker a minimal reward should he or she gain control of the daemon process. The portion that runs as root is small and audited and doesn't trust user input, making attacks on this copy significantly harder to develop effectively. The default is to enable this feature. The processes will appear as follows in your process table when a user is logged in:

```
31776 ??  Is      0:00.16 sshd: jose [priv] (sshd)
  929 ??  I       0:00.03 sshd: jose@ttyp0 (sshd)
```

These two processes correspond to the privileged and unprivileged processes.

20.6 *sftp*

OpenSSH installs and supports an FTP-like channel over an SSH-2 channel called *sftp* by default. This easy-to-use method enables you to transfer files securely using a familiar interface. Unlike *scp*, the filesystem can be readily browsed and traversed, making it easy to locate or place files. The *sshd* process receives a request to launch the *sftp* process, which then invokes the configured daemon. By default, it is **/usr/libexec/sftp-server**.

Using *sftp* is easy. Invoke the *sftp* command to connect to an OpenSSH server that supports the SSH-2 protocol. By default, the *sftp* server is enabled:

```
$  sftp 10.10.10.23
Connecting to 10.10.10.23...
The authenticity of host '10.10.10.23 (10.10.10.23)' can't be
    established.
RSA key fingerprint is 1b:de:39:88:ce:7a:22:a5:74:18:d4:a9:30:2b:c4.
Are you sure you want to continue connecting (yes/no)? yes
Warning: Permanently added '10.10.10.23' (RSA) to the list of known
    hosts.
jose@10.10.10.23's password: my password
sftp> ls
.cshrc
.cvspass
openssh
packages
...
```

At this prompt, a nearly normal FTP session can be used to browse the filesystem and to copy files using GET and PUT commands.

The *sftp* subsystem is enabled by default for SSH 2 servers and clients. It uses the **/usr/libexec/sftp-server** subsystem for such requests. Because *sftp* doesn't use a different port than normal *ssh*, firewalls do not need to be adjusted. Furthermore, it does not use multiple ports or active or passive mode, as traditional FTP does, making it easier to track. The *sftp* system uses normal system accounts and keys for authentication.

Almost all traditional FTP commands will be honored, except for the PASV commands (including EPASV) and the commands to set the file type to binary or ASCII. All transfers utilize the raw bytes of the system, so they transmit exact duplicates across systems. File ownership and modes can be adjusted, just as they are in normal FTP.

To override any subsystems, including *sftp*, comment out the following line in the configuration file:

```
Subsystem       sftp    /usr/libexec/sftp-server
```

By default, no subsystems are enabled. If none is specifically chosen, none will be active.

Part III
Advanced Features

Chapter 21

The OpenBSD Development Environment

21.1 Introduction

Having been targeted by developers for developers, OpenBSD is, of course, a rich platform for software development. The system uses the GNU C compiler suite, and it can be accessorized with additional languages, includes the powerful GNU debugger, and has an extensive selection of development tools available in both the base system and the ports tree. Several features that make the OpenBSD system a stellar development environment are outlined here.

OpenBSD is a POSIX-compliant system, meaning it conforms to well-defined standards for operating system behavior and a development environment. The popularity of this standard means that most well-written software will behave as expected on OpenBSD systems. Furthermore, OpenBSD incorporates a number of BSD-specific features, such as library functions, and several GNU enhancements. OpenBSD is, for the most part, a standard UNIX development environment.

21.2 Editors

Essential to any development effort is a text editor for the entry and editing of source code. OpenBSD includes, in the base system, the *vi* editor. This small, console-based text editor provides a rich set of editing commands. Because *vi* is often too arcane and terse for many people to use, other editors are often chosen in its stead. If you are more into *emacs*, *mg* offers an environment with similar keystrokes that is found in the base installation.

From the OpenBSD ports tree, the packages for *emacs* and *xemacs* can be installed to create a more user-friendly and rich editing environment. The *emacs* editor is a text editor with powerful features. The *xemacs* editor is a related project that focuses on the use of *emacs* in the X Window environment. A rich set of plug-ins, including development tools, are available for both of these popular editors, from the development teams for the editors as well as third parties.

Additional editors from the ports tree can be found in the **editors** subdirectory. Several of them are excellent choices for source code editing.

21.3 Compilers and Languages

Of course, central to any development environment are the compiler and the languages supported. OpenBSD supports several popular languages in the base system, and more can be added via the ports and packages system. Thus a rich set of programming languages can be supported in OpenBSD for the regular developer.

21.3.1 Base Language Support

OpenBSD includes, in the base installation, the GCC compiler suite as well as several other popular languages. The GCC included in OpenBSD from the **comp34.tgz** archive (or whatever version which is current) supports the C programming language, C++, Objective C, and Fortran 77. This support is based on the EGCS compiler from GCC.

The GCC compiler is actually a set of tools, including a compiler, a linker, and an assembler, that this is commonly referred to as the GNU Toolchain. It behaves in OpenBSD almost exactly as it does on other GCC-supported platforms. Minor changes include warnings printed for well-known security hole functions, such as `mktemp()` and `gets()`. Such messages assist the developer in performing minor software audits.

Several other languages are supported in the base installation as well. These include the popular Perl programming language, the awk programming language (based on "the one true awk," or nawk, from the original authors of the language), and the Korn shell scripting language. Additionally, the C language accessories Lex (supported by the Flex implementation) and Yacc are present in the base development environment, as well as the RPC language, supported through the *rpcgen* tool. As you see, most popular software is supported in the base installation of OpenBSD.

One interesting set of tools available in the base installation encompasses profiling tools, allowing for the tracing of the performance of an executable. This task is largely achieved through the popular *gprof* tool. Kernel profiling can be done as well, using *kgmon*, which interacts with the kernel to the *gprof* tool. Lastly, the Perl language can be profiled using the *dprofpp* utility. Taken together, these tools can greatly assist a programmer in development.

A Brief Tour of GCC

The GCC compiler contains numerous options. Because of this proliferation of options, and recognizing that the complete documentation is already included in the base system, only the major highlights will be discussed here. For complete information, see the gcc manual page of the Info page (*info gcc*). Unless otherwise noted, the same options discussed here for gcc, g++, and g77 will apply to the C, C++, and Fortran 77 compilers, respectively.

The most basic use of the GCC compiler is to invoke it on a source code file. This will compile, assemble, and link the source code into an executable named **a.out** by default:

```
$  cat temp.c

#include <stdio.h>

int
main (int argc, char *argv[])
{
        printf("Hello world.\n");
}

$  cc temp.c
$  ls -l
-rwxr-xr-x  1 jose  wheel  25564 Dec 29 08:51 a.out
-rw-r--r--  1 jose  wheel     60 Dec 29 08:50 temp.c
```

The resulting executable, **a.out**, can be invoked as follows:

```
$  ./a.out
Hello world.
```

In this example, the invocation of gcc has called the compiler cc1, the assembler as, and the linker ld to produce the final executable. By default, the C library is linked to the executable. Additional libraries must be specified manually (see below).

To change the name of the executable, use the *-o* option to gcc:

```
$  cc temp.c -o temp
$  ls -l
```

```
-rwxr-xr-x  1 jose  wheel  25564 Dec 29 08:53 temp
-rw-r--r--  1 jose  wheel     60 Dec 29 08:50 temp.c
```

Here the same executable is produced but is now named **temp**, as we specified.

This method works well if you have one simple source file with no special libraries or additional source files. However, if you want to link two or more source files together, you'll have to go through the intermediate steps involving *relocatable objects*. These are built using the *-c* option to gcc:

```
$  cc -c temp.c
$  cc -o temp temp.o
$  ls -l
-rwxr-xr-x  1 jose  wheel  25555 Dec 29 08:57 temp
-rw-r--r--  1 jose  wheel     60 Dec 29 08:50 temp.c
-rw-r--r--  1 jose  wheel    215 Dec 29 08:57 temp.o
```

By default, the resulting objects have the suffix changed from **.c** (or **.cc**, **.C**, or **.c++** for C++ source files, or **.f** for Fortran 77 source files) to **.o**. Here we explicitly controlled the building of an object using *cc -c* and the final linking steps using *cc -o*. To link two or more objects together, name them in series to the compiler:

```
$  cc -c temp.c
$  cc -c temp2.c
$  cc -o temp temp.o temp2.o
$  ls -l
-rwxr-xr-x  1 jose  wheel  25650 Dec 29 09:00 temp
-rw-r--r--  1 jose  wheel     71 Dec 29 09:00 temp.c
-rw-r--r--  1 jose  wheel    245 Dec 29 09:00 temp.o
-rw-r--r--  1 jose  wheel     50 Dec 29 08:59 temp2.c
-rw-r--r--  1 jose  wheel    187 Dec 29 09:00 temp2.o
```

Here the two source code files were built into one executable **temp** using two steps of building objects (the ***.o** files) and then a final linking step of *cc -o*. Additional files can be specified in this way.

The inclusion of additional libraries, such as the math library, needs to be done explicitly. Use *cc -l* library in the final linking step:

```
$  cc temp.o temp2.o -o temp -lm
```

Here the math library, known as **libm.a** or **libm.so**, is linked in. Static libraries use the **.a** suffix, while shared libraries use the **.so** suffix, which sometimes includes a version number as well. By default, shared libraries are used when available to protect against excessive executable sizes. This behavior can be overridden using the *-static* option to *cc* in the final linking step. The prefix **lib** is not used when referencing libraries using the *-l* option.

The default library search path is **/lib** and **/usr/lib**. If you need to specify additional library search paths, you must use the *-L* option. For example, to specify both a locally installed library, **libfoo.so**, and its location, you would execute a command similar to the following:

```
$  cc -L/usr/local/lib -o tempfoo foo.o temp.o temp2.o -lfoo
```

This will tell the compiler to look in the directory **/usr/local/lib** (from the *-L* directive) for **libfoo.so** or **libfo.a** (from the directive *-l*) and link it against the final output.

Similarly, if you have nonstandard locations for header files, they must be specified using the *-I* directive. For example, the following command will tell *cc* to look in **/usr/local/include** for any needed header files, in addition to the default search path of **/usr/include**:

```
$  cc -I/usr/local/include -c temp.c
```

The *-I* directive can be specified multiple times to build a long list of search paths. It can be done only when compiling the source code file, however—not when working with any object files. There is no corresponding *-i* directive.

Additional topics worth investigating include warning directives, such as *-Wall* to show all warnings, *-D* for definitions at compile time, and optimization commands (through the *-O* options). These are all covered in the *cc* documentation.

21.3.2 Default Security Options

The *gcc* shipped in the base OpenBSD system includes, by default, the ProPolice mechanism. ProPolice is a compile-time stack protection mechanism developed by IBM Tokyo Research Laboratories that is available as an addition to the *gcc* compiler. It will apply code to detect and thwart attacks that seek to overwrite the execution stack, which are typically attempted by an attacker who is exploiting a buffer overflow. The system will detect that the stack has been overwritten, log the event to the system logs, and terminate the application before any malicious code can execute.

Not all source code can build with this option enabled. This mechanism can be disabled per source file:

```
$  gcc -fno-stack-protector -c file.c
$  gcc -o file file.o
```

This code will build the object file **file.o** with this stack protection disabled.

21.4 Additional Languages from Ports

While the base installation includes support for various popular languages, several other development languages can be installed from the ports and packages system. These are mainly grouped in the **lang/** and **devel/** subdirectories of the ports tree.

Included in this long list of languages are the LISP programming languages, which are popular for AI programming as well as for *emacs* extensions. The Java language is available either through a source code implementation or through Linux emulation (for newer versions). Other languages include the popular scripting languages Python, Tcl/Tk (along with expect), the object-oriented language Ruby, the popular Web scripting language PHP, scheme, and smalltalk (which is available via the squeak port).

21.5 Debuggers

Debugging is, unfortunately, where most developers spend their time. Bugs happen, and debuggers make it much easier to figure out what went wrong. OpenBSD includes the GNU debugger, *gdb*, in the base installation. This utility integrates nicely with the GNU compiler, allowing for smooth bug detection.

The *gdb* program is rather simple to use. It's best applied to core dump files and executables with their debugging symbols intact (use the *-g* option in *cc*, and don't *strip* the resulting executable). An example session is shown below.

First, we deliberately create some source code that will not execute correctly. This isn't as hard as you might think. Here we misuse a function:

```
$  cat bomb.c
#include <stdio.h>

int
```

```
main(int argc, char *argv[])
{
        char *foo;
        char *template = "foo-bar";

        foo = tmpnam(template);
        printf("%s\n", foo);

        exit(0);
}
```

Now we make the executable, including debugging symbols:

```
$  cc -g -o bomb bomb.c
bomb.c: In function 'main':
bomb.c:5: warning: assignment makes pointer from integer without a cast
/tmp/cce10449.o: warning: tmpnam() possibly used unsafely; consider
using mkstem
p()
$  ./bomb
Memory fault (core dumped)
```

After building it and running the resulting executable (appropriately named **bomb**), we
have what we're after—a core dump. A core dump is nothing more than the contents of
memory that the program was using when it failed. Together with debugging symbols,
we can utilize the debugger to tell us which routine caused the problem in the execution
of this application:

```
$  gdb ./bomb bomb.core
GNU gdb 4.16.1
Copyright 1996 Free Software Foundation, Inc.
GDB is free software, covered by the GNU General Public License,
and you are welcome to change it and/or distribute copies of it
under certain conditions.
Type "show copying" to see the conditions.
There is absolutely no warranty for GDB.  Type "show warranty"
for details.
This GDB was configured as "i386-unknown-openbsd3.4"...
```

```
Core was generated by 'bomb'.
Program terminated with signal 11, Segmentation fault.
Reading symbols from /usr/libexec/ld.so...done.
Reading symbols from /usr/lib/libc.so.28.2...done.
#0  0x40089f9e in memcpy ()
```

We've loaded the executable **bomb** and its core file **bomb.core**; *gdb* will also load the debugging symbols from the libraries used by the application. This will allow us to do a full analysis of the failure in the program. We do so by issuing a "backtrace" command to examine the sequence of events leading up to the failed call:

```
(gdb)  bt
#0  0x40089f9e in memcpy ()
#1  0x5 in ?? ()
#2  0x40081a09 in fprintf ()
#3  0x40083913 in vfprintf ()
#4  0x4007c905 in snprintf ()
#5  0x4002c91b in tmpnam ()
#6  0x17c2 in main () at bomb.c:5
(gdb)
```

In this simple example, we can readily see our problem: the incorrect usage of the tmpnam() function on line 5 of **bomb.c.** The other calls, including snprintf(), are all within the library definition of tmpnam() and are not explicitly included in our source code.

A running application can also be monitored via *gdb*. To do so, provide the application name and the process ID as arguments to *gdb*:

```
$  gdb /usr/local/bin/treewm  23697
 trimmed
Attaching to program '/usr/local/bin/treewm', process 23697
```

You can now monitor the program using *gdb*, including setting breakpoints and monitoring stack variables. This powerful mechanism enables you to debug an application in its environment.

Additional tasks we can perform in *gdb* include disassembly of the executable, examination of the registers on the stack, and even stepwise tracing through the executable. This utility is a powerful tool when used correctly, even though it can be difficult to use at times. The manual page for *gdb*, along with the relevant info page, is especially worthwhile reading if you plan to use this debugger. Even more documentation is available from the Gdb project.

Sometimes the output from *gdb* isn't correct or very easy to understand. The preceding example was deliberately kept simple, but larger, more complex applications will not be as easy to decipher when something goes wrong. In combination with *gdb*, debugging statements within the application are worth using to isolate and correct problems during development.[1]

For what it's worth, the example **bomb.c** contains a handful of errors. One of the fixes is to use the function **tmpnam()** correctly and to use a character string rather than a pointer to a string. Note that the function **mkstemp()** is a significantly more secure function for creating temporary files. However, its semantics are different, and it returns a file descriptor and not a filename. Furthermore, the filename is more random than the filename created by tmpnam(). This helps to thwart a temporary file race, where an attacker tries to guess a filename and then begin controlling it. The mkstemp() function opens the file and hands it to the program that requests it directly; it also sets the permissions on the function to 0600 (which allows the owner of the program to read and write to it, but prevents anyone else from accessing the file). The resulting program looks like the following:

```
#include <stdio.h>
#include <string.h>
#include <unistd.h>

int
main(int argc, char *argv[])
{
        int foo;
        char template[1024];
        strlcpy(template, "/tmp/bomb.XXXXXX", sizeof(template));

        foo = mkstemp(template);
        printf("%s\n", template);
        close(foo);

        exit(0);
}
```

---

[1]Interested readers may wish to obtain the book *The Practice of Programming* by Brian Kernigahn and Rob Pike, which covers several facets of development, including debugging. Much of this book's coverage applies to any OpenBSD system.

When you run this program, it will output data like the following:

```
$  ./bomb
/tmp/bomb.yx2846
$  ls -l /tmp/bomb.yx2846
-rw-------  1 jose  wheel  0 Sep 18 20:04 /tmp/bomb.yx2846
```

The length of the template, which is determined by how many **X** characters are used, governs the amount of randomness possessed by the filename. It comprises a concatenation of random letters (uppercase and lowercase) and the calling process ID. Be sure to use at least eight characters for the template, because the worst-case scenario is a program with a five-digit process ID, which leaves the temporary filename having only three characters of randomness. Persistent programs, which will always have the same process ID, will have three characters of randomness in their temporary filenames; in these situations use a longer template.

21.5.1 Additional Debugging Tools from Ports

Additional development tools useful in debugging that are available in the ports tree include the DDD interface to *gdb*, the Electric Fence debugging library, and SCO's Cscope tool, useful in tracing an executable's execution.

DDD provides a Motif-based graphical interface to *gdb*, making it far more intuitive and easy to use. Together with the display windows, stack registers, source code, and trace output can be more easily examined than via the command line (at least sometimes).

The Electric Fence library can be difficult to use for a novice, but in skilled hands it can provide a rich debugging environment for dynamic memory allocation analysis. Note that the application must be modified to take advantage of these features and linked against the library.

Cscope is a console-based application, using the *curses* interface, that follows symbols through an executable. It provides a rich binary analysis interface, and can even be used to reverse-engineer binary-only applications.

21.5.2 Tracing System Calls

OpenBSD includes a facility for tracing system calls as they happen in real time, known as *ktrace*. The *ktrace* utility is read using the *kdump* tool. It is analogous to the *truss* utility on Solaris or the *strace* toolset in Linux.

Use of *ktrace* is quite simple. One invokes it, with any optional arguments, and supplies the command to be traced, with any arguments, along with it. Returning to our earlier example **temp**, we can examine how this is done:

```
$  ktrace ./temp
Hello
```

The output of the command is shown, but no traced data appears on the standard output. By default, the kernel trace data is not written in a human-readable format but instead written to a binary file called **ktrace.out**. This output file can, of course, be changed. Abbreviated output from *kdump*, the tool used to analyze this file, is shown below:

```
$  kdump -f ktrace.out
  3002 ktrace    RET   ktrace 0
  3002 ktrace    CALL  execve(0xdfbfdc47,0xdfbfdbfc,0xdfbfdc04)
  3002 ktrace    NAMI  "./temp"
  3002 temp      EMUL  "native"
  3002 temp      RET   execve 0
  3002 temp      CALL  open(0x10b1,0,0)
  3002 temp      NAMI  "/usr/libexec/ld.so"
  3002 temp      RET   open 3
```

omitted

```
  3002 temp      CALL  write(0x1,0x4000,0x6)
  3002 temp      GIO   fd 1 wrote 6 bytes
       "Hello
       "
  3002 temp      RET   write 6
  3002 temp      CALL  exit(0x1)
```

The fields are, from left to right, the process ID of the process being traced; the process name (note that *ktrace* executes first, then the process being traced—in this case, *temp*); the action, such as *CALL* or *RETURN*; and the system call being issued, such as *mmap* or *write*, along with any data to the system call.

The *ktrace* and *kdump* utilities contain a rich array of features, and actions such as process attachment can be performed. By using a binary output file, the *kdump* utility can process the data in a variety of ways to show selective or detailed output. For more information on these tools, see their respective manual pages.

One interesting use of the *ktrace* facility is to build a *chroot* environment for an application. By tracing the output of the normal execution of the application, you can ensure that the proper libraries, configuration files, devices, and any auxiliary features are available in the new environment. One of the authors has used this tool to build a *chroot* cell for the *sendmail* mail server in hostile environments.

21.5.3 Additional Source Code Development Tools

While the following tools are not quite debugging accessories, they can nevertheless be used to improve the quality of the code under development. When used in the debugging process, they can help illuminate various source code problems. These static analysis tools are used to analyze source code and to assist in the identification of problems.

One built-in tool is the C program verifier *lint*. A small semantic checker, *lint* uses the C preprocessor (*cpp*) on the input file, which is then analyzed using a two-pass lexical analysis engine. The *lint* utility is very good at being very strict about the use (or misuse) of C directives. Typical output of *lint* used on a small C source file is shown below:

```
$  lint main.c
main.c:
main.c(2): warning: foobar unused in function main
Lint pass2:
printf used( main.c(4) ), but not defined
```

In this case two minor errors appeared: an unused variable and an undefined function. Both would show up as warnings with the C compiler, though neither would prevent the proper execution of the application (a small, "hello world" type of executable).

Although *lint* can be quite verbose, its output can sometimes help locate problem code. Note that *lint* works only on C source code.

Additional programs, available as ports and packages, are similar to *lint* in that they are static analysis tools. The tool *lclint* is similar to *lint*, but can be far more rigorous in its analysis of source code. Numerous enhancements have been made to it to assist in security audits as well as large-scale analysis of source code. Note that some modification of the source code is needed to fully utilize *lclint*.

Three security-conscious tools are also available in the OpenBSD ports collection: *flawfinder*, a Python script to analyze C and C++ source code for security flaws; *its4*, a lexical analysis tool applicable to C and C++ source files; and *rats*, similar to *its4* but capable of scanning not only C and C++, but also Perl, PHP, and Python code. Each of these tools can analyze source code to identify potential security holes, useful in code audits. Note that they will identify only the "low-hanging fruit" of security problems, as none of them understands data flow.

21.6 *make*

The *make* system is a power tool to manage complex projects. Using **Makefiles**, the *make* tool handles dependencies and actions, ensuring that builds are up to date. OpenBSD includes the Berkeley-style *make* tool, which is somewhat different from the more popular GNU *make*. In large measure these styles are compatible, but in their high-end features they differ noticably.

A **Makefile** is a flat text file specifying "targets," dependencies, and actions. A simple **Makefile** is shown below:

```
all: stage1
        cc -c project.c
        cc -o project project.o -L. -lstage1
        @strip project

stage1:
        cc -c stage1.c
        ar -r libstage1.a stage1.o

clean:
        rm -f libstage1.a stage1.o project
```

In this small example, three targets are specified: *all*, *stage1*, and *clean*. The *all* target has a dependency, *stage1*, which itself has no dependencies, as does the *clean* target. The last action of the *all* target, whereby the final executable is stripped of debugging symbols, executes silently. The use of the @ symbol as a prefix of the action means that while it is executed, this action is not printed to the output. To use any of these targets, specify the command *make target*:

```
$  make all
cc -c stage1.c
ar -r libstage1.a stage1.o
cc -c project.c
cc -o project project.o -L. -lstage1
```

The *make* utility manages the complexities of the process, ranging from something as simple as the preceding example or this book, to a large, complicated project like the entire OpenBSD source tree, which is entirely managed from a handful of top-level **Makefiles**.

The BSD version of *make* has various options, including *include* directives and conditionals, allowing for a complex build process. These features are used heavily in the ports tree, for example. Several larger templates are available in **/usr/share/mk**, such as **bsd.prog.mk**. You can use these in your own programs, allowing you to have smaller, more manageable *Makefiles*. Furthermore, you can control some options, such as various types of libraries, more easily when you use this infrastructure. These capabilities are well documented in a **README** file in this directory.

The GNU version of *make*, in contrast, doesn't have support for the same *include* directives or conditionals, but does allow for greater flexibility in specifying actions based on filenames. GNU *make* is available in the OpenBSD ports tree in **devel/gmake**, and is typically installed as **/usr/local/bin/gmake**.

Indeed, *make* can be used for a variety of projects. This book, for example, was managed by using a simple **Makefile** to specify several targets for the LaTeX source files, thereby generating PS, PDF, and DVI outputs. This flexibility has led to the widespread adoption of *make*.

When invoked in the absence of a **Makefile**, *make* will execute the command *cc -O2 -o target target.c*.

Sometimes you may get an error like "line 68: Need an operator" or "line 68: Missing dependency operator" when you run *make*. The most likely explanation is that you're invoking *make*, the BSD *make* tool, on a **Makefile** that uses GNU *make*-isms. Try again with *gmake*.

For additional information on *make*, see the manual page for *make(1)*.

21.6.1 *automake*

The GNU development team has created a system for generating GNU Makefiles from templates. These are processed by the *automake* facility, available in the ports tree, to produce a file **Makefile.in**. This file is then processed by GNU's *autoconf* tool, typically through a *configure* script, to produce a **Makefile** for your setup. This can help the source code identify required libraries and tools, as well as adjust to alternative APIs.

Detailing how *autoconf* and *automake* work is beyond the scope of this book. For more information, see the GNU Info pages for *automake*.

21.6.2 *Imake* and *xmkmf*

An older method of software portability was to use the **Imakefile** facility, which was part of the X11 distribution. The **Imakefile** was processed by the command *xmkmf* so as to generate, from the system's template file, a **Makefile** suited to the system in use. In so doing, software developers could generate portable software. A regular execution of *make* would then build the software as normal.

The **Imakefile** style has fallen out of favor with most mainstream software developers in favor of the GNU *configure* script setup. However, the **Imakefile** facility is in heavy use in the X11 source tree.

21.7 Libraries

OpenBSD includes, in the base system, a number of C libraries useful for programmers. These include the *pcap* libraries, useful for packet capture, and the OpenSSL libraries. The latter are stripped of the IDEA algorithm, which is patented in Canada and, due to licensing considerations, is not included in OpenBSD by default.[2] The inclusion of XFree86 version 4 in the base system also means you have access to OpenGL libraries by default, which is useful for graphics programming. These libraries are included in the base system, along with the standard C and C++ development libraries one would expect in any UNIX system.

Included in the base C library are several additional routines that were originated by the OpenBSD team. Todd Miller created two string-handling routines, `strlcat()` and `strlcpy()`, which provide safe, NUL-terminated replacements for `strncat()` and `strncpy()`. The small check routine `issetugid()` is useful for examining the status of the current executable, to see whether it is running *setuid* or *setgid*. Lastly, the strong pseudo-random bit generator `arc4random()` provided in the base C library offers significantly stronger random bits than the routines it replaces. These routines are now commonly available on other platforms; the source is included in the portable version of OpenSSH, for example.

Other libraries can be added, of course, using the ports and packages system. These include audio libraries, graphics libraries, and the like. Add them just as you would any other port.

21.8 Shared Library and Object Tools

Several auxiliary tools for development are included in OpenBSD to assist you in debugging or examining binaries. Some deal with shared libraries; others allow you to examine the data inside a binary executable.

---

[2]You can, of course, rebuild openssl to include IDEA.

Shared libraries require a runtime link cache so that the executables can find them during their initialization. This cache is configured using the *ldconfig* command. Typically, you will not need to adjust these settings, as they're set by the boot script **/etc/rc** to the directories **/usr/lib**, **/lib**, and, if they exist, **/usr/local/lib** and **/usr/X11R6/lib**. These last two are specific to the ports tree and any added libraries and to the X Window system, respectively.

To examine the shared libraries linked to an executable, you use the command *ldd*. The linked libraries are then listed:

```
$  ldd /usr/local/bin/antisniff
/usr/local/bin/antisniff:
        -lkvm.5 => /usr/lib/libkvm.so.5.1 (0x40022000)
        -lpcap.1 => /usr/lib/libpcap.so.1.1 (0x40027000)
        -lc.25 => /usr/lib/libc.so.25.2 (0x4003e000)
```

Two environmental variables can also alter the behavior of the runtime shared library loading utilities. *LD_LIBRARY_PATH* gives a search path for shared libraries, overriding the search path set by the *ldconfig* cache. *LD_PRELOAD* gives directives for the loading of any special shared libraries; they are honored before any additional libraries are loaded. Both of these directives are ignored for any *suid* or *sgid* executables.

To examine the data within a binary executable, two utilities that are quite useful are *objdump* and *nm*. The *objdump* tool can, for example, disassemble an object file. The *nm* tool is used to display the symbol name list from an object or executable. In each case, stripping the executables can make it more difficult to examine the data in the objects.

21.9 Documentation

An important consideration for any development system is the documentation. OpenBSD documentation is quite extensive. The manual pages for library routines are well written, are checked for clarity and correctness, and often include example code. The "Programmers Supplementary Documentation," found in **/usr/share/doc/psd**, can also be very useful for developers who are new to the BSD environment.[3]

The manual page *style(9)* is worth reading for its discussions of the KNF style, which is used heavily in the OpenBSD source. It gives a very readable and well-established set of guidelines for code layout, use, and checking.

---

[3] The PSD is available as a part of the **misc*** installation set.

## Chapter 22

Packet Filtering and NAT

Since OpenBSD 3.0, the main firewall system has been the PF packet filter. Previously it was the IPF toolkit, but in light of licensing issues this selection was changed. Since then, PF has grown into a mature, full-featured packet filter.

PF's merger with the ALTQ traffic-shaping framework gives greater power to the PF package without creating complicated rules. PF is also capable of packet filtering and NAT, of course, and it has many advanced features normally found only on commercial firewalls.

This chapter introduces PF and gives a brief tour of its features. Because it is so richly endowed, only simple examples are given here. There are many places in the OpenBSD community where rulesets can be shared and discussed and new features more fully explained.

22.1 Introduction to Firewalls

In the most strict definition, a firewall is a device that sits between two network areas and enforces a communication policy between those networks. This enforcement mechanism can include packet filters and filtering routers, as well as application-layer devices such as filtering proxies and mail filters.

This chapter introduces the PF packet filter found in OpenBSD. PF is an IP-layer packet filter that can act either as a filtering router or as a transparent, filtering bridge. However, PF can do significantly more than pass or block packets: It can, for example, modulate the traffic characteristics on the network it filters. PF is a high-performance system that can scale to thousands of concurrent connections without incurring a significant load. Despite this complexity, PF has a relatively simple-to-use configuration format.

22.2 Introduction to PF

The first thing many people will need to do is to enable the OpenBSD system to pass packets from one interface to another, forwarding them through the server. If the system will merely protect itself and will not pass any data, this step isn't necessary. The PF capabilities can be enabled in one of two ways. The first is to edit the **/etc/sysctl.conf** file and make sure the following lines are present:

```
net.inet.ip.forwarding=1
net.inet6.ip6.forwarding=1
```

Both of these features are disabled by default. Changes to this file are read only upon start-up. To change the variables without rebooting the system, the *sysctl* tool could be used:

```
#  sysctl -w net.inet.ip.forwarding=1
```

This command will set the IP forwarding variable to 1, and packets will then be passed.

The next step in enabling PF is to tell the system to load the necessary rules upon start-up. This is done by editing the **/etc/rc.conf** file and setting the following:

```
#pf=NO
pf=YES
```

A few other PF settings in this file may be worth examining:

```
pf_rules=/etc/pf.conf
pflogd_flags=
```

The first setting tells PF which configuration file to load by default. The second setting gives flags to pass to *pflogd*, such as *-d 60* if you wanted *pflogd* to flush its output every 60 seconds.

Once the system is set up to be able to use PF, we need to manipulate its configuration. All user interface changes to PF are made through the *pfctl* tool.

- *-d*   Disable the firewall.
- *-e*   Enable the firewall.
- *-f*   Tell PF the file from which to read the rules. If no file is given, the default file, **/etc/pf.conf**, will be read. Unless another flag is given, *pfctl* will read and load all rules from the file. Unless a flush command is given, old rules will not be removed.

Be mindful that flushing all rules will also flush any connection state and require most connections to be reestablished.

- *-F*   Flush the firewall rules. This flag requires a second option to specify which rules to flush (e.g., *pfctl -Fs*). These rules can be abbreviated:
    - *n*   NAT rules
    - *q*   Queue rules
    - *r*   Firewall rules
    - *s*   State rules
    - *i*   Info, the statistics that are kept on an interface
    - *T*   Tables
    - *a*   All
- *-k*   Kill all state entries for a host. If a second *-k* flag is given, then kill the state entries from the first host to the second host.
- *-n*   Don't actually load the rules, just parse them. This is useful for checking syntax.
- *-s*   Show firewall information. Like the flush flag, this option requires a second option to specify what to show.
    - *n*   NAT rules
    - *q*   Queues
    - *r*   Firewall rules
    - *a*   Anchors
    - *s*   State
    - *i*   Info, the statistics that are kept on the tables
    - *l*   Labels
    - *t*   Timeouts
    - *m*   Memory
    - *T*   Tables
    - *a*   All
- *-v*   Display verbose information. The more *-v* options given, the more verbose the output will be.
- *-z*   Clear the per-rule statistics.
- **Others**   There are other options listed in the manual page for *pfctl*; these will be covered later in this chapter.

22.2.1 The PF Configuration File

The PF configuration file is a flat text file. It is parsed from beginning to end, so order is important. For firewall rules, whichever rule matches a packet last is the one that is taken.

PF supports the use of macros in the configuration file to simplify configuration and make the file more manageable. The most commonly used macro is for the interfaces:

```
EXT_IF="dc0"

pass in on $EXT_IF any
```

PF also supports lists. Rather than having to write a line for each host, a list can be used to specity all hosts:

```
block in on $EXT_IF from 192.168.0.1 to any
block in on $EXT_IF from 192.168.0.7 to any
block in on $EXT_IF from 192.168.0.12 to any
```

This could also be written as follows:

```
block in on $EXT_IF from "{ 192.168.0.1, 192.168.0.7, \
    192.168.0.12 }" to any
```

A macro for a list is also possible:

```
SERVERS="{ 192.168.0.15, 192.168.0.16 }"
```

The most important rule about macros in the configuration file is that they need to be defined before they can be used.

22.3 Firewalls with PF

Building an effective packet filter with PF is relatively painless. The rules are presented in a logical, easy-to-understand format and are well separated in terms of their actions.

When rules in PF are evaluated, the last match wins. Thus, while a rule may match early in a ruleset as it is evaluated from top to bottom, the final rule that matches the packet will set the judgment. This can be overridden via the *quick* action for any rule:

```
# an exception
pass in quick proto tcp from any to 10.1.2.3
# anything else will match and be dropped
block in all
```

Only packets inbound to the host 10.1.2.3 will be allowed to pass, with all other packets being blocked by default.

PF can understand both major IP address families, IPv4 and IPv6 (see Chapter 28). To specify which family you're using, place *inet* and *inet6* declarations in your *block* and *pass* statements. For ICMP rules, the IPv6 family rules are typically used with *icmp6* statements.

PF offers an easy-to-use ports specification mechanism. Ports can be specific ports, such as a single port, or ranges. Specific ports can be specified by name, with the mapping matching that in the file **/etc/services**. Port ranges can be specified using the angle bracket operators or equality operators:

```
# ports 0-99
pass in proto tcp from any port < 100
# only port 102
block in proto tcp to any port = 102
# ports 1001-2000
pass out proto udp from any port 1000 >< 2000
# any ports except 53
block out proto udp to any port != 53
# ports 0-99, 1001, and greater
pass out proto tcp to any port 100 <> 1000
```

This specification strategy can be used for very complicated rulesets or for very simple rulesets. For example, only ephemeral ports can be pass out if you specify a range greater than 1024.

PF boasts a rich interface for handling addresses. It works through dotted quad notation or through CIDR notation. Also, interface addresses can be implicitly stated by giving the interface's name. For example, the interface **fxp0** can be dynamically addressed (via DHCP), but the PF configuration does not need to be updated. Also, to specify the network attached to the interface and the broadcast address for the interface, you can append *:network* or *:broadcast* to the interface name.

PF can also handle arbitrary directionality for packets—either in or out. This ability can be used to block packets not just as they enter a firewall, but also as they leave the device.

One of the more interesting features of PF is that it can make packet decisions on the basis of the network process context. That is, the users and groups of the network processes can be examined by the PF firewall, but only if the firewall is a local endpoint (in or out) of the connection. For example, to control who can browse websites and use *ssh*, rules like the following would be used:

```
pass out proto tcp to any port 80 group www keep state
pass out proto tcp to any port 22 user {jose, brandon} keep state
```

This feature can be useful on a multiple-user shell host to control application usage, in addition to executable controls.

PF offers a rich set of options that can be applied to packets and connections that it has allowed to pass. These are specified with the *pass* action. For example, stateful packet analysis can be done by appending the terms *keep state* to the end of the rule. This technique can be somewhat confusing at first due to the directionality used in conjunction with the rule. Passing a rule *out* and keeping the state on the rules will allow the returning packets in the connection to come back in, but passing a connection *in* and keeping the state will not have the same effect. The state entry is applied to the reverse direction.

Stateful analysis occurs for TCP, UDP, and ICMP packets. For connectionless protocols, it works mainly through timing values and packet tuples (ports and addresses). For TCP, the sequence numbers are used, with a sliding window representing the connection. This helps prevent hijacking attacks when passing through a PF firewall.

PF can affect TCP sequence numbers for hosts behind the firewall by a technique called state modulation. Here the sequence numbers are translated to strongly random increments, which masks the operating system (identifiable by passive analysis techniques) and helps to thwart TCP session hijacking weaknesses. A simple rule that would work for any TCP connection originating from behind the PF firewall would be the following:

```
pass out proto tcp from any to any modulate state
```

The *modulate state* action implicitly sets *keep state* on the connection.

TCP flags are specified in two stages: (1) the flags to match and (2) a list of flags to test. These are specified using the *S/SA* syntax, where the flags to match are separated from the flags to be tested by a slash. Any flags not specified are not tested. Omitting the flags to match defaults to the NULL flag specification. The flags that are tested but not listed as needing to match must be unset. A common way to test for a TCP connection opening is to specify a rule like the following:

```
pass in proto tcp from any to any port 80 flags S/SA
```

This will ensure that the SYN-ACK combination is not matched and that the SYN flag is set.

PF can make routing decisions on packets it can pass in one of four ways. The first, the *fastroute* action, uses the kernel's routing table to make the decision. This is the default action for packets passed by PF. The second, the *route-to* action, specifies the next hop address. Only packets matching the direction are affected, so an asymmetric routing scenario may be created. The third action, *reply-to*, affects only the return packets and creates an asymmetric scenario in the opposite direction. The *route-to* and *reply-to* actions can be used together to create a traffic stream that bypasses a normal routing table based on arbitrary criteria. The fourth action, *dup-to*, can be useful for traffic analysis. For example, packets can be sent to their destinations, but duplicated to a monitoring station that can make additional decisions.

The routing actions in PF can be used to create streams for monitoring, such as with an IDS (by selectively passing traffic that matches a particular service), or even with a sinkhole router via the *dup-to* and *route-to* actions. Using a sinkhole router allows you to examine traffic that may be disrupting services. Packets can also be routed to the loopback address to create a blackhole router, which is often useful in thwarting a denial-of-service attack or for enforcing strict network policies.

PF can, of course, set the *block* action for packets as well. Here packets are simply dropped inside the kernel with no reply being sent. The *block policy* can be set, either globally or on a per-rule basis, to explicitly deny the traffic to the endpoint. The following rule sets up the default return policy, which will send a TCP RST for TCP connections, send ICMP unreachable messages for UDP traffic, and silently discard all other blocked traffic:

```
set block-policy return
```

The block policy can be set immediately after the *block* action and, if desired, can specify a particular packet type to return. For example, to silently drop all packets but return a TCP RST for *ident* connections, the following pair of rules would be used:

```
block in all
block return-rst in tcp port 113
```

One last, very neat feature of PF is the *antispoof* action. This method examines the networks directly connected to an interface and ensures that only traffic that can be returned via that interface is allowed in from that network. For example, if the interface **fxp0** has the network 10.1.2.0/24 attached to it, the following rule will ensure that only packets from that network are allowed to pass:

```
antispoof for fxp0
```

This is similar to reverse path filtering on commercial routers. Note that this technique works only for directly connected networks, so complex routing tables built on these interfaces will not work properly.

22.4 Introduction to Network Address Translation

PF can also perform the duties of a network address translation (NAT) device. NAT allows for the many-to-one or many-to-many translation of addresses. It can be used to share an Internet connection, for example, or to have different network mappings between two segments. The PF device will create the circuitry needed to make those associations dynamically.

To load NAT rules, use the command *pfctl -N*. Packet filtering rules will be ignored. To examine the NAT statistics, use the command *pfctl -s nat*.

22.5 NAT with PF

The basic NAT setup with PF is implemented with the *nat* action. Here the source and destination addresses and networks are specified. Blanket rules can be specified, or more specific rules can be identified. The following rule will translate any traffic from any interface on the NAT device that does not originate on interface **fxp0** to the **fxp0** device.

```
nat on fxp0 inet from ! (fxp0) to any -> (fxp0)
```

Here the interface name is used, rather than its address, because the address may change. Thus the rule can make the address determination when the rule is loaded.

NAT rules involve a many-to-one or many-to-many mapping. By definition, the system cannot map from one network size to another, such as from a /16 network to a /24 network. To map from one /24 network to another /24 network (i.e., networks of the same size), a NAT rule such as the following would be used:

```
nat on fxp0 inet from 10.1.2.0/24 -> 192.168.10.0/24
```

Here all packets originating from the 10.1.2.0/24 network will emerge from the NAT device with addresses in the network 192.168.10.0/24.

For most home users, a single rule such as this one can be useful for establishing a many-to-one mapping for a broadband or dial-up connection.

Exceptions can be designed using two NAT rules, rather than one NAT rule. In this scenario, *nat, rdr*, and *binat* rules that should apply to everything except a specific subset of traffic can be specified by first using a *no* rule and then the needed *nat, rdr*, or *binat* rule. For example, to map all traffic except the traffic for a single host, the following pair of rules would create the exception:

```
no nat on fxp0 from 192.168.7.3 to any
nat on fxp0 from 192.168.7.0/24 to any -> de0
```

Now all traffic except that from 192.168.7.3 is rewritten to the address on interface **de0**.

22.6 Redirection

Port-level redirection can be accomplished using the *rdr* action. This feature can be useful to redirect a single IP address's services to multiple machines in a network. For example, the following rules will map the external address services for *ssh* and HTTP to two different internal machines:

```
rdr on fxp0 inet proto tcp from any to (fxp0) port 22 -> 10.1.2.4
rdr on fxp0 inet proto tcp from any to (fxp0) port 80 -> 10.1.2.5
```

This strategy is useful if you need to split the services among many hosts, a basic premise of server security.

Finally, bidirectional mappings can be generated using the *binat* rule. It redirects the incoming packets to the new network addresses. For example, to set up a bidirectional mapping to allow a single host within a NAT network to communicate freely with the outside network, the following *binat* rule would be used:

```
binat on fxp0 from 10.1.2.3 to any -> 192.168.3.4
```

Here the internal address is 10.1.2.3 and the external address is 192.168.3.4.

22.7 Advanced PF Usage

While the previously mentioned features of PF will satisfy the needs of most simple installations, PF boasts a number of even more advanced features that are also very powerful. These can be used in conjunction with the simpler features to build powerful rulesets.

22.7.1 Tables

PF supports the concept of tables that contain a dynamic set of IP addresses that can be changed at the system runs without reloading the ruleset. One of the more common uses of tables would be to help a spam-blocking program add IP addresses to a table of servers that have been identified as sending spam. The following is an example of such a configuration:

```
table <spammers> persist  192.168.7.1, 192.168.7.2

block in quick on $EXT_INT from <spammers> to any
```

This would block connections from the servers in the *spammers* list. The *persist* flag says to keep the rule even if the list is empty.

Lists are manipulated using *pfctl*. There are a few flags that affect lists:

- *-t*   Specify the list.
- *-T*   Specify operations to perform on a table.
  - *k*   Kill the table; remove it from existence.
  - *f*   Flush; remove all addresses from a table.
  - *a*   Add an IP or network address to a table.
  - *d*   Delete an IP or network address from a table.
  - *r*   Replace the entire contents of a list with a new list of addresses. As an example, the following list *spammers* is truncated by one address.

    ```
    #  pfctl -t spammers -Tshow
       192.168.7.1
       192.168.7.2
       192.168.7.3
    #  pfctl -t spammers -Tr 192.168.7.1 192.168.7.5
    1 addresses added.
    ```

```
    2 addresses deleted.
#   pfctl -t spammers -Tshow
        192.168.7.1
        192.168.7.5
```

- *s*   Show the contents of a list. With the *-v* flag set, this will also show packet counters for each element in the list.

- *t*   Test to see whether an element is in a list. Matching elements are shown with a leading *M*.

```
#   pfctl -t spammers -vTt 192.168.7.3
0/1 addresses match.
#   pfctl -t spammers -vTt 192.168.7.5
1/1 addresses match.
M   192.168.7.5
```

- *z*   Clear the statistics for each element in a table. These statistics include In/Block, In/Pass, Out/Block, and Out/Pass.

- *l*   Load. When using *pfctl*, we can instruct the system to load only one type of rule—in this case, table rules.

```
#   pfctl -f /etc/pf.conf -Tl
```

It is not possible to specify a list with the *-t* command, so all lists from the file will be loaded.

Once this group of options has been set up, the spam-blocking program in our example would add addresses to the list as it runs:

```
#   pfctl -t spammers -Tadd 192.168.7.3
1/1 addresses added.
#   pfctl -t spammers -Tshow
        192.168.7.1
        192.168.7.2
        192.168.7.3
```

Note that the **/etc/pf.conf** file isn't updated when the list is changed. A script would need to be written to save the list to make sure addresses are not lost. Then, when PF is loaded, the file could be read to load the list:

```
table <spammers> persist file "/etc/spam/list"
```

This also allows for the list to be transferred between machines and distributed among other users.

Reactive Rulesets

With such tables, it becomes easy to write scripts that can react to events in logfiles. A simple script can run from *cron* every few minutes, scan a logfile, and look for any IPs addresses that match a certain violation. These addresses could be pushed into a table every time the *cron* job runs. Any type of log could be read for mail servers, FTP servers, Web servers, IDS, or other servers: The possibilities are almost endless. The one thing to be careful of is that the scripts don't try to do too much and close off too much. A smart attacker could use the script to make the firewall block addresses it shouldn't. If, for example, a script were to block anyone who sent a packet with some improper header flags set, an attacker could send a forged packet to block almost any address.

The following script could be used to block IP addresses that are running a known scanning tool against a Web server:[1]

```
#!/bin/ksh

#  Scan the specified logfile for the specified search entries.  Add
#  IP addresses found into the table www_block_ips and log IP and
timestamp into
#  the specified LOGFILE.  Dump the contents of the table to the
#  BLOCKFILE.

TABLE=www_block_ips
SEARCH='cmd.exe|cgi-bin/formmail.pl'
LOGFILE=/var/log/dyn_pf.log
BLOCKFILE=/root/www_block_ips.list
FILE=/var/www/logs/error_log
WHEN='date +"%a %b %e %H:"'
NOW='date +%Y%m%d%H%m'

for bad_address in `cat $FILE | \
        grep "$WHEN" | \
        grep -E $SEARCH | \
        awk 'print $8' | \
```

---

[1]This script is available at **http://www.crimelabs.net/openbsdbook/**.

```
        sed 's/]//' | \
        sort | uniq`
  do
  pfctl -q -t $TABLE -Ta $bad_address
  echo "Ip address $bad_address added at $NOW" >> $LOGFILE
done


/sbin/pfctl -t $TABLE -Tshow > /root/www_block_ips.list
```

This script reads the logfile and finds any host that requested the **cmd.exe** file or a **form-mail.pl** script that doesn't exist on the server. These hosts are then added to the PF table *www_block_ips* and the table is logged back to the system:

```
#  pfctl -t www_block_ips -Tshow
   61.171.119.152
   62.161.213.2
   64.8.212.90
   64.72.36.75
...
...
#  cat /root/www_block_ips_list
   61.171.119.152
   62.161.213.2
   64.8.212.90
   64.72.36.75
...
...
```

22.7.2 Anchors

PF uses anchors to mark points in the configuration file where new rules can be added or removed dynamically. One of the most common uses would be to allow a program like *authpf* to change the ruleset for a user during login. With *authpf*, as will be discussed later in this chapter, when a user logs in, the IP address from which he or she is connecting can be added to the firewall ruleset.

In the **/etc/pf.conf** file, we can have one of four types of lines:

```
binat-anchor my_binat_anchor
nat-anchor my_nat_anchor
rdr-anchor my_rdr_anchor
anchor myanchor
```

PF cares about the order of the rules, so some rules must be defined before others.[2] If our anchor has only one type of statement, like a simple NAT statement, we could use the first command. If there are multiple types of anchors, like NAT and filtering, we would need to break up the rules to make sure they are processed in the proper order.

To load rules into an anchor, we load the rules into a file and then use *pfctl* to merge or remove the rules:

```
#  echo "pass in quick proto tcp from any to 192.168.7.10 \
   port www" > anchorrules
#  pfctl -a myanchor:10_www -f anchorrules
```

Once we've added the rule to the anchor, we could just as easily remove it:

```
#  pfctl -a myanchor:10_www -F rules
```

Anchors provide a clean and compartmentalized way to manage related rules.

22.7.3 Packet Scrubbing

One type of attack on firewalls and IDS sensors seeks to malform the packets seen by the intervening device. In this scenario, fragments and odd flag combinations may be set in an attempt to confuse monitoring devices but not the end system, which will reassemble the fragments and possibly drop or ignore strange flag combinations.

PF can help mitigate such an attack through the use of the *scrub* action. This action normalizes the packets as they pass through a PF device, either inbound or outbound. The technique is based on work by Vern Paxson and others as well as work by Robert Malan and others. Such scrubbing can also be used to thwart passive operating system identification, which relies on predictable values for the TCP sequence numbers, IPID values, MSS, and TTL values. This simple interface helps make PF unique, even among commercial filtering devices.

---

[2] The *anchor* tag can't precede the *nat-anchor* tag because the translation rules must be processed before the filtering rules.

Used without any arguments, *scrub* will perform basic cleanups on IP traffic that passes through the firewall. PF will reassemble IP fragments before passing them on. If the packet is not reassembled before a timeout occurs, it is actively discarded.

Other cleanups that PF can perform with "scrub" include:

- **no-df**   PF will clean the "don't fragment" bit from matching packets, which may be inappropriately set by the node's operating system.
- **min-ttl**   PF will enforce a minimum TTL value. Note that this setting can interfere with *traceroute* and similar tools that exploit the TTL measurements.
- **max-mss**   PF will set a maximum MSS value for TCP traffic.
- **random-id**   After reassembling the fragments, PF will randomly assign IPID values. This setting is useful for thwarting OS identification as well as NAT host counting techniques as described by Bellovin and others. It is most powerfully used with a NAT device.
- **fragment crop**   PF will remove duplicate fragments and fix overlapping fragments.
- **fragment drop-ovl**   PF will selectively drop overlapping fragments, not just the portions of the overlap.
- **reassemble tcp**   This operation selectively normalizes TCP connections and their states, including keep-alive timers and TTL values.

Most installations will want to use something like the following:

```
scrub in all random-id fragment reassemble
```

This line, which is near the beginning of the **/etc/pf.conf** file, will take all packets, make sure the fragments are reassembled before they are passed on, and assign a random value to the identification field in the packet if it is going out. This is done because some operating systems use packet identifications that can be predicted. Setting the *scrub* action to handle inbound packets means that packets will be cleaned up regardless of the first interface they cross. Most rulesets benefit from using the simple *scrub in all* rule at the top of their PF configuration files.

It is important to reiterate that a single PF firewall can extend these features to all systems communicating through it, including non-OpenBSD systems. This "bump-in-the-wire" approach can greatly improve a network's security and resistance to passive information gathering.

22.7.4 Rate Limiting

Rate limiting, or "bandwidth queues" in PF terminology, regulates the speed of connections that pass through the firewall. This feature is found on very few firewall products and is not free. OpenBSD supports several industry-standard rate-limiting technologies, including Class-Based queues, Priority queues, Random Early Detection, and Explicit Congestion Notification.

- **Class-Based Queue**   A Class-Based queue (*cbq*) controls traffic by specifying bandwidth rates for each rule. The bandwidth for an interface is divided into rules that are assigned to filtering rules.

- **Priority Queue**   A Priority queue (*priority*) controls traffic by setting a priority for each rule. All traffic is processed and rules with the highest priority are handled first.

- **Random Early Detection**   Random Early Detection (*red*) helps the firewall handle traffic congestion by dropping random packets from queues that have the *red* option set. The alternative would be to just drop, for example, all *telnet* or *snmp* connections rather than just some of them. The *red* flag makes network loading more graceful.

- **Explicit Congestion Notification**   Rather than dropping a packet, PF could tag it with the Explicit Congestion Notification (*ecn*) flag in the header to tell both clients involved in a connection that there is a congestion problem and to slow down the places of sending traffic. Not all clients honor this bit. See RFC 3168.

Setting up queues is very simple for almost any system. You just turn queues on, set some defaults for the limiting interface, define the different rates for the different queues, and then specify a queue for any filter rule. For example:

```
altq on fxp0 cbq bandwidth 10Mb queue { normal, ftp, www }
queue normal cbq(default)
queue ftp bandwidth 800Kb
queue www bandwidth 1.2Mb

pass in on fxp0 from any to any port 80 queue www
```

This class-based rule enables queuing on **fxp0** with a maximum bandwidth of 10 megabits/second and then defines the queues *normal, ftp*, and *www*. If no bandwidth was specified, the link speed of the interface would have been used. The second line defines a queue called *normal* that handles any filter rules that don't have another queue set. The next queue, *ftp*, limits traffic to 100 kilobytes/second or 800 kilobits/second. The last line defines another queue at 1.2 megabits/second. A filtering rule is shown with the *www* queue set.

The other major queuing method is the Priority queue. It defines a queue and gives it a priority. Queues with the highest priority are handled first.

```
altq on fxp0 priority bandwidth 10Mb queue { ssh, www }
queue ssh priority 10
queue www priority 1


pass out on fxp0 from any to any port 22 keep state queue ssh
pass out on fxp0 from any to any port 80 keep state queue www
```

In this example, any SSH traffic will be processed before any Web traffic.

22.7.5 Transparent Filtering

A filtering router isn't the best solution for everyone. Some people need only an in-line bridge that can do packet filtering. OpenBSD and PF are also able to support this setup. If this system were utilized at a university, for example, we wouldn't want to do address translation, be a hop in the network, or deny much. For our purposes here, let's assume that we just want to prevent SMB and X traffic from going into or out of the network. Like a firewall, we want to make this machine secure and, presumably, invisible. Be sure that all services are turned off and any communication with the system is out of band.[3]

Firewalling is turned on in **/etc/rc.conf** as described above. Creating the bridge is relatively easy, and was discussed in Chapter 9. Briefly, in the two interface configuration files, set the interfaces to *up*, but don't add an IP address. For example, in the **/etc/hostname.dc0** file, we would have the following entry:

```
up
```

A similar entry would appear in **/etc/hostname.dc1**. Next, we need to specify the bridge, add the interfaces, and bring the bridge up. We will use *bridge0* and will edit the **/etc/bridgename.bridge0** file:

```
add dc0 add dc1 up
```

---

[3]Use a third network card and connect the host to an internal network behind the firewall for management.

The next step is to set up the **pf.conf** rules that will be used. PF can filter both inbound and outbound packets on a bridge device, so rules can apply to either direction on a bridge's interface. For example, to constrain IGMP to a subnet behind the **dc0** interface on a bridge and to keep out IGP (IP protocol 9) via a filter on **dc1**, the following rules would be used:

```
block in quick on dc0 proto igmp
pass in on dc0 all
block in quick on dc1 proto igp
pass in on dc1 all
```

The bridge can also be used to block outbound packets on an interface by using *block out on dc1* directives. Packets in bridges always traverse two interfaces, the one they enter on and the one they leave on.

Note that PF cannot filter traffic based on layer 2 (link-layer) addresses, as it handles only IP packets (which include TCP, UDP, and the like). Instead, use the *brconfig* command to set up link-layer filters, as described in Chapter 9.

22.7.6   Load Balancing

Another feature of PF that is rare among firewalls is its ability to support load balancing. Although many firewalls can load-balance incoming connections, PF can load-balance outgoing network connections as well. This feature is difficult to find with other products, but is native with PF.

Incoming Load Balancing

The most basic load-balancing method, and the most commonly used, is to load-balance incoming connections. The place this would typically be done would be for Web servers.

```
WWW_POOL=''{192.168.1.10, 192.168.1.20, 192.168.1.30}''
rdr on $EXT_IF from any to $WWW_IP port 80 -> $WWW_POOL source-hash
```

In this example, we will redirect any traffic going to the external IP of our Web site to the internal servers. This is done in a round-robin fashion. The *source-hash* keyword tells PF to keep directing a client to the same internal server. This technique is needed in some instances to ensure browser persistence.

Furthermore, a round-robin usage of multiple internal addresses can be performed using the *round-robin* keyword with a list of addresses:

```
rdr on fxp0 inet proto tcp from any to (fxp0) port 80 -> \
    {192.168.1.10, 192.168.1.20, 192.168.1.30} round-robin
```

This can be useful for incoming load balancing to an internal network. Addresses are chosen in a fashion that evenly distributes the requests among them.

Outgoing Load Balancing

Outgoing load balancing is one of the cooler features of PF. If a firewall resided behind a pair of network connections, it could route traffic out through both network connections. This is done using a combination of the *route-to* action, which forces a routing decision within PF, and the *round-robin* action, which evenly distributes packets across a list of addresses.

   In the following scenario, the interface **fxp0** is the internal interface on network 10.1.2.0/24, **dc0** is the primary external interface on network 192.168.1.0/24, and **dc1** is the secondary external interface on network 192.168.2.0/24. Here we balance the inbound traffic, which has the effect of causing outbound traffic to be balanced as well:

```
$int_if = "fxp0"
$ext_if1 = "dc0"
$ext_ip1 = "192.168.1.1"
$ext_if2 = "dc1"
$ext_ip2 = "192.168.2.1"
pass in on $int_if route-to { ($ext_if1, $ext_ip1), \
    ($ext_if2, $ext_ip2)} round-robin from 10.1.2.0/24 to \
    any keep state
```

Notice that the *route-to* action specifies both an interface and an address, so we have to pair these together with parentheses and then curly braces for the *round-robin* decision. Rules such as this need to be established for any traffic that is to be load balanced. PF can selectively or globally load-balance outbound traffic on the basis of the selection criteria.

22.8 Selective Filtering Based on the Operating System

OpenBSD 3.4's PF added a new feature to the system—the ability to enact rules on the basis of the target's detected operating system. This feature uses the TCP SYN operating system fingerprinting mechanism as implemented in Michal Zalewksi's *p0f* tool to make this determination. The fingerprints file is included with the base system and should work for most systems commonly found on the Internet.

Fingerprints are stored in the file **/etc/pf.os**, which contains mappings of TCP SYN packet characteristics to source operating systems. These characteristics include TCP options and their values. To use this feature, you must include the fingerprints file in your PF configuration file, **/etc/pf.conf**:

```
set fingerprints "/etc/pf.os"
```

Now PF will use this file to determine the operating system for ruleset evaluation.

A new ruleset factor, *os*, has been added to PF that makes use of this file. For example, to selectively block Linux 2.2 systems from connecting to your Web server, add a line like the following:

```
block in proto tcp from any os "Linux 2.2" to any port WWW
```

This will effectively prevent Linux 2.2 systems from crossing the PF firewall and contacting Web servers on TCP port 80.

Two big caveats are in order, however. First, the values set in the TCP SYN can be modified by the owner of the machine, so this is not a reliable detection mechanism. Nevertheless, it will work for most systems given that most people do not alter the values on their systems. Second, normalizations done by PF (and other devices) will defeat this detection mechanism. Use it with care in these scenarios.

22.9 Logging with *pflogd*

Having a firewall, but not caring about or checking the logs, is like locking the vault of a bank, but not looking at the video tapes of the criminals trying to pick the lock. PF logs packets in a native *tcpdump* format. This allows the logfiles to be passed through *tcpdump* and replayed later using *tcpreplay* or other tools.[4] It also allows the use of *tcpdump* to check through the logs for interesting traffic.

As with any network interface or pseudo-device, make sure that the interface is configured *up*:

```
#  ifconfig pflog0 up
```

To watch the logfile in a terminal, the following command is used:

---

[4]The version of *tcpreplay* in the ports tree does not support the **pflog** header format, but the version at **http://tcpreplay.sourceforge.net/** does.

```
root@firewall:/root# tcpdump -nettti pflog0
tcpdump: WARNING: pflog0: no IPv4 address assigned
tcpdump: listening on pflog0
Jun 09 21:48:47.948688 rule 6/0(match): block in on fxp0: \
    10.10.10.11 > 10.10.32.1: icmp: echo request
Jun 09 21:48:48.958257 rule 6/0(match): block in on fxp0: \
    10.10.10.11 > 10.10.32.1: icmp: echo request
Jun 09 21:48:54.342430 rule 6/0(match): block in on fxp0: \
    10.10.10.52.137 > 10.10.255.255.137:  udp 50
Jun 09 21:48:55.091389 rule 6/0(match): block in on fxp0: \
    10.10.10.52.137 > 10.10.255.255.137:  udp 50
Jun 09 21:48:55.841593 rule 6/0(match): block in on fxp0: \
    10.10.10.52.137 > 10.10.255.255.137:  udp 50
```

The output of *tcpdump* is modified to be specific to the **pflog** interface. By using *tcpdump* -*e*, processing of the packets from **pflog** is enabled, showing the rules and reasons why packets were logged. Filters for *tcpdump* can also be applied, meaning we could have used *tcpdump* to look only at specific traffic:

```
#  tcpdump -n -i pflog0 host 66.92.101.112
```

This will show only packets logged by the firewall for the host 66.92.101.112.

Logging in the background can be accomplished by using the *pflogd* daemon, which listens to the device **pflog0**. The *pflogd* service starts when PF is started from **/etc/netstart**. The default options suit most users and scenarios. However, *pflogd* also understands extended *tcpdump* filters (which understand options specific to the **pflog0** interface). While all packets can be displayed by the **pflog0** interface, selective logging of denied packets can be performed as well:

```
#  pflogd on fxp1 action block
```

This command will log all packets blocked into or out of the interface **fxp1**.

PF logging is, by default, done only on the firewall itself. To remotely send the logged packets to another host using the *syslog* system, combine the *tcpdump* examples above with the use of the *logger* command. First, set up the file **/etc/syslog.conf** to send the packets to a remote system:

```
local0.info        @firewall-loghost
```

This will send all messages of *local0* origin and at an INFO level to the host *firewall-loghost*. Next, start the log pipe:

```
#  tcpdump -nettti pflog0 | logger -p local0.info
```

This will pass all of the text output of the *tcpdump* command through the *logger* command, which provides an interface to the *syslog* facility. The *syslog* command will handle the network transport of the data. More robust scenarios can be built, but this example provides a skeleton for more complex solutions.

The header for the PF logfiles is unique to OpenBSD and PF, meaning **libpcap**-based applications will have to be modified to read them. This includes *snort* and *tcpreplay*, two popular tools. The source code changes are fairly minor and are best built using the system headers, which define the header size and structure.

22.10 Examining the State Table with pfsync

OpenBSD exposes the PF state table (which keeps track of connections) via the **pfsync0** device. This pseudo-device is written to by the kernel when the internal state table in PF is altered. The **pfsync0** device is currently useful only as a debugging aid, which can be deployed to determine whether a firewall is properly seeing and recording connections. The failure of a firewall to add an expected state entry can indicate a botched ruleset or some other networking error.

This device must be enabled in a kernel configuration to be viewed (but is not needed to keep stateful firewall rules). The needed line in the configuration is as follows:

```
pseudo-device    pfsync           # pf sync if
```

The GENERIC kernel already has this device enabled. This will create a simple **pfsync0** device, which appears as a pseudo-device in the network interface table:

```
$  ifconfig pfsync0
pfsync0: flags=41<UP,RUNNING> mtu 2020
```

This device is manipulated up or down with the *ifconfig* command. You cannot have more than one **pfsync** device on a system.

The **pfsync0** device is viewable by the *tcpdump* command in the base OpenBSD system. This version of *tcpdump* has been altered to understand the format of **pfsync0** entries, so using *tcpdump* from other systems will not work.

The **pfsync0** device was originally intended to expose firewall state changes between devices, which would allow for firewall failover without any loss of connection information. While an experimental *pfsyncd* tool has been created, it remains under development and is not part of the OpenBSD distribution. It will not be discussed here.

Using *tcpdump*, we can view the changes in the state table used by the PF system. This requires rules that use the *keep state* modifiers. A simple *tcpdump* command to view it would look like the following:

```
$  sudo tcpdump -ni pfsync0 -s 1500
tcpdump: WARNING: pfsync0: no IPv4 address assigned
tcpdump: listening on pfsync0
00:38:39.233407 DEL ST: rule 8 udp 10.10.32.1:123 -> \
    192.168.252.7:123        MULTIPLE:SINGLE
rule 8 udp 10.10.32.1:123 -> 192.168.1.43:123          \
    SINGLE:NO TRAFFIC
00:38:46.706373 INS ST: rule 8 udp 10.10.32.1:36556 -> \
    10.10.10.11:53       SINGLE:NO TRAFFIC
rule 8 udp 10.10.32.1:28473 -> 10.10.10.11:53          \
    SINGLE:NO TRAFFIC
rule 7 tcp 10.10.32.1:18246 -> 192.168.9.164:80        \
    SYN_SENT:CLOSED
```

Just as with logging for **pflog0**, using *tcpdump -e* will expose more information about the state table transitions.

The entries here are similar to the entries for **pflog0**, showing the protocol, source and destination information, and rule numbers. In addition, the device reports the changes in the state table:

- **INS**   Insert a state entry.
- **DEL**   Delete a state entry.
- **SINGLE**   A single packet was sent and reported in this time frame. This change is used with stateless protocols.
- **MULTIPLE**   Multiple packets were observed for a stateless protocol.
- **NO TRAFFIC**   The other end did not reply with any traffic.
- **SYN SENT**   A TCP SYN packet was sent to the server but no reply has been seen yet.

This information can be useful in debugging a PF state table issue, such as when a rule is not working as expected. Aside from *pfsyncd*, no other applications rely on this information, and this information is not usable by normal **pcap** applications.

22.11 Determining Firewall Rules

One of the biggest challenges in determining firewall rules is to map the services in use on a network to ports and protocols. Not every host has to accept inbound connections, but subnets typically behave the same way for all hosts inside of them.

A default accept firewall would allow any traffic into the network, with exceptions listing which hosts and services to block. This enumerated list identifies systems that cannot communicate beyond the firewall. For example, a database server may have its address blocked by the firewall, but other hosts may be able to communicate using any other services.

22.11.1 Opening Ports

A default deny firewall, in contrast, prevents any traffic not explicitly allowed. The determination of this traffic—enough to keep applications running smoothly but not too liberal to create a security hole—is somewhat of an art form. By tracking the applications in use, we can build exact firewall rules that provide the maximum coverage of the network. We do so by using the **pfsync0** interface to observe traffic in the firewall, followed by processing of this data.

The first steps seek to ensure that the **pfsync0** pseudo-device is up and then create a minimal PF configuration file. We pass all traffic but keep state entries, which are presented on the **pfsync0** interface. Finally, we capture this traffic in a *tcpdump* file:

```
#  ifconfig pfsync0 up
#  cat /etc/pf.conf
pass in all keep state
pass out all keep state
#  pfctl -e -f /etc/pf.conf
#  tcpdump -nettti pfsync0  -s 1500 -w /tmp/foosync
```

Now we let this system run for a while—for example, on a filtering bridge or a router. This will track the state changes as connections are created and torn down, saving them for later analysis.

After a period of observation, lasting anywhere from a few hours to a few days, the log can be analyzed to provide a convenient summary of the services and ports used. The following script will roll up any unprivileged port (above 1024) into the term "65535," which can be taken to be the upper bound of an unprivileged port.

```
$  tcpdump -nr /tmp/foosync | awk '{split ($4, src, '':'');
        split ($6, dst, '':'');
        if (src[2] > 1024) src[2] = 65535
        print $3 '' '' src[2] '' '' dst[2]}' | sort | uniq
```

The output of the script is concise and easy to understand. The entries are the protocol in use, the source port, and the destination port.

```
udp 123 123
tcp 65535 22
udp 65535 53
tcp 65535 80
```

The biggest drawback to this method is that it assumes that all connections are symmetrical. However, with the proper filters to the second *tcpdump* command (which is piped through *awk*), this traffic can be differentiated:

```
$  tcpdump -nr /tmp/foosync src net 10.10 ...
```

This command will show only traffic that originated on the network 10.10/16, so the summary observations will be for the outbound traffic from this network (provided it is behind the firewall). Additional **pcap** filters can be specified if necessary.

22.12 Authenticated Firewall Rules

The *authpf* system can be used to tie firewall rules to individual users. For example, one user may be allowed to use a service that is unique to that user. By controlling the loading of these firewall rules to users' periods of activity, we can improve network security.

The *authpf* method of authenticated firewall rules uses two components. The first is a user shell that tells the PF firewall that a user has been authenticated. The second is a firewall ruleset that creates the rules needed for each user.

Setting up the *authpf* shell is very simple and uses the **login.conf** file. Here, the default user class has the *authpf* shell as its default:

```
default:\
    :localcipher=blowfish,6:\
    :shell=authpf:
```

When users log into this host, they will not get a shell. Instead, they will have told the firewall that they have been authenticated.

Accounts using this system must be listed in the file **/etc/authpf/authpf.allow**. Users who cannot use this system can be explicitly listed in the directory **/etc/authpf/banned/**, with one file per username of the banned user. This file can contain a message describing why that particular user cannot use the network. By default, accounts not listed in the **allow** file cannot insert firewall rules using this system. When they log into the firewall (if they have an account), no rule changes will be created.

The PF ruleset, in **pf.conf**, must be altered slightly to accept rules in anchors from *authpf*. The following four anchors are used by *authpf*:

```
nat-anchor authpf
rdr-anchor authpf
binat-anchor authpf
anchor authpf
```

Now rules can be inserted into these anchors to control the network access for the user's IP address.

Upon seeing this user authentication from *authpf*, new firewall rules can be inserted. The rules (and macros) are listed in the file **/etc/authpf/authpf.rules**. A simple ruleset might look like the following:

```
external_if = "fxp0"
internal_if = "fxp1"
pass in log quick on $internal_if proto tcp from $user_ip to any
keep state
pass in quick on $internal_if from $user_ip to any
```

This ruleset provides no protection for the new user, but any traffic to and from the user's host can pass without objection. More complicated rulesets can be created as well. The macro **user_ip** holds the IP address of the network client.

Traditionally, *ssh* connections are used to authenticate the users to the firewall. Users log into the firewall to "turn on" their network use. Any system that can correctly establish and hold an *authpf* session should be able to work, however, that meaning a Webpage where users can authenticate is possible.

The *authpf* system is typically used for high-security installations or even medium-security wireless networks. It prevents unauthorized use of the Internet service beyond the firewall. Note that eavesdroppers can still capture traffic on the local network—they just cannot go beyond the firewall.

22.13 Firewall Performance Tuning

Very little can or needs to be done for an OpenBSD PF firewall. There are very few limitations for the firewall, and it is very efficient from the outset. Some people have reported rather high performance with even meager hardware. A few things can be done in some environments to tweak performance, but these steps are really useful only for firewalls that are being pushed near their limits.

- **Options**   PF allows for a large number of timing settings that regulate sessions. A dozen variables can be set for the various states in the TCP, UDP, and ICMP connection process. There is a general catch-all for all other protocols:

```
set timeout  tcp.first 30, tcp.opening 10
```

- **Ruleset**   Because the firewall needs to parse the ruleset for every packet it handles, how the ruleset is written can affect performance. This consideration, however, is applicable only for massive rulesets and high-utilization environments (either very high bandwidth or very slow hardware). The first strategy is to have the firewall deal with the most common packets first. For example, consider a firewall that is set up to pass out all TCP port 80 traffic and all TCP port 22 traffic. Because there should be much more port 80 traffic than port 22 traffic, the port 80 rule should be applied first so most packets are caught earlier. A second strategy is to use lists rather than individual rules. It comes into play when there are a large number of hosts in the list (or table). Third, the smaller the ruleset, the less there is to parse. Any unnecessary rules that can be combined will make the list smaller to traverse and will help speed up the firewall.

Overall, the PF firewall is extremely efficient. Solutions like those mentioned here need to be considered only in the most extreme situations.

Chapter 23

NFS: The Network Filesystem

23.1 Introduction to NFS

The Network File System (NFS) is used to share filesystems between two computers over a network. There are two pieces to the connection: a client and a server. The server shares or *exports* one or more filesystems to be used by the client. The client mounts the filesystem on its local directory hierarchy. In this way, a remote filesystem can appear to be a local filesystem. NFS is defined in RFC 1094.

NFS offers a way to share home directories between a set of workstations, to share a large data store, or to share block devices such as CD-ROM or DVD drives. Typically, it is found in situations where a set of workstations need to be identical, such as university computer labs. However, NFS is relatively painless to set up and, for many users, provides an easy way to share a significant amount of disk space between systems.

Like its cousin NIS, NFS uses the *portmap* utility to dynamically assign port numbers for requests. Also, NFS uses the RPC protocol to communicate requests between the client and the server. Communications typically take place over the UDP transport protocol. When used in combination, NIS and NFS can enable a set of workstations to appear very similar to the regular user, having the same login requirements and home directories for all machines.

NFS is designed for local networks that have low latencies between them. As such, remotely mounting a filesystem over networks is not recommended when you are using NFS.

23.2 NFS Client Configuration

From the client's perspective, mounting an NFS filesystem is almost the same as mounting a local one. The source is not a device, however, but rather a server name and exported filesystem:

```
#  mount orion:/usr/local /usr/local
```

This command will mount the exported filesystem from the server *orion* on the local system as **/usr/local**. In effect, *orion* and the local system have identical **/usr/local** hierarchies.

23.3 NFS Server Configuration

The NFS server requires three components to handle NFS client requests: the mount daemon *mountd*, the NFS daemon *nfsd*, and the file-locking daemon *rpc.lockd*. These daemons are started automatically by the system initialization script */etc/rc* if the configuration option *nfs_server* is set to "YES."

23.3.1 Kernel Configuration

To begin setting up an NFS server, ensure that the kernel has been configured to act as such a server. In the configuration file, the NFS server option must be selected and not commented out:

```
option          NFSSERVER          # Network File System server
```

The GENERIC kernel that ships with OpenBSD has this option enabled by default. Without it, NFS operations will not work.

23.3.2 Configuration of the Server

To run an NFS server, you will need a few things. The configuration file **/etc/rc.conf** uses a variable, *nfs_server*, to note that these services should be started. Setting this variable to YES will start the daemons needed to run NFS services. You will also need to have the *portmap* service running for this to work and a properly configured **/etc/exports** file.

    The *portmap* server maps RPC to TCP and UDP port numbers, thereby connecting RPC services to IP addresses. Because RPC is used by NFS, we need to have *portmap* available. To start *portmap*, simply run the command. The command *portmap -d* will start the service in foreground mode, printing debug information and errors to the standard error output. Setting the YES value for *portmap* in **/etc/rc.conf** will ensure that *portmap* becomes activated at every start-up. Once initiated, *portmap* will listen on port 111 using TCP and UDP:

```
#  netstat -na
Active Internet connections (including servers)
```

```
Proto Recv-Q Send-Q  Local Address     Foreign Address     (state)
tcp       0      0  *.111             *.*                 LISTEN
...
udp       0      0  *.111             *.*
...
```

You can view the status of *portmap* by using the command *rpcinfo*. This command can also be used to contact the local system or a remote system and find out which RPC services are available:

```
$  rpcinfo -p orion
   program vers proto   port
    100000   2   tcp    111  portmapper
    100000   2   udp    111  portmapper
```

RPC programs have numbers, with *portmap* itself having the number 100000. In the preceding example, no additional RPC services are running. Services such as NIS and NFS will be visible if they are running. The file **/etc/rpc** lists RPC programs and their numbers.

The next step in setting up NFS as a server is to configure the filesystems that will be shared with other systems. Filesystems to be shared are handled by the file **/etc/exports**. This file has the following format:

```
filesystem options
```

The *filesystem* argument gives the full path to the local filesystem or directory hierarchy you wish to share with other systems. Multiple filesystems can be specified before any options, allowing you to have a common set of options for several filesystems you are exporting. The *options* control the scope of access and the interactions that clients can have with the server's filesystem.

The valid options for NFS exports are described below:

- **-ro**   Export the filesystem as read-only by those users who can connect to it. In the absence of this option, read-write access is assumed.
- **-network**   Specify a network in IPv4 format that can mount the filesystem. In the absence of this option, any host that can reach the NFS server can attempt to connect to the filesystem (and may succeed in doing so). Example: *-network=10.65.0.0*

- **-mask**   When used with the *-network* option, limit the range of hosts that can connect. In the absence of the *-mask* option, the expected network mask (class A, B, or C) will be used. Example: *-mask=255.255.0.0*

- **-maproot**   Set the credentials of the root user coming from the remote system as it acts on the NFS filesystem. For example, you can treat the root user as having lower privileges when using the remotely mounted filesystem. Group membership can also be specified by using a colon-separated list of groups, either by name or by number. An empty list means no group memberships are mapped. In the absence of *-maproot*, the remote root user is given the user ID *-2* and the group ID *-2*. In the absence of any group directives, all of root's groups (visible in *id*) are used. Example: *-maproot=nobody:users*

- **-mapall**   Like the *-maproot* option but applies to any users coming in, not just the root user. Also, group options may be specified. In the absence of this directive, normal user ID values are used. The directives *-maproot* and *-mapall* may not be specified on the same line. Example: *-mapall=www:www*

- **-alldirs**   Allow any subdirectories of the exported filesystem to be mounted, not just the top-level directory.

As can be seen in the following example, we set first the items to export and then the options on the export.

```
/usr/local -ro -network 192.168.1 -mask 255.255.255.0
/usr/home 192.168.1.2
```

The first export sends **/usr/local** to everyone in the 192.168.1.0/24 network, making it available on a read-only basis. Clients can read the data from the filesystem but cannot alter the data, erase any files, or add files to the filesystem. The second export sends **/usr/home** to just 192.168.1.2. With no such option specified, the default is to export in read-write mode.

Once the exports file is set up, start *nfsd* and *mountd*. The *nfsd* service is usually run with the following command-line options: *-tun 4*. This means to listen to TCP and UDP and to allow four servers to be run. The number of servers should match the maximum number of concurrent servers you expect to hit the server. You cannot start more than 20 NFS servers. For consistency between reboots, the variable *nfsd_flags* in **/etc/rc.conf** is used to hold arguments to the command *nfsd*.

Having started these services, we can now see them registered with the RPC service:

```
$  rpcinfo -p orion
   program vers proto   port
```

```
100000    2    tcp    111    portmapper
100000    2    udp    111    portmapper
100003    2    udp   2049    nfs
100003    3    udp   2049    nfs
100003    2    tcp   2049    nfs
100003    3    tcp   2049    nfs
100005    1    udp    971    mountd
100005    3    udp    971    mountd
100005    1    tcp    720    mountd
100005    3    tcp    720    mountd
```

Make sure that both *nfsd* and *mountd* are running; otherwise, the clients will not be able to complete their requests to the server. The *rpcinfo* tool can be useful in debugging NFS problems.

We can use the *showmount* tool to see which systems are being exported:

```
#  showmount -e
Exports list on localhost:
/usr/local                    loopback
/usr/home                     127.0.0.1
```

23.4 NFS Security

NFS security is based entirely on network addresses, so it can be fooled via spoofing. Furthermore, any authentication information and data are sent via plaintext, allowing an attacker to eavesdrop and compromise the session or copy the files from the captured transmissions. The NFS version in OpenBSD is based on the NFSv3 specification. NFSv4 offers significantly more security via the GSS API and Kerberos, but has yet to be widely implemented or adopted. More-secure network filesystems can be created using AFS, which is complicated to set up, or the WebDAV filesystem over SSL.

Furthermore, you can control access to the NFS server by controlling *portmap* access via a packet filter to TCP and UDP port 111. This will prevent unwanted parties from communicating via the *portmap* daemon in an effort to connect to the NFS mount daemon, which listens on other ports.

Lastly, you can control access to the NFS volumes by specifying explicit maps regarding who can mount which volumes and with which permissions in the **exports** file. Control of read-write volumes is especially important, but read-only volumes can contain sensitive data as well.

Chapter 24
NIS and YP Services

24.1 Introduction to NIS

The Sun Microsystems development Network Information Service (NIS) is used for centralized management of users. Authentication databases are held and managed in a central repository, and clients request data from this central site. This data includes user accounts and their passwords, host information, and the like. NIS manages "maps," which connect data and keys, such as passwords with usernames. NIS was formerly known as YP, but this designation was eventually dropped. However, NIS services retain their *yp* prefix, such as *ypcat*, and all manual pages refer to the YP subsystem. We will call it NIS, its official name.

OpenBSD can behave as either an NIS client or an NIS server. This chapter describes how to set up an NIS client into an existing NIS domain, and how to set up a new NIS server using an OpenBSD system. Note that OpenBSD is not compatible with NIS+, an enhanced version of NIS, unless the server is set to work in NIS mode. None of the security features introduced in NIS+ is present in this mode of operation.

24.2 Client Setup

There are a few steps to take to activate a host as an NIS client. These activation steps can also be made permanent so that the configuration is set at every start-up.

First, you must ensure that the right NIS domain has been established for the system. This is done via the *domainname* command:

```
# domainname crimelabs
# domainname
crimelabs
```

The NIS domain is used to set the authentication information for each NIS region, allowing for more than one domain to exist on any network segment. To set this value permanently, enter it into the file **/etc/domainname**:

```
#  echo "crimelabs" > /etc/domainname
```

This will set the NIS domain at each start-up.

Next, the NIS client service must be started by using the command *ypbind*. This will facilitate communication between the NIS master and the clients. If the file **/etc/domainname** exists, *ypbind* will become activated at every start-up.

Lastly, you must enable the NIS mappings to be used for authentication by appending a single line to the file **/etc/master.passwd**:

```
+:*:::::::::
```

Now the local OpenBSD system should be ready to contact the specific NIS master and authenticate as a part of an NIS domain.

24.3 Server Setup

The NIS server setup is a multistep process, but rather direct. First, we set the domain name of the NIS domain. In this case we are setting it to the DNS domain name, *crimelabs*:

```
$  sudo domainname crimelabs
```

Just as with the client, this configuration can be made permanent by using the file **/etc/domainname**. Now we have to initialize the NIS master using *ypinit -m*. When we first do this, we are asked a series of questions about the NIS domain, which are relatively easy to answer:

```
$  sudo ypinit -m crimelabs
Server Type: MASTER Domain: crimelabs

Creating an YP server will require that you answer a few questions.
Questions will all be asked at the beginning of the procedure.

Do you want this procedure to quit on non-fatal errors? [y/n: n]
Ok, please remember to go back and redo manually whatever fails.
If you don't, something might not work.
```

```
At this point, we have to construct a list of this domain's YP servers.
tank is already known as master server.
Please continue to add any slave servers, one per line. When you are
done with the list, type a <control D>.
        master server   :   tank
        next host to add:   ^D
The current list of NIS servers looks like this:
tank
```

We only have one NIS server, the master (**tank**), so this list is correct. We can now create our NIS database and master.

```
Is this correct?  [y/n: y]    y
Building /var/yp/crimelabs/ypservers...
Running /var/yp/crimelabs/Makefile...
updated passwd
updated group
updated hosts
couldn't find /etc/ethers
updated networks
updated rpc
updated services
updated protocols
updated netid
couldn't find /etc/netgroup
couldn't find /etc/amd/amd.home
/var/yp/crimelabs/crimelabs-aliases: 22 aliases, longest 10 bytes, \
235 bytes total
updated aliases

tank has been setup as an YP master server without any errors.
```

We now have a large set of files in the directory **/var/yp/crimelabs**, consisting of databases and maps for the domain. These correspond to hosts and users and their pertinent authentication data. The master (and slave) server coordinates this information and makes authentication decisions for clients.

Finally, we start the listening process that handles network requests:

```
$  sudo ypbind &
Enabling yp client subsystem.
To disable: kill ypbind and remove /var/yp/binding
```

We can now handle requests from users who wish to authenticate to this domain. A single machine can be an NIS server for more than one domain, provided the domains have unique names.

Basic password support for the NIS system was shown in the previous section. The relevant entry should be made in **/etc/master.passwd** on the server using the command *vipw*. This will properly rebuild the password database.

New users are added to this master server's password database just as they would be for local users. Once added, the NIS databases and maps will need to be regenerated by running the command *make* in the directory **/var/yp/DOMAINNAME**, which is unique to any NIS domain. Specific users can be omitted by prepending their usernames with a dash; for example, *-fred* would omit the user *fred* from any NIS authentication maps. User and group ID values can also be overridden by specifying them on the master server in the master password file. This file will override any default values from the NIS maps.

Password changes on the NIS master server are handled with the daemon *rpc.yppasswdd*. This program should be started on the server when the NIS subsystem is initialized. It allows users to edit their password data over the NIS system in the same way if they were working with a local password database. Users run *passwd -y* on the client machines to edit their passwords on the NIS server. This daemon should be running to ensure that these operations can smoothly take place.

24.4 Security

NIS security concerns are well known and the system is easily abused. For starters, NIS transmits data in the clear (i.e., as a plaintext transmission) and doesn't use any cryptography to protect against an eavesdropper. Also, no integrity checking is done on the messages beyond simple checks, so an attacker can readily alter them to make a play against the data. Lastly, NIS uses weak authentication with untrustworthy credentials—namely, the host's address, which can easily be spoofed. For these reasons and many more, NIS is not considered to be secure.

If you must use NIS, make sure that you have restricted access to the domain. This step will help prevent an attacker from damaging the data. Access can be restricted by using firewalls at the borders of the domain. Also, if possible, protect the sessions by implementing VPN connectivity between the systems, such as with IPsec (covered in Chapter 27). This approach will help protect the integrity and confidentiality of the data.

NIS security was improved with the advent of NIS+. However, no open standards for NIS+ exist, so interoperability is limited and not supported in most free forms of UNIX, including current OpenBSD releases.

A more secure network authentication scheme is Kerberos, which OpenBSD supports natively. Kerberos is a widely accepted and implemented standard. See Chapter 25 for more information on how to get started with Kerberos V.

24.5 Resources

A few resources for NIS have been developed over the years, although the popularity of this system is now declining. *NFS and NIS*, published by O'Reilly and Associates, is the definitive book on these two RPC programs.

A variety of NIS and YP manual pages have been written. They are summarized and indexed in the manual page for *yp*.

## Chapter 25

Kerberos

25.1 What Is Kerberos?

Kerberos is an authentication scheme designed by the MIT Athena Project to operate under a hostile environment. By using encryption and undertaking a complex dialogue between the client and the server, the network can remain untrusted but strong authentication can be assured. The Kerberos Key Distribution Center (KDC; described later in this chapter) acts as the trusted third party, allowing the client and the target server to mutually authenticate in the absence of any trust relationships between them.

With minimal effort, many applications can be used securely with strong authentication and optional session encryption, such as *telnet* and *rsh*. This ability is commonly referred to as "single sign-on" technology, which has become a "holy grail" of sorts in the information security world. Kerberos has been providing this assurance for more than 10 years, and reliably.

Kerberos uses traditional encryption for its protection, rather than public key encryption such as Diffie-Hellman or RSA cryptography. Kerberos IV was designed to use only DES encryption and simple hash algorithms. Kerberos V has been abstracted to allow for a variety of encryption algorithms offering varying levels of protection. RFC 1510 is the official specification of Kerberos V.

This chapter describes the setup and use of Kerberos V. Note that Kerberos V supports most features and clients that present Kerberos IV credentials or requests. OpenBSD uses the Heimdal implementation of Kerberos V, rather than the MIT distribution. If you wish to use the very latest release of the Heimdal source code and it hasn't yet been integrated into the OpenBSD release, see the port **security/heimdal**.

25.1.1 Why Use Kerberos?

Kerberos offers a significant number of advantages over other network authentication schemes, such as LDAP, X.509, and NIS. Namely, it is widely deployed and accepted as a standard, unlike some proprietary schemes. For example, Sun Microsystems has developed NIS+, a notably stronger scheme than NIS, but one that is unavailable on other platforms. LDAP and X.509 are both well-documented and widely accepted standards, but authentication tools based on them are still in their infancy.

Kerberos V is available in several implementations, including those from the KTH team (Heimdal) and the original developers, MIT. As a consequence, it has been ported to a variety of platforms and widely adopted. Furthermore, it provides transparency to a variety of applications, including terminal sessions like those conducted with SSH, *telnet*, or *rsh*, and mail protocols like POP. In addition, session encryption can be provided to assure session integrity and privacy.

25.2 Key Concepts in Kerberos

Kerberos is a complex protocol, but relies on a handful of basic principles for its underpinnings. Although the terminology can confuse some people, it relates to very commonly understood ideas.

- **Realms**   Kerberos realms are domains of administration, encompassing users and privileges. Realms are usually related to DNS domains for convenience, but this is not an absolute requirement.
- **Principal**   The principal is the username within a realm. It typically corresponds to the username in the network or workstation.
- **Instances**   An instance can be thought of as a role. You can have a privileged username without granting a privileged instance, effectively limiting the permissions a user has.
- **Tickets**   Kerberos uses tickets to communicate messages between servers. These are typically encrypted to prevent eavesdropping or forgery. To protect against their reuse after theft, tickets have a finite lifetime. Typically, the more privileged the instance, the shorter the lifetime of the ticket. Lifetimes can range from a few minutes to hours, and can be renewed as needed.

  Some tickets are *ticket-granting tickets* that allow you to get other tickets from other systems. Another key concept is *ticket forwarding*, whereby the trust that's been already established is extended.
- **KDC**   The Kerberos Key Distribution Center is the primary source for tickets in the network. You can have a master KDC and slave KDCs, ensuring a reliable network.

The principal, instance, and realm are combined to provide a specific instance within the Kerberos domain. If no instances or realms are specified, the default instance and realm are assumed. The instance is typically separated from the principle name by a slash ("/"), and these are separated from the realm by an @ sign. The following examples illustrate this usage:

- **jose**   The principal name "jose," with the default instance and realm assumed.
- **root/admin**   A privileged principal and instance in the default realm.
- **jose@CRIMELABS.NET**   The principal name "jose" within a specific realm, "CRIMELABS.NET."
- **jose/admin@OTHER.COM**   A specific principal and instance in a realm, which in this case is not the default realm.

These values are typically supplied when you initialize your presence in a realm, using commands like *kinit*.

One of the strongest protections offered by Kerberos is the approach whereby the user's password never traverses the wire. Instead, it is used in the encryption process, ensuring that the correct password is submitted yet still protecting it. The design of the Kerberos protocol serves to protect against forgery attacks (often called "spoofing") targeting either the client or the server. Lastly, the only component that needs rigorous protection is the KDC. If the KDC becomes compromised, obviously the whole domain of trust can be abused. Typically, the KDC is protected physically as well as on the network, and it is not used for any other services.

25.3 Overall System Setup

25.3.1 Clock Synchronization

Because Kerberos uses ticket lifetimes, the synchronization of the clocks within the realm is vitally important. If you have a clock skew of more than a few minutes (5 minutes by default), you will get errors like this:

```
$ kinit jose
jose@CRIMELABS.NET's Password:
kinit: krb5_get_init_creds: time skew (31535986) larger than max (300)
```

In this case, the client (the author's laptop) and the server (an OpenBSD Kerberos V server set up using the techniques described later in this chapter) were off by about one year. Resetting the clock to the correct time quickly resolved this minor problem.

It is recommended that you use the Network Time Protocol (NTP), which is available in the ports tree in **net/ntp**. The *ntp* service will keep your clocks tightly synchronized when set up properly. Alternatively, you can adjust the allowed skew between the client and server clocks with the configuration option *clockskew*. To promote interoperability with a variety of clients, use *ntp* instead, and keep your clocks synchronized within a few seconds of one another.

25.3.2 Build Support for Kerberos

Many of the services in OpenBSD come ready to support Kerberos mechanisms for authentication, and some packages even require it. This includes daemon and client software. By default, Kerberos IV/V support is included. If you wish to change this default, edit the file **/usr/share/mk/bsd.own.mk** and the following values:

```
# Set 'KERBEROS5' to 'yes' to build with support for Kerberos5
# authentication.
KERBEROS5?=     yes
```

Now when you rebuild your system from sources or from any **Makefile** that includes the file **bsd.own.mk** and the appropriate support for Kerberos V, you can control how much compatibility you offer. An increasing number of sites are moving to adopt Kerberos as a major means of authentication as well.

25.4 Client Setup

Kerberos clients need to know how to connect to the local realm servers, what to ask for, and how to use Kerberos credentials once they are obtained. This section describes the basic steps needed to get a Kerberos V client working within a small realm.

25.4.1 Client Configuration

The Kerberos V client configuration file, **/etc/kerberosV/krb5.conf**, controls the behavior of the Kerberos client system and applications. This file, which is laid out in a Windows **.ini** format, can be Used on a variety of workstations and is typically shared within a realm. System-specific information is then entered and changed as needed. A basic, working configuration file for the example realm in this chapter is shown below:

```
[libdefaults]
```

```
    ticket_lifetime = 6000
    default_realm = CRIMELABS.NET

[realms]
    CRIMELABS.NET =
        kdc = uriel.crimelabs.net:88


[domain_realm]
    .crimelabs.net = CRIMELABS.NET
```

In this configuration file, we have set up the defaults for any application that uses the systemwide Kerberos libraries. We have specified a 6000-second (100-minute) lifetime for our tickets and a default realm, **CRIMELABS.NET**. This realm's basic configuration information specifies only the KDC. The *domain_realm* section maps the DNS domains to Kerberos realms. The use of the leading dot in the DNS entry specifies that it is the trailing component for a variety of hosts.

A variety of configuration options are available, including those for the tickets and encoding, all at the realm or application level. For most users, a basic configuration file such as the one used in our example should suffice, as long as the local configuration information is entered. For a full list, see the manual page for *krb5.conf*.

Note that you can have a variety of realms and options set in your Kerberos V configuration file, but only one default for any type of setting. It is possible to have multiple realms, for example, and different types of properties for them, such as home and work realms.

25.4.2 Obtaining Tickets

Having set up our client configuration, we are now able to obtain a ticket from the KDC. To do so, we can use the command *kinit* or *kauth*. Either will retrieve a Kerberos V ticket, but the *kauth* command will also retrieve a version IV ticket. By default, *kinit* assumes that the principal name within the realm is your current user name. You can specify another principal name if you wish. The *kinit* command also assumes the default instance for the user name and the realm for your client. If you wish to obtain credentials other than your defaults, you can set these values as an argument to *kinit*.

```
$  kinit jose
jose@CRIMELABS.NET's Password:  Kerberos password
```

The password used here is the one set when the Kerberos account was created. If you get an error about an unknown principal, make sure that you are working in the database. See your administrator if you need help in this area.

To view the issued tickets, use the *klist* command. By specifying various arguments to it, you can also list the attributes of the tickets.

```
$  klist
Credentials cache: FILE:/tmp/krb5cc_1000
        Principal: jose@CRIMELABS.NET

  Issued              Expires            Principal
Jan 17 17:20:12   Jan 17 17:30:47   krbtgt/CRIMELABS.NET@CRIMELABS.NET
$  ls -l /tmp/
total 4
-rw-------  1 jose  wheel  565 Jan 17 17:20 krb5cc_1000
```

Tickets are stored, being readable only to the user who requested them, in the **/tmp** directory by default. The ticket type is listed in the *Principal* section of the listed tickets. In this case we have a *ticket-granting ticket* issued for the **CRIMELABS.NET** realm. It will allow us to get tickets to use services on other systems.

If you wish to get rid of your tickets, use the *kdestroy* command. It will remove all of the Kerberos tickets in the cache.

```
$  kdestroy
$  klist
klist: No ticket file: /tmp/krb5cc_1000
```

Use this command when you step away from your workstation, for example, or disconnect your laptop from the network. Note that if someone is able to steal your tickets, he or she can impersonate you for the remaining lifetime of your tickets. After all, you have already done the hard part—authenticating with your password. The *kdestroy* command is similar to the command *ssh-add -D*, which deletes all of your *ssh* identities. It is probably wise to add this command to your logout scripts, if you have any.

If you have any tickets in your cache, specifying *kinit* without any arguments will attempt to renew the tickets in the cache. This includes expired tickets, which the client will attempt to renew. If you wish to obtain a different ticket, specify the necessary information to *kinit* so it knows what you intend to do.

At this point, you are ready to use Kerberized services, such as *ssh*, within your realm, or any realm in which you are authorized to operate. Their use is described in Section 25.6.

25.5 Kerberos Server Setup

The Kerberos server configures the realm (or multiple realms if it is set up to do so) by issuing tickets and managing principals. This system is central to the entire trust employed within the Kerberos scheme and must be protected against compromise. It is very unwise to run any additional services on the KDC, as they could open up unexpected access to the system and hence the realm.

25.5.1 KDC Configuration

The main Kerberos configuration is done in the file **/var/heimdal/kdc.conf**. Here the KDC and realm are specified, along with any major options. To set up a basic KDC, an entry like the following would be used. It creates the realm and the basic authentication requirements:

```
[kdc]
        require-preauth = no
        v4-realm = CRIMELABS.NET
        key-file = /key-file
```

This entry can be included in the file **/etc/kerberosV/krb5.conf** in the section **[kdc]**, when you specify the option *–config-file=/etc/kerberosV/krb5.conf* to the *kdc* command initialization.

Kerberos V expects its databases to reside in the directory **/var/heimdal**, which doesn't exist by default. Hence, it is wise to execute the command *mkdir/var/heimdal* before setting up the rest of the server.

25.5.2 *keytab* Creation

The *keytab* is a core part of the server setup. It is used to identify the servers and systems within the realm to one another. The creation of a Kerberos V *keytab* is shown below using the *kadmin* command:

```
kadmin>  add --random-key host/entropy.crimelabs.net
Max ticket life [1 day]:
```

```
Max renewable life [1 week]:
Principal expiration time [never]:
Password expiration time [never]:
Attributes []:
kadmin>  ext -k FILE:/etc/kerberosV/krb5.keytab \
    host/entropy.crimelabs.net
kadmin>  q
#  ktutil list
FILE:/etc/kerberosV/krb5.keytab:

Vno  Type            Principal
  1  des-cbc-crc     host/entropy.crimelabs.net@CRIMELABS.NET
  1  des-cbc-md4     host/entropy.crimelabs.net@CRIMELABS.NET
  1  des-cbc-md5     host/entropy.crimelabs.net@CRIMELABS.NET
  1  des3-cbc-sha1   host/entropy.crimelabs.net@CRIMELABS.NET
```

As you can see, multiple types of tabs can be used, and multiple hosts can be stored in a single *keytab* file.

To convert a Kerberos IV *keytab* to a Kerberos V *server tab* (**srvtab**) file, using the command *ktutil*, specify the input Kerberos IV file and the output Kerberos V *keytab* file:

```
#  ktutil copy krb4:srvtab keytab
```

Now make sure that the file **srvtab** is in the **/var/heimdal** directory, where the Kerberos V daemons *kdc* and *kadmind* can find it.

This file belongs to **/etc/kerberosV/krb5.keytab** and should be readable only by root.

25.5.3 Initialization Realm

Realm initialization is done with the *kadmin* tool. This tool can run against the data on a remote system, or it can run locally. The invocation of *kadmin -l* runs the tool locally.

```
#  kadmin -l
kadmin>  init CRIMELABS.NET
Realm max ticket life [unlimited]:
Realm max renewable ticket life [unlimited]:
kadmin>  add jose
Max ticket life [1 day]:
```

```
Max renewable life [1 week]:
Principal expiration time [never]:
Password expiration time [never]:
Attributes []:
jose@CRIMELABS.NET's Password:
Verifying password - jose@CRIMELABS.NET's Password:
kadmin>  q
```

After a few questions are answered, we can examine the status of our realm by dumping the contents of our database:

```
kadmin>  dump
jose@CRIMELABS.NET 1::16:169b4f57b9...
default@CRIMELABS.NET 1::16:7308c18...
kadmin/admin@CRIMELABS.NET 1::1:2f8...
kadmin/hprop@CRIMELABS.NET 1::1:0d7...
...
```

At this point, the realm is initialized and ready to start.

25.5.4 Controlling Access to the Administrative Server

Access controls for the realm are specified in the file **/var/heimdal/kadmind.acl**. Within this file one finds principals Kerberos and their privileges. These privileges can be either *add, change-password* (abbreviated as *cpw*), *delete, get, list*, or *modify*. The global privilege *all* should be given only to realm administrators. The responsibilities for limited administrative duties are easily managed by assigning the correct privileges.

Note that the incoming principal name is the name from the Kerberos ticket, not the user name. Thus you do not need to have similar rights on the client workstation to administer the Kerberos server.

This file is specified in a three-part format for each entry (one entry per line), with the third part being optional. The first part is the principal, specified as the entry on the ticket. The second part is the privilege granted to the principal holder. The third part specifies the limitations on the realms. In the following example, the "root/admin" principal can modify any attribute of any realm within this Kerberos system, but the principal "jose/admin" can only change passwords for users in the realm **CRIMELABS.NET**:

```
root/admin@CRIMELABS.NET    all
jose/admin@CRIMELABS.net    change-password  */*@CRIMELABS.NET
```

When used properly, such access controls can help ensure the smooth operation of a Kerberos realm by a multimember team.

25.5.5 Starting the Kerberos Server

Once the realm is initialized and the access controls are established, the Kerberos server can be started. The main component to start is the daemon that operates the Kerberos domain controller:

```
#  /usr/libexec/kdc &
```

If you wish to start the *kadmin* server so that it will be accessible from the network, you will need to start it now as well:

```
#  /usr/libexec/kadmind &
```

Alternatively, you can use the *kadmin -l* command to administer the local Kerberos administrative server when you are on this machine (i.e., networked in via *ssh*).

25.5.6 Activating Kerberos V Services at Start-up

To activate these services at start-up, edit the file **/etc/rc.conf** and set the system as either a Kerberos V master KDC or a slave KDC. (The system cannot be both.) Set the appropriate value to *YES*:

```
krb5_master_kdc=NO       # KerberosV master KDC.
krb5_slave_kdc=NO        # KerberosV slave KDC.
```

All three Kerberos V daemons—*kadmind, kdc*, and *kpasswdd*—are started by default if you set your machine up as a Kerberos V master KDC. If you wish to alter this behavior, edit the appropriate subsection in the initialization script **/etc/rc**.

25.6 Kerberizing Services

A number of network services are ready to use Kerberos V as an authentication mechanism in OpenBSD by default. This group includes the remote shell *rsh, ftp, ssh*, and a handful of others. Note that only setup information for *ssh* and *telnet* is provided in this section, but the other services follow suit.

25.6.1 Secure Shell

The secure shell *ssh* and its daemon *sshd* are already Kerberized applications. By default, they understand Kerberos V tickets and authentication dialogues. The client configuration option *KerberosAuthentication* is used to specify that this authentication method is to be attempted. It is undertaken before password or even public key authentication methods are attempted. To specify this option, edit the file **/etc/ssh_config** or the user-specified file **$HOME/.ssh/config** to set the value of *yes* for this option. If you wish to specify this option on the command line for a single instance, use the command *ssh -o KerberosAuthentication=yes*.

Using the verbose flag for *ssh*, we can see the Kerberos authentication and determine whether it succeeds:

```
$  ssh -v 10.10.10.1
...
debug1: Found key in /home/jose/.ssh/known_hosts:37
debug1: Encryption type: 3des
debug1: Sent encrypted session key.
debug1: Installing crc compensation attack detector.
debug1: Received encrypted confirmation.
debug1: Trying Kerberos v5 authentication.
debug1: Kerberos v5 authentication accepted.
debug1: Requesting pty.
debug1: Requesting shell.
debug1: Entering interactive session.
 login text begins
```

The daemon *sshd* also uses the option *KerberosAuthentication* for controlling the use of Kerberos as an authentication mechanism. By default, it is set to *yes*. Both the client and the server have to be ready to try this form of authentication before it can succeed.

25.6.2 *telnet*

The *telnet* client and daemon are both Kerberos V ready in OpenBSD by default. Thus, if Kerberos authentication is available, it will be attempted. You can see how this scheme works when we use *telnet* to connect to a *telnet* server in the realm:

```
$  telnet uriel
Trying 10.10.10.1...
```

```
Connected to uriel.
Escape character is '^]'.
[ Trying mutual KERBEROS5 (host/uriel.crimelabs.net@CRIMELABS.NET) ]
[ Kerberos V5 accepts you as "jose@CRIMELABS.NET" ]
 normal login messages
```

By default, no credentials are forwarded to the target system. The option *-f* can be used to request the credentials to be forwarded if possible. Also, Kerberos, by default, will protect only the authentication setup, not the data stream. Use *telnet -x* to request encryption of the data stream to protect the session contents.

The daemon *telnetd* is set to accept Kerberos authentication by default. This behavior can be controlled with the option *-a* to specify limited authentication types.

25.7 Windows 2000 and Kerberos V

One of the biggest news items in the information security world was the inclusion of Kerberos V in Microsoft's Windows 2000. Kerberos is a widely accepted standard for strong authentication, available on a variety of platforms. Because it is a standard, it should therefore be possible to integrate Windows 2000 into your existing Kerberos infrastructure.

Not quite. The Kerberos V specification allows for some specifics to be decided by the vendor, which could cause some interoperability problems. Microsoft has chosen to use different encryption algorithms—a tactic that is allowed for in the specification, but not widely deployed.

The Heimdal Kerberos V implementation used in OpenBSD can be used as the KDC for a Windows 2000 network. The authors have not tested this possibility, but the developers of Heimdal have provided some documentation on this scheme. To read how to do this, see the GNU Info page for *heimdal*, specifically the "Windows 2000 compatibility" node. It involves minor setup work for the OpenBSD Kerberos V server, but a number of steps on the Windows 2000 controller to establish the KDC for the system.

25.8 Security of the Kerberos Scheme

Kerberos was designed to be a strong, trustworthy authentication scheme in an otherwise hostile environment. Rather than trusting the client systems or even the servers, nothing is trustworthy except what the Kerberos KDC says. Using encryption to create confidential messages and to maintain their integrity, Kerberos provides a well-designed sign-on technology.

Nevertheless, several lines of attack may be pursued against a Kerberos realm:

- Offline attacks, which include breaking the encryption or the password used to encrypt the ticket, can take place. Given the speed of commodity systems and the pace with which the DES (or 3DES) encryption can be broken in software (even faster in hardware), this possibility represents a serious threat and could compromise the entire principle. Protection against such attacks can be improved in Kerberos IV by using strong passphrases, and in Kerberos V by using stronger ciphers.

- Ticket theft is a very real problem in Kerberos. Tickets have finite lifetimes, typically adjusted to match a working session within the realm's setting, to help thwart this threat. Nonetheless, the weakest part of the scheme is the client workstation. If a ticket is stolen, it can be used to authenticate the user to systems that utilize Kerberos authentication schemes. There is a delicate balance between ticket lifetimes and their utility. Maintaining high security on the workstations is the best solution to this problem.

- The integrity-checking algorithms used in Kerberos IV are limited to the CRC32 scheme, which is linearly dependent on the data. Kerberos V, which is significantly more flexible, allows for the use of cryptographically strong MAC algorithms, such as MD4 or MD5. An attacker could selectively alter the data to test for authentication bits by adjusting the CRC32 checksum and the data present in the ticket.

25.9 Resources

The GNU Info page for *heimdal* offers an excellent tutorial on the setup of the Heimdal Kerberos V code. Note that it doesn't cover many of the Kerberos concepts central to understanding how to develop a Kerberos realm, connect realms, or fully utilize Kerberos. The tutorial does cover how to set up slave KDC servers, a topic that is not discussed in this book.

The Heimdal Web site (**http://www.pdc.kth.se/heimdal/**) is an excellent site replete with the archives of the technical mailing list, where some discussions about troubleshooting can be found, for example. Also, the latest development code is available there if you wish to replace the OpenBSD distribution code with a more recent version.

The MIT Kerberos V distribution comes with an excellent set of documents on the key concepts, setup, administration, and use of this version of Kerberos V. While many of the commands are not the same as those found in the Heimdal distribution, the overview of Kerberos is quite thorough, and many of the configuration options are well worth studying. Visit the MIT site at **http://web.mit.edu/kerberos/www/**.

RFC 1510 covers the Kerberos V specification.

The Usenet newsgroup **comp.protocols.kerberos** is an especially helpful place for those individuals who are working with Kerberos.

25.10 Troubleshooting

1. I am continually prompted for my password even though I have run *kinit* and gotten a ticket.

   Ensure that you have been issued a valid ticket for the realm that you are attempting to network in. Also, make sure your ticket hasn't expired. You can use *klist* to view the status of your ticket. Make sure you are in the right realm and working with the expected principal name. Lastly, ensure that the target system is participating in the Kerberos realm for which you are authorized.

2. Kerberos authentication (such as with *ssh*) takes a long time before it reports that it succeeded or failed.

   This delay is most likely caused by the client attempting to obtain a DNS **TXT** record for the Kerberos V realm for the target system. Ensure that you have valid DNS entries on your client and that this information in your DNS servers is correct. (DNS is discussed in more detail in Chapter 18). Note that this check can be completed successfully in the absence of DNS servers—it just takes a few minutes.

Chapter 26

Authentication Methods

26.1 Authentication Overview

OpenBSD supports several authentication methods besides a simple password. To use these alternate login methods, the username is changed and OpenBSD processes the authentication in the background. By default, the only authentication methods that are allowed are simple passwords and S/Key. To specify a different authentication method, the username has the authentication method appended to it after a colon:

```
login:  bpalmer:skey
otp-md5 95 psid06473
S/Key Password:
```

26.2 *passwd*

The standard authentication method is the *passwd* method. It takes the name of the user, looks up the password hash in the **/etc/master.passwd** file, and compares that with the hash of the password provided by the user.

26.3 *skey*

In some installations, S/Key is the most common login method. It is used when no secure way to log in exists and a password must be entered in plain text. Examples would be either *ftp* or *telnet*, where the login is not encrypted at all. OpenBSD supports S/Key for numerous services including *ftpd, telnetd*, and *sshd*.

The problem with tools like *telnet* and *ftp* is that they use plaintext logins that pass over the network and can be sniffed. In contrast, services like *sshd* use encryption to send information without danger. Rather than using plain text, S/Key sends a challenge and the remote user sends back a response. This information is sent in plain text but it's one-time information and does not contain the password, so it does not pose any danger.

26.3.1 S/Key Setup

To use S/Key, the user must first set it up for the receiving partner. This is done as follows:

```
# skeyinit bpalmer
Reminder - Only use this method if you are directly connected
           or have an encrypted channel.  If you are using telnet
           or rlogin, hit return now and use skeyinit -s.
[Adding bpalmer with md5]
Enter secret passphrase:
ERROR: Your passphrase must be at least 10 characters long.
Enter secret passphrase:
Again secret passphrase:

ID bpalmer skey is otp-md5 99 orio71643
Next login password: WAD GALA FLAT ARTS SHOD LIEU
```

The user is first asked to specify a password (the user's normal login password) and then an S/Key password. This is done so that the S/Key password will be different than the system password or so that the user can use only S/Key (if no local system password is set). The number 99 indicates that there are 99 keys available until the user needs to repeat the *skeyinit* process.

If run as root, the *skeyinit* tool can set a password for any user:

```
root@orion:/root#  skeyinit brandon
Reminder - Only use this method if you are directly connected
           or have an encrypted channel.  If you are using telnet
           or rlogin, hit return now and use skeyinit -s.
[Updating brandon with md5]
Old seed: [md5]  orio87272
Enter secret passphrase:
Again secret passphrase:

ID brandon skey is otp-md5 99 orio87273
Next login password: DEAR ALSO MONK GINA FRET STOW
```

26.3.2 Getting Passphrases

There are two main ways to use S/Key once the keys are set up. The user either has access to an S/Key generator or has printed out the next keys in the sequence. To generate the next 10 keys, the user would issue the following commands:

```
$  skeyinfo
98 orio87273
$  skey -n 10 98 orio87273
Reminder - Do not use this program while logged in via telnet or
rlogin.
Enter secret password:
89: OH BUFF FOUL LAMB INK BALD
90: NILE FROG GRIM HANS NON ANTI
91: LEO BESS ELK NASH COIN SUNK
92: MARS HUH AMMO FAST MUCK DEAL
93: BUST ROVE AWN FRET FED BERN
94: ANTI LO VEAL HOWE BUCK RANK
95: ADDS AWRY BOCK SUIT SUN JUNO
96: CRAY SOY DOT WAST SELF SOB
97: ABEL LORD CHIN JANE TUBA SEEN
98: CASE GRIN ROOK TWIN BOG LAW
```

The first command asked what the next key would be. The system told us that it would be number 98 and key *orio87273*. This means that we could *telnet* to the system and use *CASE GRIN ROOK TWIN BOG LAW* as our next password.

```
$  telnet orion
Trying 192.168.1.3...
Connected to orion.
Escape character is '^]'.

login:  brandon:skey
otp-md5 98 orio87273
S/Key Password:
S/Key Password [echo on]:  CASE GRIN ROOK TWIN BOG LAW
OpenBSD 3.3 (GENERIC) #2: Fri Feb 21 13:16:59 MST 2003

Welcome to OpenBSD: The proactively secure UNIX-like operating system.

$
```

When asked for a username, we entered the username followed by a colon and then the login method we wanted to use, S/Key. The challenge and sequence followed. We chose to enter the passphrase with the echo on.

FTP would work in the same way.

```
$  ftp orion
Connected to orion..
220 orion. FTP server (Version 6.5/OpenBSD) ready.
Name (orion:jose):  jose:skey
331- otp-md5 96 orio87273
331 S/Key Password:
Password:
230- OpenBSD 3.3 (GENERIC) #2: Fri Feb 21 13:16:59 MST 2003
230-
230- Welcome to OpenBSD: The proactively secure UNIX-like operating
230- system.
230-
230 User jose logged in.
Remote system type is UNIX.
Using binary mode to transfer files.
ftp>
```

Of course, the user won't always be able to, nor want to, carry around a list of passphrases. Thus we need tools to generate the passphrases. A few are available for each platform:

- **OpenBSD**   The *skey* program is used:

  ```
  $  skey 97 orio87273
  Reminder - Do not use this program while logged in via telnet or
  rlogin.
  Enter secret password:
  ABEL LORD CHIN JANE TUBA SEEN
  ```

- **Palm Pilot**   The *Pilot/OTP* program can be used. It can be found through a search engine.
- **Windows**   The *winkey.exe* program is a simple tool for generating S/Key passphrases. You can find it with a Web search engine as well.

26.3.3 *sshd* Setup and Usage with S/Key

In addition to *telnet* and *ftp*, S/Key can be used with *sshd*. If *ssh* is encrypted, why would anyone need to use S/Key? Because the remote client isn't always trusted. Although public workstations are set up at a convention, for example, one can't be sure that keyboard logging systems aren't running. With an S/Key calculator running on a tool like a Palm Pilot, for instance, these can be used confidently.

The only changes needed to use S/Key are to enable *UseLogin* in the **/etc/sshd_config** file and to restart *sshd*.

```
UseLogin yes
```

To *ssh* with S/Key, use the following code:

```
hacker@unsafe:/home/hacker$  ssh brandon:skey@server
otp-md5 97 serv87273
S/Key Password:
Last login: Sun Apr  3 20:58:14 on ttyp1 from client.
OpenBSD 3.3 (GENERIC) #44: Sat Mar 29 13:22:05 MST 2003

Welcome to OpenBSD: The proactively secure UNIX-like operating system.

$
```

The OpenSSH system integrates cleanly with the login methods described here, provided they have been set up properly.

26.4 Additional Login Classes

Additional login classes can be specified in the configuration file **/etc/login.conf**. This file works by specifying a login class and then the options for that class. The following variables work for the *auth* key word, which specifies the authentication types. S/Key support would be added by using the *auth=skey* parameter.

Login classes are defined as either the default or some specified class. This is given in the file **/etc/master.passwd**, in the field after the group ID. For example, a user *friend* whom we wanted to control in the class *visitors* would have a password file entry like the following:

```
jose:$2a$06$shki2fo4.t2e7mtSAGQwoejga7rm2lb6RkjahhfCmiFysXjOCXiDi:\
    1000:1000:visitors:0:0:jose:/home/jose:/bin/ksh
```

This defines the user's class as *visitors*. Then, a login class *visitors* would be defined in the file **login.conf**:

```
visitors:
        :datasize-cur=64M:
        :datasize-max=infinity:
        :maxproc-max=256:
        :maxproc-cur=128:
        :auth=skey,radius,passwd:
```

This would allow the *visitors* class to authenticate via S/Key, *radius*, or a local password. This section discusses these authentication methods.

26.4.1 *lchpass*

OpenBSD allows the user to change his or her password using several authentication methods. The first technique is to change the user's password on the local machine.

```
$ login
login: bpalmer:lchpass
Changing local password for bpalmer.
Old Password:
New password:
Retype new password:
```

The *lchpass* approach operates almost identically as a local password change system for the user.

26.4.2 *chpass*

The next method, *chpass*, is used to change the primary password system for the user. It differs from *lchpass* in that it can change the Kerberos password if the user normally authenticates via Kerberos. It will default to changing the local password, operating as *lchpass* does, if Kerberos is not available.

26.4.3 Token-Based Authentication Methods

Varying degrees of support for token-based authentication (such as smart cards) exist in OpenBSD. However, this support is often hampered by access to such hardware. We will mention some of the tools available for such authentication, but because we also lack the needed hardware, we will not give any details on using these methods. These methods share one characteristic: use of the command *tokeninit* to initialize the system and add or remove users.

ActivCard Authentication

The *activ* authentication method works with ActivCard tokens. When the user logs in with this method, the user is looked up in the **/etc/active.db** file. This activity is controlled by the *activadm* command.

SecureNet Authentication

Another token-based authentication method utilizes SecureNet key tokens. This method is controlled via the *snk* command, which is similar to the *activadm* command.

CRYPTOCard Authentication

The *crypto* method controls the use of CRYPTOCard tokens to authenticate. It works via the command *login_crypto*. This method is controlled by the *cryptoadm* command, which is almost identical to *snkadm* and *activadm*.

SecureID

At the time of writing, there was no complete method for SecureID login. Several sites, such as **http://www.deadly.org**, continue to discuss this issue, but nothing exists yet.

26.4.4 Kerberos

Kerberos login and authentication is discussed in detail in Chapter 25.

krb-or-pwd

This authentication method first attempts to log the user in using Kerberos and then, if that fails, with a normal local login. It would be a good first method if Kerberos were installed on a system, but was not used for all users (such as root).

26.4.5 *radius* Method

If the OpenBSD server is configured with a *radiusd* server, the user can log in using that server for authentication with this method. The *radiusd* server is not discussed here, but two versions are available in the ports tree.

26.4.6 *reject* Method

The *reject* method, as the name implies, always rejects login attempts. It would be of value to prevent certain types of logins, like *ftp*, as shown in the manual page for *reject*:

```
:auth=krb-or-pwd,kerberos,passwd:
:auth-ftp=reject:
```

The user is allowed to log in with *krb-or-pwd, kerberos*, or *passwd*, but no logins are allowed of any sort are allowed for the auth-ftp class.

## Chapter 27

IPsec: Security at the IP Layer

27.1 Introduction

The traditional networking standard, IPv4, provides no security mechanisms on its own. This includes authentication (the verification of the sender or the recipient), privacy concerns (often addressed through cryptography), or integrity measures. As a consequence, IPv4 traffic is vulnerable to spoofing, manipulation, or replay attacks, as well as the ubiquitous eavesdropping, or sniffing, attack. While this shortcoming can be addressed at the upper application layers, through technologies such as SSL, existing services must be retrofitted to use this new service.

IPv6 addressed these concerns by creating two new protocols. These protocols formed an additional layer inserted as another header after the IP address header, but before other data such as the TCP header. This approach affords all network services the benefits of the new security model without any additional modification. While they represent a core part of IPv6, these extensions have since been backported to IPv4. They provide authentication, encryption, and integrity checking through cryptographic additions to IP packets.

OpenBSD fully supports IPsec in the GENERIC kernel provided with the system. This support allows services on OpenBSD systems to work with secure networks using IPsec standard practices or to be used on other devices on the same network.

27.2 IPsec Basics

Without IPsec, a typical TCP packet looks like this:

```
[IP header] [TCP header] [data...]
```

To provide these new security measures, IPsec defines two new IP protocols: ESP (Encapsulating Security Payload), which is designated as protocol 50, and AH (Authentication Header), which, is designated as protocol 51. By comparison, ICMP is designated as IP protocol 1, UDP is IP protocol 17, and TCP is protocol 6.

To exchange the cryptographic keys used in IPsec operations, upper-layer key management protocols have been developed. ISAKMP (Internet Security Architecture Key Management Protocol) comprises a complex set of mechanisms by which two IPsec nodes or endpoints can exchange first authentication data and then session information. This management protocol is popularly known as the Oakley or IKE (Internet Key Exchange) key management protocol.

Different IPsec scenarios require different setups. For example, an IPsec gateway would require the use of an endpoint—a router that has a specific route configured to use the IPsec interface. However, a single system using IPsec to link to another system would merely need to configure its encapsulation as a node.

Furthermore, IPsec includes a tunnel mode and a transport mode.

In tunnel mode, a new IP header is written that is specific to the IPsec tunnel. The original packet, including the original IP header, the protocol header, and the data, forms the payload of the new packet, which has an AH protocol header. With tunnel mode, a TCP packet would look like this:

```
[IP header] [ESP header] [IP header] [TCP header] [data...]
```

In transport mode, a new protocol header is inserted between the original IP header and the original protocol header. This authentication header covers the entire packet except for fields that will change in transit (such as the TTL). This is the same process as used in the MAC calculation.

```
[IP header] [ESP header] [TCP header] [data...]
```

Note that in these examples, "[IP header]" can be an IPv4 or IPv6 header.[1]

27.2.1 Creating x509 Keys

To set up an x509 key for *isakmpd*, which is not required, but is used for several of the examples presented later in this chapter, take the following steps:

1. Generate a key for your host using the *openssl* command.

```
# cd /etc
# openssl genrsa -out isakmpd/private/local.key 1024
# chmod 600 isakmpd/private/local.key
```

---

[1] The examples in this section are available online at **http://www.crimelabs.net/openbsdbook**.

2. Create a public key, used only on remote hosts. (The authors prefer to have all of the host public keys synchronized, so they put the local host's public key in the local host's **pubkeys/** directory, even though this is absolutely not necessary.)

```
#  pkd=isakmpd/pubkeys
#  pub=$pkd/$(hostname).pub
#  openssl rsa -out $pub -in isakmpd/private/local.key -pubout
#  mkdir -p $pkd/ipv4 $pkd/ipv6
#  ln $pub $pkd/ipv4/[your local v4 address]
#  ln $pub $pkd/ipv6/[your local v6 address]
```

3. Distribute/synchronize the **pubkeys/ipv*** directories to all hosts.

27.3 Setting Up IPsec

27.3.1 Kernel Requirements

Setup of the IPsec environment requires a small number of kernel options to be enabled. First, ensure that the cryptographic and IPsec frameworks are enabled in your kernel. These are built into the GENERIC kernel. If you are building a custom kernel, confirm that these two lines are present in your configuration if you wish to use IPsec:

```
option    CRYPTO # Cryptographic framework
option    IPSEC  # IPsec
```

Second, verify that the two main protocols used by IPsec—AH and ESP—are enabled via *sysctl* by issuing the command *sysctl -a*. On a running system, these values can be changed by using the command *sysctl -w*. The changes can be made permanent by editing the values in the file **/etc/sysctl.conf**:

```
net.inet.esp.enable = 1
net.inet.ah.enable = 1
```

On a normal system installation, both protocols are enabled by default. However, one rarely ever uses AH,[2] as ESP provides both authentication and encryption (if the packet does not decrypt to meaningful data, it does not authenticate).

---

[2]Using ESP also allows one to traverse a NAT firewall. Using AH protects the IP address header, which does not allow NAT.

At this point the two protocols for IPsec should be enabled and ready for use. Now, if you are setting up an IPsec gateway, ensure that IP forwarding is enabled on the gateway. Using *sysctl*, enable this setting. This change can be made permanent by editing the value in **/etc/sysctl.conf**:

```
net.inet.ip.forwarding = 1
```

Lastly, several IPsec-related variables are tunable via *sysctl*. For most scenarios, however, the defaults are acceptable.

```
net.inet.ip.ipsec-expire-acquire = 30
net.inet.ip.ipsec-invalid-life = 60
net.inet.ip.ipsec-pfs = 1
net.inet.ip.ipsec-soft-allocs = 0
net.inet.ip.ipsec-allocs = 0
net.inet.ip.ipsec-soft-bytes = 0
net.inet.ip.ipsec-bytes = 0
net.inet.ip.ipsec-timeout = 86400
net.inet.ip.ipsec-soft-timeout = 80000
net.inet.ip.ipsec-soft-firstuse = 3600
net.inet.ip.ipsec-firstuse = 7200
net.inet.ip.ipsec-enc-alg = aes
net.inet.ip.ipsec-auth-alg = hmac-sha1
```

The timeout values are most useful on IPsec gateway devices that are operating under a significant load. By lowering the timeout values, the number of entries can be reduced. However, for most users and IPsec gateways, the defaults will suffice.

27.4 Endpoint Setup

27.4.1 Manual Configuration

ipsecadm

With the *ipsecadm* command, you can manually configure data flows and insert keys into the kernel, which is all that is required for both ends to run a static IPsec configuration. Markus Friedl's example in Section 27.4.2 makes use of *ipsecadm*. To better understand this command, it is recommended that you read the *ipsecadm(8)* and *vpn(8)* manual pages.

A Static Configuration with rc.vpn

With the **rc.vpn** script, you can edit a few variables and set up a secure, statically configured IPsec configuration without running the *ipsecadm* command manually. Once configured, this script can be activated at system start-up by invoking it from the system initialization scripts. By default, the script resides in **/usr/share/ipsec/rc.vpn**.

27.4.2 Automatic Configuration

Markus Friedl developed the easy automatic configuration method for IPsec with ISAKMP with no configuration file that appears in this section. With his method, you need not use a firewall to make certain that packets with IPsec flows do not escape unencrypted. In this scenario, *isakmpd* merely serves as the key exchange mechanism. One obvious downfall (if it can be considered such) of this approach is that the IP addresses are fixed, so there can be no roaming road warrior.

To set up an IPsec connection between 10.0.0.10/32 and 192.168.20.1/32, you can do the following:

- Set up the IP address and policy (i.e., SPD, flow):

```
#  cat hostname.fxp1
inet 10.0.0.10
!ipsecadm flush
!ipsecadm flow -addr 10.0.0.10/32 192.168.20.1/32 \
      -src 10.0.0.10 -dst 192.168.20.1 -proto esp -out -require
!ipsecadm flow -addr 192.168.20.1/32 10.0.0.10/32 \
      -src 10.0.0.10 -dst 192.168.20.1 -proto esp -in -require
```

- Enable *isakmpd* (Use the option *-L* for *debug* in **/var/run/isakmpd.pcap**):

```
#  grep isakmpd_flags rc.conf
isakmpd_flags="-L"
```

- Set up an allow-all policy file:

```
#  cat isakmpd/isakmpd.policy
Authorizer: "POLICY"
#  chmod 600 isakmpd/isakmpd.policy
```

- Follow the x509 instructions given in Section 27.2.1. There is no need for an **isakmpd.conf** file.
- Either reboot each machine, or execute the *ipsecadm* commands and start *isakmpd*.
- Ping a peer address:

```
# ping 192.168.20.1
```

If the tunnel is not properly established, the ping operation will fail.

27.5 Testing/Debugging the Configuration

27.5.1 *tcpdump*

While one does not get decrypted data via *tcpdump*,[3] one can determine whether traffic is encrypted and identify to whom the data is being sent.

As an example, a very simple command from a host named *kyrakat* looks like this from an application standpoint:

```
kyrakat$  ping6 -c 2 shadow; ping6 -c 2 toshi
PING6(56=40+8+8 bytes) 3ffe:b00:4004::15 --> 3ffe:b00:4004::1
16 bytes from 3ffe:b00:4004::1, icmp_seq=0 hlim=64 time=2.595 ms
16 bytes from 3ffe:b00:4004::1, icmp_seq=1 hlim=64 time=2.468 ms

--- shadow.fries.net ping6 statistics ---
2 packets transmitted, 2 packets received, 0% packet loss
round-trip min/avg/max/std-dev = 2.468/2.532/2.595/0.063 ms
PING6(56=40+8+8 bytes) 3ffe:b00:4004::15 --> 3ffe:b00:4004::7
16 bytes from 3ffe:b00:4004::7, icmp_seq=0 hlim=64 time=8.219 ms
16 bytes from 3ffe:b00:4004::7, icmp_seq=1 hlim=64 time=8.04 ms

--- toshi.fries.net ping6 statistics ---
2 packets transmitted, 2 packets received, 0% packet loss
round-trip min/avg/max/std-dev = 8.040/8.130/8.219/0.089 ms
kyrakat$
```

---

[3] With OpenBSD release 3.4, *tcpdump* includes the capability to decrypt data, given the necessary information. Refer to the *tcpdump(8)* manual page for details if you have OpenBSD 3.4 or higher.

However, from the host *kyrakat*, the Ethernet packets look like this to *tcpdump*:

```
kyrakat$ sudo tcpdump -env -i wi0 icmp6 or esp
tcpdump: listening on wi0
08:10:35.900432 0:60:1d:f0:88:8e 0:90:27:62:2b:7e 86dd 70: \
    3ffe:b00:4004::15 > 3ffe:b00:4004::1: icmp6: echo request \
    (len 16, hlim 64)
08:10:35.902612 0:90:27:62:2b:7e 0:60:1d:f0:88:8e 86dd 70: \
    3ffe:b00:4004::1 > 3ffe:b00:4004::15: icmp6: echo reply \
    (len 16, hlim 64)
^C
2 packets received by filter
0 packets dropped by kernel
kyrakat$
```

In the first exchange, the data is very clear. It shows "icmp6" type, "echo request," and "echo reply." This exchange is between *kyrakat* (::15) and *shadow* (::1). The second exchange, between *kyrakat* (::15) and *toshi* (::7), shows only *ip-proto-50*, the length, and hop limit because it is encrypted via IPsec.

27.5.2 *ipsecadm monitor*

The output of the command *ipsecadm monitor* is very useful for observing the activity of the kernel IPsec code. This command will dump changes to the standard output as the IPsec parameters change.

The *ipsecadm show* command can also be used to dump the current IPsec parameters. However, it gives only a snapshot of the current IPsec scenario on the system.

27.5.3 /kern/ipsec

Viewing **/kern/ipsec** is the best way to see which SPIs are currently set up. It requires that the *kernfs* filesystem be mounted (typically on the **/kern** mount point).

27.5.4 /var/run/isakmpd.pcap

If given the -*L* command-line option, *isakmpd* uses the **/var/run/isakmpd.pcap** file to log decrypted IKE packets. One can examine this log via *tcpdump -r /var/run/isakmpd.pcap*.

27.5.5 /var/run/isakmpd.report

When a SIGUSR1 signal is sent to *isakmpd*, many details are written to the **/var/run/ isakmpd.report** file, including the active configuration file. This data is very educational when utilizing Markus Friedl's zero configuration setup (see Section 27.4.2).

27.5.6 *netstat -nr*

Because IPsec tunneling routes traffic through an encapsulating interface, the kernel routing tables will contain information about the current IPsec parameters. By running *netstat -nr*, the encapsulating routing table can be dumped and viewed:

```
Encap:
Source              Port  Destination        Port  Proto \
    SA(Address/Proto/Type/Direction)
0/0                 0     10.0.0.42/32        0     0 \
    3ffe:b00:4004::1/50/use/in
10.0.0.37/32        0     10.0.0.42/32        0     0 \
    3ffe:b00:4004::7/50/use/in
10.0.0.42/32        0     0/0                 0     0 \
    3ffe:b00:4004::1/50/require/out
10.0.0.42/32        0     10.0.0.37/32        0     0 \
    3ffe:b00:4004::7/50/require/out
default                                       0     3ffe:b00:4004::15/128 \
    3ffe:b00:4004::1/50/use/in
3ffe:b00:4004::7/128                          0     3ffe:b00:4004::15/128 \
    3ffe:b00:4004::7/50/use/in
3ffe:b00:4004::15/128                         0     default 0     0      \
    3ffe:b00:4004::1/50/require/out
3ffe:b00:4004::15/128                         0     3ffe:b00:4004::7/128 \
    0     0 3ffe:b00:4004::7/50/require/out
```

This output does not show the SPI values for the connections, however.

27.6 Example VPN Configurations

The examples in this section all use shared x509 keys; please refer to Section 27.2.1 before proceeding. These configurations illustrate how the various parameters can be combined to create a secure tunnel with various endpoints.

For further details on the **/etc/isakmpd/isakmpd.conf** file, refer to the *isakmpd.conf(5)* manual page.

27.6.1 Transport: OpenBSD–OpenBSD + Tunnel: Net–Net

isakmpd.conf Dissected

A basic VPN configuration includes a transport mode connection for host-to-host communications, and a tunnel mode connection for net-to-net communications.

The configuration file for *isakmpd* is, by default, located at **/etc/isakmpd/isakmpd. conf**. Inside, there are named sections denoted by "[" and "]". A few names are special, or reserved—for example, "[General]". The section name is followed by a newline, with each line up until the next section consisting of "tag" and "value" pairs, with "=" in between. Some may be familiar with this format, known as the .INI style.

There are two phases during IKE. The first phase includes the daemon-to-daemon authentication and encryption negotiations. The second phase is for negotiating keys for SAs, which must be completed before any ESP or AH packets can flow for the SA being negotiated.

In general, one can think of the "[Phase 1]" section as "to whom does *isakmpd* talk." If you do not have the IP address of a remote peer here, *isakmpd* will not talk to it. For the roaming laptop scenario, a "Default" label permits identifying remote hosts by means other than IP addresses.

In general, one can think of the "[Phase 2]" section as "which network combinations should speak IPsec." Here there can be a "Connections" tag whose value is a comma-separated list of connection names, which refer to sections located elsewhere in the **isakmpd.conf** file.

Our first example includes a full basic VPN configuration. We have two IPv6 peers, *kyrakat* and *toshi*. Below, each piece of the **isakmpd.conf** file is examined.

For the host named *kyrakat*, the following example configuration snippet should be used:

```
[Phase 1]
3ffe:b00:4004::1= toshiv6

[Phase 2]
Connections=  toshi-IPv6-kyrakat-IPv6,toshi-IPv6-v4tunnel-kyrakat-IPv6
```

For the host named *toshi*, the following example configuration snippet should be used:

```
[Phase 1]
3ffe:b00:4004::15= kyrakatv6
```

```
[Phase 2]
Connections=  kyrakat-IPv6-toshi-IPv6,kyrakat-IPv6-v4tunnel-toshi-IPv6
```

The rest of the configuration snippets apply to **isakmpd.conf** files on both hosts. A configuration file typically has a "[General]" section that overrides any global defaults:

```
[General]
Policy-File=            /etc/isakmpd/isakmpd.policy
Retransmits=            2
Exchange-max-time=      600
Check-interval=         15
```

At this point, a few IP addresses must be defined:

```
[toshi-IPv6]
ID-type=                IPV6_ADDR
Address=                3ffe:b00:4004::7

[kyrakat-IPv6]
ID-type=                IPV6_ADDR
Address=                3ffe:b00:4004::15

[kyrakat-net-IPv4]
ID-type=                IPV4_ADDR_SUBNET
Network=                10.0.0.0
Netmask=                255.255.255.0

[toshi-net-IPv4]
ID-type=                IPV4_ADDR_SUBNET
Network=                192.168.0.0
Netmask=                255.255.255.0
```

Next, the section names referred to in "[Phase 1]" are created:

```
[kyrakatv6]
Phase=                  1
Address=                3ffe:b00:4004::15
Configuration=          rsa-main-mode
```

```
[toshiv6]
Phase=                     1
Address=                   3ffe:b00:4004::7
Configuration=             rsa-main-mode

[kyrakat-netv4]
Phase=                     1
Network=                   10.0.0.0
Netmask=                   255.255.255.0
Configuration=             main-mode

[toshi-netv4]
Phase=                     1
Network=                   192.168.0.0
Netmask=                   255.255.255.0
Configuration=             main-mode
```

These names are to be used only as values in the "[Phase 1]" section. The "Address" denotes the IP address; both IPv4 and IPv6 are supported. The "Configuration" refers to a section defined later on. For now, it suffices to understand that it describes how to negotiate the authentication and encryption.

Once we have defined these IP addresses, we must define some Phase 2 connections. We will start with the host-to-host variety:

```
[kyrakat-IPv6-toshi-IPv6]
Phase=                     2
ISAKMP-peer=               toshiv6
Configuration=             quick-mode
Local-ID=                  kyrakat-IPv6
Remote-ID=                 toshi-IPv6

[toshi-IPv6-kyrakat-IPv6]
Phase=                     2
ISAKMP-peer=               kyrakatv6
Configuration=             quick-mode
Local-ID=                  toshi-IPv6
Remote-ID=                 kyrakat-IPv6
```

Now we define the net-to-net connections:

```
[kyrakat-IPv6-v4tunnel-toshi-IPv6]
Phase=                  2
ISAKMP-peer=            toshiv6
Configuration=          quick-mode
Local-ID=               kyrakat-net-IPv4
Remote-ID=              toshi-net-IPv4

[toshi-IPv6-v4tunnel-kyrakat-IPv6]
Phase=                  2
ISAKMP-peer=            kyrakatv6
Configuration=          quick-mode
Local-ID=               toshi-net-IPv4
Remote-ID=              kyrakat-net-IPv4
```

Finally, we include some support definitions:

```
[default-IPv6]
ID-type=        IPV6_ADDR_SUBNET
Network=        ::
Netmask=        ::

[default-IPv4]
ID-type=        IPV4_ADDR_SUBNET
Network=        0.0.0.0
Netmask=        0.0.0.0

[rsa-main-mode]
DOI=                    IPSEC
EXCHANGE_TYPE=          ID_PROT
Transforms=             3DES-SHA-RSA_SIG

[ip6-main-mode]
DOI=                    IPSEC
EXCHANGE_TYPE=          ID_PROT
Transforms=             3DES-SHA
```

```
[ip6-quick-mode]
DOI=                     IPSEC
EXCHANGE_TYPE=           QUICK_MODE
Suites=                  QM-ESP-3DES-SHA-PFS-SUITE

[ip4-main-mode]
DOI=                     IPSEC
EXCHANGE_TYPE=           ID_PROT
Transforms=              3DES-SHA

[ip4-quick-mode]
DOI=                     IPSEC
EXCHANGE_TYPE=           QUICK_MODE
Suites=                  QM-ESP-3DES-SHA-PFS-SUITE

[ip4-main-mode]
DOI=                     IPSEC
EXCHANGE_TYPE=           ID_PROT
Transforms=              3DES-SHA

[ip4-quick-mode]
DOI=                     IPSEC
EXCHANGE_TYPE=           QUICK_MODE
Suites=                  QM-ESP-3DES-SHA-PFS-SUITE
```

Simplified Configuration Creation with *m4*

While this example may seem daunting, it is highly repetitive—so much so that it was generated from a very short file with the assistance of a few *m4* macros written for this purpose. For the host *kyrakat*, the configuration file (named **isakmpd.m4**) reads like this:

```
include(common.m4)dnl

[Phase 1]
3ffe:b00:4004::1= toshiv6

[Phase 2]
Connections=  toshi-IPv6-kyrakat-IPv6,toshi-IPv6-v4tunnel-kyrakat-IPv6
```

So far, this is very similar to the above.

The **common.m4** file is where the simplicity lies. It is the same for both *toshi* and *kyrakat*:

```
[General]
Policy-File=                /etc/isakmpd/isakmpd.policy
Retransmits=                2
Exchange-max-time=          600
Check-interval=             15

include(lib.m4)dnl

hostdef6(toshi,3ffe:b00:4004::7,rsa)
hostdef6(kyrakat,3ffe:b00:4004::15,rsa)

hostdef4(toshiint,10.0.0.37)
hostdef4(kyrakatint,10.0.0.42)

sadef6(toshi,kyrakat)
sadef6(kyrakat,toshi)

tunnel4in6(kyrakat,toshi,kyrakatint,toshiint)
tunnel4in6(toshi,kyrakat,toshiint,kyrakatint)
```

Here, there are four "hosts" defined: two IPv6 hosts and two IPv4 hosts.

Next, four SPIs (Security Parameter Indexes) are made: a host-to-host connection and a tunnel that uses the IPv6 protocol to transport an IPv4 tunnel.[4]

The contents of **lib.m4** are somewhat arcane and cryptic. They have been placed in Appendix G.

27.6.2 Transport: None + Tunnel: Net–Net

You don't have to use a tunnel, of course. You can instead have just an OpenBSD-to-OpenBSD (i.e., host-to-host) IPsec security arrangement.

For *toshi*, the **isakmpd.m4** file would be

```
include(common.m4)dnl
```

---

[4]Yes, four SPIs are created, one for each direction.

```
[Phase 1]
3ffe:b00:4004::15=        kyrakatv6


[Phase 2]
Connections=              toshi-IPv6-kyrakat-IPv6
```

For *kyrakat*, the **isakmpd.m4** file would be

```
include(common.m4)dnl

[Phase 1]
3ffe:b00:4004::7=         toshiv6


[Phase 2]
Connections=              kyrakat-IPv6-toshi-IPv6
```

For both machines, the **common.m4** file would be

```
[General]
Policy-File=              /etc/isakmpd/isakmpd.policy
Retransmits=              2
Exchange-max-time=        600
Check-interval=           15

include(lib.m4)dnl

hostdef6(kyrakat,3ffe:b00:4004::15,rsa)
hostdef6(toshi,3ffe:b00:4004::7,rsa)

sadef6(kyrakat,toshi)
sadef6(toshi,kyrakat)
```

For *toshi*, the **isakmpd.conf** file would be

```
[General]
Policy-File=              /etc/isakmpd/isakmpd.policy
```

```
Retransmits=            2
Exchange-max-time=      600
Check-interval=         15


[kyrakat-IPv6]
ID-type=                IPV6_ADDR
Address=                3ffe:b00:4004::15

[kyrakatv6]
Phase=                  1
Address=                3ffe:b00:4004::15
Configuration=          rsa-main-mode

[toshi-IPv6]
ID-type=                IPV6_ADDR
Address=                3ffe:b00:4004::7

[toshiv6]
Phase=                  1
Address=                3ffe:b00:4004::7
Configuration=          rsa-main-mode


[kyrakat-IPv6-toshi-IPv6]
Phase=                  2
ISAKMP-peer=            toshiv6
Configuration=          ip6-quick-mode
Local-ID=               kyrakat-IPv6
Remote-ID=              toshi-IPv6

[toshi-IPv6-kyrakat-IPv6]
Phase=                  2
ISAKMP-peer=            kyrakatv6
Configuration=          ip6-quick-mode
Local-ID=               toshi-IPv6
Remote-ID=              kyrakat-IPv6
```

```
[Phase 1]
3ffe:b00:4004::15=      kyrakatv6


[Phase 2]
Connections=            toshi-IPv6-kyrakat-IPv6

[default-IPv6]
ID-type=        IPV6_ADDR_SUBNET
Network=        ::
Netmask=        ::

[default-IPv4]
ID-type=        IPV4_ADDR_SUBNET
Network=        0.0.0.0
Netmask=        0.0.0.0

[rsa-main-mode]
DOI=            IPSEC
EXCHANGE_TYPE=  ID_PROT
Transforms=     3DES-SHA-RSA_SIG

[ip6-main-mode]
DOI=            IPSEC
EXCHANGE_TYPE=  ID_PROT
Transforms=     3DES-SHA


[ip6-quick-mode]
DOI=            IPSEC
EXCHANGE_TYPE=  QUICK_MODE
Suites=         QM-ESP-3DES-SHA-PFS-SUITE

[ip4-main-mode]
DOI=            IPSEC
EXCHANGE_TYPE=  ID_PROT
Transforms=     3DES-SHA
```

```
[ip4-quick-mode]
DOI=                    IPSEC
EXCHANGE_TYPE=          QUICK_MODE
Suites=                 QM-ESP-3DES-SHA-PFS-SUITE
```

27.6.3 Transport: OpenBSD–OpenBSD + Tunnel: None

A tunnel mode security arrangement isn't strictly necessary either. You can have just a transport security arrangement. These configuration files build on the *m4* processing system described earlier.

For *toshi*, the **isakmpd.m4** file would be

```
include(common.m4)dnl

[Phase 1]
3ffe:b00:4004::7=       toshiv6

[Phase 2]
Connections=            kyrakat-IPv6-v4tunnel-toshi-IPv6
```

For *kyrakat*, the **isakmpd.m4** file would be

```
include(common.m4)dnl
[Phase 1]
3ffe:b00:4004::15=      kyrakatv6

[Phase 2]
Connections=            toshi-IPv6-v4tunnel-kyrakat-IPv6
```

For both machines, the **common.m4** file would be

```
[General]
Policy-File=            /etc/isakmpd/isakmpd.policy
Retransmits=            2
Exchange-max-time=      600
Check-interval=         15

include(lib.m4)dnl
dnl
```

```
hostdef6(kyrakat,3ffe:b00:4004::15,rsa)
hostdef6(toshi,3ffe:b00:4004::7,rsa)dnl

hostdef4(kyrakat-net,10.0.0.0,,255.255.255.0)
hostdef4(toshi-net,192.168.0.0,,255.255.255.0)dnl

tunnel4in6(kyrakat,toshi,kyrakat-net,toshi-net)
tunnel4in6(toshi,kyrakat,toshi-net,kyrakat-net)dnl
```

For *toshi*, the **isakmpd.conf** file would be

```
[General]
Policy-File=              /etc/isakmpd/isakmpd.policy
Retransmits=              2
Exchange-max-time=        600
Check-interval=           15


[kyrakat-IPv6]
ID-type=                  IPV6_ADDR
Address=                  3ffe:b00:4004::15

[kyrakatv6]
Phase=                    1
Address=                  3ffe:b00:4004::15
Configuration=            rsa-main-mode

[toshi-IPv6]
ID-type=                  IPV6_ADDR
Address=                  3ffe:b00:4004::7

[toshiv6]
Phase=                    1
Address=                  3ffe:b00:4004::7
Configuration=            rsa-main-mode

[kyrakat-net-IPv4]
ID-type=                  IPV4_ADDR_SUBNET
```

```
Network=                10.0.0.0
Netmask=                255.255.255.0

[kyrakat-netv4]
Phase=                  1
Network=                10.0.0.0
Netmask=                255.255.255.0
Configuration=          main-mode

[toshi-net-IPv4]
ID-type=                IPV4_ADDR_SUBNET
Network=                192.168.0.0
Netmask=                255.255.255.0

[toshi-netv4]
Phase=                  1
Network=                192.168.0.0
Netmask=                255.255.255.0
Configuration=          main-mode


[kyrakat-IPv6-v4tunnel-toshi-IPv6]
Phase=                  2
ISAKMP-peer=            toshiv6
Configuration=          quick-mode
Local-ID=               kyrakat-net-IPv4
Remote-ID=              toshi-net-IPv4

[toshi-IPv6-v4tunnel-kyrakat-IPv6]
Phase=                  2
ISAKMP-peer=            kyrakatv6
Configuration=          quick-mode
Local-ID=               toshi-net-IPv4
Remote-ID=              kyrakat-net-IPv4

[Phase 1]
3ffe:b00:4004::7=       toshiv6
```

```
[Phase 2]
Connections=             kyrakat-IPv6-v4tunnel-toshi-IPv6

[default-IPv6]
ID-type=        IPV6_ADDR_SUBNET
Network=        ::
Netmask=        ::

[default-IPv4]
ID-type=        IPV4_ADDR_SUBNET
Network=        0.0.0.0
Netmask=        0.0.0.0

[rsa-main-mode]
DOI=                    IPSEC
EXCHANGE_TYPE=          ID_PROT
Transforms=             3DES-SHA-RSA_SIG

[ip6-main-mode]
DOI=                    IPSEC
EXCHANGE_TYPE=          ID_PROT
Transforms=             3DES-SHA

[ip6-quick-mode]
DOI=                    IPSEC
EXCHANGE_TYPE=          QUICK_MODE
Suites=                 QM-ESP-3DES-SHA-PFS-SUITE

[ip4-main-mode]
DOI=                    IPSEC
EXCHANGE_TYPE=          ID_PROT
Transforms=             3DES-SHA

[ip4-quick-mode]
DOI=                    IPSEC
EXCHANGE_TYPE=          QUICK_MODE
Suites=                 QM-ESP-3DES-SHA-PFS-SUITE
```

27.6.4 Wireless Laptop to a Secure Gateway

For this example, *shadow* is the secure gateway, and *kyrakat* is the wireless laptop. There is one trick not used in the other examples that appears here—the default route over IPsec.

For *shadow*, the **isakmpd.m4** file would be

```
include(common.m4)dnl

[Phase 1]
3ffe:b00:4004::15=      kyrakatv6

[Phase 2]
```

For *kyrakat*, the **isakmpd.m4** file would be

```
include(common.m4)dnl

[Phase 1]
3ffe:b00:4004::1=       shadowv6

[Phase 2]
Connections=    kyrakat-IPv6-v6default-shadow-IPv6,kyrakat-IPv6-v4default
                -shadow-IPv6
```

For both machines, the **common.m4** file would be

```
[General]
Policy-File=            /etc/isakmpd/isakmpd.policy
Retransmits=            2
Exchange-max-time=      600
Check-interval=         15

include(lib.m4)dnl

hostdef4(kyrakatint,10.0.0.42,rsa)

hostdef6(kyrakat,3ffe:b00:4004::15,rsa)
hostdef6(shadow,3ffe:b00:4004::1,rsa)
```

```
[kyrakat-IPv6-v6default-shadow-IPv6]
Phase=                  2
ISAKMP-peer=            shadowv6
Configuration=          quick-mode
Local-ID=               kyrakat-IPv6
Remote-ID=              default-IPv6

[kyrakat-IPv6-v4default-shadow-IPv6]
Phase=                  2
ISAKMP-peer=            shadowv6
Configuration=          quick-mode
Local-ID=               kyrakatint-IPv4
Remote-ID=              default-IPv4
```

For *kyrakat*, the **isakmpd.conf** file would be

```
[General]
Policy-File=            /etc/isakmpd/isakmpd.policy
Retransmits=            2
Exchange-max-time=      600
Check-interval=         15

[kyrakatint-IPv4]
ID-type=                IPV4_ADDR
Address=                10.0.0.42

[kyrakatintv4]
Phase=                  1
Address=                10.0.0.42
Configuration=          rsa-main-mode

[toshiint-IPv4]
ID-type=                IPV4_ADDR
Address=                10.0.0.37

[toshiintv4]
Phase=                  1
Address=                10.0.0.37
```

```
Configuration=              rsa-main-mode

[kyrakat-IPv6]
ID-type=                    IPV6_ADDR
Address=                    3ffe:b00:4004::15

[kyrakatv6]
Phase=                      1
Address=                    3ffe:b00:4004::15
Configuration=              rsa-main-mode

[toshi-IPv6]
ID-type=                    IPV6_ADDR
Address=                    3ffe:b00:4004::7

[toshiv6]
Phase=                      1
Address=                    3ffe:b00:4004::7
Configuration=              rsa-main-mode

[toshi-IPv6]
ID-type=                    IPV6_ADDR
Address=                    3ffe:b00:4004::7

[toshiv6]
Phase=                      1
Address=                    3ffe:b00:4004::7
Configuration=              rsa-main-mode


[shadow-IPv6]
ID-type=                    IPV6_ADDR
Address=                    3ffe:b00:4004::1

[shadowv6]
Phase=                      1
Address=                    3ffe:b00:4004::1
Configuration=              rsa-main-mode
```

```
[kyrakat-IPv6-v6default-shadow-IPv6]
Phase=                  2
ISAKMP-peer=            shadowv6
Configuration=          quick-mode
Local-ID=               kyrakat-IPv6
Remote-ID=              default-IPv6

[kyrakat-IPv6-v4default-shadow-IPv6]
Phase=                  2
ISAKMP-peer=            shadowv6
Configuration=          quick-mode
Local-ID=               kyrakatint-IPv4
Remote-ID=              default-IPv4

[kyrakat-IPv6-toshi-IPv6]
Phase=                  2
ISAKMP-peer=            toshiv6
Configuration=          quick-mode
Local-ID=               kyrakat-IPv6
Remote-ID=              toshi-IPv6

[toshi-IPv6-kyrakat-IPv6]
Phase=                  2
ISAKMP-peer=            kyrakatv6
Configuration=          quick-mode
Local-ID=               toshi-IPv6
Remote-ID=              kyrakat-IPv6


[kyrakat-IPv6-v4tunnel-toshi-IPv6]
Phase=                  2
ISAKMP-peer=            toshiv6
Configuration=          quick-mode
Local-ID=               kyrakatint-IPv4
Remote-ID=              toshiint-IPv4

[toshi-IPv6-v4tunnel-kyrakat-IPv6]
Phase=                  2
```

```
ISAKMP-peer=              kyrakatv6
Configuration=           quick-mode
Local-ID=                toshiint-IPv4
Remote-ID=               kyrakatint-IPv4


[Phase 1]
3ffe:b00:4004::1=        shadowv6


[Phase 2]
Connections=    kyrakat-IPv6-v6default-shadow-IPv6,kyrakat-IPv6-v4default
                -shadow-IPv6


[default-IPv6]
ID-type=        IPV6_ADDR_SUBNET
Network=        ::
Netmask=        ::


[default-IPv4]
ID-type=        IPV4_ADDR_SUBNET
Network=        0.0.0.0
Netmask=        0.0.0.0


[rsa-main-mode]
DOI=                     IPSEC
EXCHANGE_TYPE=           ID_PROT
Transforms=              3DES-SHA-RSA_SIG


[ip6-main-mode]
DOI=                     IPSEC
EXCHANGE_TYPE=           ID_PROT
Transforms=              3DES-SHA


[ip6-quick-mode]
DOI=                     IPSEC
EXCHANGE_TYPE=           QUICK_MODE
Suites=                  QM-ESP-3DES-SHA-PFS-SUITE


[ip4-main-mode]
```

```
DOI=                      IPSEC
EXCHANGE_TYPE=            ID_PROT
Transforms=              3DES-SHA

[ip4-quick-mode]
DOI=                      IPSEC
EXCHANGE_TYPE=            QUICK_MODE
Suites=                  QM-ESP-3DES-SHA-PFS-SUITE
```

27.6.5 OpenBSD–OpenBSD Through an OpenBSD PF NAT Firewall

There is nothing specific about the OpenBSD **pf.conf** setup needed to allow *isakmpd* to negotiate through NAT. Typical uses of *isakmpd* do not involve AH, and this protocol cannot be used in this scenario. By default, PF will treat ESP as a generic protocol, making a mapping between an internal machine and an external machine. For this reason, only one internal machine may connect to each unique remote VPN gateway.

At C2K3, in Canada, one of the authors used his laptop to connect to his machine on the Internet. In general, he had to tell the laptop its internal address for a few sections, and the gateway external public IP address for a few more sections. The same thing was necessary for the remote machine.

Prior to establishing the connection, x509 preshared keys were selected. They allowed the full configuration file to be inspected, as no secrets were included. (See Section 27.2.1 for advice about generating x509 keys.)

Next, the **isakmpd.conf** files were loaded on each host, and *isakmpd* was started via */sbin/isakmpd*.

One other item of note: The author chose to use the FIFO interface to bring the connection up. Debugging programs could then be prepared before any IPsec packets started flying around the network.

After loading the laptop configuration described below, you would then echo the following string to the **/var/run/isakmpd.fifo** file:

```
C laptop-IPv4-remote-IPv4
C laptop-IPv4-v6tunnel-remote-IPv4
C laptop-IPv4-v6default-remote-IPv4
```

The "trick" to using IPsec over a NAT tunnel is to tweak a few entries so as to have the public IP address of the NAT gateway on the remote VPN server, yet to insert the internal IP address of the laptop on the laptop for those same entries.

Laptop Configuration
This information is for inside the NAT machine:

```
[General]
Policy-File=               /etc/isakmpd/isakmpd.policy
Retransmits=               3
Exchange-max-time=         600


[laptop-IPv4]
ID-type=                            IPV4_ADDR
Address=                            192.168.78.128

[laptopv4]
Phase=                              1
Address=                            192.168.78.128
Configuration=                      rsa-main-mode

[remote-IPv4]
ID-type=                            IPV4_ADDR
Address=                            66.210.104.215

[remotev4]
Phase=                              1
Address=                            66.210.104.215
Configuration=                      rsa-main-mode

[FRIESNET-c2k3-IPv6]
ID-type=                            IPV6_ADDR_SUBNET
Network=                            3ffe:b00:4004:c283::
Netmask=                            ffff:ffff:ffff:ffff::

[FRIESNET-c2k3v6]
Phase=                              1
Network=                            3ffe:b00:4004:c283::
Netmask=                            ffff:ffff:ffff:ffff::
Configuration=                      ip6-main-mode
```

```
[FRIESNET-remote-IPv6]
ID-type=                               IPV6_ADDR_SUBNET
Network=                               3ffe:b00:4004:200::
Netmask=                               ffff:ffff:ffff:ffff::

[FRIESNET-remotev6]
Phase=                                 1
Network=                               3ffe:b00:4004:200::
Netmask=                               ffff:ffff:ffff:ffff::
Configuration=                         ip6-main-mode

[laptop-IPv4-remote-IPv4]
Phase=                                 2
ISAKMP-peer=                           remotev4
Configuration=                         ip4-quick-mode
Local-ID=                              laptop-IPv4
Remote-ID=                             remote-IPv4

[remote-IPv4-laptop-IPv4]
Phase=                                 2
ISAKMP-peer=                           laptopv4
Configuration=                         ip4-quick-mode
Local-ID=                              remote-IPv4
Remote-ID=                             laptop-IPv4

[laptop-IPv4-v6tunnel-remote-IPv4]
Phase=                  2
ISAKMP-peer=            remotev4
Configuration=          ip4-quick-mode
Local-ID=               FRIESNET-c2k3-IPv6
Remote-ID=              FRIESNET-remote-IPv6

[remote-IPv4-v6tunnel-laptop-IPv4]
Phase=                  2
ISAKMP-peer=            laptopv4
Configuration=          ip4-quick-mode
Local-ID=               FRIESNET-remote-IPv6
```

```
Remote-ID=                   FRIESNET-c2k3-IPv6


[default-IPv6]
ID-type=          IPV6_ADDR_SUBNET
Network=          ::
Netmask=          ::

[laptop-IPv4-v6default-remote-IPv4]
Phase=                   2
ISAKMP-peer=             remotev4
Configuration=           ip4-quick-mode
Local-ID=                FRIESNET-c2k3-IPv6
Remote-ID=               default-IPv6

[rsa-main-mode]
DOI=                                    IPSEC
EXCHANGE_TYPE=                          ID_PROT
Transforms=                             3DES-SHA-RSA_SIG

[ip6-main-mode]
DOI=                                    IPSEC
EXCHANGE_TYPE=                          ID_PROT
Transforms=                             3DES-SHA


[ip6-quick-mode]
DOI=                                    IPSEC
EXCHANGE_TYPE=                          QUICK_MODE
Suites=                                 QM-ESP-3DES-SHA-PFS-SUITE

[ip4-main-mode]
DOI=                                    IPSEC
EXCHANGE_TYPE=                          ID_PROT
Transforms=                             3DES-SHA

[ip4-quick-mode]
DOI=                                    IPSEC
```

```
EXCHANGE_TYPE=                            QUICK_MODE
Suites=                                   QM-ESP-3DES-SHA-PFS-SUITE

[Phase 1]
66.210.104.215= remotev4
```

Remote Configuration
This information is for the public remote VPN:

```
[General]
Policy-File=              /etc/isakmpd/isakmpd.policy
Retransmits=             3
Exchange-max-time=       600


[laptop-IPv4]
ID-type=                                  IPV4_ADDR
Address=                                  209.5.161.192

[laptopv4]
Phase=                                    1
Address=                                  209.5.161.192
Configuration=                            rsa-main-mode

[remote-IPv4]
ID-type=                                  IPV4_ADDR
Address=                                  66.210.104.215

[remotev4]
Phase=                                    1
Address=                                  66.210.104.215
Configuration=                            rsa-main-mode


[FRIESNET-c2k3-IPv6]
ID-type=                                  IPV6_ADDR_SUBNET
Network=                                  3ffe:b00:4004:c283::
Netmask=                                  ffff:ffff:ffff:ffff::
```

```
[FRIESNET-c2k3v6]
Phase=                              1
Network=                           3ffe:b00:4004:c283::
Netmask=                           ffff:ffff:ffff:ffff::
Configuration=                     ip6-main-mode

[FRIESNET-remote-IPv6]
ID-type=                           IPV6_ADDR_SUBNET
Network=                           3ffe:b00:4004:200::
Netmask=                           ffff:ffff:ffff:ffff::

[FRIESNET-remotev6]
Phase=                              1
Network=                           3ffe:b00:4004:200::
Netmask=                           ffff:ffff:ffff:ffff::
Configuration=                     ip6-main-mode


[laptop-IPv4-remote-IPv4]
Phase=                              2
ISAKMP-peer=                       remotev4
Configuration=                     ip4-quick-mode
Local-ID=                          laptop-IPv4
Remote-ID=                         remote-IPv4

[remote-IPv4-laptop-IPv4]
Phase=                              2
ISAKMP-peer=                       laptopv4
Configuration=                     ip4-quick-mode
Local-ID=                          remote-IPv4
Remote-ID=                         laptop-IPv4


[laptop-IPv4-v6tunnel-remote-IPv4]
Phase=                   2
ISAKMP-peer=             remotev4
Configuration=           ip4-quick-mode
```

```
Local-ID=                FRIESNET-c2k3-IPv6
Remote-ID=               FRIESNET-remote-IPv6


[remote-IPv4-v6tunnel-laptop-IPv4]
Phase=                   2
ISAKMP-peer=             laptopv4
Configuration=           ip4-quick-mode
Local-ID=                FRIESNET-remote-IPv6
Remote-ID=               FRIESNET-c2k3-IPv6



[default-IPv6]
ID-type=        IPV6_ADDR_SUBNET
Network=        ::
Netmask=        ::


[laptop-IPv4-v6default-remote-IPv4]
Phase=          2
ISAKMP-peer=    remotev4
Configuration=  ip4-quick-mode
Local-ID=       FRIESNET-c2k3-IPv6
Remote-ID=      default-IPv6


[rsa-main-mode]
DOI=                            IPSEC
EXCHANGE_TYPE=                  ID_PROT
Transforms=                     3DES-SHA-RSA_SIG


[ip6-main-mode]
DOI=                            IPSEC
EXCHANGE_TYPE=                  ID_PROT
Transforms=                     3DES-SHA


[ip6-quick-mode]
DOI=                            IPSEC
EXCHANGE_TYPE=                  QUICK_MODE
Suites=                         QM-ESP-3DES-SHA-PFS-SUITE
```

```
[ip4-main-mode]
DOI=                            IPSEC
EXCHANGE_TYPE=                  ID_PROT
Transforms=                     3DES-SHA

[ip4-quick-mode]
DOI=                            IPSEC
EXCHANGE_TYPE=                  QUICK_MODE
Suites=                         QM-ESP-3DES-SHA-PFS-SUITE


[Phase 1]
209.5.161.192=   laptopv4
```

## Chapter 28

IPv6: IP Version 6

The Internet Protocol (IP) was designed in the early days of the Internet. At the time, the Internet was a much smaller collection of networks, mainly involving researchers. Several current realities facing the Internet were inconceivable at the time. As a result of this failure to plan ahead, the currently popular IP standard, IPv4, faces a number of limitations.

Size is merely one of the large issues facing the current IPv4 Internet. The size of the IPv4 address space, 32 bits, can allow for a maximum of more than 4 billion hosts. However, due to use of many of these addresses for network numbers, broadcasts, and reserved networks, the number actually possible is smaller than the maximum allowed. Furthermore, a number of large networks are unused, due to political or technical reasons. This brings the actual number of networkable addresses down to a number that faces a serious crunch as the twenty-first century starts.

Additionally, IPv4 addresses can be readily spoofed, as they do not allow for any mechanism for authentication or nonrepudiation. Additions such as IPsec, originally mandated in IPv6 and now optionally available for IPv4, can provide these capabilities, however. Lastly, one serious problem relates to routing and the network layout. The current IPv4 Internet exists as an ad-hoc network, with no geographical or hierarchical layout.

Many of the limitations facing IPv4 have been addressed in IPv6, the next generation of the IP standard.[1] They include the following:

- **Addressing**   Using a larger address space—128 bits as opposed to 32 bits— several million million hosts are possible on the network. A common anecdote is

---

[1] IPv6 is often referred to as IPng, or IP Next Generation; this older term was used for the evolving standard before it was finalized. What happened to IPv5? There were two different standards, Internet Streaming Protocol and Internet Streaming Protocol 2, that were collectively called IPv5. Where did it go? We don't know either.

that every square inch of the planet Earth could have several thousand hosts under this new networking standard.

- **Topology**   The layout of the network has been designated to be geographical, allowing for a hierarchical layout. As such, neighboring regions can also be network neighbors. This should ease the table size for backbone routers, for example.

- **Host configurations**   Positioning a host on the network has become infinitely more user-friendly. IPv6 includes, in its base design, an ad-hoc configuration mechanism known as *rtsol*, which enables hosts to determine valid addresses for their network space and to adapt themselves to the network. This is analogous to the use of DHCP in IPv4.

- **Bandwidth usage**   Quality-of-service provisions are implicit in the design of IPv6, thereby allowing networks that move varying types of data with varying bandwidth and quality requirements to more smoothly handle these competing requests.

- **Security**   Authentication headers are provided by default, allowing for the verification of the source of IPv6 packets and traffic.

A massive overhaul of the Internet would be required to fully deploy IPv6, as well as vendors' large-scale adoption of the appropriate implementations. This is currently the bottleneck in IPv6 deployment. Nevertheless, several IPv6 research networks are spreading, allowing for the real-world testing of this emerging standard. RFC 2893 describes a transition mechanism for network administrators that seek to adopt the new IPv6 standard, which could otherwise be a headache. Significant support for IPv4 networks is inherent in IPv6, however.

OpenBSD fully supports IPv6 natively.[2] The **GENERIC** kernel that is installed has full IPv6 support built in, and most, if not all, of the base networking systems support IPv6.[3] If you wish to compile the kernel's support for IPv6 separately, remove the INET6 and related options in your kernel configuration file and rebuild your kernel (see Chapter 32). No damage is done if you have IPv6 enabled but not in use.

---

[2]This code comes mainly from the KAME project, at http://www.kame.net/, a Japanese group developing IPv6 and IPsec support for BSD systems. Some portions come from the WIDE project, which also do a fair amount of IPv6 work for BSD kernels.

[3]Note that some ports, at this time, do not support IPv6 correctly. One example, at the time of this writing, is the *mozilla* port. Note that this is being worked on to ensure the correct handling of a useful port, such as this.

28.1 How IPv6 Works

IPv6 can be thought of as an expanded IPv4. Addresses are still hierarchical, just as they are in IPv4. Normal TCP, UDP, and ICMP packet types still exist, and the standard ports for services are in use. The biggest change comes in the packet format, which has slightly larger headers and more options via chained headers.[4]

Because there are so many IPv6 options, including them all in any packet would leave little room for the packet's payload. Because of this, protocol options are chained in additional headers as needed, leaving more room for data payloads.

28.1.1 Special Addresses

The addressing scheme in IPv6 has several facets. First is the "link local" address with which each interface is initiated. These addresses are immediately obvious by their prefix **fe80**. They are built using this prefix and the MAC address of the interface. A typical link local configuration of an interface is as follows:

```
$  ifconfig wi0 inet6
wi0: flags=8843<UP,BROADCAST,RUNNING,SIMPLEX,MULTICAST> mtu 1500
        inet6 fe80::205:5dff:fef2:cb11%wi0 prefixlen 64 scopeid 0x14
```

While this appears to be a valid IPv6 address, it is difficult to use correctly. The *scopeid* limits the locality of the address, as it may not be globally unique. This address is then used to gain a valid local IPv6 network address via either stateless autoconfiguration (described below) or stateful autoconfiguration (such as through DHCP), or it is ignored entirely for manual configurations of the interface.

Unlike IPv4, IPv6 doesn't have a concept of a broadcast address. Rather, multicast addresses, such as for all nodes or all routers, are used. Furthermore, IPv4 broadcast addresses are discarded by IPv6 to prevent swamping IPv4 networks.

IPv6 also supports the anycast address. This address is used for services that can reach a variety of machines, with any of them responding. In recent years, it has become popular for distributed content caching systems. This scheme is difficult to implement cleanly in IPv4, but in IPv6 it is part of the format. The anycast address has the following

---

[4]A common misconception is that IPv6 will make the header size four times larger. The IPv6 header actually casts aside many parts of the IPv4 header, mainly to limit the size increase, but also as a result of chaining headers. In reality, IPv6 headers are 40 bytes long and IPv4 headers are 20 bytes long.

format for the *any* router address: *n* bits of subnet prefix with 128*n* bits of zeroes. Other anycast addresses have identifiers and scoping as well.

Multicast addresses are also supported in IPv6. Two well-known multicast addresses are the all routers (ff02::2) and all nodes (ff02::1) addresses. Additional fields in the most significant bits of the address can be used to identify the scope and nature of the address. Other well-known multicast addresses are identified in the least significant bits of the address.

Two other address schemes are popular in IPv6. The "all address," which maps to 0.0.0.0 in IPv4, is the all-zero address in IPv6, which collapses to ::. The localhost address, typically 127.0.0.1, is ::1 in IPv6.

The format of the addressing scheme in IPv6 is similar to that in IPv4, but with some additional structure included. The most significant bits of the address are the subnet identifier, with the least significant bits comprising the node address. In IPv4, the concept of a netmask for a class C would be 255.255.255.0. Another way of stating this would be in CIDR format, or "/24". This "/24" concept is used by IPv6 and is called a prefixlen (prefix length). There is no such thing as an IPv6 netmask in the RFCs, only a prefixlen. Unlike IPv4, IPv6 has a suggested prefixlen that is to be valid for all Ethernet segments. The "/64" prefixlen is recommended for use by all IPv6 networks. This approach clearly separates the "network" portion of the addresses from the "host" portion of the addresses, and it facilitates renumbering—just change the upper 64 bits and you're good to go. Before being configured for networking, any IPv6 host has a link local address, which is built using the fe80:: prefix along with the node's link-layer address. This address allows the host to communicate with nodes on the local network but should not be passed by the router. Addresses can also be scoped, identifying how globally unique they are.

28.1.2 Tunneling IPv4 and IPv6

Central to the deployment of IPv6, during the trasition period, is the use of *tunnels* to allow for connectivity to the growing IPv6 backbone network. The initial testbed network, nicknamed **6bone**, is accessible via a number of avenues. If you have only IPv4 access through your upstream, there is no need to worry. Using a tunnel, you can pass IPv6 packets through an IPv4 network. Furthermore, using various edgepoints on the **6bone** cloud, you can connect even if you do not have a static IPv4 address.

As of the time of this writing, there is a proposal for an RFC that will disband the **6bone** addresses, "3ffe::/16". Enough "production" addresses are now in use that tunnel providers such as **he.net** have switched from providing **6bone** addresses to providing real production addresses. In reality, not much is different, save the first 16 bits of the address, as all public IPv6 networks are fully routable to and from one another.

The method preferred to tunnel from an IPv4 network to an IPv6 network in OpenBSD is to use **gif** devices. These generic interface devices can be used to tunnel IPv4 or IPv6 data over an IPv4 or IPv6 tunnel. The required support for the **gif** device is built into the kernel in the **GENERIC** device. We will show how an automatic **gif** tunnel is set up later in this chapter.

28.1.3 Kernel Setup

To enable the use of IPv6 in your kernel, make sure that the *INET6* option is enabled, along with *INET*, which is a dependency. This option is enabled in the **GENERIC** kernel and is installed by default.

28.1.4 Userland Setup

To enable the use of IPv6 in the userland, some tools need to be compiled with the option *-DINET6*, which is on by default. These userland applications include *ifconfig, route, ping6, traceroute6, tcpdump, netstat, ndp, ifmcstat* (used to show multicase statistics), and *systat* (e.g., *systat netstat*). Note that if you have IPv6 enabled but are not using it, you are not hurting your system.

28.2 Normal Use

28.2.1 Manual Configuration

To configure an interface to support a valid IPv6 address, you can use the familiar *ifconfig* tool. However, this process is labor intensive and prone to error. It is far easier to use host autoconfiguration, which is built into the IPv6 protocol.

If we wanted to have this sort of configuration occur between reboots, we could manually enter the information in the file **/etc/hostname.if**—in this case, **/etc/hostname.ep0**:

```
inet 10.10.10.1 255.255.0.0 NONE media 10baseT
inet6 3ffe:501:ffff::205:5dff:fef2:fb11 64
```

The first field is, as usual in this file, the address family—in this case, *inet6* for IPv6. The second field is the address. The third field is the *prefix length*, commonly abbreviated *prefixlen*; it is similar to the *netmask* in IPv4 addresses. Default router support for IPv6 is not automatic, but a simple statement like the following in **/etc/rc.local** adds support for a file like **/etc/mygate6**:

```
if [ -e /etc/mygate6 ]; then
    route add -inet6 default 'cat /etc/mygate6'
fi
```

This will use this file in the exact same way that the file **/etc/mygate** is used in IPv4 networking.

An alternate IPv6 router setting could be used:

```
inet6 3ffe:501:ffff::205:5dff:fef2:fb11
!/usr/sbin/route6d -q
```

This will automatically install the local routing table if the local IPv6 router has *route6d* running, which is highly recommended. Then no **/etc/mygate6** file needs to be present. More information about *route6d* can be found on its manual page, which provides a fairly clear description of its operation.

A third way of creating the router setting would be to add the following to the file **/etc/hostname.ep0**:

```
!route -n add -inet6 default 3ffe:501:ffff::1
```

This manual configuration may be required for an IPv6 router. Because routers provide network information to the hosts using *stateless autoconfiguration* (described later in this chapter), they themselves cannot benefit from this configuration option. They can, however, take advantage of configuration from other routers using dynamic routing protocols, the preferred method for IPv6 routing information propogation. Even so, the node's address will have to be manually configured as described previously.

28.2.2 Configuring a Router for IPv6

To enable your IPv6 router to talk to other routers and receive routing updates via the RIPng protocol, you must enable and configure the *route6d* daemon. It is configured in the file **/etc/rc.conf**:

```
route6d_flags=          # for normal use: ""
```

This will start *route6d* services and update the kernel routing tables appropriately. The configuration and use of *route6d* are beyond the scope of this book (their discussion would require an introduction to routing and IPv6 routing specifics). All of the IPv6 routing configurations shown here center on a single IPv6 router that is manually configured.

To enable the system to start advertising IPv6 configurations, you can edit the file **/etc/rc.conf**:

```
rtadvd_flags=sis0 sis1    # for normal use: list of interfaces
```

This value contains a space-separated (unquoted) list of interfaces on which to advertise the IPv6 network configuration. For each of these interfaces, the *rtadvd* daemon will run and handle autoconfiguring clients. Note that if any of the interfaces are invalid, *rtadvd* will not run correctly on that or any other interfaces.

Just as is needed for IPv4 routers, IPv6 forwarding must be enabled. To ensure that this setup persists, edit the key in **/etc/sysctl.conf**:

```
net.inet6.ip6.forwarding=1
```

This will allow IPv6 traffic to pass through your router and on to the destination.

28.2.3 Configuring a Host for IPv6 Automatically

A host is defined as a network node that receives packets on the network but is not configured to forward packets. Typically, a host receives only packets addressed to itself. This includes both workstations and servers. Manual configuration information for such machines was described earlier. The preferred way to configure a host, however, is through automatic methods, using Neighbor Discovery Protocol and IPv6 ICMP6 router solicitations, a technique called *stateless autoconfiguration.*

IPv6 has automatic configurations of hosts built into the protocol. Using IPv6 ICMP *router solicitation* messages, local IPv6 routers can dispense valid network configurations for a host requesting such information. This is far less error prone because it uses the link local addresses (valid only on the local network). This scheme is very similar to the *DHCP* option in IPv4, but also mixes in elements of the ICMP Router Discovery Protocol. However, this approach is built into IPv6, and every valid IPv6 network will support this configuration choice. It is preferred to manual configurations by a wide margin.

To have this autoconfiguration run at start-up, you can have a very simple interface configuration file. Just as you would for IPv6 DHCP configuration, you can use *rtsol* in your **hostname.if** file to have the system configure the interface using IPv6 stateless autoconfiguration. The file would then look like this for a wireless interface **wi0**:

```
$  cat /etc/hostname.wi0
rtsol
```

This will invoke automatic configuration of the interface during network initialization at start-up. Also, you must enable the acceptance of router advertisements via *sysctl*. To ensure that this information persists across reboots, add the following line (or edit the existing entry) to your configuration file **/etc/sysctl.conf**:

```
net.inet6.ip6.accept_rtadv=1    # 1=Permit IPv6 autoconf
```

Without this line, your system will not be able to accept the configuration advertisements from an IPv6 router.

The client program *rtsol* is invoked to send out *router solicitations*, basically seeking out IPv6 routers for configuration. The format of the packet appears as shown below, using the "all routers" multicast address ff02::2 as a target address and the link local address as the source:

```
00:40:39.140226 fe80::210:5aff:fe8a:bfe3 > ff02::2: icmp6: \
    router solicitation
  0000: 6000 0000 0010 3aff fe80 0000 0000 0000   '.....:.......
  0010: 0210 5aff fe8a bfe3 ff02 0000 0000 0000   ..Z........
  0020: 0000 0000 0000 0002 8500 4632 0000 0000   ..........F2....
  0030: 0101 0010 5a8a bfe3                        ....Z.
```

Having seen this message, the IPv6 router can send out a *router advertisement* message, which contains information about the network and valid addressing information. Such messages are also periodically broadcast by IPv6 routers for hosts that are listening to these advertisements. The response address is not the target host but rather the multicast address for "all IPv6 nodes," ff02::1, and the source address is the link local address for the router:

```
00:40:39.202580 fe80::2a0:ccff:fe7b:af92 > ff02::1: icmp6: \
    router advertisement
  0000: 6000 0000 0038 3aff fe80 0000 0000 0000   '....8:.......
  0010: 02a0 ccff fe7b af92 ff02 0000 0000 0000   .{........
  0020: 0000 0000 0000 0001 8600 e92d 4000 0708   ...........-@...
  0030: 0000 0000 0000 0000 0101 00a0 cc7b af92   ...........{.
  0040: 0304 40c0 0027 8d00 0009 3a80 0000 0000   ..@.'....:.....
  0050: 3ffe                                       ?
```

This packet contains the information needed for the IPv6 host to configure itself for the local IPv6 network, including the router IPv6 address, the network's prefix length, and any additional parameters for local configuration.

The table of IPv6 neighbors can be viewed using the *ndp* program:

```
$ ndp -a
Neighbor                              Linklayer Address    Netif Expire     \
    St Flgs Prbs
3ffe:501:ffff::1                      0:a0:cc:7b:af:92      ep0 23h57m10s \
    S  R
3ffe:501:ffff:0:210:5aff:fe8a:bfe3 0:10:5a:8a:bf:e3        ep0 permanent \
    R
fe80::2a0:ccff:fe7b:af92%ep0          0:a0:cc:7b:af:92      ep0 23h43m12s \
    S  R
```

The *ndp* program works very much like the *arp* program in IPv4, mapping link-layer addresses to IP addresses. Similarily, you can delete entries and add static entries—all controls you have in *arp*. Furthermore, entries expire in IPv6. The only permanent entry (in the absence of any static entry you may create) is your local address. The pair of addresses at the link-layer addresses 0:a0:cc:7b:af:92 belong to the default router—in this case, at **3ffe:501:ffff::1**. In the preceding example, the first entry is the IPv6 address of the router, and the third entry is the link local address of the router.

The router solicication program *rtsol* is rarely run as such. Instead, you typically have the solicitation daemon *rtsold* running in the background. It initiates and sends a small number of router solicitations. Furthermore, it caches router advertisements, allowing your host configuration to remain correct for your network. This works well if you are moving from network to network, for example. To start *rtsold* at start-up, edit the value of *rtsold_flags* in **/etc/rc.conf** and list the interfaces on which you need IPv6 autodiscovery:

```
rtsold_flags="wi0 fxp0"       # start rtsold on wi0, fxp0
```

Also, ensure that you are not set to forward IPv6 packets and that your kernel can accept router advertisements. To do this, use the command *sysctl -w net.inet6.ip6.accept_rtadv=1*.

28.3 Getting on the IPv6 Network

There are several ways to access the IPv6 Internet. If your provider has IPv6 enabled to your nearest hop, that's the most obvious route to take. If that's not a direct option, consider asking the provider to build a tunnel to your nearest hop. Of course, in either case you'll probably have to be a large customer for your upstream provider to get this service. Not all providers are tied into the IPv6 backbone, and not all will be willing to build a tunnel your way. It is, after all, a lot of work on their part.

Don't run away in fear, though: You can still get on the **6bone**, even if you have only one IPv4 address. This scheme includes dial-up access. For starters, the address will have to be globally unique, meaning it is not a reserved network like 10/8 or 192.168/16. Many providers use this network for their customers; if you're in this situation, you're out of luck.

28.3.1 Freenet6

One way to access the Internet as an IPv6 host is through a tunnel broker, such as Freenet6, located online at **http://www.freenet6.net/**. Freenet6 is chartered with assisting people interested in using the Internet in the **6bone** cloud for free. It offers delegations of /48 network segments (Freenet6 itself has a /32 pTLD delegation).

Getting the network segment allocated via Freenet6 is easy. Simply visit its site and obtain a username and password. This system prevents tunnel abuse and ensures that the parties using it are properly authenticated. Then obtain the tool *tcpc* and use it to configure the tunnel **gif0** as an interface to the outside world. (Obviously, if you have a **gif0** tunnel established with something else, you can use **gif1**.)

A simple **tcpc** configuration file would look like the following after some modification:

```
$  cat tcpc.conf
# Freenet6 config file
tsp_version=1.0.0
tsp_dir=/home/jose/papers/ipv6/freenet6-0.9.5
auth_method=any
client_v4=auto
userid=myname
passwd=password
template=openbsd
server=tsps1.freenet6.net
if_tunnel=gif0
```

Launching the client is then quite easy to do. Just launch the client with the interface specified as your external network interface, which will be the physical interface for your **gif** tunnel:

```
#  ./tspc -vs ep0
tspc - Tunnel Server Protocol Client
```

```
Loading configuration file

Using [129.22.210.63] as source IPv4 address taken from ep0.
Connecting to server

Send request

Process response from server

TSP_HOST_TYPE              host
TSP_TUNNEL_INTERFACE       gif0
TSP_HOME_INTERFACE
TSP_CLIENT_ADDRESS_IPV4    129.22.210.63
TSP_CLIENT_ADDRESS_IPV6    3ffe:0b80:0002:4418:0000:0000:0000:0002
TSP_SERVER_ADDRESS_IPV4    206.123.31.114
TSP_SERVER_ADDRESS_IPV6    3ffe:0b80:0002:4418:0000:0000:0000:0001
TSP_TUNNEL_PREFIXLEN       128
TSP_VERBOSE                1
TSP_HOME_DIR               /home/jose/papers/ipv6/freenet6-0.9.5
--- Start of configuration script. ---
Script: openbsd.sh
Setting up interface gif0
Adding default route to 3ffe:0b80:0002:4418:0000:0000:0000:0001
writing to routing socket: No such process
delete net default: not in table
add net default: gateway 3ffe:0b80:0002:4418:0000:0000:0000:0001
--- End of configuration script. ---
Closing, exit status: 0
Exiting with return code : 0 (0 = no error)
```

At this point, the tunnel is complete. Note that the IPv6 address is assigned to the **gif** interface and not the Ethernet interface. This is because the routing for IPv6 uses the **gif** tunnel.

```
# ifconfig -a
...
gif0: flags=8051<UP,POINTOPOINT,RUNNING,MULTICAST> mtu 1280
        physical address inet 129.22.210.63 --> 206.123.31.114
```

```
        inet6 fe80::210:5aff:fe8a:bfe3%gif0 -> :: prefixlen 64 \
          scopeid 0x10
        inet6 3ffe:b80:2:4418::2 -> 3ffe:b80:2:4418::1 prefixlen 128
ep0: flags=8863<UP,BROADCAST,NOTRAILERS,RUNNING,SIMPLEX,MULTICAST> \
          mtu 1500
        media: Ethernet 10baseT
        inet6 fe80::210:5aff:fe8a:bfe3%ep0 prefixlen 64 scopeid 0x14
        inet 129.22.210.63 netmask 0xfffffc00 broadcast 129.22.211.255
...
#  route -n show -inet6
Routing tables

Internet6:
Destination     Gateway             Flags
default         3ffe:b80:2:4418::1  UG
::1             ::1                 UH
...
```

Setup is now complete, and you can use **6bone**.

At this point, it is easy to check for connectivity to the outside world. First, to make sure the tunnel is functional, you can do this:

```
$  ping6 -n -w ff02::1%gif0
PING6(72 bytes) fe80::290:27ff:fe62:2b7e%gif0 --> ff02::1%gif0
38 bytes from fe80::290:27ff:fe62:2b7e%gif0: shadow.fries.net.
40 bytes from fe80::290:27ff:fe17:fc0f%gif0: rap.viagenie.qc.ca.
38 bytes from fe80::290:27ff:fe62:2b7e%gif0: shadow.fries.net.
40 bytes from fe80::290:27ff:fe17:fc0f%gif0: rap.viagenie.qc.ca.
^C
--- ff02::1%gif0 ping6 statistics ---
2 packets transmitted, 2 packets received, 0% packet loss
```

The ff02::1 address is a special multicast address, "all nodes," as mentioned earlier. Presuming things are working, you will get a response from both your local machine and the remote machine. This will not work for all tunnel providers (for example, **he.net**).

Here a simple *ping6* command checks both hostname resolution and IPv6 networking to a well-known IPv6 host:

```
$  ping6 www.kame.net
PING6(56=40+8+8 bytes) 3ffe:b00:4004::4:2 --> \
    2001:200:0:4819:210:f3ff:fe03:4d0
16 bytes from 2001:200:0:4819:210:f3ff:fe03:4d0, icmp_seq=0 \
    hlim=54 time=301.937 ms
16 bytes from 2001:200:0:4819:210:f3ff:fe03:4d0, icmp_seq=1 \
    hlim=54 time=311.008 ms
16 bytes from 2001:200:0:4819:210:f3ff:fe03:4d0, icmp_seq=2 \
    hlim=54 time=309.272 ms
16 bytes from 2001:200:0:4819:210:f3ff:fe03:4d0, icmp_seq=3 \
    hlim=54 time=330.662 ms
^C
--- apple.kame.net ping6 statistics ---
4 packets transmitted, 4 packets received, 0% packet loss
round-trip min/avg/max/std-dev = 301.937/313.220/330.662/10.630 ms
$
```

We can *traceroute* through this tunnel to the IPv6-only site at **kame.net**:

```
$  traceroute6 -n www.kame.net
traceroute6: Warning: apple.kame.net has multiple addresses; \
    using 3ffe:501:4819:2000:210:f3ff:fe03:4d0
traceroute6 to apple.kame.net (3ffe:501:4819:2000:210:f3ff:fe03:4d0) \
    from 3ffe:b00:4004::4:2, 64 hops max, 12 byte packets
 1  3ffe:b00:4004::3:5  0.594 ms  0.442 ms  0.313 ms
 2  3ffe:b00:c18::2e  92.75 ms  97.697 ms  96.231 ms
 3  3ffe:b00:c18::13  185.211 ms  *  255.583 ms
 4  3ffe:1800:0:3:2d0:b7ff:fee1:35bc  376.299 ms  324.834 ms  \
    334.718 ms
 5  3ffe:1800:0:3:230:48ff:fe41:4e4f  316.66 ms  321.87 ms  \
    357.344 ms
 6  2001:200:0:1800::9c4:2  396.252 ms  389.607 ms  395.05 ms
 7  2001:200:0:1c04:201:64ff:fea3:ec55  413.256 ms  367.347 ms  \
    400.572 ms
 8  2001:200:0:1c04::1000:2000  407.372 ms  *  309.173 ms
 9  2001:200:0:4819::2000:1  314.913 ms  361.782 ms  320.384 ms
10  3ffe:501:4819:2000:210:f3ff:fe03:4d0  327.792 ms  305.043 ms  \
    309.139 ms
$
```

These are clear indications that your connectivity to the IPv6 network is working. Notice that the lag is somewhat increased over the normal IPv4 traffic (in this case, about 10-fold).

If you need to clear the interface and tunnel, use the *ifconfig* command on the interface **gif0** and the *route* command to clear the IPv6 routes. This can be done to remove the configured information should you need to reestablish your Freenet6 link under a different IPv4 address. The following commands will accomplish this task for us, a step we have to take before we can reinitialize the tunnel:

```
#  ifconfig gif0 deletetunnel
#  route delete default -inet6
#  ifconfig gif0 down
```

Now you can reinitialize the tunnel using the Freenet6 tool. If you are using a different **gif** interface for another purpose and a different **gif** interface for your Freenet6 tunnel, clear the appropriate interface.

28.3.2 IPv4 and IPv6 Proxying

Native IPv6 support for Web browsers in OpenBSD is present but not fully available for all of them. The Konquerer browser, from KDE, supports IPv6 fully. Mozilla has code for IPv6 but, as of this writing, it does not get enabled. Lynx and w3m, two popular text browsers, also support IPv6 fully. Luckily, a local IPv4 and IPv6 translator can be built for Web browsing with all browsers. This is easily accomplished using a small proxy for your system.

One such proxy is the tool *www6to4*.[5] This small program can act as a local, minimal-configuration HTTP proxy that can handle IPv4 requests as well as IPv6 requests, and translate between the two.

There are several things to note about *www6to4*. First, it has no built-in authentication mechanisms, so you have to make sure it's accessible only to yourself or to those you wish to use it. By default, it binds only to the local host, so you don't have to worry about this issue. However, if you wish to bind it to an external interface and share the capability with others around you, you will have to perform some form of access control (such as with *pf*) or look into a more serious IPv6-capable proxy (such as *squid*). Second, *www6to4* can handle pure IPv6 and IPv4 networks and requests, so there is no need for drastic changes to your network. Lastly, you will need some tie-in to the IPv6 Internet, such as with Freenet6.

---

[5] Available for download at **http://www.vermicelli.pasta.cs.uit.no/ipv6/**.

Installing *www6to4* is quite simple. Just download, extract, and run the **Makefile** and it's ready to go. Install the configuration files, **www6to4.conf** and **www6to4_forward.conf**, in **/etc**, and you can begin working. The configuration file **www6to4.conf** looks like this:

```
# the forwardfile defines domain-specific routing
forwardfile /etc/www6to4_forward.conf

listen-to 127.0.0.1,::1
listen-port 8000

# patterns that cause short timeout when found:
pattern .gif
pattern .png
pattern .jpg
pattern size=
pattern sz=
pattern doubleclick

# default timeout used is short for URLs that match a given
# pattern and 60 seconds for all else.
# You can multiply the timeout values by a factor.
#timeout-factor 2
```

The forwarder file controls domain- and application-level specific actions. For example, if you have an IPv6-capable FTP proxy, you can configure it here. Here's a sample **www6to4_forward.conf** file:

```
# This feature allows routing of HTTP requests via multiple proxies.

# The syntax of each line is
# [proto://]target_domain[:port][/path] forwarding_domain[:port]
# proto can be ftp, http, https
# target_domain may contain a '*' wildcard

# A '.' in the forwarding domain/port means that requests made to the
# target domain are not forwarded but are made directly by the proxy
#
# Lines are checked in turn, and the last match wins.
```

```
* . # this is default implicit base config

# Note that www6to4 does not support ftp requests itself, i.e., it
# can only forward them to some other proxy that does support them.
#ftp://*        proxy.uit.no:5555


:443            .
```

You may wish to edit these files, particularly the forwarder file, to remove the references to the authors' proxies. Start the tool in the background and you are almost done:

```
$  /usr/local/sbin/www6to4 &
```

This will fork in the background and listen on the specified interfaces and ports—by default, both 127.0.0.1 and ::1 on port 8000/TCP.

To have Netscape work with the proxy, you must edit the configuration of your browser. In Netscape 4.7, in the Edit menu, edit the preferences—specifically, the "advanced" section. Manually enter the address of your *www6to4* proxy—by default, 127.0.0.1 on port 8000. You can now use an IPv4-only Netscape 4.7 to view IPv6-accessible sites.

Note that there are a few issues to watch for with this approach. First, errors in getting the files will return a generic error in Netscape, "page contains no data." Second, the proxy will default to the IPv4 address if the site is accessible by both IPv4 and IPv6. Lastly, the timeout values may need some adjustment. Using this method, the authors have found that many images on image-laden pages do not load fully. Edit the timeout values in the configuration file if you want to remedy this situation.

28.4 Some IPv6-Ready Applications

Many client applications in OpenBSD are built by default with IPv6 support. There is no global option for the userland sources to enable or disable IPv6 support (such as an *INET6* flag in **/etc/mk.conf**); each file does it on its own. These clients include *telnet, ftp, ssh, bind, sendmail,* and the *netcat (nc)* command.

In the ports and packages tree, notable IPv6-ready applications include the W3C browser *w3m,* in **www/w3m**, and *rsync,* in **net/rsync**.

28.5 Service Support for IPv6

To make services in OpenBSD work with IPv6, several mechanisms are available. For daemons that support IPv6 and can be run from *inetd*, use the *tcp6* keyword for the socket type. For example, to have an IPv6 FTP server along with an IPv4 FTP server, the following lines in **/etc/inetd.conf** would be used:

```
ftp     stream  tcp   nowait  root    /usr/libexec/ftpd     ftpd -US
ftp     stream  tcp6  nowait  root    /usr/libexec/ftpd     ftpd -US
```

This will leave two FTP sockets open on the system, using port 21/TCP: one in IPv4 listen mode (the line with the *tcp* keyword used) and the other listening for IPv6 connections (specified with *tcp6*).

```
$ netstat -na
Active Internet connections (including servers)
Proto Recv-Q Send-Q  Local Address   Foreign Address    (state)
tcp        0      0  *.21            *.*                LISTEN
..
tcp6       0      0  *.21            *.*                LISTEN
```

At this point the *ftp* service is listening on both IPv4 and IPv6 sockets. It is possible to have an IPv6-only server, too—the IPv4 version does not need to be enabled.

We can connect to these sockets as we would any other *telnet* system:

```
$ ftp 127.0.0.1
Trying 127.0.0.1...
Connected to 127.0.0.1.
220 tank.my.domain FTP server (Version 6.5/OpenBSD) ready.
Name (localhost:todd):
```

To connect to the IPv6 host (in this case available on localhost), use the following:

```
$ ftp ::1
Trying ::1...
Connected to ::1.
220 tank.my.domain FTP server (Version 6.5/OpenBSD) ready.
Name (localhost:todd):
```

While the preceding example has been used for TCP connections, UDP connections can also listen on IPv6 sockets for IPv6-aware UDP applications using the keyword *udp6* in **/etc/inetd.conf**.

Access control can be provided using both the *tcpd* mechanism, which supports IPv6, and the packet filter mechanism *pf*, described in Chapter 22. The use of IPv6 filtering in *pf* is described in this chapter.

Note that not all services in **/etc/inetd.conf** support IPv6, including Kerberized services, X11, and RPC services.

28.5.1 *sendmail*

Some services, such as *sendmail*, have their configuration files set up to listen on IPv6 addresses by default. The default configuration of *sendmail* listens on localhost only, to both IPv4 and IPv6 sockets. The additional "incoming mail" configuration also listens to both IPv4 and IPv6 by default.

The *DaemonPortOptions* option with an address family of *inet6* is used, with the same keyword used in the earlier *ifconfig* example. For the localhost configuration, the following lines are used in **/etc/mail/localhost.cf**:

```
# SMTP daemon options

O DaemonPortOptions=Family=inet, address=127.0.0.1, Name=MTA
O DaemonPortOptions=Family=inet6, address=::1, Name=MTA6,  M=O
O DaemonPortOptions=Family=inet, address=127.0.0.1, Port=587, Name=MSA,
    M=E
O DaemonPortOptions=Family=inet6, address=::1, Port=587, Name=MSA6, M=O,
    M=E
```

To specify that *sendmail* should listen on all IPv6 interfaces, the "all zero" address is used in **/etc/mail/sendmail.cf**:

```
# SMTP daemon options

O DaemonPortOptions=Family=inet, address=0.0.0.0, Name=MTA
O DaemonPortOptions=Family=inet6, address=::, Name=MTA6, \
    M=O
O DaemonPortOptions=Family=inet, address=0.0.0.0, Port=587, Name=MSA,
    M=E
```

```
O DaemonPortOptions=Family=inet6, address=::, Port=587, Name=MSA6, M=O,
   M=E
```

This will allow the server to accept mail on any valid IPv6 interface. Of course, you can specify particular addresses to bind to if you wish to have, for example, a dual-homed machine listening on one side only for incoming mail.

28.5.2 Secure Shell Daemon

The secure shell daemon, *sshd*, fully supports the use of IPv6. The selective listening on IPv6 addresses or ignoring of IPv6 can be accomplished either from the command line or from the configuration file, **/etc/sshd_config**.

To force *sshd* to listen *only* on IPv6 addresses, specify the command *sshd -6*. To have *sshd* ignore IPv6 entirely, you can force it to listen only to IPv4 addresses using *sshd-4*.

By default, *sshd* will listen on all available interfaces. To force use of a specific interface, the *ListenAddress* directive is used in the configuration file or on the command line. For example, to have an IPv6 *sshd* listen only on the localhost interface, the following line would be used in the configuration file **/etc/sshd_config**:

```
ListenAddress ::1
```

Of course, you can specify a particular address on which to listen by supplying an interface's IPv6 (or IPv4) addresss. A particular port can be specified as well. Specifying the zero address in IPv6 (::) does not enable the zero address in IPv4 (0.0.0.0); it must be explicitly enabled.

Because X11 services cannot take advantage of IPv6 addressing, *ssh* X11 forwarding cannot be used on an IPv6-only host.

28.5.3 DNS

Because of the change in addresses for IPv6 as opposed to IPv4, a new set of record formats was created. Originally known as the **A6** format (the equivalent of the IPv4 **A** record), it is now properly called the **AAAA** record. Version 4.9.8 of BIND, which ships with OpenBSD versions earlier than 3.3, can service the **AAAA** address, but cannot bind to an IPv6 socket. The version in OpenBSD 3.3 and later, based on ISC BIND 9.2.2, can not only serve IPv6 addresses but also provide DNS for IPv6 clients.

To do both (i.e., handle **AAAA** records and bind to an IPv6 socket), BIND9, included in the OpenBSD system since version 3.3, can be used. The format of the address lines for BIND4 and BIND9 will then look like the following:

```
host1      IN      AAAA    3FFE:800::2A8:79FF:FE32:1982
```

Other record types, such as **CNAME**, remain the same.

28.5.4 Apache

The version of Apache that ships with OpenBSD is based on the 1.3 series, which requires patches to bind to IPv6 sockets. These patches are updated infrequently and are not supported by either Apache or OpenBSD . They are available at **ftp://ftp.piuha.net/pub/misc/**.

28.5.5 Routing Daemons

Dynamic routing protocol support for IPv6 is available in the base system through the *route6d* daemon. However, this daemon supports only RIPng for IPv6. For additional routing protocols in IPv6, such as OSPFv3 and BGP-4+, the third-party package *zebra* can be used. It is available in the ports tree as **net/zebra**.

28.5.6 DHCP Daemons

Although stateless address autoconfiguration is available, DHCPv6 is sometimes necessary to pass DNS server addresses, NTP server addresses, and other information. Standardization of DHCPv6 is ongoing, however, so no server/client is yet available on OpenBSD.

28.5.7 IPsec with ISAKMP

IPv6 has native support for IPsec. The configuration files (discussed in Chapter 27) use the options *IPV6_ADDR* and *IPV6_ADDR_SUBNET* in place of their IPv4 cousins. Everything else should be similar.

28.5.8 Kerberos V

The OpenBSD Heimdal implementation of Kerberos V fully supports IPv6 for both servers and clients.

28.6 Programming with IPv6

OpenBSD supports the IPv6 sockets API as described in RFC 2292 and RFC 2553. This API includes the following library calls: `ip6(4)`, `inet6(4)`, `inet6_option_space(4)`, and `inet6_rthdr_space(4)`. These functions are built into the base C library in the system.

28.7 IPv6 and Security

The spread of IPv6 around the world will inevitably increase concerns about IPv6-related security issues. The complexity of IPv6 brings new opportunities in security, such as AH and ESP protocol support and an increased number of packet types that can be used in secure networks. Of course, the complexity of IPv6 brings some new problems as well.

First and foremost in this problem arena is the lack of tools for profiling and securing IPv6 networks. A wide array of tools exist to monitor, map, profile, and characterize IPv4 networks, including rigorous port scanners, intrusion detection systems, and firewalls. Only a handful of these tools support IPv6 natively, and so far no widely available tools can adequately mirror their IPv4 cousins in terms of power or utility.

Second, administrators will have to learn to use a significant number of new technologies, along with their implications, as they incorporate IPv6 in their network infrastructure. For example, is it wise to allow any and all IPv6 traffic in, given the lack of IPv6-specific features in some firewalls? What about "next hop" headers in IPv6 traffic—how are those handled?

These are just a few of the many questions that arise regarding the secure deployment of IPv6 networks. The protocol's complexity, while providing for new features and options, also means significantly more complex interactions will take place between these options, which can bring unexpected results in IPv6 networks.

28.7.1 Firewalling IPv6 with *pf*

The PF firewall in OpenBSD has native support for firewalling with IPv6. By using the protocol specification of *inet6*, IPv6 processing is enabled for packets being evaluated. This operation is described in detail in Chapter 22.

28.8 Resources

The IPsec and IPv6 kernel code, found at **kame.net**, is an excellent source of IPv6 information. The IPv6 mailing list, **ipv6@openbsd.org**, is also somewhat useful for debugging IPv6 problems in an OpenBSD system. The book *IPv6 Essentials* by Silvia Hagen (2002,

O'Reilly) offers an excellent treatment of the standards and background material for IPv6 networking. It does not contain much information about setting up IPv6 on a network node.

Another Web site for IPv6 information that acts as a clearinghouse for all OSs is **hs247.com**.

28.9 Troubleshooting

Perhaps the most helpful tool in debugging IPv6 connectivity problems is *tcpdump*. Looking for traffic in both directions is essential to diagnosing the problem.

1. Soliciting for IPv6 router advertisements with *rtsold* reports "rtsold: kernel is configured not to accept RAs."

   The value of *net.inet6.ip6.accept_rtadv* isn't set to 1. Use *sysctl -w* to set it correctly.

2. Soliciting for IPv6 router advertisements with *rtsold* doesn't yield any valid configuration information. I'm stuck with just the link local address.

   First, check your *pf* ruleset and ensure that IPv6 ICMP messages (IP protocol 58) are being allowed in and out. Second, check the interface connectivity and ensure that the interface can communicate with the IPv6 router at the link layer. Third, make sure that you are on a network with an IPv6 router doing stateless autoconfiguration. Using *tcpdump* to watch for IPv6 router advertisements is a useful exercise here.

3. I am unable to reach a host via *ping6* or *traceroute6*.

   First, check your firewall rules and ensure that IPv6 ICMP and UDP (in the case of *traceroute6*) are allowed through. Second, make sure a route to the host is specified—typically the **default** route for your IPv6 networking. Lastly, it is possible that the other end of the communication channel has ICMP6 blocked at its firewall. Rather than *ping6*, use *traceroute6* to ensure proper IPv6 networking.

   Another common firewalling mistake is to not allow through the IPv6, which is actually the IPv4 packets that the **gif0** interface creates. A line such as the following will be necessary if you have a "block all" site:

```
lte="129.22.210.63"  # local gif0 tunnel endpoint
rte="206.123.31.114" # remote gif0 tunnel endpoint
```

```
pass in on $ext_if proto IPv6 from $rte to $lte
pass out on $ext_if proto IPv6 from $lte to $rte
```

4. I was able to get my laptop working with *rtsold* but when I removed the card and reinserted it, the laptop stopped working.

   The interface index probably changed, confusing *rtsold*. Kill *rtsold* and start it again.

5. I was able to get router advertisements working, but since I disconnected and reconnected my network, it doesn't provide any advertisements.

   The interface index may have changed (when the status changed from active to inactive, and then back to active). Restart *rtadvd*.

6. I am unable to connect to other hosts over IPv6, even though I have a valid IPv6 address and can use *ping6* to reach them.

   First, check your *pf* rules and ensure that IPv6 traffic is being passed. You may want to temporarily flush the ruleset with *pfctl -F a* to clear all of the rules or to allow IP protocol 41 through (the generic IPv6 protocol). Second, verify that the route is sound using a tool like *traceroute6 -n*. Lastly, try connecting via the numerical (as opposed to named) address to ensure that a DNS failure has not occurred.

7. I am unable to use *scp* to specify the IPv6 address in hexadecimal form (i.e., *scp user@3ffe::201::1: /filename*). It hangs or reports "host 3ffe not found."

   The *scp* command uses the colon ":" as its own field separator, separating the hostname from the filename. Because IPv6 uses the colon as a field separator in the hexadecimal representation of the address, this confuses the *scp* program, and it reads only the first part of the address as the hostname. Bracket the IPv6 address in square brackets so it reads like *user@[3ffe::201::1]: /filename*. Alternatively, use the hostname of the target host.

8. I am not configured to connect to **6bone**. How can I use IPv6 on my local network?

   The *ping6* command can be used to probe the link local network:

```
$ ping6 -n -w ff02::1%le0
PING6(72 bytes) fe80::a00:20ff:fe7c:514a%le0 --> ff02::1%le0
37 bytes from fe80::a00:20ff:fe7c:514a%le0: flare.fries.net.
39 bytes from fe80::201:2ff:fec9:ee06%le0: eclipse.fries.net.
40 bytes from fe80::2e0:29ff:fe70:5133%le0: poohbear.fries.net.
38 bytes from fe80::290:27ff:fe62:2b7e%le0: shadow.fries.net.
37 bytes from fe80::a00:9ff:fe5f:de12%le0: hppa5.fries.net.
```

```
37 bytes from fe80::a00:7ff:fe86:62f9%le0: cloud.fries.net.
37 bytes from fe80::260:1dff:fef0:888e%le0: toshi.fries.net.
36 bytes from fe80::260:1dff:fef1:67af%le0: tube.fries.net.
^C
--- ff02::1%le0 ping6 statistics ---
1 packets transmitted, 1 packets received, +7 duplicates, 0% packet loss

$
```

You can also use the addresses found via this probe to connect to a link local node,
regardless of the IPv4 or IPv6 "global" routable address:

```
$  telnet fe80::290:27ff:fe62:2b7e%le0 25
Trying fe80::290:27ff:fe62:2b7e%le0...
Connected to fe80::290:27ff:fe62:2b7e%le0.
Escape character is '^]'.
220 fries.net ESMTP Sendmail 8.12.6/8.12.2; Mon, 24 Feb 2003 \
    15:11:33 -0600 (CST)
 quit
221 2.0.0 fries.net closing connection
Connection closed by foreign host.
$
```

Chapter 29

systrace

29.1 Introduction

The OpenBSD default system comes with a policy enforcement tool named *systrace*, which provides a way to monitor, intercept, and restrict system calls. The *systrace* facility acts as a wrapper to the executables, shepherding their traversal of the system call table. The *systrace* facility then intercepts the system calls and, using the **systrace** device, processes them through the kernel and handles the system calls.

Getting started with *systrace* is quite easy. You can run your programs under *systrace*, generate policies based on the observed behavior, and then enforce this policy on the program in subsequent runs. There are, however, two problems with this approach:

- This approach assumes that the executable behaves entirely correctly and within the expected bounds. Violations of this assumption can include the use of a modified executable that has been reconfigured by an attacker. Subsequent uses of *systrace* will allow the malicious behavior to continue. To remedy this problem, policies should be reviewed after their generation to ensure that the anticipated behavior is observed, and trusted executables should be used in policy generation. Generally, automated policy generation should be undertaken only with trusted applications. Unknown applications can be used with interactive policy generation, so that decisions can be made before any damage is done by a rogue application.

- This approach assumes that the initial runs of the *systrace* policy generator fully exercise the range of actions for which the policy is intended. In reality, the *ls* executable, for example, may not know that it is allowed to list the files in a publicly allowed directory that was skipped in the original run.

To remedy this situation, it is possible to bootstrap the policy that *systrace* knows about by using arbitrary external policies and the *-f* flag. In this scenario, a base policy can be built and extended. Furthermore, one can generate filters that use wildcards, which eliminate the need for fully itemized lists:

```
native-open: filename match "$HOME/*" and oflags sub "ro" then permit
```

In this example, one can read (but not write to) any files and directories under the current user's home directory. This filter is forward adaptable and condensed.

Executables run under the *systrace* facility can pass policies on to their children and inherit policies from their parents. This is useful for login shells, for example, where you may wish to restrict a user's behavior using *systrace*. Any children from this shell will have a policy that has been inherited from their parent. A simple *systrace* login shell would look like the following:[1]

```
#include <sys/types.h>
#include <sys/wait.h>
#include <stdio.h>

int
main(int argc, char *argv)
{
        char            *args[4];

        args[0] = "-Ua";            /* system policies, auto enforce */
        args[1] = "/bin/ksh";       /* run ksh */
        args[2] = "-l";             /* login shell */
        args[3] = NULL;
        if (execv("/bin/systrace", args) < 0) {
                fprintf(stderr, "loging in failed.");
                exit(-1);
        }
        /* NOTREACHED */
        return (0);
}
```

---

[1] Newer, more flexible versions are maintained by one of the authors and are available at **http://monkey.org/ jose/software/stsh/**.

The series of steps to enable this system for users would look like the following:

```
$  mkdir -p /usr/local/src/bin/stsh/
$  vi /usr/local/src/bin/stsh/stsh.c
   enter above code
$  gcc -o /usr/local/src/bin/stsh/stsh /usr/local/src/bin/stsh/stsh.c
$  sudo cp /usr/local/src/bin/stsh/stsh /bin/stsh
$  sudo vi /etc/login.conf
   edit the variable ''shells'' to be /bin/stsh
```

This can be applied in the *default* class for all users or just to users in a particular login class.

Before you begin, make sure you have a policy for **/bin/sh** in the directory **/etc/systrace** (saved as **bin_sh**). Now test this setup (leaving at least one user with a normal shell for login purposes). Also, this method disables the utility *chsh*, which users can use to change their shells. They cannot disable their use of *stsh* and use a non–systrace-wrapped */bin/ksh*, for example. Instead, their parent shell will always be a *systrace*-wrapped */bin/ksh*. Newer versions of *stsh* can spawn any shell the user chooses, wrapped in *systrace*.

The target uses of *systrace* are threefold. First, it is designed for untrusted data paths, such as executables from potentially untrusted sources or applications that handle untrustworthy data. These can include daemon processes, for example, which are open to the world. By using *systrace*, an administrator can restrict the arbitrary execution of commands. Second, this program is very useful for machines with untrusted users operating in their shells. By spawning the login shell under the control of *systrace* and then forcing children to inherit this policy, transparent sandboxing of the system can occur. Third, *systrace* can protect users from their own processes. Some applications are untrusted or otherwise potentially damaging to the system or accept untrusted data from the network. Cradeling their execution by using *systrace* can help mitigate any damage they may cause.

Global system policies live in the system directory **/etc/systrace**. Examples policies exist for two daemons, *lpd* and *named*, which provide robust sandboxing for the executables. These examples show what can be done to secure a system using *systrace*.

User-specific policies are found in **/home/*username*/.systrace**. If a user modifies a global policy, the modified version is saved in his or her home directory. This prevents one user from modifying the execution environment of other users' applications.

Note that *systrace* does require a modest level of understanding regarding system calls and their consequences. It is easy to write a policy that is impossible to use by ignoring fundamental actions, which is why it is advisable to start with automatically generated policies. Also, some large, complex applications may be difficult to run under *systrace* due to the large number of system calls they make. In these situations, it may be wise to attempt to allow nearly everything except a subset of commands. For example, your Web browser may be allowed to open arbitrary sockets above 1024 but not allowed to spawn a child shell.

29.1.1 Example Use

As described previously, it is possible to use *systrace* to automatically generate a policy for an executable. With the *-A* flag set, *systrace* will accept all actions as permitted and use them to build a policy. The following example shows the geneation of a simple policy allowing **/bin/ls** to read the user's home directory:

```
$   cd
$   systrace -A ls
```

By default, *systrace* will store the generated policies in the directory **/home/*username*/ .systrace**. For our example run of *ls*, a policy named **bin_ls** will appear with the contents of the policy for that executable:

```
Policy: /bin/ls, Emulation: native
    native-_sysctl: permit
    native-mmap: permit
    native-mprotect: permit
    native-ioctl: permit
    native-getuid: permit
    native-fsread: filename eq "/etc/malloc.conf" then permit
    native-issetugid: permit
    native-break: permit
    native-fsread: filename eq "/home/jose" then permit
    native-fchdir: permit
    native-fstat: permit
    native-fcntl: permit
    native-fstatfs: permit
    native-getdirentries: permit
    native-lseek: permit
    native-close: permit
    native-write: permit
    native-munmap: permit
    native-exit: permit
```

This simple, minimalistic policy is nevertheless very restrictive. When we try to use this policy to enforce actions, we can see the effect. Using the command *systrace -a*, we can automatically enforce the policy we have installed:

```
$ systrace -a ls /etc/
ls: /etc/: Operation not permitted
```

Additionally, a message is logged to the central system logs via the *syslog* mechanism. By default, these messages will appear in the file **/var/log/messages**. Reading these messages can be useful for security monitoring or policy review and adjustment purposes:

```
May 30 07:12:11 superfly systrace: deny user: jose, prog:
/bin/ls, pid: 1664(0)[17057], policy: /bin/ls, filters: 129, syscall:
native-dup2(90), args: 8
```

The denial of system calls can be controlled by using the specific signal sent to the executable making the request. For example, it may be advisable to send *ls* a "permission denied" signal when it attempts to show the files in the **/etc** directory. The *ls* command gracefully reports the error to the user and exits.

More complicated policies can be generated interactively. When the X11 environment is available, the application *xsystrace* is used to provide responses to policy queries. In a text-only environment, the responses are handled on the command line. Responses are "permit" and "deny" with options that match those found in the policy file. For example, generating a policy for *tcpdump* would look like the following:

```
# systrace tcpdump
/usr/sbin/tcpdump, pid: 8159(0)[0], policy: /usr/sbin/tcpdump,
filters: 0, syscall: native-issetugid(253), args: 0
Answer:  permit
```

Note that *systrace* uses the shell from which it was started to make these policy queries. If the shell has been closed, the application will hang while waiting for a policy decision.

The *systrace* system understands the following environmental variables and expands them as macros:

- **HOME**   The user's home directory (e.g., **/home/jose**).
- **USER**   The user's name (e.g., *jose*).
- **CWD**   The current working directory (also known as **.**).

These variables can be substituted in the *systrace* policy and allowed to expand. An example setup using such macros would appear as follows:

```
native-fsread: filename eq "$HOME/.gaim" then permit
native-fswrite: filename eq "$HOME/.gaimrc" then permit
```

These examples were taken from a policy for the IM chat client *gaim*, generated automatically by *systrace -A*, and then smoothed over by manual editing.

29.2 Creating Policies

Creating a *systrace* policy for an application is relatively straightforward, but entails an interactive series of steps. Policies must be edited to support matching arbitrary versions of shared libraries of network sockets, for example. The steps outlined here illustrate how the policy for the chat client program *gaim* was developed on one of the authors' systems.

Creating an initial policy is done using the built-in *systrace -A* command:

```
$   systrace -A gaim
```

At this stage, an initial policy is created (in this case, in the directory **/home/jose/.systrace/ usr_local_bin_gaim**). It contains specific network addresses, shared library versions, and filenames. Many of these can be edited to support arbitrary versions.

29.2.1 Editing Policies

Policy editing consists of two main questions. The first question is "which attributes can be generalized into expressions to match, rather than specific instances?" Here the policy is edited to move from "eq" tests to "match" tests with some form of globbing. The second question is "What kind of filesystem limitations should be added?" For applications that write to the filesystem, it may be worthwhile to control the directories to which they have access.

For network applications, one of the major issues in policy editing is the handling of name servers. The file **/etc/resolv.conf** allows for multiple DNS servers, yet the application typically uses only one:

```
native-connect: sockaddr eq "inet-[192.168.4.3]:53" then permit
```

In editing this entry, it is important to examine both the resolver configuration and the network environment. A laptop that uses DHCP on several networks and unknown DNS servers should edit the line to look like the following:

```
native-connect: sockaddr match "inet-*:53" then permit
```

Here any IP address on port 53 can be accessed. If a predefined list of servers is sufficient, then they can be enumerated:

```
native-connect: sockaddr eq "inet-[192.168.4.1]:53" then permit
native-connect: sockaddr eq "inet-[192.168.4.3]:53" then permit
native-connect: sockaddr eq "inet-[192.168.4.4]:53" then permit
```

In the case of *gaim*, the client connects to a variety of servers for load-balancing efforts and possibly on different ports, depending on the protocol. Here blanket socket connections could probably be allowed.

In the case of filenames, specifically for shared libraries, one can convert the policy to use the "match" operator and globbing rules. For example, a policy rule such as

```
native-fsread: filename eq "/usr/lib/libc.so.29.0" then permit
```

is easily rewritten as

```
native-fsread: filename match "/usr/lib/libc.so.*" then permit
```

and made more portable when the system is upgraded. If you wish to allow arbitrary library access and not enumerate libraries by name, the entries

```
native-fsread: filename eq "/usr/lib/libz.so.2.0" then permit
native-fsread: filename eq "/usr/lib/libperl.so.8.0" then permit
native-fsread: filename eq "/usr/lib/libm.so.1.0" then permit
native-fsread: filename eq "/usr/lib/libutil.so.8.0" then permit
native-fsread: filename eq "/usr/local/lib/libintl.so.1.1" \
    then permit
native-fsread: filename eq "/usr/local/lib/libiconv.so.3.0" \
    then permit
native-fsread: filename eq "/usr/lib/libc.so.29.0" then permit
```

can be rewritten as follows:

```
native-fsread: filename match "/usr/lib/*" then permit
native-fsread: filename match "/usr/local/lib/*" then permit
```

The application can now read any file in the directory **/usr/lib** or **/user/local/lib**. Note that it will not be allowed to write to any file in that directory unless an action is stated to permit that operation.

After editing the policy, the application should be rerun with the policy used:

```
$ systrace gaim
```

Errors will be handled in two ways. First, with no auto-enforcement (*systrace -a*) in use, the system will ask you how you want to handle policy violations. Second, denied actions will be logged to the system's logs:

```
/var/log/messages.1.gz:Jan 25 23:58:29 tank systrace: deny user: jose,
prog: /usr/local/bin/gaim, pid: 27552(0)[0], policy: /usr/local/bin/gaim,
filters: 104, syscall: native-connect(98), sockaddr: inet-[192.168.4.2]:53
```

After examining both of these feedback mechanisms, the policy can be edited to remove them and gracefully handle errors. As stated earlier, this strategy involves an interactive process of policy editing and testing.

29.2.2 The Benefit of a Local Caching Name Server

One of the complexities of a *systrace* policy with respect to a dynamic system (such as a laptop) is the variety of networking changes it generates as it travels around. For example, the DNS servers used by the system will change for each network used, as reflected in the varied entries in **/etc/resolv.conf**. As network client applications are used, they will contact these new DNS servers. If the *systrace* policy is restrictive in terms of the IP address of the socket used for DNS, then the application will fail as it enforces this policy.

One option is to build a generic *systrace* policy that can connect to any address on port 53 (for DNS):

```
native-connect: sockaddr match "*:53" then permit
```

Any IP address will then be matched and DNS will be allowed.

Another option is to use a local, caching-only DNS server as your primary DNS system, along with a configuration that keeps this option static. For example, a name server entry in the file **resolv.conf** that specifies *nameserver 127.0.0.1* will cause client applications to use the local DNS server. For DHCP users, not requesting the *domain-name-servers* option will also be useful. In the file **/etc/dhclient.conf**, such a configuration will request other information, but not DNS server information, and actively reject the DNS server information offered:

```
interface "fxp0" {
    request subnet-mask, broadcast-address, time-offset, routers,
        domain-name, host-name;
    supersede domain-name-servers 127.0.0.1;
}
```

Now the local DNS server will be used. On the one hand, this scheme requires the additional complexity of running a local, caching-only DNS server, which is not desirable for some systems. On the other hand, it gives a static *systrace* option for all network client applications.

29.3 Privilege Elevation with *systrace*

The *systrace* system can also be used to remove *setuid* and *setgid* binaries. Normally, only a single step or two needs to be performed as an elevated privilege user. This can include binding to a low-numbered socket or reading a protected file.

In *systrace*, the *permit as* action can be used to allow a system call to proceed as a specified user. For example, an application that captures packets from the network will have to read these packets using the BPF devices as root. This privilege can be allowed for non-root users using the *permit as root* option:

```
    native-fswrite: filename eq "/dev/bpf0" then permit as root
    native-fswrite: filename eq "/dev/bpf1" then permit as root
```

Note that the parent *systrace* command must be run as root for this technique to work, as arbitrary users cannot run various system calls as elevated privilege users. Failure to do so will result in an error in the execution of the program:

```
$  systrace dnstop wi0
Privilege elevation not allowed.
```

The program will attempt to operate normally under these circumstances, but will typically fail. Instead, use the *-c* option to *systrace* to set the user ID (and optionally the group ID) for the child process. Here, root runs the *dnstop* program as user 1000, but is still allowed to open the BPF devices (normally accessible only by root):

```
# systrace -c 1000:1000 -a dnstop wi0
```

This approach can be used to greatly limit the scope of programs that would otherwise require root privileges.

29.4 Where to Use *systrace*

One ideal place to run *systrace* with complete and restrictive policies is on network servers. Protecting the execution environment of exposed services with *systrace* can considerably minimize the ability of an attacker to cause a dameon program to begin executing arbitrary actions. This can include remote SSH servers, name servers, and Apache Web servers. Generating these policies can be a bit time-consuming. Nevertheless, with *systrace -A*, a thorough exercise of the program, and a review of the policies, security can be enhanced.

For publicly accessible shell servers—for example, on common lab systems—one target for *systrace* policies is the control of *setuid* root executables. Wrapping the execution of these programs in a controlled policy minimizes the potential damage that can be generated by a malicious user. The *setuid* root bit can be removed, and operations that require privileges can be replaced by *permit as* statements in the *systrace* policy. Wrapping the executable in a small program that ensures it is run under *systrace* can complete this security enhancement.

On network clients, Internet-exposed client applications can be wrapped in *systrace* policies. The earlier example, which showed the generation of a policy for the *gaim* client, can be extended to a variety of network clients, including *irc* clients and *ssh* usage. The *systrace* system can protect the local system from malicious servers or P2P clients that might attempt to execute arbitrary actions on the client system.

29.5 System Coverage with *systrace*

Achieving total system coverage with *systrace*, where no avenue remains in which to execute arbitrary commands or handle user-supplied data, is the ultimate goal for a system protected by *systrace*. It is best accomplished by performing three actions. The first action is to ensure that complete, up-to-date policies have been generated for the applications. It is perhaps best to run the system using *systrace -A* for a short while to fully exercise applications. The second action is to start any network daemons that are launched from processes such as **/etc/rc** using *systrace*, which requires minor amounts of script editing. The third action is to give users shells wrapped in *systrace*. Any executable that the users will run will require a policy, as *systrace* also wraps child processes.

This difficult-to-achieve process requires an in-depth understanding of the system as well as the implications of system calls. For most users, running *systrace* on their network daemons will suffice.

29.6 Additional Uses for *systrace*

Beyond application sandbox enforcement, the *systrace* facility has other uses. These are just now starting to be explored.

29.6.1 Software Testing

One interesting use of *systrace* is to test the error-handling abilities of various applications. The *systrace* system can be used to reliably and predictably force failures with various error conditions on a per-system call level. For example, to examine how a process reacts if it is unable to read the configuration file for *malloc*, a line such as the following would be integrated into a *systrace* policy for the process:

```
native-fsread: filename eq "/etc/malloc.conf" then deny[enoent]
```

This would return a "file not found" error for this file. The application's handling of this error condition could then be tested to look for graceful handling of the error. Note that denying an application the right to peform a *native-exit* will force it to abort, which will produce a core dump.

29.6.2 IDS Logging

Another use of *systrace* is as an intrusion detection logging system. This is best done with the logging of *native-exec* entries. For example, to enable logging of all file openings by a network daemon process, the *systrace* policy for the daemon would include a line like this:

```
native-fsread: filename eq "*" then permit log
```

Now every file opening carried out by the process will be logged by the application. An otherwise complete policy will have to be created for the process as well.

29.7 Limitations of *systrace*

Despite its many features, *systrace* has a number of limitations that bear mentioning. First, it lacks a facility to specify that you can "permit once" for a system call, such as binding to a socket. This can allow an attacker to recycle a system call, potentially at elevated privilege.

Second, system calls have no exclusive or. For example, an application might be permitted to open a file or a device, but not both. This weakness could ultimately be leveraged by an attacker who seeks to do more than a program was intended to do.

Lastly, the parent process has no control over spawned processes. For example, if you allow */bin/sh* to be executed, you cannot control it beyond its own *systrace* policy. One way to get around this limitation is to specify a policy for the child process to inherit if it is to be less liberal than the normal system policy. This would be done via *systrace -i*.

29.8 Resources

Niels Provos, the primary author of *systrace*, presented a paper at Usenix 2003 on the architecture of *systrace*. Users who are interested in the internal workings and design of the system may want to read his paper.

Niels also maintains the Web site **http://www.systrace.org**, which houses information on *systrace*. Various example policies are available there.

Chapter 30

Network Intrusion Detection

30.1 Introduction

Security-minded administrators will establish a perimeter with a firewall, and this security perimeter will monitor for known attacks and probes. Such a monitor is called a network intrusion detection system (NIDS). This chapter covers these kinds of software programs, which are outside of the base OpenBSD installation, but are popular third-party packages in the ports tree.

Network monitoring with a NIDS solution typically utilizes one or more network sensors. These sensors can be stand-alone systems (i.e., complete inspection and reporting systems) or part of a larger, distributed system in which multiple collectors pass data to a single analysis system.

Most NIDSs perform packet-level inspection, looking at each packet individually. The packet headers and the payload are examined and compared with known signatures in an effort to detect the signs of an attack or a probe.

OpenBSD makes a low-cost, high-performance, secure, and scalable NIDS available. The networking subsystem is a robust and scalable TCP/IP implementation. OpenBSD supports many high-performance interfaces, and the base system itself is compact and secure. All of these features make OpenBSD a natural choice for a NIDS platform.

30.2 Snort

Snort is a widely supported, open-source, and feature-rich NIDS implementation. Originally developed by Marty Roesch, it now has a dedicated team of skilled developers and signature generators who are constantly improving the system.

This section covers the installation and basic use of the Snort 2.0 series of software. Installation via the official OpenBSD package is shown. Users can adapt this information if they wish to download other versions of Snort. Additional sources of Snort-related information are given at the end of the chapter.

The Snort base system can be extended via modules (i.e., optional feature sets). This base product uses rules to evaluate the traffic. These rules, or signatures, are the characteristics of the packets that Snort works to detect. They include the packet headers, such as the protocols and ports seen in the packets, along with a description of the payload. For example, a Snort signature for the Code Red worm would look like the following:

```
alert tcp $EXTERNAL_NET any -> $HTTP_SERVERS 80 (msg: "WEB-IIS CodeRed C
   Worm Attempt"; flags: A+;
   uricontent:"/default.idaXXXXXXXXXXXXXXXXXXXXXXXXXXXXXXXXXXXXXXXXXX
   XXXXXXXXXXXXXXXXXXXXXXXXXXXXXXXXXXXXXXXXXXXXXXXXXXXXXXXXXXXXXXXXXX
   XXXXXXXXXXXXXXXXXXXXXXXXXXXXXXXXXXXXXXXXXXXXXXXXXXXXXXXXXXXXXXXXXX
   XXXXXXXXXXXXXXXXXXXXXXXXXXXXXXXXXXXXXXXXXXXX%u9090%u6858%ucbd3%u
   7801%u9090%u6858%ucbd3%u7801%u9090%u6858%ucbd3%u7801%u9090%u9090%u8
   190%u00c3%u0003%u8b00%u531b%u53ff%u0078%u0000%u00=a";
   nocase;reference:cert,ca-2001-19; classtype: attempted-admin; sid:
   9259; rev: 1;)
```

This signature tells Snort to issue an alert for any traffic that comes from outside the home network to any of the listed HTTP servers that contain the payload of the worm's attack. Additional information includes the alert message and the classification of the attack.

30.2.1 Installation

Installing the Snort base package is very simple because it is a standard OpenBSD port. It is typically installed from the list of precompiled packages, which saves a significant amount of time and eliminates much potential confusion in building it. For OpenBSD 3.4, both Snort 1.9.1 and Snort 2.0.0 are available. Version 2.0.0 is recommended, as earlier versions contain known security problems. Additionally, the performance and features of the 2.0 series are significantly more impressive than those found in earlier versions.

The package can be installed via *pkg_add*:

```
#  pkg_add snort-2.0.0.tgz
The Snort rule examples have been installed in
   /usr/local/share/examples/snort
```

This will install the base version of Snort as **/usr/local/bin/snort**. However, this version lacks some features that other users may want, including database integration (to

PostgreSQL or MySQL) and the FlexResponse feature, which allows the Snort system to issue reply packets. To include these features, you must build the port from the ports tree. For example, to build the version of Snort that ties into the MySQL database system and also issue reply packets, build both the *mysql* and *flexresp* flavors:

```
# env FLAVOR="mysql flexresp" make
```

This version of Snort will have new dependencies. The following list describes the available flavors and their dependencies:

- **mysql flavor**   Provides features to make the Snort installation able to insert data into a database. Requires **lib/mysql/mysqlclient**.
- **flexresp flavor**   Allows the Snort system to build and send reply packets, which can be useful in shutting down an attack. Requires the *Libnet* package to be installed.
- **postgresql flavor**   Provides database integration with Snort and a Postgres database, allowing the Snort sensor to insert data into a Postgres data store. Requires **databases/postgresql**.
- **smbalert flavor**   Allows the Snort installation to issue alerts using SMB messages to a Windows system. Requires **net/samba/stable**.

Clearly, Snort's functionality can be greatly enhanced using this external system integration. Building these packages should take only a short while on a modern-speed processor system. Note that the database versions will require that a database server be installed somewhere. The schemas for the tables that Snort uses are left in the Snort source directories, so you will have to retrieve them before you clean up the port-building process.

Sensor Installation

The installation of the Snort sensor ultimately depends on the network topology. Ideally, you will monitor the communications of sensitive systems with untrusted hosts. This group can include Web servers in a DMZ network. By placing the Snort sensor interface (the NIC that actually captures the traffic) on this network, you can observe the traffic.

In a switched environment, you will need to use a span or mirror port, as Snort needs to see other systems' traffic. In a normal switched environment, this is possible only with a configuration change. You will also want to choose a higher-speed link for this monitoring port than you have on your switch; for example, use a gigabit-speed port for this purpose if you have a 100bT switching layer. This will help mitigate the effects of as many dropped packets as possible.

If your switching equipment does not support the configuration of mirror ports, it may be possible to insert a Snort system as a logging bridge between the switch and the router. In this scenario, a bridge (as described in Chapter 9) is set up for PF (as described in Chapter 22) with a simple ruleset. This ruleset allows all traffic to pass, but it is also logged. Thus the traffic is visible to the Snort system on the **pflog0** interface. If it were using two *sk** interfaces (SysKonnect fiber gigabit Ethernet interfaces), a sample ruleset would look like this:

```
pass in log all on sk0
pass out log all on sk0
pass in log all on sk1
pass out log all on sk1
```

After the **pflog0** interface was prepared for use (by issuing the command *ifconfig pflog0 up*), Snort would be told to monitor packets on this interface. This technique may provide a way to pass packets to the Snort system without resorting to an expensive switch purchase.

Obviously, a wireless or hub environment will not need this infrastructure, as all packets are already visible to all parties in the collision domain.

30.2.2 Configuration

The next steps in the Snort installation process are to move all of the example rules to the system rules directory and to create a new user for the Snort process to run as. This will help mitigate weaknesses in the Snort software that could lead to an attack. Finally, we'll set up the logging for Snort.

```
#  mkdir -p /etc/snort/rules
#  cp /usr/local/share/examples/snort/* /etc/snort
#  mv /etc/snort/*.rules /etc/snort/rules/
#  useradd -c "Snort" -m -s /sbin/nologin -d /var/log/snort snort
#  mkdir -p /var/log/snort
#  chown snort.snort /var/log/snort
#  chmod 0700 /var/log/snort
```

Next, edit the file **/etc/snort/snort.conf** to establish your *HOME_NET* variable; it is the network specification for your local network. Everything outside of this area is considered "external." Next, point the variable *RULE_PATH* to the directory **/etc/snort/rules**.

Lastly, configure Snort to become active at every start-up by appending this code to the **/etc/rc.local** script:

```
if [ -x /usr/local/bin/snort ]; then
    /usr/local/bin/snort -i fxp0 -t /var/log/snort
    -c /etc/snort/snort.conf -u snort -g snort -D
fi
```

Now the Snort system will start on interface **fxp0** (edit the argument to *-i* to adjust this location) as the user *snort* in daemon mode. Furthermore, it is set to *chroot* itself to **/var/log/snort**, which is also useful in mitigating attacks against the sensor.

30.2.3 Loading New Rules

The rules and signatures for Snort are what drive its utility. These rules define which traffic characteristics will trigger alerts. The basic ruleset that comes with Snort is adequate for triggering alerts on some common attacks and probes, but not enough to defend a network on a day-to-day basis.

Rules are easily installed once they are downloaded. The Snort Web site maintains a database of commonly accepted rules that is periodically updated and available for the public to download at **http://www.snort.org/snort-db/**. Furthermore, the user community maintains a mailing list to discuss and develop new rules, available at **http://lists. sourceforge.net/lists/listinfo/snort-sigs**. Here, new and updated rules are disseminated, often within a short time of them being needed (such as during a rapid worm outbreak).

Once you download the rules, place them in the directory **/etc/snort/rules** and restart the Snort process. This will reread the rules database and begin matching traffic using the new rules. Rules can also be deleted if they don't work well or provide too many false-positive warnings.

Writing new rules is both a science and an art. Once you have observed enough traffic to make a judgment about the common features of the traffic, you can write a new rule. One easy way to do so is to take a similar situation's rule and copy it to the new rule, edit the file for the attributes and payload of the packet, and install the new rule. Because this is a time-intensive and laborious process, we won't cover it here. However, the Snort Web site and mailing list archives are excellent sources for information on this process.

30.2.4 Snort Add-Ons

By itself, Snort is a great package. It has a significant number of features and is finely tunable. Nevertheless, it may not satisfy all of the demands of the NIDS console administrator.

To meet these needs, various add-ons have been developed. Two of these are mentioned here, but many others exist as well.

The ACID front end to Snort was developed partly by the CERT organization. It provides for easy navigation of your Snort alerts in your Web browser. This program also allows you to link to content about the attack and make decisions about the scenario in near real time. ACID is available at **http://www.andrew.cmu.edu/rdanyliw/snort/snortacid.html**.

The "flex response" flavor of Snort allows you to shut down a connection when an alert is triggered by known bad traffic—for example, an ICMP port unreachable for UDP traffic and a TCP reset for a TCP connection. By taking this step, an attack's progress can be thwarted. This program combines a Snort package flavor with rules that have been configured to send reply packets.

Snort can also output alerts in XML format, allowing the alerts to be parsed and then displayed or aggregated in various ways. This capability can include using an XSLT to display the data in a Web browser.

30.2.5 Integration with PF

A reactive IDS solution can be built that uses the Snort detection engine and rulsets along with the OpenBSD PF firewall. This integrated approach can give your network a reactive stance to identified threats.

Stephan Schiedar has written a tool called *snort2pf*, which actively polls the Snort logs and inserts the addresses of offensive hosts into a PF anchor. The tool is based on a small Perl script available at **http://unix-geek.info/codedocs/snort2pf.txt**. The script comments contain information on installing and configuring the script.

The benefits of this approach are debatable. Drawbacks include the polling interval of any log analysis system, the chance of false positives, the frequency of false negatives, and self-induced denial-of-service attacks assisted by forged attack source addresses. However, if an inline, reactive-IDS system is required, this approach may be worth investigating as it uses entirely free software on commonly available hardware.

30.3 Other IDS Solutions

While Snort is a full-featured IDS solution, other components in the OpenBSD ports tree can be used to build a home-grown solution. These pieces can be fit together using freshly written software or even added to a Snort installation to improve its detection capabilities.

The *scanlogd* tool is a simple port-scan detection system. It observes the traffic on your system and can alert you when a port scan occurs. This utility can be run on individual hosts. The tool is available in **security/scanlogd**.

Another tool that is commonly installed on a Snort sensor is *p0f*. It reads the TCP traffic captured and can determine the remote operating system of the source of the traffic. This tool can differentiate between Windows versions and Linux or BSD systems. It can also map your network on a per-host basis. The *p0f* utility is available in the ports tree as **security/p0f**.

The tool *arpwatch* is another useful network mapping tool. It can be used in conjunction with a Snort sensor to map IP addresses to MAC addresses and to detect shifts or hijacking. This tool also produces a fine-grained map of the local network—allowing for an inventory, for example. It is available in the ports tree in **/usr/ports/net/arpwatch**.

30.4 Important Notes

This chapter has merely scratched the surface of the complex issue of network intrusion detection. There are multitudes of ways that attackers can fool a sensor (and ultimately the administrator), which we cannot possibly cover in this chapter. Any NIDS operator should be well versed in TCP/IP networking and all of its complexities. This knowledge will help administrators understand the false positives and negatives generated by the sensor and make more accurate assessments of their networks' security.

30.5 Resources

The Snort Web site (**http://www.snort.org/**) is a fantastic resource for most of the Snort community. It has links to mailing lists, software updates, and new rules, as well as popular add-ons.

Chris Paul has written a detailed document on setting up Snort with ACID under OpenBSD 3.3. It gives step-by-step instructions regarding how to build and configure the Snort sensor and the secure communications with the ACID console. Find it at **http://www.rexconsulting.net/acid_openbsd.html**.

Chapter 31

Upgrading

31.1 Upgrading an Installation

If you already have an OpenBSD installation on your system and you wish to upgrade to a later version, there is no need to clean the system and reinstall from scratch. The upgrade path will affect only installed binaries and such—not the disk layout, home directories, or system configuration. Upgrading can be done by two main methods: using binary sets, such as from a release or a snapshot, or from source. Both methods are described in this chapter.

Upgrading from version 3.3 and before to version 3.4 and beyond on the i386 platform is a special process, as the binary format changed. A simple upgrade from source process cannot occur, so special care must be taken. This process is described later in this chapter. This consideration is also important for other architectures that made a similar executable format transition, such as SPARC (at about OpenBSD 3.2).

31.2 CVS and Branches

OpenBSD produces a stable release every six months. These releases can be bought on CD or downloaded for free. A release means tagging all source files in the CVS server, branching the tree. Afterward, new features will be committed to the *-current* branch, which developers follow. But normal users will not take that route, as it may introduce instability. For their purposes, a *-stable* branch is created after each release, where urgent bug and security fixes found after the release are committed. A responsible OpenBSD administrator must know about the *-stable* branch and be able to follow it.

Fixes are announced on mailing lists. After a fix is committed, the administrator will have to either apply patches to his or her local source tree or update it through *-stable* CVS, and then rebuild the system. OpenBSD doesn't provide binary patches or updated release CDs. Luckily, urgent bug fixes are less common on OpenBSD (a dozen per year is a very bad year). If an installed system is not patched in a timely manner, however, the "secure" OpenBSD host sits vulnerable in the cold—and makes an inviting target.

The branches have the CVS branch tag of *OPENBSD_3_4* for OpenBSD 3.4, *OPENBSD_3_3* for OpenBSD 3.3, and the like. This *-stable* branch incorporates important security and reliability fixes, but no other changes. Releases, which are tagged at a single date, have names like *OPENBSD_3_4_BASE* for the OpenBSD 3.4 release. This branch *does not change* and no fixes are brought into it.

To CVS checkout a particular branch, use the *-r* option to *cvs* along with the branch tag:

```
$ cvs checkout -P -rOPENBSD_3_4 src
```

This will check out the source tree (src) for the OpenBSD 3.4 *stable* tree. With this tree checked out, you can build it as described later in this chapter and incorporate fixes as needed. You can also upgrade this tree using *cvs* in a manner similar to the following command:

```
$ cvs -q up -rOPENBSD_3_4 -Pd
```

This will CVS upgrade (*cvs up*) the sources in the OpenBSD 3.4 *stable* branch, incorporating any code changes.

OpenBSD-*stable* branches are maintained for one year after their creation at the time of a release, but no longer than that.

31.3 System Preparation

A key step in the preparation of a system to be upgraded is to ensure that any users or groups that will be needed are added. This is done so that programs can run as non-root and non-nobody, thereby improving system security.

An example is the *ssh* user and group, added with the introduction of the privilege separation mechanism in OpenSSH. Without these user and group additions, the daemon process will fail to start.

These changes are typically well marked in the release notes of the new versions of the system. The "Upgrade Mini-FAQ" is found on the OpenBSD Website at **http://openbsd. org/faq/upgrade-minifaq.html**.

31.4 Upgrading from Binary Sets

To upgrade an OpenBSD installation, you can start the system from the installation floppy and decide to use the upgrade path instead. As the floppy system boots, the kernel will display its messages. You will then be prompted to identify which path you wish to use:

```
erase ^?, werase ^W, kill ^U, intr ^C, status ^T
(I)nstall, (U)pgrade or (S)hell?  u
```

At this prompt you can choose the "upgrade" option by typing "u".

This choice will start the binary update procedure, which differs from the installation process in several ways. First, rather than allowing you to partition the disk, the upgrade routine will examine your disks and find the root filesystem. Second, rather than setting up networking, the upgrader will configure the network as it is set up on the installed system. Each of these steps is indicative of the overall simplicity of the upgrade path, in which you are asked fewer questions than during the installation process. Third, you will be unable to choose the **etc** set to install, because it would conflict with the installed system. Other than these differences, the upgrade procedure will look like the installation procedure.

The upgrader will find the sets on a local disk, such as the CD-ROM or even the system disk, or over the network. They are extracted and installed, and the upgrade routines will finish. You can then reboot to utilize the freshly updated system. You must upgrade the **/etc** directory manually, as described later in this chapter.

31.5 Upgrading from Source

One way that many of us stay current with the development version of OpenBSD is by using the latest sources and doing regular builds. Staying up-to-date with daily CVS pulls isn't typically needed, unless you're doing system development. Instead, weekly pulls are generally frequent enough to stay in step with the current version of the system. Weekly or even monthly builds are probably regular enough for the typical user to keep up-to-date with the latest features, bug fixes, and cutting-edge support. As with any development project, a period of instability and bugs is inevitable before the code is slowly stabilized as features and capabilities are added. Maintaining currency can sometimes be a risky venture.

Note that when you upgrade from source, you will install all of the software from all of the sets distributed with the OpenBSD distribution. Thus, even if you didn't intend to install the **games** set, you will do so when you upgrade via source. Obviously, you'll need to have a working compiler, from the **comp** set, installed. Furthermore, installing the new software will surely trigger any host-based file integrity-checking utilities, such as Tripwire or Aide. Rebuild the database when your upgrading is complete.

It's also important to have enough disk space to hold your sources, their object files, and final binaries. For kernel sources, this space is approximately 25MB. For both kernel and userland sources, it is about 220MB for a whole build. (Yes, we're overestimating here, which is a safe thing to do in this era of cheap disks.) If you run out of disk space, you'll undoubtedly crash the build process. Use *make clean* to clean out the source tree when you're done, cutting back on the disk space used.

The Build Process

You may want to first build a new kernel to support new options available in the userland sources. Chapter 32 provides details on how to do this. After you build your new kernel, install it and then reboot it. Of course, you should always keep a backup kernel in case something goes wrong. We will first build our userland sources, and then our X11 sources. They're maintained in different trees, as the XFree86 group is the main source for X11 software.

Having installed the latest sources, obtained via CVS (see Appendix A), and placed them in **/usr/src**, you can now build your system from source. First, make a directory to hold the object files, the ***.o** files. Keeping this directory outside the source tree is a handy way to prevent it from becoming corrupted with stale objects and hindering a new build. Issue the commands first to build the object tree links and then to build the source. The steps would be as follows:

```
#  mkdir /usr/obj
#  cd /usr/src
#  make obj
 lots of output
#  make build
 lots of output
```

After this series of steps has completed successfully, you can reboot. Rebooting ensures that any settings that required the new userland utilities were successfully and correctly installed. This step is recommended because various **ioctl** interfaces change, for example, during the development cycle.

If you encountered any problems, you should go back, identify where they occurred, and fix the error. Sometimes it's useful to clear out the source tree, refetch it, and then rebuild from scratch.

Both a userland and a kernel build typically take a few hours on current i386 hardware. This process includes cleaning the tree, building the software, and rebooting with the new kernel. Faster or slower hardware will decrease or increase this time, of course.

Building the X11 source tree is slightly different. Again, after fetching the source tree from the OpenBSD CVS servers using CVS, place them in **/usr/XF4** (for the XFree86 4.x series software). Then build the directory **/obj** and make the links to it. Finally, build the software and install it.

31.6 Upgrading Configuration Files

As noted earlier, when you upgrade an installation you have to manually merge the files in **/etc**. They may include the new **rc** scripts, utility configuration data, or new users in the password database. The simplest technique is to unpack the set containing the **/etc** files in a temporary directory and then manually *diff* the files against the ones in the existing **/etc** tree. Changes can then be merged manually to prevent overwriting local configuration settings. When you upgrade from source, the directory **/usr/src/etc** contains most of the files that make up the **/etc** tree, along with architecture-dependent files in the subdirectory **etc.*arch***, such as **etc.i386**. Note that software configuration files that are installed as part of the software build process are not included here.

31.6.1 Using *mergemaster*

The *mergemaster* command is a third-party tool designed to assist in the upgrade of OpenBSD systems. The *mergemaster* command finds the text and configuration files not normally handled gracefully by the *make build* process of upgrading and installs them. It allows you to have updated manual pages, configuration files, and key system files to ensure smooth operation of your upgraded system. For example, new options in the *pf* system may cause it to operate incorrectly. The *mergemaster* tool assists your upgrade procedure by ensuring that all volatile files are found and their differences relative to the installed versions are noted.

Installation of *mergemaster* is quite simple. It is available from the third-party packages collection or in the ports tree in the directory **/usr/src/sysutils/mergemaster**. This small shell script and manual page install without any trouble. Because *mergemaster* modifies system configuration files and reads system-level configuration files not accessible to normal users, it is typically best run as the root user.

The first thing that *mergemaster* does is build a fake system directory hierarchy. Created in the directory **/var/tmp/temproot**, it contains files from most of the text and configuration files in the system. These are pulled from the source tree installed by default in **/usr/src**:

```
$  mergemaster

*** Creating the temporary root environment in /var/tmp/temproot
*** /var/tmp/temproot ready for use
*** Creating and populating directory structure in /var/tmp/temproot

if [ ! -d /var/tmp/temproot/. ]; then
    install -d -o root -g wheel -m 755 /var/tmp/temproot;
fi
mtree -qdef mtree/4.4BSD.dist -p /var/tmp/temproot/ -U
missing: ./altroot (created)


*** Beginning comparison


========================================================================


*** Displaying differences between dev/MAKEDEV and installed version:

--- /dev/MAKEDEV        Wed Jul 31 14:15:10 2002
+++ ./dev/MAKEDEV       Wed Dec 25 23:00:18 2002
@@ -3,8 +3,8 @@
 # THIS FILE AUTOMATICALLY GENERATED.  DO NOT EDIT.
 # generated from:
 #
-#  OpenBSD: etc.i386/MAKEDEV.md,v 1.14 2002/06/18 00:33:00 fgsch Exp
-#  OpenBSD: MAKEDEV.mi,v 1.49 2002/06/18 00:53:45 fgsch Exp
+#  OpenBSD: etc.i386/MAKEDEV.md,v 1.15 2002/10/16 15:48:31 todd Exp
+#  OpenBSD: MAKEDEV.mi,v 1.52 2002/10/16 15:48:31 todd Exp
 #  OpenBSD: MAKEDEV.sub,v 1.7 2002/02/16 01:19:52 deraadt Exp
 #
 #

  Use 'd' to delete the temporary ./dev/MAKEDEV
  Use 'i' to install the temporary ./dev/MAKEDEV
  Use 'm' to merge the temporary and installed versions
```

```
Use 'v' to view the diff results again

Default is to leave the temporary file to deal with by hand

How should I deal with this? [Leave it for later]
```

If you choose "m", the two versions of the file (the newer one in the fake filesystem and the installed one) are merged. You are then presented with a question for every "chunk" of file differences:

```
                    > >biocenter.helsinki.fi  # Univ of Hel
                    > 128.214.58.174          # afsdb1.bioc
                    > 128.214.88.114          # afsdb2.bioc
%
l:      use the left version
r:      use the right version
e l:    edit then use the left version
e r:    edit then use the right version
e b:    edit then use the left and right versions concatenated
e:      edit a new version
s:      silently include common lines
v:      verbosely include common lines
q:      quit
%
```

In the above example there is no chunk on the left-hand side, so choosing the right-side material enters it into the system's files. This operation can be time-consuming, so it is typically easier to either install the new file, keep the old file, or just ignore the differences. Note that every difference is caught, including CVS tags, so not every difference affects functionality.

Some files shouldn't be merged, such as the password databases **/etc/passwd** and **/etc/master.passwd**, the file specifying who can use the *sudo* command (**/etc/sudoers**), and PF configuration files. Merging these files will overwrite any locally configured attributes in the system. Other files that are modified, such as **/etc/sysctl.conf** and **/var/www/conf/httpd.conf**, are probably best merged one chunk at a time.

There are also several options to *mergemaster* available. The key options are *-i*, which tells the tool to install new files as needed, and *-t directory*, which tells *mergemaster* to use a new directory for its temporary files. The latter option is useful if you don't have enough disk space or want to keep several versions around. The default is **/var/tmp/temproot**. The configuration file **.mergemasterrc** can be used to set up the environment and tell the command which scripts to source prior to running.

Even if you have upgraded by using binary sets, the upgrade process can be completed with the assistance of *mergemaster*. Simply download the source files, unpack them, and then allow *mergemaster* to identify the differences.

31.6.2 Manual Merging

The alternative to using mergemaster is to identify differences in files by hand and then to incorporate the changes and update manually. This operation is typically done with the current configuration files in place. The new configuration files that will be found in **/etc** are installed in a temporary location, and then *diff -u* is run over the directories. This command will show the old and new files and can be used to generate files that can be applied using the *patch* command. All of this activity is carried out manually, so it is labor intensive and error prone.

When this step is done, mainly configuration files are left to be merged. Many other flat files, such as executable scripts, merely need to be installed. An example of a script that would be updated is **/etc/netstart**, which is not normally modified by the user. Instead, that configuration files that it reads are modified. The file **/etc/rc.conf** is an example of a configuration file that changes slightly from one release to the next and is altered by an administrator after installation.

It is for this reason that the volatile configuration of the system and the scripts that process this configuration are separated. This setup allows for the controlled upgrade of a system while incurring minimal damage.

31.7 Binary Format Changes and Upgrades

On some platforms, a binary change from **a.out** executables to ELF executables has occurred. This group includes the i386 platform for the OpenBSD 3.3 migration to 3.4 and beyond releases, as well as the SPARC 3.1 to 3.2 migration.

Upgrades are not possible as they are normally presented, via source or binary snapshots, due to kernel booting issues. The *boot* program, which worked for the **a.out** kernel, cannot start the ELF kernel. In contrast, the ELF kernel *boot* program can boot the **a.out** kernel. Once the system has begun booting, the file format of the *boot* program no longer matters. Upgrading from source is typically not possible, as it requires major compiler changes. Snapshots are typically the best way to upgrade for users on *-current* systems, or binary release sets for formal releases.

Also, note that your previously built software, such as ports and packages, will not continue to work on the new binary system. It is best to remove such software before you begin. It is wise to track all of the packages you have installed, however

```
$ pkg_info -a > all-packages
```

Now this file can be read and the same packages can be loaded again.

The following instructions combine the authors' experiences as well as a recipe from Brent Graveland. To upgrade via a binary release, first download all of the new release sets and store them on a local disk. This includes the kernel files. For this example, they will be in **/usr/dist**. Second, obtain the sources for the new *installboot* program via CVS:

```
# cd /usr/src
# cvs up -Pd
```

Third, build the new version of *installboot*:

```
# cd /usr/src/sys/arch/i386/stand/installboot
# make clean obj depend
# make
# cp obj/installboot /usr/mdec/installboot-new
```

It is advisable to prepare a few files from the old **a.out** format to help you if you should experience difficulties in the next few steps:

```
# cp /bsd /bsd.aout
# cp /sbin/reboot /sbin/reboot-aout
# cp /bin/sync /bin/sync-aout
```

At this point you are ready to unpack the new binary boot system (this example assumes that your root disk is **wd0** and that the whole disk is available for your OpenBSD system):

```
# cp /usr/dist/bsd /
# cp /usr/dist/bsd.rd /
# mv /boot /boot.aout
# tar -zxvpf /usr/dist/base34.tgz -C / ./usr/mdec
# cp /usr/mdec/boot /
# /usr/mdec/installboot-new -v /boot /usr/mdec/biosboot /dev/rwd0c
```

Finally, you can unpack the system sets:

```
#  for file in xshare xserv xfont xbase misc man game comp base; do
      tar -C / -xzpf /usr/dist/${file}34.tgz
 done
#  /sbin/sync-aout
#  /sbin/reboot-aout
```

At this point your system should reboot and come up with the new kernel and binary format. If you need to run the installer, you can boot the **bsd.rd** kernel, which is exactly like the installation CD.

The upgrade procedure can proceed normally from here, including the upgrade of the **/etc** files.

The next best alternative to this method—and the one officially suggested—is to wipe the current OpenBSD installation and reinstall the OS from scratch. Personal files are backed up, the configuration is stored somewhere, and the OS is reinstalled. The local files are reapplied to restore the system configuration. The biggest advantage of this technique is that it produces a guaranteed system state for all files, with no stale files or binaries lying around. The authors have found that periodically wiping the system and reinstalling from a clean system help keep disk usage at the appropriate level, as stale library versions are removed.

Chapter 32

Kernel Compilation

The OpenBSD kernel comprises a set of files that build a single executable, the kernel. The heart of the system, the kernel controls the use of the hardware. By default, systems use the kernel that was built with the GENERIC configuration file.

Most users will want to keep using the GENERIC kernel configuration for several reasons: Almost all hardware is supported in this kernel, the settings for memory and other options are tuned, and this configuration has been tested and is consistently supported. When you change the kernel configuration, problems may be introduced. It is also unlikely that you will find adequate support for your changes. Most changes that a user will want to make are available via the *sysctl* tool.

32.1 Why Recompile a Kernel?

For most people the GENERIC kernel suffices, giving them the needed support for their devices and options. As such, users may not feel driven to rebuild the kernel. Nevertheless, there are a number of reasons you may want to rebuild your kernel:

- **Size**   A GENERIC kernel, with all of those devices supported, is rather large. On some systems with memory issues, its size poses a real problem. Rebuilding the kernel and choosing only those options you actually need can help alleviate the strain on your system.

- **Functionality**   Although the GENERIC kernel supports almost every common option, some options are not supported by default. Rebuilding your kernel is the only way to gain these features. This includes the *USER_LDT* option, which is used in Wine.

- **Performance**   A rebuilt kernel can be tweaked to support the processor type you are using, rather than a range of processors. This change can manifest itself as a significant speed gain, at the cost of portability. Because you typically use your kernel on only one type of hardware, this issue is moot.

- **Devices**   The GENERIC kernel doesn't support all devices, some of which you may need. Rebuilding your kernel will add the support you need for these devices.
- **Options**   Some options, such as the *apm* option, have variable settings. These settings are coded into the kernel, and some of them cannot be changed except by rebuilding your kernel.

Many people come to OpenBSD from Linux and, therefore, are used to working with an interactive configuration tool. OpenBSD lacks such a tool, instead relying on flat text configuration files. It's up to you to make sure that your dependencies are correct, but they are noted once you have asked the system to configure itself based on these files.

There are two ways to adjust a kernel: a total rebuild of the kernel and an adjustment of a built kernel. Both of these methods will be covered here.

32.1.1 Why Not Reconfigure and Rebuild Your Kernel?

Many users, in a premature attempt to optimize their systems, remove important options that break the system's operation in subtle ways. In case of a problem (e.g., a repeated kernel crash), a non-GENERIC kernel is useless (as no one will have the very same kernel, and no one is likely to be willing to install the same kernel just to aid debugging). As a consequence, the user will be forced to try to repeat the problem with a GENERIC kernel first.

Not easily reproducible problems with non-GENERIC kernels have a very low chance of getting resolved. In short, using non-GENERIC kernels creates an unsupportable system. The defaults are tuned to support almost all average users, and most changes can be made by adjusting the exposed variables via *sysctl*.

32.2 Where to Get the Source and How to Compile

The OpenBSD kernel is not like the Linux kernel—that is, no big version releases exist outside of an entire system release. Instead, the userland and the kernel are developed in tandem. As a result, you cannot download a kernel source tarball and expect it to work on your system. Userland *include* files need to be up-to-date, and some userland tools need to be rebuilt, including *top* and *pfctl*.

However, you can use CVS to update the **src/sys** module, where the kernel sources are kept. There are two main ways to get sources via CVS. The first, as discussed in Appendix A, uses SSH as the transport layer. The second uses the CVS *pserver* and logs into the CVS server using the *anoncvs* password. Using the *pserver* method to get only the i386 kernel source and needed common pieces would rely on a command like this:

```
$  export CVSROOT=:pserver:anoncvs@anoncvs.ca.openbsd.org:/cvs
$  cvs login
(Logging in to anoncvs@anoncvs1.ca.openbsd.org)
CVS password:  anoncvs
$  cvs get ksrc-i386 ksrc-common
```

Using the SSH transport method, you would choose a CVS mirror from the list and use it as your *CVSROOT* variable, as described in Appendix A. Then you would check out the sources:

```
$  cd /usr
$  cvs co src/sys
```

This will download all of the kernel sources, not just the i386-specific components.

Compiling the GENERIC kernel is a relatively easy process. The configuration file for this kernel is supplied as a complete system. In this example, replace the keyword *somearch* with your architecture, such as i386 or SPARC. To build the GENERIC kernel for your system, issue the following commands:

```
#  cd /usr/src/sys/arch/somearch/conf
#  config GENERIC
#  cd ../compile/GENERIC
#  make
```

This will create the kernel **bsd** in the directory **/usr/src/sys/arch/***somearch***/compile**. This kernel can then be moved to the root directory and booted. It is typically a wise idea to save the older kernel as **/bsd.old** or some unique name. This preventive measure can prove very helpful if your new kernel fails to boot.

The build process usually proceeds over the course of an hour or so for modern i386-class systems. If the build is interrupted by an error, it is best to abort it entirely, fix the error, and restart the build process from the ground up.

32.3 Information to Be Set in the Configuration Files

A brief walk through the GENERIC configuration file reveals the structure of a typical kernel configuration file. It is typically split into two files: one that controls global, architecture-independent options, and one that controls architecture-dependent options. Only the major options are shown here.

The kernel-independent configuration files typically live in the directory **/usr/src/sys/conf**. The GENERIC architecture-independent configuration file is located here. Some of the major options are described below:

- **DDB**   Controls whether the kernel is built with a debugger installed. Turned on by default, it is useful for developers.
- **CRYPTO**   Required by many key systems in the kernel and in userland. It is enabled by default and is best left enabled.
- **SYSVMSG, SYSVSEM, SYSVSHM**   System V shared memory structures, used by many userland components. They are best left enabled.
- **COMPAT_23, COMPAT_25, COMPAT_43, TCP_COMPAT_42**   Control compatibility with older OpenBSDand BSD versions. They are best left untouched.
- **FFS, FFS_SOFTUPDATES**   Filesystem options. The default filesystem is FFS. Soft updates are covered in Chapter 14.
- **GATEWAY**   Controls IP forwarding. It also available via the *sysctl* system.
- **INET, INET6**   Networking options. You can remove *INET6* if you do not expect to use IPv6 networking.
- **BOOT_CONFIG**   Allows for start-up configuration of the system (via *boot -c*).
- **sl, ppp, sppp**   Parallel and serial IP linkages. They are rarely needed today.
- **bpfilter**   Controls how many */dev/bpf* devices will be available. Don't increase this number without adjusting kernel memory allocation and knowing how to properly calculate these values.

These are just a handful of the many options available to tweak in the configuration files. The system can be fine-tuned in the hands of a knowledgable builder, but it is also easy to introduce significant instability. For most users, the GENERIC kernel options will work very well.

The list of options can be viewed in detail from the manual pages for *options* as well as device driver files, such as **fxp** and **em**. The *options* manual page controls platform-independent options, while the architecture-specific kernel options are listed in their manual pages.

If you plan to modify the kernel configuration, it is best to copy the GENERIC kernel configuration file and rename it to something specific. The convention is to take the hostname and use it in uppercase—for example, the kernel name TANK is the laptop *tank's* specific kernel. This naming convention allows you to track changes across versions as well as to identify the specific build. Kernels also have incrementally numbered versions, which are automatically created by the build process.

It is easy to make a mistake in the kernel configuration steps and omit a needed option, such as a general driver class. Here, in an example from a recent kernel compile by one of the authors, two such mistakes were made. The options for `usscanner?` and `isp?` were commented out, but two drivers that depend on their presence remained:

```
# config TANK
TANK:119: scsibus* at usscanner? is orphaned
 (nothing matching usscanner? declared)
TANK:220: scsibus* at isp? is orphaned
 (nothing matching isp? declared)
```

This error is quite easy to understand. Such an error occurred in the configuration file **TANK** at lines 119 and 220, generating two orphans. By satisfying this dependency and reading `usscanner?` (for example), or by commenting out `scsibus*`, this error can be cleaned up.

Many options are either self-documenting or documented in the manual page for *options*. If you don't understand a variable or its consequences, it is best to leave the variable untouched.

32.4 Tweaking a Built Kernel

Several options in the kernel are malleable, meaning that they can be modified without much need to recompile a kernel. They include the disabling of some drivers, such as when a conflict arises, and the editing of various flags for drivers, such as ISA memory addresses. Rather than rebuilding a kernel to make these changes, editing of the kernel binary can be done.

To do so, the *config* tool is used with the major option *-e*. This allows for the editing of a kernel binary. The other option, specifying an output kernel file, must also be done. In this example, one of the authors forgot to edit the flags for *apm0*, the kernel APM support, to work with his laptop. The default flags are 0×0, but flag values of 0×10000 were needed for proper hibernation of his laptop with in suspend mode. The kernel **bsd** was edited and the new kernel **bsd.new** was generated with this minor change.

```
# config -e -o bsd.new bsd
OpenBSD 3.4 (TANK) #0: Wed Nov  5 13:12:12 EST 2003
    jose@tank:/usr/src/sys/arch/i386/compile/TANK
Enter 'help' for information
ukc> help
```

```
    help                            Command help list
    add     dev                     Add a device
    base    8|10|16                 Base on large numbers
    change  devno|dev               Change device
    disable attr val|devno|dev      Disable device
    enable  attr val|devno|dev      Enable device
    find    devno|dev               Find device
    list                            List configuration
    lines   count                   # of lines per page
    show    [attr [val]]            Show attribute
    exit                            Exit, without saving changes
    quit                            Quit, saving current changes
    timezone   [mins [dst]]         Show/change timezone
ukc> list
  0 audio* at clct* flags 0x0
  1 nsphy* at aue*|fxp*|fxp*|ep* phy -1 flags 0x0
  2 nsphyter* at aue*|fxp*|fxp*|ep* phy -1 flags 0x0
  3 qsphy* at aue*|fxp*|fxp*|ep* phy -1 flags 0x0
 truncated
121 apm0 at bios0 flags 0x0
 truncated
ukc> change apm0
121 apm0 at bios0 flags 0x0
change [n] y
flags [0] ? 0x10000
121 apm0 changed
121 apm0 at bios0 flags 0x10000
ukc> q
Saving modified kernel.
# ls -l bsd*
-rwxr-xr-x  1 root  bin  3674272 Nov  5 13:12 bsd
-rwxr-xr-x  1 root  bin  3674272 Nov  5 13:14 bsd.new
```

Using the option *list*, all of the kernel options that can be modified using the interactive kernel editor were listed. Only one line (line 121) was needed for the *apm* settings. The *change* command was used and the flags altered to reflect a new value. Next, the *config* tool was quit and the new kernel was made. Note that the size of the kernel remained unaffected by this operation.

The new kernel can be installed just as any new kernel and must be booted to begin using the new settings. At the `boot)` prompt, enter the name of the new kernel—in this case, **bsd.new**—to boot using this new system image. Once you have done so, you can modify the name of the kernel to make it be the default kernel loaded at start-up.

32.5 Kernel–Userland Synchronization

One often-forgotten caveat in the OpenBSD world for regular users is the importance of keeping the userland and the kernel "in sync." Simply put, the kernel data structures accessed by some userland tools need to be "in sync" with what the tools are expecting. This includes the process namespace for commands like *ps* or *top* as well as networking subjects like IPsec functionality. "*Userland*" is the term commonly employed to discribe non-kernel executables and files.

You may notice problems when using a kernel built on a different system from the existing userland toolset. This may include downloading a new kernel from a snapshot without upgrading the userland sets as well. Potential errors include the message "proc size mismatch" when attempting to execute the command *ps* or worse:

```
$ ps
ps: proc size mismatch (11520 total, 732 chunks)
$ fstat
fstat: proc size mismatch (26880 total, 732 chunks)
$ top              doesn't execute
```

Note that the system will be largely usable, but some options may not work correctly. If the kernel and userland systems are dramatically outdated and significant changes have occurred, such as to the firewall configuration options, the userland configuration utilities may not function as expected.

For these reasons, it's important to ensure that your kernel was built based on the userland set you actually use. This is typically not a problem, but it should be noted anyway. A discrepancy can occur if you boot a kernel built on a different system or build a userland set against a different kernel. Kernels reconfigured using the *config -e* options, described earlier, do not suffer from this problem.

Chapter 33

Bug Reports with OpenBSD

33.1 Introduction

OpenBSD is a continually evolving system that is under constant development. New features are added, new hardware is supported, and—most importantly—bugs are fixed. Bug fixes can come about only if clear, accurate descriptions of bugs are reported. A variety of tools have been made available to the community for this purpose. Their use is described here.

Above all, the most important step in avoiding problems is to ensure that you are working with the most up-to-date source code. If you experience a legitimate problem in a major area that many people will use, chances are that it's already been diagnosed and fixed. If you're using old code, your efforts will merely be redundant. Check the latest versions and update your OS (using a method like CVS) as needed.

The second most important thing is to assume that the problem you are experiencing is a local problem. Such a problem can come about through misuse of a tool or command, or as the result of a local configuration error. This isn't to say that the most users are mistaken, but you should nevertheless try and ensure that the problem is legitimate before reporting it more widely. If you need assistance, several bug-related resources are listed in Appendix F, including mailing lists and Web sites. It's wise to assume that something is not a bug until proven otherwise.

Lastly, make sure you are using commands properly and the problem is real. The OpenBSD team has developed extensive documentation, including the FAQ on the Web site, extensive manual pages, and the like, to assist you in using the software correctly. What may appear to be a bug may, in fact, be misuse of the software. Read the documentation and confirm that you're using it correctly. If you can, check the source code if you feel technically inclined. "Read the FAQ" is an all too common reply when basic problems arise, simply because it's true—problems are most often covered in the FAQ (or the manual page).

33.2 Diagnosing a Problem

The first step in diagnosing a problem is to demonstrate reproducibility of the error. Intermittent problems are not uncommon on any system. Given the number of moving parts in a typical system, an occasional failure is to be expected. However, if you can reproduce the problem, then chances are good that it's a real problem.

To check the reproducibility of a problem, make careful notes about the conditions under which you find a problem. In the following example, the command *ls* is broken. The first hint of a problem is an error on a newly installed system:

```
$  pwd
/home/jose
$  ls .
Memory fault
```

One of the first things to do is to test the command in another directory. In this case, this step is the equivalent of giving the command different input to see its reaction.

If this effort fails and gives an error, the next thing to do would be to verify the integrity of the input, or the filesystem in this case. Filesystem integrity is best checked using the *fsck* command, discussed in Chapter 14. After the integrity of the input is verified, attempt the command again and determine the result—an error or successful execution.

If you have the opportunity, it would be wise to check the command on a second machine with the same setup. A number of minor nuances could be responsible for the error, aside from a software problem, including disk or memory problems. If a redundant system is not available, do not worry—you can ask others to do it for you.

33.3 Check with Others

A problem is a real issue worth solving only if others have it as well. If it affects only one person, the problem should be dealt with locally. However, if it affects many people, it's worth fixing. This criterion can also be used to determine whether a problem is real.

Using the resources listed in Appendix F, including mailing lists and Usenet groups, post a full description of the problem and solicit additional information from others. Does it affect them? Is it a real problem? Does anyone know of a workaround?

For the preceding example problem for the *ls* command, a sample posting to a list such as **misc** would be as follows:

To: misc@openbsd.org
Subject: ls in -current core dumps

Hi all. I've been using -current on i386 and found a small problem, possibly. When I use the "ls" command I get segmentation faults and core dumps, occasionally. Has anyone else seen this?

Some brief information on my setup. I'm using FFS (soft updates are not enabled) on an IDE disk (wd0) on i386. It only affects a few directories like /home/jose and /tmp. When I run "fsck" on the filesystems they come back clean.

Any ideas? Thanks.

Do not forget to provide the *dmesg* for the machine on which you are experiencing the bug. This data may seem of no importance to you, but in most cases developers need more information about your system. That includes a full *dmesg*—not just snippets you find important. Components interact with one another, so failures might be caused by supposedly unrelated components.

With the preceding message, you've clearly communicated the problem, giving others enough information to begin to diagnose the problem. With luck, others can follow up and confirm (or deny) the problem for you. Be prepared to provide more information as needed to help others diagnose the problem. Sometimes others will jump in immediately with confirmations and, if it's a well-known problem, a fix. This happened, for example, with the *boot* problems experienced by some 3.0 releases, which quickly became a well-known problem with a well-known workaround. At other times no one will provide any additional information. The response ultimately depends on several factors, including the popularity of the command or tool and the platform. The VAX architecture isn't as popular as the i386, for example, so relatively few people will be able to chime in with follow-up information.

The **misc@openbsd.org** list, or the Usenet group **comp.unix.bsd.openbsd.misc**, is probably the best place to start, simply due to the nature of the discussions. Almost any mail inquiring about the system from a user's perspective belongs here. The next best place to check would be the **bugs@openbsd.org** list, an open list with both the GNATS entries and follow-up responses as well as some high-end discussion. The **tech@openbsd.org** list is a similarly high-end list, mainly useful for very technical discussions on the OpenBSD system. The **tech** list isn't meant for the discussion of bugs, but rather for proposed code changes or hardware development.

33.4 Develop a Solution

If possible, it's wise to attempt to find a solution to the problem you have identified. This may take the form of a workaround, such as disabling a portion of a service or application, or a source code patch if you are able to develop one.[1] There is usually a

[1]Patches, and ways to generate them, are discussed in Appendix B.

place to provide the proposed solution so that the OpenBSD developers may be able to remedy the real problem more quickly. Furthermore, if the flaw persists for a long period of time, a workaround helps other users continue to use the system, despite its limited functionality.

One way to examine a potential fix is to debug the output of the crashed component and obtain a backtrace. The steps for doing so are described in Appendix E. Note that a debugging-symbol-enabled version of the software will be required for the backtrace to return useful information. By default, installed software has these symbols stripped to reduce the binary size.

33.5 The OpenBSD Bug Tracking System

The OpenBSD project uses the GNATS bug tracking system. GNATS allows for multiple types of administration, including various administrators, stages in the life cycle of a bug, and several types of bugs. Bugs are assigned types and numbers, such as "user/2301" (the number of the bug shown later in this chapter, in fact). A simple Web interface is also available to the user community, allowing for the searching of bugs and their viewing.

The OpenBSD Web interface to the GNATS tool can be reached through the "Bug Tracking System" link from the side bar on the main page, or at **http://www.openbsd.org/query-pr.html**. This interface to the GNATS database is suitable for use by the general community. Here you can retrieve bug reports identified on the basis of a variety of criteria.

The first search option presented is retrieval by the PR (problem report) number. Use the bug number, if you know it. For example, to pull up number 1001 (a message about the Christmas holiday), enter "1001" as the PR number and click "View existing PR." The report will come up in a plain text view, including any follow-up information related to the problem.

The next two buttons are useful for getting summary statistics. The summary for bugs by status and person allows you to sort the two GNATS-identified "people" who handle OpenBSD bugs—the GNATS administrator and the bug list—according to status and show summary numbers. A more useful metric is the summary by status and category. In each case a small list, with links, comes up for the types of data sorted. You can click the links to get the expanded summaries for the categories and the status numbers, if you like.

The third section is probably the most useful one for sorting bugs when you are looking for advice and don't know the PR number. This section allows you to search the bug reports based on various criteria, including status and text words. If an entry is omitted from any of the fields, the wildcard entry is supplied. This approach can be useful, for example, for looking at all outstanding bugs (status "open") in the system. You can select multiple status values, if you wish. You can also restrict yourself to various categories, such as architectures, kernel issues, or whatever, in the "category" pull-down menu.

The difference between "text" and "multitext" searches is that the "text" search looks only in the header information of a GNATS entry, while the "multitext" search also looks in the last few sections for matches, including the problem description and fixes. Note that the latter search technique can be slower, sometimes.

Of course, you can mix and match the options—say, to restrict yourself to closed i386 kernel bugs. Playing with the bugs database is recommended.

Use the GNATS database and this Web form to determine whether someone else has reported a similar problem before you submit a bug report. It's possible that someone has beat you to the punch, and perhaps a workaround has already been suggested or a fix implemented.

33.6 Reporting Bugs with *sendbug*

The primary tool employed by the user community to communicate problems to the development team via the GNATS database is the *sendbug* utility. Relying on flat text files and an e-mail transport layer, *sendbug* is an easy-to-use tool with which to enter bugs into the GNATS system.

Once invoked, *sendbug* uses a template to fill an editor buffer. The editor, as specified by the *VISUAL* environmental variable, is used to fill in this form. The lines and sections are used to provide information about the problem, the environment where it is found, and any fixes that may be available.

The following is an actual problem report (PR 2301) sent in by one of the authors with annotations provided. It illustrates how to fill out a *sendbug* report to enter a bug into the GNATS database.

```
SENDBUG: -*- sendbug -*-
SENDBUG: Lines starting with 'SENDBUG' will be removed automatically,
SENDBUG: as will all comments (text enclosed in '<' and '>').
SENDBUG:
SENDBUG: Choose from the following categories:
SENDBUG:
SENDBUG: system user library documentation ports kernel sparc i386
```

```
SENDBUG: m68k mips ppc arm alpha ns32k vax sparc64
SENDBUG:
SENDBUG:
To: gnats@openbsd.org
Subject: xman breaks on ports/packages manpages
From: jose@cwru.edu
Cc:
Reply-To: jose@cwru.edu
X-sendbug-version: 3.97


>Submitter-Id: net
>Originator: jose
>Organization:  net
>Confidential: no
>Synopsis: pointing xman to ports/packages manpages segfaults
>Severity: non-critical
>Priority: low
>Category: user
>Class: sw-bug
>Release: 3.0-current
>Environment:
<machine, os, target, libraries (multiple lines)>
System     : OpenBSD 3.0
Architecture: OpenBSD.i386
Machine    : i386
>Description:
xman, the X11 interface to the 'man' utility, will segfault and
dump core if possible. using debug code and gdb, it appears to be
in the function Format in misc.c. the following is a gdb of the
coredump from xman's barfing on the ddd manpage (installed from ports):

(gdb) bt
#0  0x40233c52 in fgets ()
#1  0x82ff in Format (man_globals=0x9a600,
    entry=0x27ee0 "/usr/local/man//man1/ddd.1") at misc.c:435
#2  0x7ea3 in FindManualFile (man_globals=0x9a600, section_num=0,
    entry_num=172) at misc.c:284
```

```
#3   0x6c86 in DoManualSearch (man_globals=0x9a600, string=0xa9770
     "ddd") at search.c:343
#4   0x6afb in DoSearch (man_globals=0x9a600, type=0) at search.c:271
#5   0x389b in Search (w=0xae400, event=0xdfbfdb34, params=0xa9680,
     num_params=0xa9668) at handler.c:548
#6   0x400bc0f2 in _XtMatchAtom ()
#7   0x400bc55d in _XtMatchAtom ()
#8   0x400bcab0 in _XtTranslateEvent ()
#9   0x40096f01 in XtDispatchEventToWidget ()
#10  0x400978a5 in _XtOnGrabList ()
#11  0x40097ae0 in XtDispatchEvent ()
#12  0x40097fbb in XtAppMainLoop ()
#13  0x73ee in main (argc=1, argv=0xdfbfdc08) at main.c:216


>How-To-Repeat:
fire up xman. point it at a port's manual page (several tested
will repeat this, including ddd, dsniff, scanssh), wait for a
segfault.
>Fix:
i honestly have no idea. its stringy X code ... not my favorite
place to muck.
```

Quitting the editor and saving the changes will have the *sendbug* utility submit the bug report to the database. At this point, you should be prepared for one of several things to happen.

First, the code may be fixed without any further involvement by you. A simple e-mail stating that the problem has been addressed and the bug is closed is typically received.

Second, you may receive a request for a follow-up discussion from the person assigned to investigate the bug report. It might include an e-mail requesting additional information (such as the output of the *dmesg* command or other diagnostics) or even a request for your assistance in testing a proposed patch.

Third, nothing at all may happen. Your bug report may not generate any interest from anyone, and it may remain unfixed. There is little you can do if your report doesn't appear on anyone's agenda.

Part IV

Appendixes

CVS Basics

OpenBSD is a system created by developers for an audience consisting of developers. Don't let this stated mission stop you from using it, though, because it works very well for the typical end user. OpenBSD is constantly in development and is freely and openly available, so the source code can always be accessed. As with the other free BSD projects, NetBSD and FreeBSD, this source code is publicly available via the Concurrent Versions System (CVS).

CVS is a powerful system that supports the controlled development environment required in a large, distributed project. By using CVS, developers around the world can obtain, or "check out," parts of the source code, work on it, and then "check in" their changes. CVS is intelligent, allowing for the easy resolution of "conflicts," which may arise when two separate developers attempt to contribute contradictory changes. CVS is also efficient, storing not the entire component at every stage, but rather keeping track of the changes. These changes are logged as well, enabling others to see what changes have been implemented and what comments the developer has made.

Despite its power, CVS remains easy to use. This appendix is not designed to be an authoritative discussion of CVS, but rather a gentle introduction allowing you to use it to keep your system up-to-date with the project's most recent source code. The resources list at the end of this chapter explains where to get more information on CVS, some of which is specific to the OpenBSD project, such as repositories, mirrors, and "modules."

A.1 How to Set Yourself Up for CVS

CVS operations are controlled via the *cvs(1)* command. It usually takes the following form:

```
$ cvs options action file ...
```

The major options and actions are discussed here. The *file* can be a filename, a CVS module, or a path within a module.

Only one environmental variable needs to be set up for CVS to work properly, although two are typically used for security reasons. The main variable, *CVSROOT*, specifies the location of a repository from which you will be working. It has the form *user@hostname:path*, where *user* specifies the username on the remote system *hostname*, and *path* is the path to the CVS repository location on that remote system. This username is typically set to *anoncvs* for OpenBSD mirrors; for most of the servers, **/cvs** is the path to use. To set this variable in your shell, you can use the following command in Bourne shells like *ksh*:

```
$  export CVSROOT=anoncvs@openbsd.citi.umich.edu:/cvs
```

In *csh* derivatives, such as *tcsh*, use this type of command:

```
%  setenv CVSROOT anoncvs@openbsd.citi.umich.edu:/cvs
```

Alternatively, this location can be set on the command line using the *-d* argument to *cvs*:

```
$  cvs -d anoncvs@openbsd.citi.umich.edu:/cvs   action
```

The other CVS-related shell variable that is usually set is *CVS_RSH*, specifying the method by which you will be connecting if you are not using a *pserver* (discussed in Section A.1.1). Because *rsh* has a number of security problems, *ssh* is typically chosen as the method for connecting to a CVS server. Again, this variable may be set in *ksh* or other Bourne shell derivatives:

```
$  export CVS_RSH=/usr/bin/ssh
```

If you are using a *csh* family shell, you will use the following command or something similar:

```
%  setenv CVS_RSH /usr/bin/ssh
```

If you decide to make these changes permanent, you can edit your shell initialization file to always set these variables. For *ksh* or other *sh* users (such as *bash*), make the file **~/.profile** look something like this (showing only the CVS-related lines):

```
# sh/ksh initialization
export CVSROOT=anoncvs@openbsd.citi.umich.edu:/cvs
export CVS_RSH=/usr/bin/ssh
```

If you are using a *csh* family shell, edit the file ~/**.cshrc** to look like this (again showing only CVS-related lines):

```
# csh initialization
setenv CVSROOT anoncvs@openbsd.citi.umich.edu:/cvs
setenv CVS_RSH /usr/bin/ssh
```

Now, having set up our environment to accommodate CVS, we can begin working with it.

A.1.1 CVS and the *pserver*

CVS has an option to skip right past using *ssh* or *lsh* and make its own socket for connecting to a client. In this setup, the CVS server runs a *pserver*. Users will notice this setup when the CVS repository is specified as something such as *:pserver:anoncvs@openbsd.citi.umich.edu:/cvs*. In this situation, you will use the value of *CVSROOT* but any value of *CVS_RSH* will be ignored.

To begin using a CVS *pserver*, you must first login, even if you do so as an anonymous server:

```
$  cvs -d :pserver:anoncvs@openbsd.pserver.someplace.com:/cvs login
Logging in to :pserver:anoncvs@openbsd.pserver.someplace.com:/cvs
CVS password:  type the password here
```

Now you can perform the CVS operations described later in this chapter. Note that a CVS *pserver* generally doesn't allow for any encryption—only if you are using the Kerberos authentication system. This option will not be covered here.

A.2 Using CVS

CVS can be used to pull down sources from the OpenBSD repositories, allowing you to keep your OS up-to-date. In the following examples, we'll assume that you are storing your source code in **/usr/src** and your ports tree in **/usr/ports**. These are the standard installation locations, but they can be adjusted if you like.

Sources, and the ports tree, can be obtained either by initiating a CVS "checkout" of the module or by unpacking the archive from the CD. The latter can be helpful if you are using a slower link and want to update the tree via CVS.

To check out the source tree, in the module named **src**, use the CVS "checkout" or "get" option:

```
$  cd /usr
$  cvs co src
cvs server: Updating /src
U src/Makefile
 output omitted
```

The action *co* is a synonym for "checkout" or "get." In this example, we first enter the directory **/usr** and then tell CVS to get the module **src**. The CVS server responds by sending the current source files it knows about. Using this approach, we can get any of the modules that exist in OpenBSD through CVS. At the time of this writing, they included the following:

- **src**   The main source tree branch, including kernel sources.
- **X11**   The XFree86 version 3.x import, not maintained.
- **XF4**   The XFree86 version 4.x import, the currently used X server.
- **sys**   The complete kernel sources for all platforms.
- **ports**   The ports tree.
- **www**   The OpenBSD Web site.

Any of these modules can be specified as an argument to CVS to obtain the current module. Submodules can also be specified, should you want only a small portion of the tree:

```
$  cd /usr
$  cvs co src/usr.bin/make
```

This command will download only the directory in the source tree **usr.bin/make**, containing the sources for the *make* utility.

Updating via CVS is also rather easy. You simply use the action *update* or *up*:

```
$  cd /usr
$  cvs up src
```

This will update the sources locally to match those of the remote server in the named module.

Additional arguments worth specifying to CVS, so as to ensure a clean source tree, are *P*, *A*, and *d*. *P* is used to prune any empty directories; *A* is used to reset any "sticky" tags or dates, thereby ensuring you have an up-to-date source tree; and *d* will perform directory creation as needed for new entries. The recommended update CVS command is given here:

```
$  cd /usr
$  cvs up src -PAd
```

This command is best used for maintaining a clean and properly updated source tree. The same options can be used on any of the other modules, such as **ports**.

A.3 CVS and Tags

Central to the CVS theme is the "tag." It is exactly what it sounds like—a tag on the versions of software created for some larger version. For example, one may tag a release of a project as **RELEASE_1_0**, and it may contain version 1.15 of file A, version 1.2 of file B, and version 1.76 of file C. Anyone who uses CVS to pull down **RELEASE_1_0** will retrieve these versions of the files, regardless of any later, more up-to-date versions that may exist. The CVS server knows, due to its filesystem, which versions to grab for you.

Current OpenBSD tags for the OS software are as follows:

- **OPENBSD_3_3**   The OpenBSD 3.3 release with all patches and errata applied. This is the *-stable* branch.
- **OPENBSD_3_4**   The OpenBSD 3.4 release with all security and reliability patches applied. This is the *-stable* branch.
- **OPENBSD_3_4_BASE**   The OpenBSD 3.4 release with *none* of the after-release patches applied. This is the source tree as it is shipped on the released CD.
- **No special tags**   In the absence of any tags, the *-current* sources are pulled. These development sources may not be stable. All patches, however, have been applied to this code.

These are just a few of the tags on the source code. Using them, you can grab any versions of the source at any time and inspect them for changes. The OpenBSD maintainers usually keep only two versions *-stable* at any one time—the two previous releases. At the time of this writing, they were versions 3.3 and 3.4.

Files in a CVS repository are usually tagged with a marker to show their current version, last date of change, and last person to make a change. For example, the source file for this appendix has the following tag:

```
# $OpenBSD: cvs.tex,v 1.14 2003/11/12 04:17:23 bpalmer Exp $
```

A.4 Speeding Up CVS

CVS can sometimes be slow, because it has to work with a lot of files and typically over the Internet. There are at least three ways you can help speed up your CVS actions.

A.4.1 Choosing a Mirror

The first way to speed up your CVS checkouts and updates is to choose a mirror that is geographically close and linked by high-bandwidth lines. Some portions of the world are linked to the North American headquarters of the OpenBSD project by slower lines, but have high-bandwidth infrastructures. In this situation, the best option is to select a mirror that is within the same geographic region as you to take advantage of the high-speed links.

A list of anonymous CVS servers is available on the OpenBSD Web site at **http:// www.openbsd.org/anoncvs.html**. Examine this list to find the server nearest you. In doing so, you allow a single server to consume the bandwidth to the project's main CVS server, keeping your consumption of that bandwidth at a minimum.

A.4.2 Compression

The second way you can speed up your CVS actions is to use compression. The *cvs* program can work with the *gzip* program to increase the compression between the two endpoints by using a sliding window. Over long-haul links with fast endpoints, the speedup can be appreciable. Note that the tradeoff is CPU usage on either side.

The command *cvs -z 3* would specify a compression level of 3, which is the default for *gzip*. Higher numbers indicate a higher level of compression, at the expense of increased CPU usage. To realize level 5 compressed checking using CVS of the ports tree, for example, use the command *cvs -z 5 co ports*.

A.4.3 Ignoring Parts of the Tree

One of the slower operations in the CVS update process is the examination of all of the subdirectories for their current state. This scrutiny can be time-consuming, even if there are only a few files to update.

If you find yourself regularly ignoring parts of the tree, you can use **.cvsignore** files to tell your CVS client to skip over these parts of the tree. Such a file contains one name per line of a directory relative to the current directory of paths that will be skipped when doing any CVS actions. For example, if you find yourself not using any of the astronomy or *plan9* ports, in the file **/usr/ports/.cvsignore** you would have entries like these:

```
astro
plan9
```

Now the CVS client will ignore those subdirectories in the ports tree when you do any CVS work. The larger the portion of the tree skipped, the more pronounced a speedup you will notice.

It is important to not skip parts of the tree that actually do matter for your work. For example, although you may not realize it, some ports have dependencies that must be satisfied. If you let these parts of the tree grow stale, you will wind up breaking the software with which you are trying to work.

A.5 Resources

The OpenBSD project maintains a short introduction to using CVS, along with a list of its recognized official mirrors, on the Web at **http://www.openbsd.org/anoncvs.html**.

The CVS manual page, *cvs(1)*, is a great resource for working with CVS. It covers not only the end-user options discussed here, but also the options you would use to set up your own CVS system.

The CVS book *Open Source Development with CVS*, is a complete resource for understanding CVS and managing large software projects with it. The core chapters on using CVS are available free of charge on the Web in PostScript and some other formats. They can be downloaded from **http://cvsbook.red-bean.com/**.

Applying Source Code Patches

B.1 What Are Patches?

OpenBSD is mainly distributed in source code form, with updates coming not as the full source code file but rather as differences between it and a preceding version. These differences constitute a source code patch. Applying a patch to the source code by hand is a simple process and allows you to update your OS as necessary.

Source code patches are often distributed for reliability fixes, security fixes, and new features. Sometimes they come from the project; at other times they come from other developers. If you choose to add a patch manually, you will usually employ the *patch* tool.

B.2 The Structure of a Patch

Patches usually have a well-defined structure. Typically they are generated by the application of the command *diff -ur oldfile newfile > file.patch*. The options *-ur* to the *diff* command generate a *unified diff* (described below) and, if directories are being compared, *recurse* through them to find differences. The redirection (>) is important, as *patch* takes its input from the standard input, not a filename.

The unified *diff* format is the standard format used in patches. It is appealing because it is intuitively obvious which parts are being added and which parts are being removed. Comments can appear at the head of the patch, perhaps explaining what the patch does and how to apply it; these comments do not affect the patch being applied.

The patch itself begins with two important lines. The first line begins with - - - and a filename, typically *filename.orig*. This is the soon-to-be-former file, which will get moved to *filename.orig*. The second line begins with +++ and a filename. The next line sets up the locations and size in lines of the patch, which is somewhat tricky to understand—we won't cover here.

The meat of the patch follows. The context to the patch is typically included, which helps the *patch* tool align itself within the source. This can be handy if the lines are transposed up or down but remain constant, as *patch* can usually handle this structure correctly. This can happen if code above has been removed or added but the block being patched is unaffected. Lines beginning with ‐ (minus) are removed, and lines beginning with + (plus) are added. This operation is intuitive to the user, and also consistent with the head of the patch and the filenames. We know, based on this plus/minus syntax, which lines are new and which are old.

The *patch* tool uses this information to alter the files based on differences. It can be very useful in reducing the amount of overhead in distributing fixes to source code. This approach is also used by tools like CVS and *rsync* internally to keep up-to-date information on files and to identify the differences between revisions. The patches automatically applied to the ports when they are built (Chapter 13) are also handled in this fashion. There the **Makefile** takes care of that process.

B.3 Using the *patch* Tool

The *patch* tool takes a *diff* output between two files and applies the changes. In the following example, part of the patch to OpenBSD 3.0 presented as a reliability fix for IP-in-IP encapsulation (patch 010)—a sanity check—is added.

```
--- sys/netinet/ip_ipip.c          2001/08/19 06:31:56      1.21
+++ sys/netinet/ip_ipip.c          2001/12/13 19:18:13
@@ -208,6 +208,13 @@
        /* Remove outer IP header */
        m_adj(m, iphlen);

+       /* Sanity check */
+       if (m->m_pkthdr.len < sizeof(struct ip))  {
+               ipipstat.ipips_hdrops++;
+               m_freem(m);
+               return;
+       }
+
        m_copydata(m, 0, 1, &v);

        switch (v >> 4) {
```

This patch is applied as follows:

```
$  cd /usr/src
$  patch -p0 < patch-010
```

The argument *-p* to the *patch* command strips leading directories in the patch. In this case we are in the right place, so we used *-p0*. If we had been one directory deeper, we would have used *-p1* to strip one directory off of the top, and so forth.

A properly applied patch will generate output similar to the following:

```
Patching file ip_ipip.c using Plan A...
Hunk #1 succeeded at 208.
done
```

The patch succeeded. Because this patch contained only one "hunk," we see just that message. In reality, patches can contain multiple points of action, each being a distinct "hunk." Sometimes one will succeed and one will fail, for example.

When a patch fails, errors such as the following may be produced:

```
Patching file sys/netinet/ip_ipip.c using Plan A...
Hunk #1 failed at 208.
1 out of 1 hunks failed--saving rejects to sys/netinet/ip_ipip.c.rej
done
```

Alternatively, if the system is confused, a question such as the following may be posed:

```
Hmm...  Looks like a unified diff to me...
The text leading up to this was:
--------------------------
|--- sys/netinet/ip_ipip.c.orig      2001/08/19 06:31:56
|+++ sys/netinet/ip_ipip.c      2001/12/13 19:18:13
--------------------------
File to patch:
```

Simply put, the patch and the path don't quite line up. In this case, the patch is attempted in the **sys/netinet/** directory but was called with *-p0*, so leading directories in the filenames are not stripped away. The answer to the question is then **ip_ipip.c**.

B.4 Obtaining Patches for OpenBSD

OpenBSD distributes patches using its FTP servers and announces them via various mailing lists. All patches for OpenBSD systems, including all versions, can be found at **ftp://ftp.openbsd.org/pub/OpenBSD/patches/**. Here patches are sorted by release version and either *common* or architecture-specific directories. Some patches, for example, are specific only to one platform, such as the Altivec instruction patches to the *macppc* platform. Patches are numbered and given a one-word description, and each patch contains a header with a brief summary of the reason for the patch and instructions for its application.

Important patches related to security matters are announced on the mailing list **security-announce@openbsd.org** and typically on other OpenBSD resource sites. Included in each advisory is a URL indicating where the patch can be downloaded along with instructions on how to install it.

Patches are, of course, applied to the current source code and are always available by CVS (Appendix A). Most are applied to the *-stable* source code branch. After a release, a *-stable* branch is created that contains important security and reliability fixes. Because of the difficulty in keeping older releases up-to-date, *-stable* branches are maintained for only one year after their creation. This means that as version 3.2 is released, 3.0-*stable* ends its life.

Appendix C

Tuning the Kernel
with *sysctl*

The OpenBSD kernel includes a number of variables that can be tuned at runtime in a dynamic fashion. The same interface is used to read kernel state values. While everyone can read these variables, only the superuser can modify them.

Some of these variables are adjusted at the kernel start-up to enable features such as the acceptance of IPv6 router advertisements, the control of IP forwarding, and kernel memory allocation values. Most of them can, of course, be modified at any time during system operation.

Various aspects of tuning an OpenBSD kernel have been described in another paper by OpenBSD developers. This paper is available at **http://www.openbsd.org/papers/tuning-openbsd.ps**.

C.1 What Are Tunable Parameters?

Various kernel parameters are adjustable, allowing you to tweak them to better suit your environment. While many of these require a recompilation of the kernel, a number allow for the selective adjustment of variables in the system. Additionally, you can turn on or off support for such things as networking protocols and swap encryption.

C.2 Using *sysctl*

Most of the kernel tuning operations are done with the *sysctl* command. Variables are presented in MIB format, similar to how SNMP variables are organized. In this way it is easy to understand their relationship to the system and to one another.

C.2.1 Reading Variables

The basic use of reading variables is done using *sysctl*. The value of the variable is then shown:

```
$  sysctl vm.swapencrypt.enable
vm.swapencrypt.enable = 0
```

You can view a family of variables by specifying the family:

```
$  sysctl kern.tty
kern.tty.tk_nin = 183222
kern.tty.tk_nout = 3812437
kern.tty.tk_rawcc = 182809
kern.tty.tk_cancc = 413
```

Not all variables are viewable by *sysctl*. To get the list of tables that are supported by additional tools, use *sysctl -A*:

```
...
vfs.ffs.sd_dir_entry = 0
sysctl: use nfsstat to view nfs information
...
```

In this case you could call up the statistics for NFS networking by using the *nfsstat(1)* command. Similar tools include the familiar *netstat, vmstat,* and *dmesg*.

To print only the value of the field, use the command *sysctl -n*:

```
$  sysctl -n net.inet6.ip6.accept_rtadv
1
```

This check can be readily included in scripts:

```
#!/bin/ksh
if [ `sysctl -n net.inet6.ip6.accept_rtadv` == 0 ]; then
        echo "The kernel isn't set up for RA's"
else
        echo "Your kernel is ready for IPv6"
fi
```

The *-n* flag may be combined with *-a* or *-A* to show all of the values of the system variables.

C.2.2 Writing to Variables

The superuser—and only the superuser—can write to the fields using *sysctl*. This restriction is imposed due to the sweeping changes one can make to a system using *sysctl*. To write to a field and set a value, use *sysctl -w*:

```
#  sysctl -w net.inet6.ip6.forwarding=1
net.inet6.ip6.forwarding: 0 -> 1
```

You have to set variables one at a time, however. If you wish to have these fields set automatically at start-up, the system boot scripts will go through the file **/etc/sysctl.conf** and set the variables as specified there. Not all variables are adjustable, however, and some are read-only.

C.3 The Variable Hierarchy

A brief tour of the *sysctl* MIB hierarchy is shown below. Values of common interest are described as well.

- **kern.***   Controls core kernel values, such as memory allocations, security levels, and random numbers. Many fields are not adjustable and are only readable.

- **net.***   Used to adjust networking aspects, including IP options, protocol enabling, and TCP control options. Notable fields include *net.inet.ip.forwarding*, which controls the forwarding of IPv4 packets (use *net.inet6.ip6.forwarding* for IPv6 forwarding); *net.inet.esp.enable* and *net.inet.ah.enable* to control IPsec-specific protocols; and *net.inet6.ip6.accept_rtadv* for IPv6 routing advertisements.

- **hw.***   Lists hardware variables, such as memory sizes, byte order, and disk statistics.

- **machdep.***   Controls machine-dependent options. Some options are only available for certain hardware platforms.

- **user.***   Controls several userland parameters.

- **ddb.***   Sets options for the kernel debugger.

- **vfs.***   Controls filesystem-specific options.

C.4 Filesystem Improvements

Disk-based input/output (I/O) is a common bottleneck for system performance. The options of using soft updates, mount options for disks, and memory-based filesystems are discussed in Chapter 14.

The VFS options that are controllable by *sysctl* are typically tuned to sound defaults for most users. The options for soft dependencies, which are found in the *vfs.ffs.sf_** tree, are also tuned for most common filesystem sizes and situations, meaning they balance filesystem reads and writes. These options are available to administrators who wish to fine-tune their settings. For example, in a read-intensive environment, the soft dependency tree will be of little help, but the option *vfs.ffs.doclusterread* should be set to 1 (to enable this option).

A *dmesg* Walkthrough

The kernel's messages at start-up and afterward can be useful for gathering diagnostic information as well as understanding the system's health. The kernel ring buffer, which is structured as a fixed-size buffer (meaning older entries get pushed out when newer ones are inserted) is viewed using the *dmesg* command.

The basic use of *dmesg* is with no arguments, which causes the command to display the current kernel buffer messages. This group can include the boot messages, but it may also include messages from the kernel generated after start-up. The kernel's boot messages are always stored in the file **/var/run/dmesg.boot**, so you can go back and review them at any time.

You can also extract information from other kernels using *dmesg*, or system core dumps (saved via *savecore*, not normal program core files). To do so, use *dmesg -N* to give an alternate kernel name (the command assumes **/bsd**, although you may boot with a different kernel image). Alternatively, you can point the tool at a different system memory image (a system core dump) using the command *dmesg -M*. These options can be combined to test the kernel messages from an experimental kernel by using a command like this:

```
# dmesg -M /var/crash/savecore/bsd.0.core -N /bsd.new
```

In this example, a new kernel was booted but we want to evaluate its crash state.

D.1 What Does *dmesg* Give Us?

The *dmesg* command can be used for several purposes. First, it tells us what hardware the system does and does not see. This information can be a critical element in debugging—it may explain why some hardware works and other pieces do not. The kernel will display diagnostic information about the devices it finds and their configuration. Negative messages would contain a brief note such as "not configured," meaning the system was unable to properly configure the device.

Second, the *dmesg* output gives information about which drivers the system loads for which hardware. This can include information about multiple network interfaces, ways to address a disk, or any USB devices attached. We can use this information to begin configuring devices, now that we know their names. Furthermore, we can use it when paring down a kernel configuration to ensure that we do not remove critical devices. Remember to look at the device chain, such as a network interface connecting to an ISA bus.

Third, the kernel messages help us keep track of the system's health. Critical errors in the system may be reported by the kernel, indicating that an administrator's attention is needed.

D.2 What Do the Messages Mean?

One of the more common messages but one that doesn't appear regularly is the warning that the filesystems were not properly unmounted. In this situation the system was turned off ungracefully—that is, it crashed. This message appears as the system prepares to initialize itself after the kernel has booted:

```
WARNING: / was not properly unmounted
```

At this point the system will check the disks and prepare them for use.

When the system has recoverable disk errors, you may see messages like the following in your active *dmesg* buffer:

```
wd0: transfer error, downgrading to Ultra-DMA mode 1
wd0(pciide0:0:0): using PIO mode 4, Ultra-DMA mode 1
wd0a:  aborted command, interface CRC error reading fsbn 114416 of
  114416-114431 (wd0 bn 114479; cn 113 tn 9 sn 8), retrying
wd0: soft error (corrected)
```

In this case the system detected an error related to the disk and corrected it. This problem can indicate a failing disk, so the frequency of these messages during uninterrupted runs (as opposed to *apm* sleep cycles) should be taken seriously.

D.2.1 The Boot Messages

The system's boot messages are the most visible kernel messages, and perhaps the most perplexing. Below is a set of messages from the start-up of a desktop system with brief explanations:

```
OpenBSD 3.3-stable (GENERIC) #2: Mon May 19 18:29:14 EDT 2003
    jose@tank:/usr/src/sys/arch/i386/compile/GENERIC
```

This output gives the kernel identification information. The version, the build date, the user who built it, and the configuration name are given. This data is useful for determining the kernel build revision.

```
cpu0: Intel Pentium II (Klamath) ("GenuineIntel" 686-class, 512KB L2
    cache) 299 MHz
cpu0: FPU,V86,DE,PSE,TSC,MSR,PAE,MCE,CX8,SYS,MTRR,PGE,MCA,CMOV,MMX
```

This CPU information is useful to ensure that the system correctly identifies the CPU.

```
real mem  = 268009472 (261728K)
avail mem = 242683904 (236996K)
using 3297 buffers containing 13504512 bytes (13188K) of memory
```

The system has 256MB of memory, approximately 234MB of which is addressable and usable by the system.

```
mainbus0 (root)
```

This is the root device to which everything attaches.

```
bios0 at mainbus0: AT/286+(94) BIOS, date 02/23/00, BIOS32 rev. 0 @
    0xfd7a0
apm0 at bios0: Power Management spec V1.2
apm0: AC on, battery charge unknown
pcibios0 at bios0: rev. 2.1 @ 0xfd7a0/0x860
pcibios0: PCI IRQ Routing Table rev. 1.0 @ 0xfdf30/176 (9 entries)
pcibios0: PCI Interrupt Router at 000:07:0 ("Intel 82371FB PCI-ISA"
    rev 0x00)
pcibios0: PCI bus #1 is the last bus
bios0: ROM list: 0xc0000/0x8000 0xe0000/0x4000! 0xe4000/0xc000
pci0 at mainbus0 bus 0: configuration mode 1 (no bios)
```

These messages come from the first round of device identification. The PCI bus is identified, as is the PCI BIOS and the system BIOS.

```
pchb0 at pci0 dev 0 function 0 "Intel 82443BX PCI-AGP" rev 0x03
ppb0 at pci0 dev 1 function 0 "Intel 82443BX AGP" rev 0x03
pci1 at ppb0 bus 1
vga1 at pci1 dev 0 function 0 "ATI Rage Fury" rev 0x00
wsdisplay0 at vga1: console (80x25, vt100 emulation)
wsdisplay0: screen 1-5 added (80x25, vt100 emulation)
```

This output is the main display information, identifying the kernel driver and the core functions.

```
pcib0 at pci0 dev 7 function 0 "Intel 82371AB PIIX4 ISA" rev 0x02
pciide0 at pci0 dev 7 function 1 "Intel 82371AB IDE" rev 0x01: DMA,
    channel 0 wired to compatibility, channel 1 wired to compatibility
wd0 at pciide0 channel 0 drive 0: <ST340016A>
wd0: 16-sector PIO, LBA, 38166MB, 16383 cyl, 16 head, 63 sec, 78165360
    sectors
wd0(pciide0:0:0): using PIO mode 4, Ultra-DMA mode 2
pciide0: channel 1 ignored (disabled)
```

This information identifies the main drive (**wd0**) and the PCI IDE chain to which it attaches.

```
uhci0 at pci0 dev 7 function 2 "Intel 82371AB USB" rev 0x01: irq 9
usb0 at uhci0: USB revision 1.0
uhub0 at usb0
uhub0: vendor 0x0000 UHCI root hub, class 9/0, rev 1.00/1.00, addr 1
uhub0: 2 ports with 2 removable, self powered
"Intel 82371AB Power Mgmt" rev 0x02 at pci0 dev 7 function 3 not
    configured
```

OpenBSD has included support for USB for some time now, with improvements to this support coming after version 3.3 was released.

```
isa0 at pcib0
isadma0 at isa0
pckbc0 at isa0 port 0x60/5
```

```
pckbd0 at pckbc0 (kbd slot)
pckbc0: using irq 1 for kbd slot
wskbd0 at pckbd0: console keyboard, using wsdisplay0
pms0 at pckbc0 (aux slot)
pckbc0: using irq 12 for aux slot
wsmouse0 at pms0 mux 0
```

The legacy devices include a PC keyboard and an ISA bus. The mouse is driven by the **wsmouse** kernel device.

```
ep0 at isa0 port 0x300/16 irq 10: address 00:20:af:05:93:fc,
    utp/aui (default utp)
pcppi0 at isa0 port 0x61
midi0 at pcppi0: <PC speaker>
sysbeep0 at pcppi0
lpt0 at isa0 port 0x378/4 irq 7
npx0 at isa0 port 0xf0/16: using exception 16
pccom0 at isa0 port 0x3f8/8 irq 4: ns16550a, 16 byte fifo
pccom1 at isa0 port 0x2f8/8 irq 3: ns16550a, 16 byte fifo
fdc0 at isa0 port 0x3f0/6 irq 6 drq 2
fd0 at fdc0 drive 0: 1.44MB 80 cyl, 2 head, 18 sec
biomask 4240 netmask 4640 ttymask 56c2
pctr: 686-class user-level performance counters enabled
mtrr: Pentium Pro MTRR support
```

The **lpt** ports are the parallel ports (named for the line printers to which they attached in the past), and the main network card of the machine is a 3COM-class device with the **ep** driver. The serial ports are given as **pccom** devices, although they have other device names in the **/dev** tree.

```
dkcsum: wd0 matched BIOS disk 80
root on wd0a
rootdev=0x0 rrootdev=0x300 rawdev=0x302
```

The system is ready to boot. It has found the root disk device and is ready to begin using it.

Appendix E

Core File Evaluation

Application development usually involves several stages, many of which inevitably include crashing. Debugging an application, or a system, that has crashed can prove to be a tricky exercise, but one that is sometimes needed.

This chapter discusses two built-in debuggers in the base OpenBSD system: *gdb* and *ddb*. The *gdb* tool is employed in userland to debug applications that crashed but left the system intact. The *ddb* command, in contrast, is called upon when the kernel crashes, resulting in a stoppage of the system.

Debugging steps are not for everyone, but they are sometimes required to produce a detailed system analysis or a bug report. The notes in this appendix by no means instruct you in application or kernel analysis—they merely provide a cursory tour of these commands. The goal is to enable the extraction of enough information to file a comprehensive bug report.

Crashes typically leave behind a "core" file. Its name dates from the historical days when memory consisted of an actual spool of wire. This core of memory was dumped so its state could be examined. Today, files are appended with the suffix "core" to indicate their nature, which is a full memory dump of the application's memory or the system memory (in the event of a kernel crash).

E.1 Applications That Crashed

Userland applications that crash will sometimes leave a file around—namely, one with the executable's name with the suffix "core" appended. For example, a crash of the Korn shell would leave behind a **ksh.core** file. These files are typically useless if the application has been built without debugging symbols or has been stripped of these symbols (to conserve space).

To prepare an application for extensive debugging, the first step is to build the source with debugging symbols enabled. The *cc -g* command is used to link in support for the *gdb* debugger:

```
$  cc -g -o application application.c
```

In this case a single application source file was compiled and linked with debugging symbols enabled. Now, if it crashes, the core file will contain useful symbol data, enabling you to step through the application's actions on its way to the crash.

Once the application is built and subsequently crashes, you use the *gdb* command (the GNU debugger) to examine this file. Targeting a core dump is easy:

```
$  gdb
GNU gdb 4.16.1
Copyright 1996 Free Software Foundation, Inc.
GDB is free software, covered by the GNU General Public License, and
you are welcome to change it and/or distribute copies of it under
certain conditions. Type "show copying" to see the conditions. There
is absolutely no warranty for GDB.  Type "show warranty" for
details. This GDB was configured as "i386-unknown-openbsd3.4".
(gdb)  file stsh
Reading symbols from stsh...done.
(gdb)  target core stsh.core
```

This tells *gdb* to use the executable named with the *file* command (in this case *stsh*, the *systrace* shell from Chapter 29). The core file is also specified, which tells *gdb* to load the symbols:

```
(gdb)  target core stsh.core
Core was generated by 'stsh'.
Program terminated with signal 11, Segmentation fault.
Reading symbols from /usr/libexec/ld.so...done.
Reading symbols from /usr/lib/libc.so.29...done.
#0  0x4008230a in vfprintf ()
```

We can now ask *gdb* to tell us which steps preceded this crash by asking *where* the crash occurred:

```
(gdb)  where
#0  0x4008230a in vfprintf ()
#1  0x4005ab3c in printf ()
#2  0x1853 in main ()
```

This command presents a list of operations that the application attempted as it crashed. The output is called a "backtrace" capture.

The second column in the backtrace gives the address in memory of the instruction. We can examine the data at any of these addresses by using the *x* command with the memory address:

```
(gdb) x  0x4008230a
0x4008230a <vfprintf+3366>:      0xd1f7aef2
```

This output shows the values of the registers at this address. You can also examine the values of any variables on the stack at the time, by using *print* and the variable name. From a debugging session with another program:

```
(gdb)  p p
$1 = (pcap_t *) 0x0
```

Here we had a NULL value for the value of *p*, which in this case is a *pcap_t* type object (used in **pcap** routines).

Breakpoints can also be set to catch a program before it hits the problem code. To do so, first wrap the execution of the program within the debugger and then set the breakpoint. In the following example, also using the *stsh* program, we tell the debugger to stop execution when the routine _get_shell() is hit:

```
(gdb)  file stsh
Reading symbols from stsh...done.
(gdb)  break_get_shell
Breakpoint 1 at 0x189d
```

Now the program can be *run*:

```
(gdb)  r
Starting program: /home/jose/software/stsh/stsh

Breakpoint 1, 0x189d in _get_shell ()
```

Once the breakpoint is hit, registers can be examined, variables can be displayed, or the execution can occur in single steps:

```
(gdb)  s
Single stepping until exit from function _get_shell,
which has no line number information.
0x1815 in main ()
(gdb)  s
Single stepping until exit from function main,
which has no line number information.

Program received signal SIGSEGV, Segmentation fault.
0x4008230a in vfprintf ()
```

This technique lets you slowly approach the offending action, perhaps indicating a cascading problem that ultimately leads to the program's crash.

For most bug reports in OpenBSD problems, a simple backtrace will suffice when a crash has occurred.

E.2 Kernel Crash Dump Analysis

Debugging in kernel space is significantly more difficult than running a debugger on a userland application. The primary reason is that kernel crashes result in a total system failure, which means that any work that was not saved is lost, a reboot has to occur, and it is difficult to rapidly debug the problem. However, some options can be used in *ddb* to facilitate this analysis.

E.2.1 Using *ddb*

The *ddb* kernel debugger requires both setting a kernel option and tuning via *sysctl* variables. The kernel option, which is included in the GENERIC kernel, is self-explanatory:

```
option          DDB              # in-kernel debugger
```

The *sysctl* variables for *ddb* are largely irrelevant to most users. They include the screen size and tab stops.

```
ddb.radix = 16
ddb.max_width = 80
ddb.max_line = 24
ddb.tab_stop_width = 8
```

```
ddb.panic = 1
ddb.console = 0
```

The important *sysctl* variables are *ddb.panic* and *ddb.console*, which control whether the kernel will drop to *ddb* when it panics (or will simply reboot instead) and where the debugger will be shown. Both variables can safely be set to 1. The console variable respects the setting for the console given in the file **/etc/ttys**, which defaults to the local screen output.

The kernel debugger is similar to the userland debugger. Both allow for backtraces and stack variable examination, but the kernel debugger also allows for process table inspection. The commands *bt* and *ps* show a backtrace and the process table output, respectively:

```
ddb>  bt
...
ddb>  ps
...
```

This output is useful for getting an idea of what occurred and where. Typically it suffices to know which processes were running and which area of the kernel (e.g., filesystem, memory allocation) was being accessed.

E.2.2 Post-Reboot Analysis

Because the kernel debugger halts the system, the state cannot be saved automatically as a userland core dump can. Instead, you must explicitly state which boot method to use. Two boot methods, *dump* and *crash*, will save the system and kernel memory. The *dump* method will *sync* the disks to their current state, dump the system memory image, and reboot. The *crash* method will skip the disk synchronization step.

```
ddb>  boot dump
  or
ddb>  boot crash
  system reboots and you log in as root ...
#  savecore
```

Once the system has rebooted, this image can be saved to disk using the *savecore* command. It produces two files: a kernel snapshot and the system memory core from the previous crash. These can be examined using *gdb* to target a kernel core dump:

```
$  gdb /bsd bsd.0.core
...
(gdb)   target kcore bsd.0.core
(gdb)   where
```

At this point the fundamental *gdb* commands are available. They make kernel debugging significantly easier than attempting to work within the confines of *ddb*.

E.2.3 Examining the Process Table

The *gdb* tool cannot show the process table from the system memory core, but the *ps* command can be targeted at files containing the preserved kernel and the memory footprint. Using *ps -N*, you can specify a specific kernel to use rather than the current kernel; you can specify a memory image to use with *ps -M*. Hence, a pair of files dumped by *savecore* can be examined by *ps*:

```
#  ps ax -Opaddr -N bsd.gdb -M bsd.0.core
```

This output can be useful in identifying the processes residing in particular memory areas. This information helps in kernel debugging when userland processes initiated the failure.

Kernel bug reports that result in a crash are best filed with the backtrace information along with the process table. It is simply too difficult to determine what may have gone wrong without this information.

Other OpenBSD Tools and Resources

F.1 Web Pages

The OpenBSD Web site attempts to be a complete resource for the OpenBSD community. Detailed information is available on obtaining, installing, and running an OpenBSD system. A FAQ is maintained as well; it answers most questions. The FAQ, which is split into sections for easier navigation, can be found at **http://www.openbsd.org/faq/**. Topics covered include installation, migration to OpenBSD from Linux, networking setup, and the like.

The site "OpenBSD Journal," which Jose has been co-editing for several months, is devoted to OpenBSD news. It features links to stories, software, and developments within the OpenBSD community and project. It can be found at **http://www.deadly.org/**.

F.2 Software Mirrors

A number of software mirrors around the world are available for use. They include not only the distribution of OpenBSD software, both in release and current source code forms, but also additional software for UNIX and UNIX variants (OpenBSD included). Much of this software will build, sometimes with modification, on an OpenBSD system.

F.2.1 BSD-Specific Software

The OpenBSD and BSD communities have a strong, worldwide network of software sites where you can grab the latest releases or new software for BSD systems. These include both the official OpenBSD mirrors and other sites from the BSD community. Several are listed here.

- *Official mirrors* run by OpenBSD include FTP, HTTP, AFS, and *rsync* mirrors. A complete list of these servers is available on the OpenBSD Web site. For performance reasons, you should always work with a server geographically near you and, ideally, on the same network as your system. If you have access to Internet2, a new high-speed research backbone, you may wish to find a mirror on it—typically, a U.S. academic mirror.

http://www.openbsd.org/ftp.html
http://www.openbsd.org/anoncvs.html (CVS-specific)

- *BSD Central* sells CDs of various BSD releases, including OpenBSD releases, and collections of software ported to the various BSD flavors.

http://www.bsdcentral.com/

- *Maximum BSD* is a news site, similar to Slashdot, for all things BSD. Decent coverage of OpenBSD is included.

http://www.maximumbsd.com/

F.2.2 Generic Software Sites

The free and open-source software community is highly productive, releasing large amounts of software. Much of this software can be built and run on OpenBSD systems. Several key sites are listed below.

- *Freshmeat* is a popular software announcement site for tools and applications geared toward free UNIX systems. While most of the development targets Linux systems, much of the software will compile on OpenBSD equally well. Note that major applications are also announced here. The site has begun providing a tracking service, allowing you to monitor its announcements about new software releases.

http://www.freshmeat.net

- *Packetstorm* is a large repository of hacker and security-related software and important disclosure information. Much of the software can be used to secure or safely monitor networks, not just break into networks.

http://packetstormsecurity.org

- *TUCOWS* was started as a freeware site for Windows software, but has grown to support UN*X systems as well. It even has a BSD section.

http://www.tucows.com

F.3 Mailing Lists

The OpenBSD Web site lists several mailing lists of use to the community. They can be subscribed to (and, of course, unsubscribed from), searched on various off-site archives, and used to answer almost any question. Whatever your issue, chances are it's been discussed on one of the lists.

The OpenBSD Web site maintains a list, with descriptions, of the available mailing lists at **http://www.openbsd.org/mail.html**. Here are the major ones to know about:

- **Misc** The **misc** mailing list is the catch-all list, allowing for open discussions on almost every facet of OpenBSD by a general audience. It is a large traffic list, so keep this broad audience in mind.
- **Tech** The **tech** list is for advanced users and developers. It is not a list for general questions and answers.
- **Source-changes** This automated mailing list sends to its members a log message of each CVS operation on the tree. It can be high traffic and, to many, banal. It is not meant for discussion.
- **Security** This low-traffic list contains important security advisories about the OpenBSD system are sent here. Not for discussion.
- **Announce** This very-low-traffic list contains only announcements about the OpenBSD project, such as new releases.
- **Advocacy** The **advocacy** list is meant for the discussion of how to advocate and promote the OpenBSD system to people. It is a nontechnical list.
- **Ports** The ports list is mainly intended for the maintainers of ports—that is, people who build software packages for the OpenBSD project. Sometimes it is useful to send a note to the list asking for assistance related to a problem related to the ports system that cannot be addressed on a general list like **misc**.
- **bugs** The **bugs** list is used by the GNATS bugs database as well as open submissions to serious bugs in the system. This low-traffic list has relatively little discussion.

These mailing lists are usually populated by a mix of users much like yourself and the developers. Asking a well-phrased question here will usually get an answer, providing you're on the appropriate list.

The primates at **monkey.org**, which include some OpenBSD developers, maintain the **openbsd-mobile** list, a mailing list for people who use OpenBSD on their laptops. This list is usually i386-specific, although people with MacPPC laptops have been known to appear. Visit **http://www.monkey.org/openbsd-mobile/** to obtain more information on this mailing list or its archives.

F.4 User Groups

User groups exist for BSD users, not just Linux or Windows users. Note that the lesser popularity of BSD, as compared with Linux, means there are fewer user groups that specialize in BSD. However, many Linux user groups have members who also use BSD. The OpenBSD Web site lists most of the known OpenBSD user groups.

> **http://www.openbsd.org/groups.html**

F.5 Newsgroups

The Usenet newsgroups for OpenBSD users and developers behave much like the mailing lists, albeit with slightly less traffic:

- **comp.unix.bsd.openbsd.misc**   This newsgroup is much like the **misc** mailing list, acting as a catch-all for many discussions about OpenBSD issues. It is a very good source of information. Several members of the OpenBSD development team are regulars here.
- **comp.unix.bsd.openbsd.announce**   This newsgroup is much like the **announce** mailing list—very low traffic, no discussions, and only important announcements about OpenBSD systems.
- **comp.security.ssh**   This newsgroup, while not specific to OpenBSD systems, covers many of the issues surrounding the tool *ssh*, including OpenSSH development, announcements, and assistance. Several members of the OpenSSH development team are regulars on this newsgroup.

Usenet and its archives at **http://groups.google.com/** are an especially easy way to get answers to many questions. You can also post new articles from the site.

F.6 RFC Availability

RFC documents are "Request for Comments" papers put out by influential members of the Internet Engineering Task Force (IETF) and selected individuals. Some are informational; others are standards. While complying with RFCs is voluntary, by doing so a vendor or implementer ensures the connectivity of its system with others over the same protocols.

RFC documents can be obtained from the IETF Web site (the authoritative source) as well as several mirrors. Currently numbering well over 3000, they define how the Internet works and how we communicate. They are sometimes boring, dense, obtuse, or simply frustrating, but you may have to read them to understand what is going on. RFCs are usually referred to by number and sometimes by topic, but rarely by title.

http://www.ietf.org/

IPsec *m4*

The *m4* processing script found in **lib.m4** was built by Todd Fries to process simplified IPsec configuration files. Use these scripts as directed in Chapter 27.

```
dnl
dnl XXX revisit this when time permits, the Authorization= must
dnl match on both
dnl     ends and by default this encourages them to not match
dnl
define('hostaddr',
'ifelse('$2','',
'Address=                $1',
'Network=                $1
Netmask=                 $2')''dnl
')dnl
define('hosttype',
'ifelse('$1','','','_SUBNET')')dnl
dnl
define('hostdef4','hostdef($1,$2,4,$3,$4)')dnl
define('hostdef6','hostdef($1,$2,6,$3,$4)')dnl
dnl
define('hostdef','''dnl
define('host_$1_v$3','$2')dnl
dnl # hostdef(1: $1, 2: $2, 3: $3, 4: $4, 5: $5)dnl
[$1-IPv$3]
ID-type=                 IPV$3_ADDR''hosttype($5)
hostaddr($2,$5)
```

```
[$1v$3]
Phase=                      1
hostaddr($2,$5)
ifelse('$4','rsa',
'Configuration=             rsa-main-mode
','$4','',
'Configuration=             main-mode
',
'Authentication=            $4
Configuration=              main-mode
')''dnl
')''dnl
dnl
define('sadef4','sadef($1,$2,4)')dnl
define('sadef6','sadef($1,$2,6)')dnl
define('sadef','[$1-IPv$3-$2-IPv$3]
Phase=                      2
ISAKMP-peer=                $2v$3
Configuration=              quick-mode
Local-ID=                   $1-IPv$3
Remote-ID=                  $2-IPv$3
')dnl
dnl
define('ptp4in6','_tunnel($1,$2,6,4,$1,$2,ptp)')dnl
define('ptp6in6','_tunnel($1,$2,6,6,$1,$2,ptp)')dnl
define('ptp4in4','_tunnel($1,$2,4,4,$1,$2,ptp)')dnl
define('ptp6in4','_tunnel($1,$2,4,6,$1,$2,ptp)')dnl
define('tunnel4in6','_tunnel($1,$2,6,4,$3,$4,tunnel)')dnl
define('tunnel6in6','_tunnel($1,$2,6,6,$3,$4,tunnel)')dnl
define('tunnel4in4','_tunnel($1,$2,4,4,$3,$4,tunnel)')dnl
define('tunnel6in4','_tunnel($1,$2,4,6,$3,$4,tunnel)')dnl
define('_tunnel','[$1-IPv$3-v$4''$7''-$2-IPv$3]
Phase=                      2
ISAKMP-peer=                $2v$3
Configuration=              quick-mode
Local-ID=                   $5-IPv$4
Remote-ID=                  $6-IPv$4
```

```
')dnl
dnl
dnl for() loop
dnl
define('copy','$1')dnl
dnl Usage - for('1 2 3 4 5',var,string)
dnl
dnl   Example:  for('1 2 3 4 5','x',' hey there x ')
dnl
dnl                hey there 1
dnl                hey there 2
dnl                hey there 3
dnl                hey there 4
dnl                hey there 5
dnl
dnl
define('findfirst','ifelse(index('$1','$2'),-1,'$1',substr($1,0,\
\index('$1','$2')))')dnl
define('findrest','ifelse(index('$1','$2'),-1,'',substr($1,\
incr(index('$1','$2')))))')dnl
define('for','ifelse('$1','','','pushdef('action_$2', \
'$3')''pushdef('$2',copy(findfirst('$1',\
'')))''action_$2''for(findrest('$1',' '),'$2','$3')')')dnl
dnl
dnl
dnl define({test},{ifelse({$1},{},{},{countdown: \
    copy(findfirst({$1},{ }))
dnl test(findrest({$1},{ }))})})
dnl
dnl dumpdef()
dnl
dnl ff: findfirst({1 2 3 4},{ })
dnl fr: findrest({1 2 3 4},{ })
dnl test({1 2 3 4})
dnl
dnl for({1 2 3 4},{num},{hi there num
dnl })
```

```
dnl
define('mesh',
'define('mesh_Phase2_$1','$2')''dnl
define('mesh_Phase1_$1','$2')''dnl
for('$2','_MESH_',
'$3($1,_MESH_)
ifelse('$4','','','$4($1,_MESH_)
')''dnl
')')''dnl
dnl
define('mesh_connections','for(mesh_Phase2_$1,
'_host_',
'divert(0)''dnl
ifdef('_notfirst_',',','define('_notfirst_')')''dnl
$1-IPv6-_host_-IPv6,$1-IPv6-v4ptp-_host_-IPv6''dnl
divert(5)'#' c $1-IPv6-_host_-IPv6
'#' c $1-IPv6-v4ptp-_host_-IPv6
divert(0)''dnl
')''dnl
')''dnl
dnl
define('showip','host_$1_v6')''dnl
define('mesh_Phase1',
 'for(mesh_Phase1_$1,
'_host_',
'showip(_host_)=          _host_''v6
')''dnl
')''dnl
divert(5)
dnl
dnl Here are some default settings that just make things easier
dnl
[default-IPv6]
ID-type=        IPV6_ADDR_SUBNET
Network=        ::
Netmask=        ::
```

```
[default-IPv4]
ID-type=         IPV4_ADDR_SUBNET
Network=         0.0.0.0
Netmask=         0.0.0.0

[rsa-main-mode]
DOI=                  IPSEC
EXCHANGE_TYPE=        ID_PROT
Transforms=           3DES-SHA-RSA_SIG

[main-mode]
DOI=                  IPSEC
EXCHANGE_TYPE=        ID_PROT
Transforms=           3DES-SHA

[quick-mode]
DOI=                  IPSEC
EXCHANGE_TYPE=        QUICK_MODE
Suites=               QM-ESP-3DES-SHA-PFS-SUITE
divert(0)''dnl
```

Index